African Economic Development

This book challenges conventional wisdoms about economic performance and possible policies for economic development in African countries. Its starting point is the striking variation in African economic performance.

Unevenness and inequalities form a central fact of African economic experiences. The authors highlight not only differences between countries, but also variations within countries, differences often organised around distinctions of gender, class, and ethnic identity. For example, neo-natal mortality and school dropout have been reduced, particularly for some classes of women in some areas of Africa. Horticultural and agribusiness exports have grown far more rapidly in some countries than in others. These variations (and many others) point to opportunities for changing performance, reducing inequalities, learning from other policy experiences, and escaping the ties of structure, and the legacies of a colonial past. This study rejects teleological illusions and Eurocentric prejudice, but it does pay close attention to the results of policy in more industrialized parts of the world. Seeing the contradictions of capitalism for what they are – fundamental and enduring – may help policy officials protect themselves against the misleading idea that development can be expected to be a smooth, linear process, or that it would be were certain impediments suddenly removed.

The authors criticize a wide range of orthodox and heterodox economists, especially for their cavalier attitude to evidence. Drawing on their own decades of research and policy experience, they combine careful use of available evidence from a range of African countries with political economy insights (mainly derived from Kalecki, Kaldor and Hirschman) to make the policy case for specific types of public sector investment.

Praise for the Book

This is a stunningly good book: historically grounded, rich with evidence and examples, skeptical of the conventional wisdom, and infused with a realistic 'bias for hope' that counters the over-pessimistic and over-optimistic analyses of many far less thoughtful writers. Read it and be inspired.

Deborah Brautigam, Bernard L. Schwartz
Professor of International Political Economy,
Director of the SAIS China Africa Research Initiative,
Johns Hopkins School of Advanced International Studies (SAIS)

Somewhere between a bird's eye view of Africa's development dilemmas and a pragmatic assessment of the intricacies of policy making the authors of this book found a superb niche: to guide us through what is essential because it is often different from the common views. A masterful undertaking that will become essential reading for African policy makers eager to deepen their thoughts.

Carlos Lopes, Professor, Nelson Mandela School
of Public Governance, University of Cape Town

Cramer, Sender and Arkebe do an excellent job of looking at the theories of economic development from a refreshing perspective. And I highly welcome their belief in African policymakers to make good decisions when presented with robust evidence. Development practitioners around the world will benefit immensely from this book, as it challenges accepted economic theory, while providing intriguing alternatives.

K.Y. Amoako, Founder and President,
African Center for Economic Transformation,
and former Executive Secretary
of the UN Economic Commission for Africa

African policy makers generally struggle to find evidence to support initiatives they would like to pursue. Pressure on them to find such evidence has grown as the number of 'stakeholders' interested in the outcomes has grown. This book on economic development in Africa is designed to help them in their pursuit of what is good economics, relevant and more easily manageable. It is a great complement to the recent volumes on African development, offering a refreshingly different approach that appeals to common sense and the new realities of the region.

Ernest Aryeetey, Secretary-General of the African Research
Universities Alliance, former Vice Chancellor of the University of Ghana

In this remarkable book, Cramer, Sender, and Oqubay present a view of Africa unlike anything we have seen. Facing head on the brutality of capitalism in Africa—as elsewhere—they show how nonetheless it has brought about significant, if uneven, progress in human welfare. Analysing trends in structural transformation, they never lose sight of the welfare of ordinary people. Acknowledging the weight of history, they show how a country's prospects are mainly shaped by what a country does, not what it is and has. They offer realistic optimism for a continent where policies have too often been crippled by fatalism. It is one of those very rare books that make you see the world differently after you have read it.

Ha-Joon Chang teaches economics in the University of Cambridge
and is the author of books including: *Kicking Away the Ladder* and
Economics: the User's Guide

Cramer, Sender and Oqubay offer us in this book not only their deep knowledge of African economies and their challenges—with their inherent diversity—but also of other development experiences. Based on the evidence that these experiences provide, as well as an interdisciplinary framework, they put forwards an ambitious agenda for investment and structural change for African development that overcomes the over-pessimism but also the over-optimism of many alternative proposals.

José Antonio Ocampo, Professor Columbia University,
and Chair of the UN Committee for Development Policy

Africa is a fascinating continent, and this superb book provides the depth of insight that is often missing in other commentary which tends to the extremes of pessimism or over-optimism based on simplistic notions of how economies function and evolve.

Tony Addison, Chief Economist/Deputy Director, UNU-WIDER

Arguing against both 'African pessimism' and the naïve optimism of 'Africa rising', this innovative book makes the case for 'possibilism'. This is not just another economics textbook on Africa: it is deeply interdisciplinary and draws not only on history, politics, anthropology, and soil science, but strikingly too on the world of art and literature. The authors offer an unmistakeably progressive political economy, unafraid to challenge weak arguments of radical 'left' economists as much as the worn-out narratives of the mainstream.

Vishnu Padayachee, Distinguished Professor and
Derek Schrier and Cecily Cameron Chair in Development Economics,
School of Economics and Finance, University of the Witwatersrand,
Johannesburg; life-Fellow of the Society of Scholars,
Johns Hopkins University, Baltimore and Washington DC

African Economic Development

Evidence, Theory, Policy

CHRISTOPHER CRAMER, JOHN SENDER,
AND ARKEBE OQUBAY

OXFORD
UNIVERSITY PRESS

OXFORD
UNIVERSITY PRESS

Great Clarendon Street, Oxford, OX2 6DP,
United Kingdom

Oxford University Press is a department of the University of Oxford.
It furthers the University's objective of excellence in research, scholarship,
and education by publishing worldwide. Oxford is a registered trade mark of
Oxford University Press in the UK and in certain other countries

Published in the United States of America by Oxford University Press
198 Madison Avenue, New York, NY 10016, United States of America

British Library Cataloguing in Publication Data
Data available

Library of Congress Control Number: 2020930019

ISBN 978–0–19–883233–1

Printed and bound by
CPI Group (UK) Ltd, Croydon, CR0 4YY

Acknowledgements

In writing this book we have received help from a wide range of people and organizations. We cannot list every individual but, for example, all the participants in our courses on political economy and on Africa have encouraged us not to be boring and forced us to think. We have been helped by generations of students studying at SOAS, University of London; at the University of Cambridge; at the University of the Witwatersrand in South Africa; on the African Programme on Rethinking Development Economics (APORDE) and Industrial Policy for Policy Makers (IPPM) residential schools run with support from the DTI and IDC in South Africa and on their predecessor course, the Cambridge Programme on Rethinking Development Economics (CAPORDE); on the Governance for Development in Africa residential schools run by the Centre of African Studies at SOAS and funded by the Mo Ibrahim Foundation; on Masters programmes for public sector officials in Mozambique, South Africa, and Namibia run through the Centre for International Education in Economics (CIEE) at SOAS that involved, among other things, classes held during wartime at the Universidade de Eduardo Mondlane in Maputo (Mozambique) and in Parliament in Cape Town in the first year of South African democracy in 1994; and on other short courses and programmes. These students included first year undergraduates, Masters students, PhD candidates, and trade unionists, NGO staff, government and civil service officials, and senior policy makers and politicians in a number of countries.

Versions of this book took shape in discussions and drafts over many years, some of these including close SOAS colleagues to whom we owe a great deal, especially Deborah Johnston and Carlos Oya.

Most of the issues discussed in this book were presented and discussed among the three authors and with former Ethiopian Prime Minister Hailemariam Desalegn. In a series of carefully planned sessions on economic policy we covered topics including macroeconomic theory, trade and exchange rate policy, taxation and fiscal policy, labour markets, industrial policy, gender, the economics of Albert Hirschman, poverty, agriculture, and the historical background and policy experiences of modern economic development in China. Guests who joined some of these sessions included: Ken Coutts, Jonathan Di John, Michael Kuczynski, Peter Nolan, Jonathan Pincus, and Stephanie Seguino. We are very grateful to them for their contributions. They gave substantial amounts of unpaid time and effort to support what we were trying to do. Each session involved three full days of presentations and discussion in Addis Ababa, with a sustained focus on the direct policy relevance of the material. Above all, we would like to thank

Desalegn for giving us the opportunity and for the intense economic policy discussions. These helped us hone the arguments of the book.

We also organized and led a High Level policy workshop for senior Ethiopian officials at SOAS, University of London, in June 2017. It was a privilege to learn from discussions with these officials. They asked to meet and benefited from talking to economists who could offer different points of view and fill some of the many gaps in our own knowledge. These economists not only made a major contribution to the sessions but also shaped some of the arguments developed in this book. For these contributions we would like to thank Kate Bayliss, Ken Coutts, Jonathan Di John, Michael Kuczynski, Peter Nolan, and Elisa van Waeyenberge.

We are grateful to the New Venture Fund in Washington, which funded the High Level Policy Workshop. The Fund has been generous in supporting this book in other ways too. It covered the costs for two of us to be able to devote more time to the project, and it funded the invaluable work of our research assistant Camilla Bertoncin. Her skills in presenting data, as well her enthusiastic commitment to the project, have made this book more visually stimulating than would have otherwise been possible. Haddis Tadesse and Dr. Philipp Krause of the Bill and Melinda Gates Foundation showed an early interest in our project and we are very grateful to them for that, and for steering us towards the New Venture Fund. We would also give special thanks to Deborah Mekonnnen, Tsion Kifle, and Helena Alemu for extremely able administrative support throughout this project (and others).

Jonathan Di John always reminds us of a prolific writer and poet (Robert Graves) who said there is no good writing, only good rewriting. A number of people have helped us improve our arguments and writing and for that we are thankful. Adam Swallow, our commissioning editor at OUP, is pretty much the last word in professionalism, clarity, and calm support and he has given excellent advice at every step from before the first formal proposal for the book to the latter stages of its writing. Ken Barlow has also clarified our writing, helping us pare back a text that was getting out of hand. Jessica Mitford advised that to write well one has to 'murder your darlings': we are very glad to have enlisted Ken as a hired assassin and he helped us grow in confidence in our own mass murder of writerly darlings. Others have helped greatly too: Adam Aboobaker, Fantu Cheru, Richard Dowden, Ben Fine, Ernesto Latchmoor, Matthew Kentridge, Hein Marais, Nicolas Meisel, Helena Perez-Niño, Jonathan Pincus, Nicolas Pons-Vignon, Carlos Oya, Simon Roberts, and Michela Wrong all read chapter drafts and gave us valuable comments. We are grateful to Gus Casely-Hayford for his generosity in providing a photograph for us to use of a Benin bronze cockerel and to Kate Fountain for help with photograph searching and editing.

We also thank William Kentridge for his generosity in letting us use one of his images for the front cover of the book. Our book sympathizes with policy makers in Africa who metaphorically struggle to breathe in an atmosphere thick with ideas. Put in terms captured by Kentridge's image, they risk being deafened by a cacophony of amplified policy instructions from multiple sources.

We have abused the patience of those closest to us with all our absences and obsessions (and lectures at the dinner table). We are lucky that Nigisty, Kate, and Suzie, and all our children, have put up with the long process of writing and even appear to be interested in some of the ideas in this book.

Contents

List of Figures

PART I

CONTEXT

1

Introduction

A Fresh Outlook on Evidence, Analysis, and Policy for Economic Development in Africa

1.1 The Air that Policy Officials Breathe

Every day policy officials are tasked with coming up with solutions to complex puzzles. They must do this in a context of (often) inadequate staffing levels and unreliable data; multiple claims on the resources at their disposal; and having to think strategically while under intense pressure to address short-term issues. At the same time, they must field the attentions of an array of domestic political forces and international agencies (international financial organizations, bilateral partners, international non-governmental organizations (NGOs), and a stream of beltway consultants).

All the while, they are breathing in an atmosphere thick with ideas. Some they may have absorbed while ploughing through a standard textbook on economics; some are part of the popular discourse of African nationalism; and some are supposed 'universal truths' about global political economy. Often, these ideas contradict each other. In short, being a policy official in an African—or any— country is difficult.

In this book, we will attempt to introduce some fresh ways of thinking about the complex economic policy problems facing many African countries. However, this does not mean we claim to know the policy answers. Policies have to be designed in detailed ways, addressing the specific needs of individual countries (and parts of countries) at particular times. Furthermore, as we argue in this book, often the most interesting policy design issues emerge *during* the process of policy imple-mentation, where they either fail or at least do not turn out as was intended— policies can then be adjusted, improvised, and improved in response to these unpredicted problems.

Policy is made within a global and a structural context. In other words, countries are shaped by their histories, and their current options may be con-strained by the often hostile characteristics of the international environment. Even so, we strongly argue that the keys to generating sustained economic growth and development lie *within* African countries, in the form of policy and investment strategy decisions. In this sense, following the economist Albert Hirschman,

African Economic Development: Evidence, Theory, Policy. Christopher Cramer, John Sender, and Arkebe Oqubay, Oxford University Press (2020). © Christopher Cramer, John Sender, and Arkebe Oqubay.
DOI: 10.1093/oso/9780198832331.001.0001

we argue that policy officials can achieve better results by widening their horizons and adopting an attitude of 'possibilism' (see Chapter 5).

Sceptics, while perhaps acknowledging that the arguments and evidence presented in this book may be well founded, will doubtless assert that there is little chance that any policies arising from them can or will be implemented in Africa. Some might argue that there are too many 'failed states'; too many economies dominated by rent-seeking, patrimonialism, and the 'politics of the belly'. Others might argue that the weight of the continent's colonial past is too heavy; that the noose of global economic governance rules is too tight. Contrary to this, we argue that while the policymaking process is complex, and its trajectory uncertain, there is often unexpected scope for adroit policy reasoning. Policies are designed and implemented through shifting coalitions among political leaders and policy officials, often blending conflicting interests and logics. The evidence—gathered both from our own long experience of working with African governments and from the work of others—is that there are in fact cadres of thoughtful, public-spirited policy officials and even politicians; and furthermore that there is ample demand from wage workers and the intelligentsia for industrial policies rooted in evidence rather than abstruse economic theory. This positive assessment is confirmed by discussions with thousands of policy officials attending more than ten years of residential schools through the African Programme on Rethinking Development Economics (APORDE), as well as those taking part in APORDE's predecessor at Cambridge and in residential schools in African countries funded by the Mo Ibrahim Foundation/SOAS Governance for Development in Africa (GDiA) programme, not to mention by our more direct experiences of policymaking.

1.2 How This Book Differs from Others on the Economics of Africa

The spirit of possibilism is one of the things differentiating this book from other economics texts on Africa. Many of these are afflicted either by a profound pessimism—that, due to the legacy wrought by the continent's colonial past and the current strictures of global economic governance imposed by the World Trade Organization (WTO) and the Bretton Woods Institutions, there is little that can be done—or by the overly optimistic idea that if only this or that barrier could be removed then a smooth, sustained, and inclusive path to economic development would naturally unfold. Possibilism, by contrast, is a form of realism: it reflects a 'bias for hope' but is rooted in a pragmatic, often somewhat depressing, awareness of the cruel historical record in Africa and globally. A record that is, in fact, the history of capitalist development.

It is important to state that this book it is not merely an 'economics' text, confining itself to narrow economic theory or research. Instead, we draw on the work of historians, anthropologists, and political scientists; agronomists, soil scientists, and engineers; and here and there—for illustrative purposes—on works of art and literature. Economies and economic policies do not exist in a vacuum, sealed off from the social relationships, historical patterns of behaviour, power relations, and physical environments of which they are a part. Women's participation in wage labour markets, for example, cannot simply be 'read' from abstract models of labour supply and demand, or from game theoretic models of household bargaining. Rather, this is often a product of skewed power relations and violent coercion within households and wider social institutions. Throughout the book, our approach to discussing gender relations is to offer thicker descriptions of the ways in which the majority of African women are struggling to survive.

There are two consequences of taking 'interdisciplinarity' seriously. First, there is an unusually wide range of references in this book. Despite citing an array of experiences and perspectives, we have, inevitably, failed to be comprehensive. Many gaps have been left, with the rationale for our specific choices the subject of some further discussion in Section 1.3. We do not expect most readers to follow up every thread and scholarly reference, but we hope at least that the references pique the curiosity of some, allowing them to delve further into their own areas of special interest and discover a variety of publications that economists often overlook. Unpublished doctoral dissertations (readily available on the web) are also rarely cited in textbooks, but can be an important resource and one of which we have made use.

There are other reasons to include a wide range of references. The most important of these is that we cite arguments with which we disagree. Too often, economics publications feature scant citation, with what little they do cite produced by a familiar stable of data-crunching workhorses. That prevents readers seeing where contrary arguments come from, or even sometimes realizing that contrary points of view exist at all. We are happy to cite arguments made by the economists of the World Bank and Department for International Development (DFID); as well as official reports produced by organizations such as the International Monetary Fund (IMF) but also the United Nations Conference on Trade and Development (UNCTAD), the International Food Policy Research Institute (IFPRI), the International Labour Organization (ILO), and so on. Many African intellectuals distrust the Washington institutions especially, and in this book we provide a number of reasons for querying much of the economic analysis promoted by the World Bank and the IMF. At the same time, we recognize that these institutions are not monolithic, that they are subject to internal conflicts and ideological shifts over time, and that they have been able to marshal unparalleled resources to undertake economic research in Africa. However, we also cite many other economists, from Adam Smith to Karl Marx, Joan Robinson through to Alice Amsden and Prabhat

Patnaik. This is done not to make a display of our erudition, but to expose readers to a range of different arguments, to support explanations given in the book, and to encourage policymakers, students, and scholars to be more confident in formulating their own nuanced responses to the pronouncements of mainstream economists traipsing through Africa.

The second consequence of taking interdisciplinarity seriously is that we understand the relationship between economics and other 'disciplines' differently from the way most mainstream economics scholars appear to. There is a strong current within neoclassical economics that claims to be able to explain not only market transactions but virtually every other kind of social phenomenon as well—a tendency amounting to 'economics imperialism'. Some economists, for example, believe they can 'explain' the incidence and causes of civil (and other) wars in Africa though the application of neoclassical economic theory. Our approach, by contrast, comes closer to the 'trespassing' idea espoused by Albert Hirschman (see Chapter 6). We are open to learning from non-economists and advocate humility regarding the relative strength (and many weaknesses) of the methods employed by economists.

We also draw on historical experiences of capitalist development. This is not, we stress, due to some notion that everything will ultimately work out the same way it has in, say, the UK or South Korea; or that the path of African economies is determined by colonialism or its legacy. The outcomes and trajectories of capitalist expansion vary hugely and unfold through conflict and contingency. The implication of this is that past 'lessons' should not be relied upon, and that development trajectories are unlikely to repeat past experiences. Ethiopia will not follow the same pattern of development as Taiwan, nor Ghana that of Malaysia. Nonetheless, we remain convinced that a close study of the historical record of industrialization and uneven technological change is important. One reason is that it at least offers some evidence regarding the complexity of how economic change comes about, and what the implications of this are for employment and welfare. The historical evidence, though, should not be used lightly in order to highlight failure—for example, the alleged 'failure' of the Green Revolution in Africa—or as a cast-iron guide to appropriate policy in contemporary economies. There is, however, a hierarchy of plausibility, and evidence from a wide range of countries trumps anachronistic claims based primarily on ideological assumptions.

1.3 Types of Evidence in This Book

Throughout the book, we make use of the kinds of statistical evidence commonly employed by economists, both for individual countries and in cross-country comparisons. In doing so, we present a number of charts illustrating trends in variables, drawing on both national and international statistical agencies. All this said, we take far more seriously than the majority of economics texts the charge that much of this statistical evidence is unreliable.

Huge numbers of academic papers and many well-known economics books are published without much thought being given as to whether the underlying data are accurate and comparable over time or between countries (or even parts of countries). This is not mere nit-picking. We argue, again and again, that policy officials cannot be expected to design, implement, monitor, and refine effective policies without the quality of evidence being taken more seriously. This applies to everything: do we really know how much coffee is produced in Ethiopia, or how much maize is produced in Malawi? Just how sure can we be about pronouncements on the level and rate of food availability growth in a given economy? How accurate are current estimates of the total population or the level and rate of urbanization in a specified country? There are a number of technically advanced econometric models laying claim to explaining patterns of growth across African economies, the majority of which have very little to say about the evidence being fed into their equations. Even if the underlying theories, concepts, and models appear sophisticated, such exercises cannot be taken at face value because of the lack of attention paid to the quality of evidence—in effect, it is 'garbage in, garbage out'. Sometimes, the situation is even worse than a misguided faith in such econometric models. On several occasions, we have listened to senior economists make evidence claims in order to serve an ideological purpose, in the full knowledge that such assertions are misleading.

This points to one of the main purposes of this book: providing readers with the tools and confidence to question 'expert' evidence, claims, and arguments. It is also why we devote considerable space to the difficulties of economic analysis where evidence is poor. One of the key priorities for any effective policy official should be to constantly question the evidence, which is why in this book we cite authors with whose arguments we disagree. Readers—whether policy officials, graduate students, or researchers—need the tools to critically interrogate a wide range of positions before coming to their own conclusions.

Similarly, difficulties in trusting the evidence mean we do not restrict our analysis to 'large-N' statistical evidence, but also draw on other kinds of evidence where available and appropriate. It is worth noting here that our examples are 'biased' towards particular places in Eastern and Southern Africa, specifically Ethiopia, Mozambique, and South Africa. This is not because these countries are in any way statistically 'representative', but rather because of our general scepticism about evidence. We have more direct experience of policy debates in these countries and have carried out considerable primary research in them. Additionally, we have greater knowledge of what other sources of evidence are available, and why some published evidence may be unreliable. This is not to say we know everything there is to know about these countries either. For Ethiopia, for example, we draw on research evidence from the Upper Awash Valley, but not, say, from the Raya Valley. Some of our evidence is unashamedly anecdotal, deployed with the aim of helping readers digest large doses of theoretical political economy. In short, we are happy to acknowledge that our coverage of Africa is far from comprehensive.

1.4 How the Book is Organized and the Main Arguments It Develops

Inevitably, policy officials will have limited time to devote to reading books from cover to cover. Thus, we have organized the book into four clearly defined sections.

Part I, opening with this chapter, sets the stage for later analysis and arguments. Chapter 2, on the contradictions of development in Africa, provides contextual evidence from a range of countries, as well as a wide array of socio-economic indicators, ranging from gross domestic product (GDP) growth rates to the incidence of teenage pregnancy. Going beyond this, however, the chapter makes two closely related arguments. First, capitalist development is everywhere, and always has been, a messy, non-linear, and often brutal process. It is, therefore, not possible to know at any particular moment where it is 'headed'. This is an important point. Many commentators indulge in 'African exceptionalism', marking the continent out as different from the rest of the world. In reality, many of the things people point to as being peculiar problems of African economic development closely resemble historical experiences that have occurred in many places across the globe. Urban slums or abusive exploitation of mine and child workers are not pathologies of African development but have been at the heart of capitalist development everywhere. To be clear, while this does not mean we think African economies will evolve in exactly the same way as other parts of the world, there are important features worth abstracting and highlighting from global experiences of economic change. The second argument put forward in Chapter 2 emphasizes the extraordinary variety and *contradictory* characteristics of recent economic experiences both across and within African countries. If 'Africa is not a country'—and it is remarkable how easily many people still resort to sweeping continent-wide generalizations—it is just as true that 'Nigeria is not a country'. And beyond mere diversity, we argue that capitalist development in African countries, as elsewhere, has been contradict-ory: all good things do not go together.

In Chapter 3, we return to the atmosphere of ideas that policy officials inhale: the common-sense notions that are rarely questioned and that condense and then rain down in a repertoire of phrases and assumptions we refer to as 'rhetorical commonplaces'.[1] We suggest that many of these influential ideas can be categorized as either naively optimistic or overly pessimistic, and in doing so aim to liberate policy officials from the institutionalized ideas they inherit and are under pressure to accept. What is distinctive about our argument is that we show how people who regard themselves as sharply opposed to each other often in reality share attitudes and even assumptions that are excessively optimistic or pessimistic. Nor are the ideas swirling around the policymaker consistent. For example, in some African cities it is possible to identify a poisonous atmosphere that combines elements of 'neoliberalism' with a Third World nationalism that in theory ought not to sit easily with neoliberal instincts. The ideas surveyed in Chapter 3 echo many of the ideas and analyses examined throughout the book. For example, a critique of naive hopes for 'capitalism with a human face' picks up the argument developed in Chapter 2 about the way capitalist economic development is and has always been messy, non-linear, and brutal, even as it produces historically unprecedented advances in welfare and human potential. Meanwhile, a critique of the pervasive 'small is beautiful' notion rehearses arguments developed in, for example, Chapter 6's discussion of mega-projects and Chapter 9's analysis of the productivity of small farms.

Part II addresses policy questions at the core of strategies for sustained economic growth, productivity improvements, employment creation, and foreign exchange generation. Chapter 4, the principal focus of which is investment, is noticeably longer than other chapters, the reason being that it makes a point of avoiding false distinctions between 'macro' and 'micro', or between macroeconomic policies and industrial policy. In it, we argue that African governments should as a matter of urgency raise their share of investment in GDP. Furthermore, they should proactively direct such investment towards activities that have the highest potential for increasing returns of scale and scope, for raising demand for labour, and for earning foreign exchange.

Access to foreign exchange is critical. If developing countries grow quickly, this inevitably results in a huge thirst for and therefore growth in imports, which can be very difficult to keep up with. Borrowing abroad or making requests for foreign aid can certainly help, but both potentially introduce new forms of uncertainty and can threaten the coherence of development strategies. Chapter 5 deals with these and other international dimensions of economic strategy. In doing so, it discusses trends in Africa's net barter terms of trade and how these may affect policy choices, exchange rate policy, and the place of regional African (as opposed to broader international) trade within overall strategies of growth and development. In brief, we argue that sustained, broadly welfare-improving growth depends on maintaining a high growth rate of imports, which, in turn, requires

---

[1] Jackson (2006).

rapid export growth. A modestly competitive—that is, undervalued—exchange rate is one (necessary but not sufficient) way of supporting such growth. Regional integration among African economies may also have some positive consequences (though probably mostly in helping the largest firms in the most advanced economies across the continent). However, we argue that regional trade should not be promoted above exporting to large and growing high-value markets further afield. African intra-trade may be a complement to, but is certainly not a substitute for, an ambitious global trade strategy.

Our arguments about trade exemplify the possibilism we advocate throughout Part II and the book as a whole. This possibilism also extends to 'big projects' (e.g. large-scale irrigation) as well as to an overall strategy of rejecting all recommendations for balanced growth. Hirschman's approach, discussed in Chapter 6, is not reducible to making the case for unbalanced growth versus balanced growth, but rather represents a profound difference in undertaking economic analysis and thinking about projects and policies in low-income economies. Above all, we take to heart Hirschman's observation on how a country's prospects for economic development should be considered. The great majority of economists—whether 'left' or 'right', mainstream or heterodox—seem to think that a country's prospects are determined by what that country has and is: its previous history, its factor endowments, its linguistic fragmentation and geography. Hirschman argued that, instead, a country's prospects are determined by what a country *does*, and by what it becomes as a result of this.[2]

Part III extends some of the arguments made in Part II and draws out their implications. Above all, it is concerned with the broad welfare of people in African countries, especially those on lower incomes, and women in particular. Chapter 8 argues that many myths and problems abound in how economists and international organizations define and measure poverty and how they design policies for poverty reduction, and that these myths help account for the record of such programmes. We contrast these with very different 'stylized facts' about who exactly the poorest people are. The poorest people live in small, not large, households. Also, while they live in households with a relatively high number of women, this is not the same as saying they live in 'female-headed' households. Additionally, the poorest people depend for their survival on access to wage labour opportunities—much of the problem results from the fact that such opportunities are often few and far between, and even when they are available the pay and conditions for the work involved are pitiful.

Wage employment—generating more and better jobs—is at the heart of this book. This, too, is surprisingly unusual, with many influential texts on Africa barely even mentioning employment. Even when they do, the focus tends to be on

---

[2] Hirschman (1967: 5).

small farmers, the self-employed, and entrepreneurial start-ups rather than on those working for wages. In fact, many people still classify as self-employment economic activities that are really wage employment. An example of this is the young men paid a wage for carrying passengers on motor cycles or for touting and ticketing car and mini-bus passengers.

The macroeconomic policies discussed in Part II have wage employment expansion as one of their main objectives. Chapter 8 argues that an overwhelming majority of the very poorest people have to work for wages—casually, seasonally— in order to survive, but that their poverty is exacerbated if the demand for wage labour in rural Africa is not sustained. Chapter 7 brings together a range of arguments about wage labour markets and relations, and again emphasizes the lack of good-quality data on labour markets and employment status as a serious failing of national and international organizations, as well as a major impediment to progressive policy design.

Chapter 7 is also where we argue that the prospects for rising productivity and poverty reduction are likely to improve in circumstances where strong trade union organizations can develop. Throughout the long history of capitalist development, trade unions and other workers' organizations have played extremely important roles in protecting and bringing about improvements in working conditions. Many of these improvements were achieved after periods of protracted social conflict, rather than being the inevitable result of a smooth working out of shifting supply and demand, rising skills, and increases in productivity. For example, during the 1920s and 1930s Norway and Sweden were relatively poor economies, having some of the highest levels of industrial strife in the world.[3]

Unions have also played an important role in economies such as China, where, despite there being clear repression of unions, worker organizations have been able to generate changes in the law that have dramatically improved working conditions.[4] And unions have been very important in African development, having been central to bringing about the end of apartheid and, more recently, at the forefront of the movement calling for regime change in Sudan.[5]

Raising agricultural productivity acts as a foundation for broader sustained economic development and should therefore be a priority for policy officials. This is so for a number of reasons. First, most of the poorest people in Africa will, despite rapid rates of urbanization, continue to live in rural areas for some time to come. Both small- and medium-sized farms, as well as functionally landless people reliant on wage incomes, depend for their welfare on rising agricultural productivity. Second, higher productivity in the output of food crops bought and consumed by African wage workers is a key part of a non-inflationary strategy to sustain profitability, investment, and growth (as well as political stability). Third,

---

[3] Moene and Wallerstein (2008); Bengtsson (2019).   [4] Chan (2019).
[5] Marais (2013: 56ff.); Webster and Englert (2020: 6); El-Gizouli (2019: 7–9).

agriculture is central to securing foreign exchange earnings that can allow for the expansion of imports, thereby fuelling investment and growth. Fourth, there is increasingly scope for agricultural production and processing to reap productivity and other gains previously associated exclusively with manufacturing, and that have wider spill-over effects throughout the economy. Chapter 9 is devoted to understanding the constraints on raising agricultural productivity in African economies, querying conventional arguments concerning the role of extension advice and micro-credit in raising yields, and to presenting arguments for what needs to and could be done.

Finally, in Chapter 10 (Part IV) we draw together the policy priorities that flow from earlier chapters. In doing so, we emphasize strategic policy priorities—and their rationale—rather than setting out a lengthy 'must do' blueprint. We have little faith that such a blueprint would stand any chance of becoming operational across such a diverse range of contexts and uncertainties, given that policy choices are in reality products of technocrats and politicians having to respond to the pressures of prevailing economic conditions as well as to powerful and often conflicting class interests. Additionally, all policies, once introduced, will probably have unintended and unpredicted consequences that can fundamentally change their dynamic.

We hope that this book provides officials with the confidence to raise questions, as well as the means to design, implement, monitor, and refine specific policies. We also aim to present students of economics with material that is both more challenging and exciting, and features fewer bland platitudes about Africa, than many other textbooks.

Our own arguments are explicit and many of them are deliberatively provocative. We do not hold back when criticizing work on African policy issues by other social scientists. We justify our many and robustly expressed criticisms because we make a consistent effort to outline alternative theoretical and practical proposals. For example, we not only show the limitations of the most popular approaches to rural labour markets and poverty, but constructively argue the case for a very different approach. In attempting to encourage debate and further reading, we try to emphasize how and why we differ from many widely accepted and fashionable views. Some of these differences are highlighted in Figure 1.1.

Figure 1.1 Contrasting outlooks on African economic development

2

Uneven, Contradictory, and Brutal Economic Development in Africa

2.1 Introduction

This chapter sets out the context for the analytical and policy discussions under-pinning this book, emphasizing the importance of variation across and within countries as a spur to policy possibilism. In doing so, we make three points fundamental both for understanding how African economies perform and for considering policy design.

First, capitalism is contradictory always and everywhere. Even where capitalist expansion brings about dramatic and, in many ways, progressive changes, it is contradictory, uneven, and brutal. Thus, the contradictions of development in Africa should come as no surprise, nor is there any reason to mark out African countries as tragically different. These contradictions also mean that any attempt to fit Africa into a simple narrative—a narrative of 'tragic growth' or of 'Africa Rising'—is bound to fail. For capitalism is never linear and smooth, never friction-free in its expansion. Benign statements suggesting that 'all good things go together', such as the combination of growth, market liberalization, democracy, and poverty reduction, are pure fantasy.[1]

Second, unevenness and diversity form a central fact of African economic experiences. It is not only the differences *between* countries we highlight, but also the astonishing differences in experience *within* countries, differences often organized around distinctions of gender, class, and ethnic identity. Despite this, economists continue to smother variations with averages, making sweeping claims about the entire African continent based on only a few countries.[2]

Third, the variety, diversity, and unevenness of performance within and across countries is not descriptive exoticism. Although some of this variation—such as in girls' access to schooling or in export performance—is a function of different histories, nonetheless variation is a font of possibilism. That is, it suggests there is scope for *changing* performance, learning from other policy experiences, and

---

[1] See Mills et al. (2017: 1) for an example.
[2] See, for example, a widely read academic journal article claiming to know the secret behind 'Africa's growth tragedy' (Easterly and Levine, 1997), or the sweeping statement that for 'forty years, Africa stagnated while other developing regions grew' (Collier and O'Connell, 2008: 77).

African Economic Development: Evidence, Theory, Policy. Christopher Cramer, John Sender, and Arkebe Oqubay, Oxford University Press (2020). © Christopher Cramer, John Sender, and Arkebe Oqubay.
DOI: 10.1093/oso/9780198832331.001.0001

escaping the ties of structure, legacies of the past, and prior 'endowments'. For instance, if neonatal mortality can be reduced rapidly in some African countries, it is surely worth understanding why, in order to assess the prospects of accelerating improvements elsewhere.

Policymakers are in a difficult position. Constrained by storylines of linear development imposed by (some) scholars and aid agencies, they are also under pressure to deliver rapid and smooth growth and development. We argue that it is useful, as a platform from which to launch policies, to form a more realistic understanding of the history of capitalist development, and of the varied trajectories of economic change within African countries.

2.2 Contradictory, Brutal, and Uneven

Urban Deprivation

Suffering in sub-Saharan Africa, for example in rapidly growing urban slums, is often lamented as being somehow unique to the region. These horrors are real, but they are far from being exceptionally African. They have always been a central feature of capitalist growth. Urban squalor is not a good indication of stagnant capitalism in Africa or of 'tragic' growth; this squalor and other forms of suffering are historically compatible with growth, structural change, and development. These are the kinds of formative calamity characteristic of capitalist development everywhere.

The living conditions of poor people—often recent migrants to the city—in late nineteenth-century London, provide a good example,[3] with people crammed into tiny spaces and wracked by illness, scraping together the very barest of livings. This squalor seems little different to the 'endless and uniform sea of shacks, overcrowded and impoverished, with an ever-growing population' observed in, for example, Khayelitsha on the fringes of Cape Town.[4] Despite Cape Town being regarded as the second wealthiest city in Africa, in some sections of Khayelitsha in 2006 less than a quarter of people had access to taps and less than half could use toilets connected to sewage infrastructure. Furthermore, levels of unemployment were extremely high, with many people scrabbling to earn something from activities with 'vanishingly small economic rewards'.[5]

Contradictory, brutal, and uneven development is nothing new. Early modern capitalist expansion in England (and elsewhere) brought with it grime and immiseration in rural areas and in the slums of the new towns and expanding cities— 'filthy, disease ridden, gin-sodden hell holes'.[6] Real wages stagnated, especially in the

---

[3] Wise (2009).   [4] Seekings (2013: 2).   [5] Du Toit and Neves (2007: 23).
[6] Hilton (2006).

first half of the nineteenth century, and inequality increased. Furthermore, the record of socio-economic development within Europe in the first half of the twentieth century showed profoundly contradictory trends. The period 1913–45 'was littered with civil wars, famines, economic depression, population displacements, ethnic cleansings and World Wars',[7] but even so, declining mortality rates led to a huge increase in the European population. In 1913, there were much higher mortality rates in Eastern and Southern Europe compared to the rest of the continent, but by 1945 there had been dramatic convergence in mortality rates, despite the traumas suffered after 1914.

In this chapter we will show the importance of variation and contradictory developments within Africa, and why this matters. We have insisted on similarities between the unevenness and contradictions experienced in Africa and in Europe; but we deny that our references to economic history and to contingent outcomes in England, for example, is evidence of Eurocentric prejudice or teleological illusions.

Forced and Prison Labour

Capitalism—one of the defining features of which is a 'free' labour market—has in many places and times resorted to forced labour. In post-Civil War Spain, for example, the government used the forced labour of thousands of political prisoners to construct irrigation canals benefitting landowners who had backed the military coup.[8] Convict labour, meanwhile, was concentrated in some of the fastest-growing and most important sectors of the US economy—including lumber businesses, railways, and state-run mines; in the nineteenth and twentieth centuries 'the bearers of modernity frequently [carried] with them its antithesis'.[9] Forced labour continues to be widespread, though some question how much distinction there is between this category and the broader phenomena of extremely exploitative working conditions.[10]

So, there is nothing especially surprising or uniquely 'African' about substituting prisoners for wage labour. In 2013, for example, the manager of a private sector Ethiopian coffee plantation near Jimma was not at all embarrassed to give costed details (to two of this book's authors) about how he was paying to lease prison labour. The widespread use of prison labour on large-scale private farms in Uganda has been investigated in more detail.[11] Nor is it an anomaly that in Angola in the early 2000s, armed forces ran some diamond mines using forced labour.[12]

---

[7] Millward and Baten (2010: 233).   [8] Preston (2012).   [9] Lichtenstein (1996).
[10] Lerche (2007).
[11] Todrys and Kwon (2011); https://www.bbc.co.uk/programmes/w3cswf5b.
[12] Marques de Morais and Falcão de Campos (2005).

In one of the best-known African historical examples, French colonial rule in West Africa normalized forced labour through various bureaucratic forms, including mandatory prison labour on public works and the *prestation* or labour tax system, which was organized through local chiefs and frequently mobilized children and women to build roads.[13] While King Leopold of Belgium's drive to join the club of modern colonial capitalist powers led to extreme, and infamous, uses of forced labour,[14] the effects of forced labour under Belgian colonialism at a later period appear to have had more complex and contradictory effects. For example, when some of the forced recruits into the colonial army returned to their villages as non-commissioned officers after seven years, they became very successful—much to the consternation of the historically dominant leaders of the Kuba who had recruited them.[15]

Order and Discipline

One aspect of modern capitalism's expansion has typically been the effort by capitalists—in particular in capital-intensive mines and in large-scale factories—to persuade a free labour force to stick to the rhythms of production regimes. There are plenty of constraints on the successful development of modern factories but, as Freeman shows in a history of large factories, 'they paled before the problem of discipline'.[16] Employers often resort to a gendered approach to controlling and 'socializing' a new capitalist labour force:

> Many local men proved . . . unwilling to submit to the unaccustomed close supervision and discipline that came with them. In any case, . . . owners did not want adult men for most positions, preferring women and children whom they could pay less.[17]

Experiences of industrialization in England and America were very similar in this respect to recent experiences in African economies such as Ethiopia, where the creation of a labour force internalizing the rhythms and requirements of industrial capitalism has challenged employers.[18] Elsewhere in Africa, recruiting, retaining, and disciplining wage workers has long been difficult, as discussed by Frederick Cooper.[19] In the early 1990s, the general manager's attitude to the workforce on one South African gold mine remained very simple: 'Let's rubberize them and we will have them back to work.'[20]

---

[13] Tiquet (2018: 135).   [14] See Hochschild (1999).   [15] Vansina (2010: 327).
[16] Freeman (2018: 18).   [17] Ibid.   [18] Oya (2019).
[19] Cooper (1992); see also Gibbon (2011).   [20] Donham and Mofokeng (2011: 125).

In one dispute during the rapid industrialization of South Korea in the 1970s, management tried to prevent union elections by nailing shut the door to the women's dormitory, having already cut off their water and electricity supply. When striking women were confronted by riot police, they believed that if they undressed the police would not attack them—to no avail. Two years later the managers of this factory encouraged an attack on the union office by men using buckets of human excrement.[21] And, just as British police claimed to be acting in self-defence when inflicting violence on striking miners in the 1980s, so too did their better armed South African counterparts at Marikana in 2012, where the mine owners provided helicopters and logistical support. In the latter case, police shot dead 34 workers.[22] Earlier, the Zimbabwean security forces were guilty of even greater brutality in 'the Chiadzwa massacre' of October 2008. Having killed miners and terrorized the local population they were easily able to use forced labour, including child labour, to mine diamonds in Marange.[23]

Child labour also made a major contribution to industrialization in Europe and the USA. In England, many girls migrated to work in urban factories in the nineteenth century, although most children working for wages in 1870 were still employed in agricultural and rural occupations.[24] In Europe, 'traffic in children was managed by Foundling Homes, orphanages or poor relief authorities; in the German and Scandinavian countryside, poor children were also put up for public auction'. These children, who 'played a particularly important role in early industrial development', were often physically and sexually abused.[25] Overseers tortured them with long working hours:

[I]f a child becomes sleepy . . . there is an iron cistern filled with water. He takes the boy by the legs and dips him in the cistern, and then sends him back to work.[26]

The Greenhouse Grind

Today, celebrities and even politicians criticize abusive labour conditions in East Asian garment and other factories. But agricultural workers rarely get the same attention, just as was the case in the late nineteenth and early twentieth centuries in the UK and USA, when the 'long-standing exploitation of agricultural workers, domestic producers, servants . . . and others went largely unnoted by politicians, journalists, and writers'.[27]

For example, thousands of seasonal migrants work on horticultural and fruit farms in the USA and live in uninsulated and insanitary labour camps hidden

---

[21] Kim (2011).   [22] Bench Marks Foundation (2012).   [23] Towriss (2013: 106).
[24] Horrell and Humphries (2018: table 1a); on girls working in factories see Rawson (2017).
[25] Honeyman (2016: 7).   [26] Ibid.   [27] Freeman (2018).

from public view. Among these female pickers there is a high incidence of premature births and developmental malformations.[28] Migrant workers have been even more abused in other parts of the world, including in Sicily's greenhouses and parts of Africa.[29] Contradictions within this sector include the tension between providing much-needed wage employment opportunities for women and evidence suggesting that increased exposure to pesticides—especially among poorly educated and weakly organized workers—may lead to adverse health outcomes, including morbidity and spontaneous abortion.[30] Attempts to unionize in this sector stoke conflict: in 2010, for example, police viciously set about a group of women who went on strike at Uganda's largest rose-exporting farm in Entebbe.[31] In Tanzania, 20 migrant agricultural workers protesting about the failure of the state-owned sugar company to pay their wages were shot by the field force in July 1986.[32]

A further reason why less attention is paid to working conditions in agriculture is that rural wage employment is not thought to be very important in African economies. Later chapters, especially Chapter 7, dispel this myth. Wage employment is a dominant feature of rural lives.

Capitalist White Elephants

Resources are often wasted on grandiose or ill-conceived infrastructure projects. The delays, overspending, and repeated redesign of the Inga hydropower dams on the Congo make for an easy—and fair—target. But again, there is no African exceptionalism when it comes to big scheme waste and slowness. To give just one example, Berlin's new airport was scheduled to open in 2011. By 2018 it had still not opened and was some €5 billion over budget.[33] Meanwhile, in Nacala (Mozambique), a new airport terminal *did* open for business, in 2014. It has capacity for 500,000 passengers and 5,000 tonnes of cargo annually. However, it operated for just three years at only 4 per cent of capacity, amid (as was also the case with Berlin) rumours of corruption. We will discuss other African mega-projects in Chapter 7, where arguments in favour of large projects are also introduced.

The Bad, the Ugly, and the Good in the Extractive Industry

Contradictions may be especially concentrated in mining. Many development economists treat the extractive industries with distaste, citing statistics that 'show

---

[28] Holmes (2013: 266, 553).   [29] Tondo and Kelly (2017); Cole and Booth (2007).
[30] Handal and Harlow (2009); Mrema et al. (2017).
[31] http://www.monitor.co.ug/News/National/688334-851606-ca2dt2z/index.html.
[32] https://www.tzaffairs.org/1987/01/tanzania-in-the-international-media-18/.
[33] https://www.bbc.co.uk/programmes/w3csy81k. Delays, huge cost overruns, and accusations of political corruption and malfeasance have often been documented in the USA, for example in Boston's $15 billion urban transport project—finally completed after 15 years in 2007 (Smith, 2010).

a penalty for living in a resource-rich country compared with a non-resource rich country in Africa'.[34] While mining may contribute to foreign exchange earnings, it may also leave an economy exposed to volatile commodity prices. And although the value of production in the mineral extraction sector in Africa is immense (around $176 billion a year in 2010–12), African governments collect a mere 3 per cent of that in tax revenue, with some 'not selling national assets', but effectively 'giving them away' to foreign mining companies.[35]

Mining may crowd out foreign exchange earnings from, and investment in, other activities. It is commonly assumed to be an enclave activity with only negative spread effects to the national economy. These negative effects include pollution, which may reduce agricultural productivity and output growth. Oxfam alleges that women suffer disproportionately as mining leads to a depletion of firewood and restricted access to, and greater pollution of, water. Women may have to devote more time to collecting water and firewood. And because of this, women may be unable to find paid work and become increasingly dependent on men.[36]

There may be other negative effects of mining if, for example, greater fiscal flows lead to greater corruption rather than increased public goods provision. One well-documented example is the Marange alluvial diamond mine in Zimbabwe. When it was discovered in 2006, huge numbers flocked there to work as artisanal miners. But the state security services soon moved in, launching a series of violent attacks in Chikorokoza Chapera (Operation End Illegal Trading). By 2008, the remaining artisanal miners had been brutally evicted and the Marange diamond field was absorbed by a regulated sector dominated by security and political elites.[37]

However, investment by large-scale foreign corporations has been shown to deliver some benefits to people living near mines. Large-scale open-pit gold mines have expanded in a number of African economies in recent years, including Burkina Faso, the Democratic Republic of the Congo (DRC), Ethiopia, Ghana, the Côte d'Ivoire, Senegal, and Tanzania. These mines do cause terrible pollution, which might be expected to reduce agricultural yields and negatively affect infant mortality in surrounding areas. However, survey evidence shows there have instead been rapid *declines* in infant mortality, possibly linked to women's employment and improved access to health care.[38] A study of gold mining in Ghana, Mali, and Tanzania also found some positive outcomes: the chances of finding work throughout the year improve for women closer to the gold mines compared to those living further away;[39] infant mortality fell in Ghana in

[34] Chuhan-Pole et al. (2017b: 3).   [35] Moore, Prichard, and Fjeldstad (2018: 92, 258).
[36] Oxfam International (2016: 7).   [37] Towriss (2013); Rutherford (2018).
[38] Benshaul-Tolonen (2018).   [39] Chuhan-Pole et al. (2017b: 137–8).

communities nearer gold mines; in Mali there were *higher* cereal yields near mines than in other areas.[40]

Capitalist Instability, 'Post-Development', and the Possibility of Progress

The contradictory and indeterminate character of capitalism is more than a quirk of early English industrial history or a blighted feature of twenty-first-century African capitalism. Rather, it is such an enduring and central feature of capitalism that most theories of capitalism focus on its instability and proneness to crisis. The outcomes of capitalism are so uncertain that its very future has often been questioned.[41] Indeed, one of capitalism's contradictions is that it has repeatedly outlived predictions of its demise, rescued by shifts in technology or dramatic reconfigurations of politics and regulation. Another glaring contradiction is that while capitalist expansion has often been regarded as a source of peace, in reality capitalism has often been rescued by militarism. The idea that capitalism, by repressing the 'passions' or greater evils in the quest for 'interests' or lesser evils, may *nurture* peace is not new.[42] Some neoclassical economists and neoliberal ideologues have, despite the horrific experiences of the twentieth century, resuscitated the idea of blaming violence on the poor and on the lack of capitalist development to support a 'liberal peacebuilding' approach to international intervention.[43]

Within an overall pattern of instability, inequality, and war, many astonishing gains in welfare have been secured, but only through protracted political struggle and often at extremely high costs. Seeing the contradictions of capitalism for what they are—fundamental and enduring—may help policy officials protect themselves against the misleading idea that development can be expected to be a smooth, linear process, or that it would be were certain impediments suddenly removed. Across the ideological spectrum 'grand narratives', supporting the idea of unstoppable development and progress, have held strong appeal. Some have been attracted by simplistic, Stalinist versions of Marxism,[44] while others have fallen for the promise of 'automatic convergence' wrapped in Solow–Swan neoclassical growth models. These models predict that 'if' states could only stop distorting market prices then, given mobile capital and diminishing returns, low-income countries would attract investment flows and converge on the Organisation for Economic Co-operation and Development (OECD) countries in terms of income per capita.[45]

Wariness of grand narratives, combined with the myriad disappointments of development and twenty-first-century capitalism, with its frequent financial crises

---

[40] Sanoh and Coulibaly (2015: 25–6).   [41] For a recent example, see Streeck (2016).
[42] Hirschman (2013).   [43] Cramer (2006).
[44] Cohen (2001: 134–74); Howard and King (1992).   [45] Barro and Sala-i-Martins (1992).

and environmental catastrophes, has also led to the idea of a 'post-development' phase. Anthropologists Ferguson and Li write of the 'failure of long-established transition narratives, notably the narrative centred on a universal trajectory from farm-based and "traditional" livelihoods into the "proper jobs" of a modern industrial society'.[46] But these and similar criticisms of 'transition' narratives ignore a rich history—less crassly teleological—of writing about the unevenness, contradictions, and indeterminacy of capitalist development. Charles Dickens captured this famously:

> [I]t was the season of Light, it was the season of Darkness, it was the spring of hope, it was the winter of despair, we had everything before us, we had nothing before us . . .[47]

And some sociologists, such as Göran Therborn, do not hesitate to acknowledge that capitalist development can achieve real progress: 'Trend lines are discernible—in scientific-technical knowledge, economic growth, and life expectancy, for example.'[48] Humanity is at a peak of its capabilities and a survey of its achievements suggests that there has 'been real progress in the development of human resources and human freedom'.[49] Political economists regard this progress as fundamental: the development of labour power is at the centre of the development of the productive forces (the combination of labour power with the means of production to generate products), which in turn shape and underpin an economic structure (a set of production relations).[50]

The Empirical Imperative

The remainder of this chapter traces the 'trend lines' identified by Therborn across the landscape of economic development in Africa. We do not rely on charting gross domestic product (GDP), a composite indicator that is extremely useful but has well-known limitations.[51] Nor do we try to summarize Africa's experience by referring to the Human Development Index, the Multidimensional Poverty Index, or other poverty indicators—discussed in Chapter 6. Instead, we make use of selected individual indicators.

We emphasize two points. The first is, as already discussed, that capitalist development *always* shows inconsistent and messy patterns of advances in technology and welfare alongside persistent failure, wastage, exploitation, and misery. The second is that patterns of development are, typically, distinctly varied. This is very much the case in Africa, where rates of change and levels of performance on a

---

[46] Ferguson and Li (2018); Li (2017).   [47] Dickens (2003: 17).   [48] Therborn (2016).
[49] Ibid.   [50] See Cohen (1978; 2001: 42).   [51] Coyle (2015); Pilling (2019); Jerven (2013).

range of indicators vary hugely between and within countries, and even within villages. So we ignore Binyavanga Wainaina's satirical advice:

> In your text, treat Africa as if it were one country. It is hot and dusty with rolling grasslands and huge herds of animals and tall, thin people who are starving. Or it is hot and steamy with very short people who eat primates. Don't get bogged down with precise descriptions.[52]

2.3 Telling Poor Stories about African Development

Ignoring complexity and contradictions in capitalist economic development, many economists tell stories marred by three common flaws: first, oversimplifying the protagonist by homogenizing sub-Saharan Africa ('Africa is a country'); second, resorting to hyperbole (Africa is 'beyond any doubt . . . the most tragic example of a growth disaster');[53] and, third, a cavalier attitude to evidence.[54] Before criticizing these stories, we turn to very different types of evidence to tell a story of our own—about the complex dynamics and ironies of African history.

A sculpture produced by the Núcleo de Arte in Maputo (Figure 2.1) brings to mind several contradictory ideas. This elegant bird resembles the black-winged stilt that features on Mozambican stamps. The metal figure is delicately balanced as it strides forward on webbed feet. On closer inspection, we realize that the elegance and balance of this symbol of peace are made from the most brutal components—pieces of stripped-down assault rifles, the decommissioned scraps of the millions of small arms imported in the 1970s, 1980s, and 1990s to wage wars in Mozambique.[55] A cruel history literally underpins sculptures now in such fashionable demand in the metropoles.[56] The bird and this history recall Walter Benjamin's insistence that there is no document of civilization that is not at the same time a document of barbarity.[57]

Another, older bird sculpture embodies an even wider range of contradictions and horrors. Now hidden out of sight somewhere in Jesus College, Cambridge, in response to student demands for its return to Nigeria, this proud and fierce cockerel embodies power (Figure 2.2 shows a similar bronze held in the Smithsonian). In the late nineteenth century it probably stood on the altar of the Queen Mother inside the Oba's compound in Benin.[58] The altars in the royal compound from which so many works of art were looted by British forces in 1897 were described by the British Consul-General as 'covered with streams of dried human blood and the stench was too frightful'.[59]

---

[52] Wainaina (2005).   [53] Smits (2006: 1); Collier and Gunning (1999: 4).
[54] On sweeping statements about African growth failure see Sender (1999).
[55] Elmquist (2005).   [56] Verhagen (2017).   [57] Benjamin (1992: 128).
[58] Ezra (1992: 86).   [59] Admiral Rawson, cited in Bodenstein (2018).

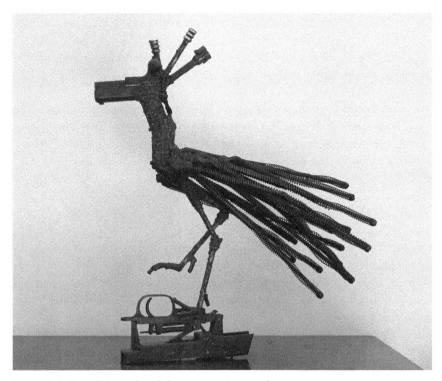

Figure 2.1 Swords into ploughshares, guns into sculptures
Source: J. B. Sender, photo C. Cramer.

Figure 2.2 Benin bronze cockerel
Note: Image provided by the Smithsonian Institute.

The aim of the British had been to eliminate barriers to trade; the gory and exaggerated descriptions of the 'stench' of human sacrifices served as an excuse for deploying Maxim guns and burning the entire city; lurid descriptions also enhanced the exotic allure on the international art market of Benin objects by adding the frisson of a cruelly 'barbaric' provenance. The magnificent plumage and naturalistic realism of the bird, subtly achieved through the brass casters' repeated use of abstract and ornamental motifs, cannot now be openly displayed in Cambridge. When it is eventually displayed to a wider public, viewers will pay tribute to Edo cultural achievements and condemn colonial atrocities, but their attention should also be drawn to Robin Law's scholarly work on pre-colonial inequality and human sacrifice.[60]

The Africa Dummy

Mainstream economists have placed a dummy variable into their regressions to tell a story about African growth failures that combines dubious data, homogenization, and hyperbole. They were trying to explain why, *on average*, African economies appeared to be growing *slower* than the rest of the world, by about 1.5 percentage points per year.[61] Variables were stacked up on top of variables in the pursuit of the mystery of the Africa dummy, but the more variables were dreamed up, the less these exercises had to do with any coherent theory of growth and change in Africa.[62] Too many of these variables were empirically questionable, both in terms of their design and in terms of the provenance and credibility of the actual data. For example, unreliable quantitative indices were constructed to measure the quality of 'African' institutions, governance, and the degree of ethno-linguistic fractionalization.

The regressions also relied on estimates of GDP per capita growth that are *not* reliable. Even in OECD economies, the techniques and assumptions behind GDP estimates shift over time. Where a great deal of economic activity goes unrecorded, as is the case in many low- and middle-income and African economies, GDP involves guestimates of the scale of activity in agriculture, services, and small-scale unregistered manufacturing enterprises. Guesses about the size of the 'shadow', or unrecorded, economy in Africa range from almost 60 per cent of GDP in Zimbabwe, Tanzania, and Nigeria, to around 30 per cent in Botswana, Cameroon, and South Africa.[63]

When we do fieldwork, we routinely ask the largest farmers if a government official had ever visited to collect data or for any other reason. They laugh at the naivety of our question. But one farmer in Mozambique said: 'the Labour

---

[60] Law (1985). [61] Jerven (2011). [62] Deaton (2009). [63] Schneider (2005).

department did visit once—because we gave them a lift'. Thus it is unsurprising if estimates of the scale and dimensions of output, employment, and earnings—or other aspects of the rural economy—are unreliable (see Chapters 7 and 8). A former Ugandan official described the lack of resources in the Bureau of Statistics in the 1990s: the national accounts were totted up by hand for lack of computers, and the office had a single roadworthy vehicle. The upshot is that a reported growth rate in an African economy of 4 per cent a year may actually mean growth was up to 6 per cent a year or it may mean it was zero.[64]

Calculating GDP is one thing: measuring GDP per capita runs into an altogether different, often highly political, challenge of population census data. Problems with population data in Africa are discussed in Chapter 7.

So the data need handling with a great deal of care. But the shortcomings of the cross-country regression approach were not only a product of bad data (though 'garbage in' most definitely guaranteed 'garbage out'), but also of a reliance on sweeping averages to capture what in reality were highly varied patterns of economic performance over time. The simple stories often told about the experience of 'African' growth are plain wrong. It seems clear that there was a concentration of weak growth episodes and growth reversals in the 1980s and 1990s, when around half of the African economies for which we have long-run data contracted.[65] However, for most of the 1950–2016 period, the majority of countries were growing, some modestly, some fairly rapidly. Growth rates and cumulative growth *differed* between African economies, as shown in Figures 2.3 and 3.1 (Chapter 3).

Although very few countries recorded extremely low rates of growth in *all* periods, the Africa dummy regression analyses offered few insights into growth dynamics, or into episodes of rapid growth or growth reversals in different African economies at different times.[66] In other words, they had nothing to say about contradictory developments, their implicit assumption being that 'all good things go together' (and hence bad things go together too). The regressions had further, technical deficiencies: for example, many include variables that are endogenous to growth (fertility or institutions, for example) on the 'explanatory' right-hand side of the equation, meaning they cannot capture causal effects.

If Africa's relatively slow growth is 'explained' by its institutions, what accounts for the lack of appropriate institutions in so many African countries? Acemoglu, Johnson, and Robinson attempt to answer this question, claiming that when Europeans ventured out to the rest of the world from around 1500, they met with essentially accommodating conditions in some places (Australasia, North

---

[64] Jerven (2013).

[65] This refers to the 43 African countries covered by the Maddison Project Database: https://www.rug.nl/ggdc/historicaldevelopment/maddison/.

[66] Some of the flaws in the Africa dummy literature are discussed in Imam and Salinas (2008).

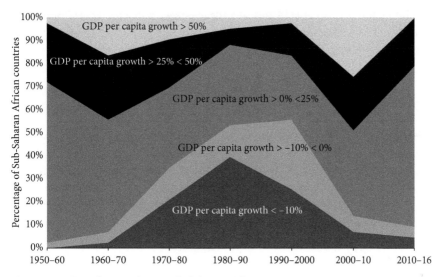

Figure 2.3 Growth episodes in sub-Saharan Africa, 1950–2016
Source: Maddison Project (2018).

America), but were stymied by inhospitable climates and diseases such as malaria elsewhere (in Africa and parts of Asia).[67] In the former, they settled and brought with them the 'inclusive' institutions that provided building blocks for long-run capitalist development. In places such as 'Africa', they found it difficult to settle, and opted instead for 'extractive' institutions, making it difficult for sustained economic growth to emerge.

Compressing 500 years of history like this has attracted criticism from more informed historians.[68] There has also been criticism of the notion that Western European institutions could be described, at least for much of the past 500 years, as resembling transparent and accountable democracies with secure private property rights. A related critical point is that many parts of the world have managed to 'catch up' with the already advanced economies, but often by violating the liberal principles of 'good' institutions or governance. It has been suggested that institutions and markets 'co-evolve': that apparently weak institutions may be useful in the creative development of new markets, but as a market expands there will be increasing pressure for institutional changes to help consolidate that market. This argument has been made, for example, about processes of institutional change and poverty reduction in China since the mid-1970s.[69] A different way

---

[67] Acemoglu, Johnson, and Robinson (2002).   [68] Austin (2008) and Bayly (2008).
[69] Ang (2016). See Chapter 6 on whether this can be applied to make sense of the rise of the Nigerian film industry, Nollywood.

of putting this is to say that historical evidence suggests that growth is a non-linear process, while much of the growth literature in economics deals in linear programming models (see also Chapter 5).[70]

Mal-integration through a Perverse Logic

The pessimistic assumptions behind econometricians' use of an Africa dummy match the fundamental pessimism of scholars influenced by dependency theory and 'world systems' interpretations of capitalism. Just as neoclassically trained economists bemoan 'market distortions' in low-income economies, so many radical economists highlight 'distorted' forms of capitalism in Africa. If orthodox economists have in mind a fantasy benchmark of perfectly competitive markets, so many of their critics invoke the fantasy of an undistorted, 'natural' capitalism in the 'core' countries.

For these critics, respected by many African intellectuals, development prospects throughout Africa are shackled by the rules of a rigged game; and they have no wish to play for the prize of 'second-class, hand-me-down capitalism, ludicrous and doomed'.[71] The theory is that Africa is prey to a 'perverse capitalist logic of disarticulated accumulation' or is a victim of 'mal-integration' into the world economy.[72] Again, the point to emphasize here is the lack of room for contradictions in development—for the possibility of a complex and uneven mix of both success and failure. The arguments and (weak) evidence for this strand of pessimism are discussed further in Chapter 3.

2.4 The Worst of Times: South Africa

Violent Democracy

There is no shortage of fodder for pessimistic outlooks on African economic development. We begin by selecting South Africa to provide negative examples illustrating one side of capitalist development—'the worst of times'—partly because so many people expected better outcomes in the most obviously industrialized economy in sub-Saharan Africa. South Africa can be described as a 'violent democracy'.[73] Not only is there a great deal of violence—pogroms against foreigners, rapes, widespread sexual violence, abuse by teachers and nurses, beatings, abuse and neglect of children—but the institutions and practices

---

[70] Rodríguez (2008).   [71] Achebe (1987: 141).
[72] Shivji (2009: 70); Moyo in Patnaik, Moyo, and Shivji (2011: 72).
[73] Bruce (2014); Taylor (2002); Johnston (1996); and von Holdt (2014).

of democracy and the state are frequently vicious. Assassinations linked to political positions have been an alarmingly common feature of South African politics, with an estimated 450 political killings taking place between 1994 and 2012. Murderous factional rivalries resulted in the assassination of many local councillors between 2011 and 2017, while threats to inflict physical harm were commonplace.[74]

Institutions of the state, especially the police, are directly involved in other forms of violence. While the most infamous example in recent years was the Marikana shooting in 2012 (see Section 2.2), the police also condoned and perpetrated violence in the grape-growing regions of the Western Cape. First, they were accused of turning a blind eye when Zimbabwean migrant workers had their homes torn down and their possessions ransacked in De Doorns in November 2009.[75] Then, in late 2012, when tens of thousands of people were involved in 'farm worker strikes' that spread from De Doorns to some 25 other towns in the area, police fired rubber bullets, struck protesters with batons, and shot dead three people.[76]

As the conflict on and around mines and farms in South Africa makes clear, it is not easy to separate out violence directly involving and concentrated in state institutions, violence in and around labour relations, violent antipathy towards Africans born in other countries, and violence in other social (including family) contexts. The outburst of rage arguably displaced onto foreign scapegoats in De Doorns in 2009 is often cast in the general, problematic, term of South African 'xenophobia'. 'Xenophobic attacks' on non-South African Africans, and their property and businesses, have been common, flaring up, for example, in 2008 and 2019, and on a smaller scale on many other occasions.[77]

Violent Society

Violence pervades much of South African society. It has a death from injury rate double the global average (Figure 2.4) and the incidence of women killed by intimate partners is six times the global average. About 40 per cent of reports of rape to the police concern girls younger than 18, but the 55,000 reported rapes each year are the tip of the 'iceberg of sexual violence'. The actual number is thought to be around nine times higher. Rapes are part of a continuum of sexual violence that also includes intimate partner violence, intimidation, threats, and abuse and neglect of young girls. Twenty per cent of women attending antenatal

---

[74] SALGA (2017).   [75] Kerr and Durrheim (2013).   [76] Eriksson (2017).
[77] Fauvelle-Aymar and Segatti (2012); Mlilo and Misago (2019); https://www.bbc.com/news/world-africa-47800718.

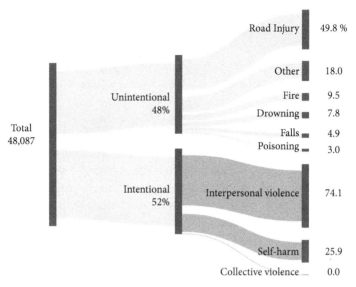

Figure 2.4 Estimated deaths in South Africa caused by intentional and non-intentional injuries in 2016
Source: WHO Global Health Estimates (2018).

clinics in Soweto reported sexual violence by their intimate partners, while 68 per cent of them reported exposure to psychological abuse (including threats of violence, insults, and controls on their movement).[78] A survey of more than 3,500 children in Mpumalanga and Western Cape found a 56.3 per cent prevalence of physical abuse; a 35.5 per cent prevalence of emotional abuse; and that 9 per cent had at some point experienced sexual abuse.[79]

Intimate partner violence and highly unequal gender relations increase the risk that young women will risk exposure to HIV/AIDS.[80] The prevalence rate for all 15–49 year olds is around 19 per cent; the prevalence rate for women is higher— 23.7 per cent. One urban survey carried out in 2016 found that 60 per cent of women patients aged 30–39 were HIV positive.

Maternal Mortality, Neonatal Mortality

South Africa has had a woeful record on maternal mortality. One longitudinal study carried out in a rural location in northern KwaZulu-Natal characterized by high HIV prevalence and unemployment found a local maternal mortality rate of

---

[78] Seedat et al. (2009); Jewkes and Abrahams (2002).   [79] Reported in Day and Gray (2017).
[80] Jewkes et al. (2010).

650 per 100,000 live births during the 2000–14 period. This is significantly higher than the least developed country average of 436 per 100,000 live births. Rural women in South Africa often have long travel times to antenatal clinics, very high costs of delivery, and unacceptably poor-quality service.

Large numbers of South African mothers die in or shortly after childbirth, but so too do many babies. The number of neonatal deaths is 'unacceptably high for a lower-middle-income country like South Africa' and also appears to be linked to poor investment in properly trained health staff.[81] Underinvestment is a major factor explaining why many clinic staff neglect pregnant women, turning them away in early pregnancy. This is on top of a generalized lack of blood for transfusions, a lack of emergency transport facilities, poor referral systems, and inadequate intensive care provision in rural areas.[82]

Dismal Economic Performance

Underpinning many of these dismal signals has been the poor overall performance of the South African economy. Investment dropped off from 1976 (the year of the Soweto uprising) and, as a share of GDP, carried on falling until 1993. After that, gross fixed capital formation stuttered for a few years, before climbing to a post-apartheid peak of 23.5 per cent of GDP in 2008 (still significantly below the 32 per cent of GDP level of 1976—see Figure 2.5). After 2008, however, it again fell away and by 2018 was at only 18 per cent of GDP. In marked contrast, the 18 most successful emerging economies, (as defined by McKinsey), have managed to *sustain* an average investment-to-GDP ratio of 30 per cent since 1965.[83] We will argue in Chapter 4 that high investment rates are associated with sustained economic growth and structural change. By structural change we mean the shift of resources over time from lower to higher-productivity economic activities.

South Africa's weak investment record has been accompanied by high unemployment. By the first quarter of 2019 the official unemployment rate was 27.6 per cent. Furthermore, Statistics South Africa adopts a 'strict' definition of unemployment which excludes 'discouraged workers'—those who very much want to work but who live in poor areas where search costs are high and the probability of finding employment is so low they do not formally 'search' for jobs. Yet panel data tracking individuals over time show that the 'non-searching' unemployed (the discouraged) are no less likely to find employment than the 'searching' unemployed, providing strong grounds to include discouraged workers in the South African unemployment figures.[84] When 'discouraged

---

[81] Rhoda et al. (2018).   [82] Tlou (2018), Silal et al. (2012), Sender (2016).
[83] McKinsey Global Institute (2018: 48).   [84] Posel, Casale, and Vermaak (2014).

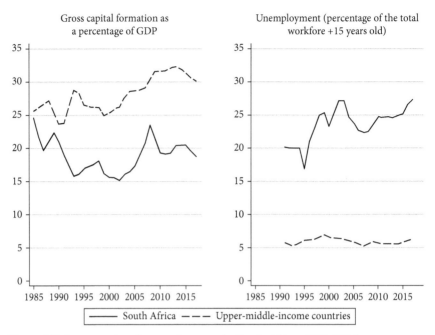

Figure 2.5 Investment and unemployment in South Africa, 1985–2016

Source: ILO for unemployment data. World Bank Indicators for Gross Fixed Capital Formation Database (2018).

workers' are included, the estimated unemployment rate in early 2019 was 40 per cent. The 'New Growth Path', announced in 2011, reasserted the need for a very orthodox, contractionary fiscal policy. Despite international applause, it did not do the trick.[85] More recent government macroeconomic policy proposals have reproduced the fiscal orthodoxy—yet again—and are unlikely to succeed.[86]

There does appear to have been a genuine tragedy of economic growth in South Africa: investment has been sluggish; unemployment is high; inequality rose after the end of apartheid and has remained extremely high, the main reason being high inequality in the labour market; and the real rate of GDP growth has stuttered like a car running out of fuel for decades.[87] The element of inevitability about this tragedy stems from religious adherence to economic policies following the 'treasury' line, favouring minimal state intervention, an overvalued currency, and a prioritizing of anti-inflation through macroeconomic 'prudence'.

[85] Tregenna (2011).   [86] Adelzadeh (2019).
[87] Leibbrandt, Finn, and Woolard (2012); Finn and Leibbrandt (2018).

2.5 Disappointment, Violence, and the Oppression of Women in Sub-Saharan Africa

Violent Conflicts

While evidence on violence is unreliable everywhere in Africa, an especially high number of deaths have been directly linked to armed conflicts in some countries in 2017. Figure 2.6 shows high estimates of casualty levels in Nigeria, South Sudan, Somalia, and DRC. The latter is a classic example of problems with data on violence. Global media paid attention to International Rescue Committee (IRC) estimates of 5.4 million fatalities in warfare in DRC between 1998 and 2007. It became clear that the IRC had used inappropriate assumptions to extrapolate from specific survey sites that had experienced particularly intense fighting. An alternative approach, covering the same period and drawing on the same survey evidence but making different assumptions about pre-conflict mortality rates, came up with a much lower estimate—less than a million.[88]

Between 1989 and 2017, Rwanda, Ethiopia, DRC, Sudan, and Nigeria recorded fatality numbers from organized violence that were among the highest

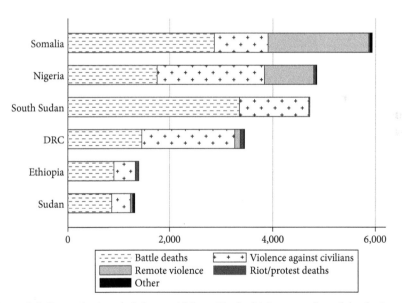

Figure 2.6 Countries in sub-Saharan Africa with the highest number of deaths in violent conflicts, 2017
Source: ACLED (2017).

[88] Human Security Report (2013).

anywhere in the world. Between 2016 and 2017, the number of non-state conflicts in African countries increased dramatically, including several different conflicts in Nigeria, Sudan and South Sudan, DRC, and the Central African Republic (CAR).[89] There is evidence that the greatest suffering caused by all types of violent conflict is experienced by women and girls, who are affected by the indirect effects of war, such as reduced access to food, health services, and clean water. This may be reflected in a narrowing—across a wide sample of conflicts—of the gender gap in life expectancy between women and men.[90]

Intimate Violence and the Blaming of Girls

With or without large-scale armed conflicts, violence against women and girls is prevalent. Intimate partner violence is, again, extremely difficult to measure accurately, but it seems to be a commonplace feature of African women's lives, as Achebe suggests:

> [A] concerned neighbour once called the police station and reported that a man was battering his wife and the Desk Sergeant asked sleepily: 'So Therefore?' So, behind his back, we call him Mr 'So Therefore'.[91]

Figure 2.7 uses the best available data in 2018 to suggest that in several African countries more than 20 per cent of surveyed women between the ages of 15 and 49 had experienced intimate partner violence within the past year, with the figure rising to well over 30 per cent in some countries. In Sweden and the UK the figure is around 6 per cent.

As discussed in Chapter 8, teenage pregnancy is an excellent predictor of poor life outcomes for both children and women.[92] In a number of African countries, a very high percentage of women have at least one child before they are 18. Mozambique is perhaps the most extreme case, with the proportion of women giving birth before they turned 18 (40 per cent) having barely changed between the early post-war years and 2012. But in the rural areas of some other countries (Chad and the CAR) close to 50 per cent of young women give birth before they are 18. And, in both rural and urban Africa, girls living in the poorest households are most at risk of teenage pregnancy.[93]

---

[89] Pettersson and Eck (2018); https://www.acleddata.com/data/.
[90] Plümper and Neumayer (2006). [91] Achebe (1987: 35).
[92] Jeha et al. (2015); Corcoran (1998).
[93] https://data.unicef.org/topic/maternal-health/adolescent-health/.

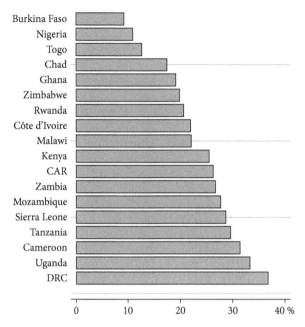

Figure 2.7 Proportion of women reporting physical and/or sexual violence in selected sub-Saharan African countries
Source: UNDS (2018).

One obvious explanation for these high rates of early childbearing is enforced child marriage. Data from Amhara regional state in Ethiopia show that well over half of rural women and girls are married before they turn 18, with 15 being the median age at first marriage among 20–49-year-old women.[94] In some countries a very high proportion of women, especially unmarried women, have unmet contraception needs. In Uganda, for example, well over half of unmarried women aged 15–49 expressed unmet demand for contraception (Figure 2.8). Social attitudes, often reinforced by political leaders (or their wives), compound the often-coercive conditions that young women must endure. In 2017, Tanzania's President insisted that pregnant students be excluded from schools, with Burundi's Minister of Education following suit in 2018.[95]

If the welfare of teenage girls is harmed by policy choices or neglect, it is unsurprising that some countries have lagged behind the more general African trend (discussed in Section 2.8) towards declining fertility rates. In Angola, Uganda, Chad, and Nigeria, for example, average fertility rates are still exceptionally high, at more than 4.5 live births per woman.[96]

---

[94] Jones et al. (2018: 45).
[95] Martínez, Odhiambo, and Human Rights Watch (Organization) (2018).   [96] UN (2017).

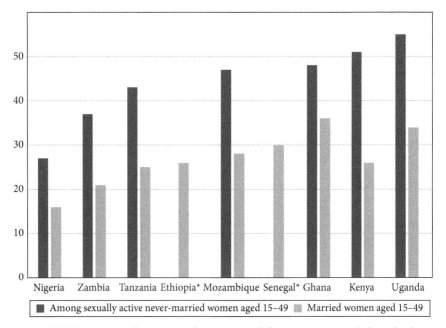

Figure 2.8 Percentage of women with unmet need for contraception (selected sub-Saharan African countries)
Source: Guttmacher (2016).

Dying Young

West and Central Africa suffer the highest rates of under-5 mortality (U5MR) anywhere in the world: on average 98.7 deaths per 1,000 live births across these regions. That is roughly 15 times higher than the high-income country average. There are U5MRs higher than 100 per 1,000 live births in Angola, Chad, Somalia, CAR, Sierra Leone, Mali, and Nigeria. However, U5MRs in Africa cannot be explained at the national level. Instead, it is necessary to look at the *local* factors increasing mortality risks. Researchers from Stanford University conclude that not only are U5MRs in sub-Saharan African nations highly heterogeneous but that subnational factors account for more than three-quarters of the overall variation in mortality.[97] Their results support the policy case we make for targeting (in Chapter 8).

2.6 The Best of Times: South Africa

Electricity provision can fundamentally improve living conditions—allowing reading at night and much safer cooking, for example. There is no doubt that

---

[97] Burke, Heft-Neal, and Bendavid (2016).

South Africa has made great strides since the early 1990s, when access levels were less than 40 per cent. By 2012/13, more than 85 per cent of households reported being connected to the electricity grid.[98]

Neonatal deaths may still be unacceptably high in South Africa but in fact the U5MR in the country has been falling dramatically, from around 80 per 1,000 live births in 2003–5 (the peak of the AIDS epidemic) to 37 per 1,000 live births by 2015. This has not been the only positive demographic change in South Africa. The rise in the percentage of girls giving birth before they are 18 has tailed off and may be in decline. National Adolescent Friendly Clinic Initiative facilities are providing reproductive health advice targeted at young people. These facilities have been associated with extended schooling for girls, higher wages among employed young adult women, and improved health for children born to young women.[99]

By 2015, 92 per cent of 5 and 6 year olds (pre-school age) were in some form of educational establishment, a rise of 38 per cent since 2002. In three provinces (Gauteng, the Free State, and the Western Cape) more than 90 per cent of children have access to safe water. Though easy access to safe water remains inadequate in Limpopo, KwaZulu-Natal, and the Eastern Cape, dramatic progress has been made in the latter two provinces.[100]

After years of massive losses of life and disability-affected life years (DALYs), the government was forced to abandon its AIDS denial stance. A surge in funding after 2005 resulted in, among other things, the world's largest anti-retroviral programme.[101] More than 98 per cent of pregnant women attending antenatal clinics were tested for HIV and more than 92 per cent of HIV-positive pregnant women received treatment.[102] More broadly, there have been important improvements in health-care capacity. Between 1996 and 2016, the estimated number of physicians per 1,000 people rose from 0.593 to 0.818. There were only about 2,000 black African medical practitioners in the public sector in 2001 but by 2016 there were nearly 7,500. Meanwhile, the number of nurses on the South African Nursing Council register rose by 74,000 (a 35 per cent increase) between 2008 and 2017.[103]

2.7 Sub-Saharan Africa: Light at the End of the Tunnel?

After 2000, when African growth seemed to be outstripping much of the rest of the world, a new oversimplified narrative replaced that of the 'Africa dummy'.

[98] Harris, Collinson, and Wittenberg (2016).   [99] Branson and Byker (2018).
[100] Jamieson et al. (2017).   [101] Mayosi and Benatar (2014).   [102] Cooper et al. (2016).
[103] https://data.worldbank.org/indicator/SH.MED.PHYS.ZS?locations=ZA; http://www.sanc.co.za/stats/stat2017/Growth%202008-2017.pdf.

Now the story was of 'Africa Rising': there were hyperbolic celebrations of growth spurts and fables of 'Lions on the Move'; and the discussion of policy lessons focused on the positive contribution of governance 'improvements' and elections. Facts that had previously heralded a dark and hopeless future, such as the 'youth bulge', were now turned into the stirrings of development resurgence. So the age composition of Africa's population and its rate of growth came less to define a 'security demographic' fear, but now promised a valuable 'dividend'—a rapidly growing consumer market and source of (cheap) labour.

Despite exaggerated prognoses, there actually is evidence of socio-economic changes in much of Africa that are remarkable by historical standards. These changes—the improvements in women's welfare above all—go deeper than a brief spurt in GDP growth or momentary upticks in 'doing business' scores.[104] In this book, we will outline important evidence of development across a range of indicators in Africa. However, we also stress that this experience of economic and social change has been *uneven*, both over time and across (and within) countries. We underline the need to consider a more complex protagonist in narratives of development in Africa.

We have already shown that in some African countries a very high percentage of women give birth as adolescents. This, though, is only part of the picture. Figure 2.9 shows that in a number of other African countries a far smaller share of women experience teenage pregnancies. This figure also shows that there have been *declines* in the incidence of teenage live births in a few countries, with Senegal being just one example (down from 27 per cent to 18 per cent between 1998 and 2016).

The prospects for further reductions are encouraging. Not everywhere has political leadership that stokes the stigmatization of schoolgirl mothers and limits access to condoms.[105] Many African countries have already enacted laws protecting the rights of young women to return to school after giving birth. Some have addressed particular barriers to their return by removing school fees and indirect costs; others, for example Senegal and Cape Verde, have provided facilities for breastfeeding mothers; and Zambia allows for flexible learning timetables.[106]

There is evidence of dramatic and deep fertility declines, as can be seen in, for example, Ethiopia and Rwanda since the early 1990s (Figure 2.10). Overall, the fertility transition (the decline in the average number of births per woman to a

---

[104] If the Doing Business Index was not already questionable, its weakness became widely recognized when the then World Bank chief economist, Paul Romer, suggested that Chile's ranking had been politically manipulated to reflect badly on particular Chilean administrations (https://eurodad.org/doing-business-report).

[105] In Uganda, Pentecostalist campaigns supported by Janet Museveni have explicitly and repeatedly opposed the marketing and distribution of condoms (Bompani and Brown, 2015).

[106] Martínez, Odhiambo, and Human Rights Watch (Organization) (2018: 11).

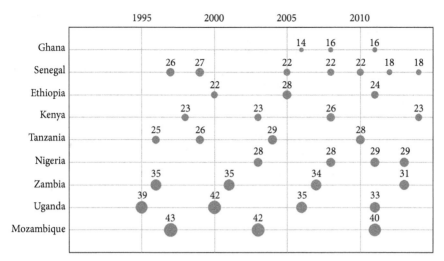

Figure 2.9 Percentage of women who had at least one child by the age of 18 (selected sub-Saharan African countries, 1995–2016)
Source: UNICEF (2018).

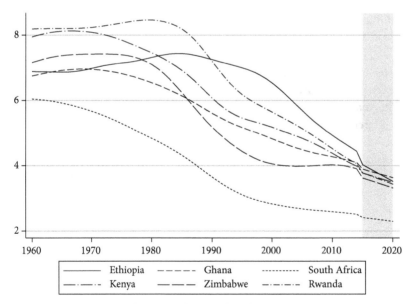

Figure 2.10 Rapid fertility decline (selected sub-Saharan African countries)
Source: UN (2017).

generally agreed figure of two) has advanced quite rapidly in Africa's urban areas. The fertility transition is almost complete in Botswana, Lesotho, Swaziland, urban Kenya, and, remarkably given income levels, urban Ethiopia. Set against this, in five countries that have been through wars and not had effective family planning policies—Angola, Mozambique, DRC, Congo (Brazzaville), and Cameroon—the rural fertility transition has barely begun.[107]

With fewer very young women becoming pregnant and with better public health and improved living standards reflected in falling fertility rates, some of the risks of maternal mortality fall away. On average, the maternal mortality rate in sub-Saharan Africa fell from 987 deaths per 100,000 live births in 1990 to 546 per 100,000 in 2015. This, of course, masks wide variations, with improvement in the maternal mortality rate especially striking in some countries. In Ethiopia, for example, the rate fell from 1,250 to 353; while in Rwanda it fell from 1,300 to 290.[108]

We could present additional demographic statistics to illustrate disparities in rates of improvement in women's well-being within and between African countries. We could, for example, chart dramatic trends in the educational status of women—such as the exceptional acceleration after 2000 in the median number of women enrolled in tertiary education in Ghana, Tanzania, Côte d'Ivoire, and, above all, in Ethiopia.[109] We prefer, however, to shift gear—to provide a different type of illustration of changes in the status of some African women. In 2017, an all-female African crew (Figure 2.11) took charge of a Boeing 777 flight from Addis to Lagos; they are emblematic of an expanding cohort of female technical graduates who have begun to find it possible to overcome daunting historical prejudices.[110]

Millions of women continue to suffer because, as noted, a high proportion of their children die before reaching the age of 5—especially in West and Central Africa. But 90 per cent of sub-Saharan African countries had a *faster* average rate of reduction (ARR) of U5MR between 2000 and 2015 than they had in the 1990s. In 21 of these countries the 2000–15 ARR was either a reversal of a negative trend in the 1990s or represented a tripling of the 1990s ARR.[111] Nine sub-Saharan African countries achieved a steady, linear decline in U5MR over the entire 1950–2000 period. Some recent trends captured by the data on armed conflict have clearly contributed to improvements in infant mortality. In countries as diverse as Angola, Burundi, Ethiopia, Rwanda, and Uganda, levels of fatalities directly caused by armed conflict have *declined sharply* in the past 10 to 25 years.

Most violent conflicts—state-based or otherwise—affect relatively small geographical areas of African countries, except in Somalia. In addition, armed conflict has become less violent, at least in the sense that the number of battle deaths is

[107] Garenne (2018).   [108] https://data.unicef.org/topic/maternal-health/maternal-mortality/.
[109] http://data.uis.unesco.org/.   [110] Egne (2014).   [111] You et al. (2015).

Figure 2.11 The first all-female air crew on Ethiopian Airlines
Source: Ethiopian Airlines.

relatively modest. Fatalities from state-based conflict and one-sided violence have both fallen markedly since around 2000 compared to the 1990s.[112]

Progress in addressing the AIDS/HIV epidemic, in the provision of safer water and in access to electricity is not restricted to South Africa. Wider access to anti-retroviral drugs (ARVs) has led to a striking recovery in overall life expectancy.[113] The World Health Organization (WHO) estimates that 43 per cent of people in sub-Saharan Africa gained access to an improved drinking water source between 1990 and 2015.[114]

In 1990, a mere 16 per cent of sub-Saharan Africans had access to electricity; by 2016 this figure had risen to 43 per cent.[115]

2.8 Nigeria is a Country

The very idea of a homogeneous 'country' or economy like Nigeria needs to be pulled apart. There are many sources of variation in Nigeria (as in other countries). One very striking indicator is the regional disparity in girls' education. In

---

[112] Bakken and Rustad (2018).   [113] UNAIDS (2016).   [114] WHO and UNICEF (2015).
[115] World Development Indicators.

2015, women of reproductive age in Ekiti state had an average school attainment level of 11.3 years. This was the highest average in Nigeria. In several northern Nigerian states the attainment level was less than two years (e.g. in Kebbi, Sokoto, Yobe, and Zamfara).[116]

Under the radar of Nigeria's allegedly debilitating 'resource curse', the production of some crops in Nigeria has begun to expand steadily. Nigeria has become Africa's biggest cashew nut exporter and the second-largest cashew producer in the world after Vietnam. Cashew production is now nine times higher than in Mozambique, which was in the 1970s the world's largest cashew producer (see Chapter 3).[117]

The Nigerian national context might be considered unfavourable for expanding production, investment, and capital accumulation. The country experienced 'civil war' in the 1960s, low-intensity on-off insurrection in the Delta, 'state-based conflict' with Boko Haram (and with Islamic State [IS]) in the north, as well as a proliferation of 'non-state conflicts', including between Fulani pastoralists and more settled agriculturalists. But this is the same context within which Aliko Dangote not only built a cement industry that operates in much of Africa, but has embarked on an industrial complex that is set to include a $12 billion oil refinery, a petrochemicals plant, and a fertilizer plant with capacity for 3 million tonnes of urea a year. This complex benefitted from Lagos State government incentives, and is just one sign of the revival of Lagos in recent years, where the quality of state interventions raises questions for stereotypes about Nigerian capabilities. The literacy rate among 15–25 year olds in Lagos State is around 95 per cent; more than 90 per cent have access to improved water sources; and more than 90 per cent live in homes with a mobile phone. All these are streets ahead of the wider Nigerian average.[118]

Variation and the Scope for Policy

Appreciating variation may be a gateway to policy potential. It is more difficult to throw up one's hands in despair, to blame a colonial past or adverse conditions and rules of the game in the global economy, if it becomes clear that some countries in the same region (and some people within the same country) have managed to perform better; if those adverse conditions are not consistently debilitating; if countries with—in some respects—similar 'cultures' have nonetheless reduced the incidence of teenage pregnancy, for example.

---

[116] Graetz et al. (2018: 49).
[117] FAOSTAT (Food and Agriculture Organization Statistical Database).
[118] Pilling (2018).

Variation also often provides clues to explanation. If some features of a set of economies have been fairly similar, but outcomes or performance vary, then the quest to explain outcomes may edge forwards. We argue that variation in performance generally ought to expand the space for the 'art of the possible' (see Chapter 6).

Perhaps the clearest example of the scope for policy is the variation in rural fertility decline. By 2010, the fertility transition in rural Rwanda was over halfway to being achieved, compared to a mere 5.6 per cent transition in rural Burundi.[119] These are two countries with many similarities, from terrain and population to colonial experience. The difference lies in Rwanda's far more comprehensive and resolutely implemented family planning policies, leading to a greater prevalence of contraception. In rural Kenya, fertility fell very fast between 1980 and 2010 to the point where again a fertility transition had been roughly half achieved. But in rural Uganda fertility rates remained very high for a longer period. Again, Kenya, which had had the highest fertility rate in the world at independence, had a long post-independence history of family planning policies and institutions, with various forms of contraception remaining free, widely disseminated, and accessible to most of the population. A similar story holds for the contrast between Ghana— with sustained, clear family planning policies and a rapid reduction in rural fertility—and Nigeria, where policy has been less consistent, opposition from Islamic and Catholic groups has been more strident, and progress in fertility transition has been more uneven and slower.[120]

There are similar disparities in the rate at which African countries have reached the level of at least one insecticide-treated bed net (ITN) per household. While Benin, for example, achieved dramatic increases in the percentage of households with at least one ITN (from 25 to 80 per cent between 2006 and 2011/12), Angola managed only a paltry rise from 28 per cent to 35 per cent. Thirteen out of 19 African countries also improved the *equity* of distribution of ITNs across wealth levels, while there was no change in two and a worsening of distribution in four countries. Again, the differences appear to be driven by variations in policy at the national level.[121]

Another illustration is the difference in the rates of change in child mortality in Tanzania and Uganda. In 1995, both countries were at very similar levels in terms of child mortality. They also received similar amounts of foreign aid for the health sector over the following 12 years. They have broadly similar climatic conditions and colonial histories, similar levels of income per capita, and similar economic structures. Yet in recent years Tanzania achieved a dramatic reduction in child mortality and Uganda did not. In Tanzania, the government gave high and

---

[119] This is a very widely observed trend, whereby as economic development proceeds the average fertility rate—the mean number of children a woman has—falls from high to low.
[120] Garenne (2018). See also Sharan et al. (2011).   [121] Taylor, Florey, and Ye (2017).

sustained priority to the health sector, as well as protecting the independence of health research by both government researchers and the external researchers to whom they were linked. In Uganda, by contrast, health interventions have been prey to privatization ideology and to the evolving politics of the regime. The biggest differences seem to be in policies preventing and treating malaria. Meritocratic appointments, technical autonomy, and continuity of individuals in key posts were features of the National Malaria Control Program (NMCP) in Tanzania. In Uganda, meanwhile, 'there were numerous examples of political interference in technical NMCP matters, high-profile and well-documented instances of corruption, and high levels of staff turnover in the NMCP over the period in question'.[122]

The same principle—analysing variation as a first step in identifying a role for policy—works for variation within a country. An example is the assessment of the relative performance of three different manufacturing subsectors in Ethiopia, carried out by one of the authors. Ethiopia has had a single economic strategy and a common approach to industrial policy, but performance across subsectors—including floriculture industry, leather and leather goods, and cement—varied markedly in recent years. Assessing variation pointed to possible explanations, which, in turn, provided a clearer understanding of where inter-sectoral differences accounted for variation and of where, despite and because of these differences, there was scope for new policies to improve performance.[123]

2.9 Conclusion: Beware the 'Dominican Model'

The aim of policymakers and their advisers should always be to learn much more about the heterogeneity of social and economic experiences in Africa, between and within countries. Our argument is they should begin with a careful analysis of the 'effective reality' in specific places and moments. We have also emphasized the contradictory, often horrific, characteristics of development in Africa, arguing that these are only to be expected given the history and theoretical dynamics of capitalism. Both these points should reinforce the guard that policy officials need to put up against analyses and prescriptions that smother complex diversity under a blanket of averages and that repress the contradictions in bland summary mash-up indices. We have also argued that variation in welfare outcomes and patterns of economic performance can provide insights when considering the potential for policy interventions.

Many policy prescriptions followed by African policy officials are based on standard diagnoses that draw on the simplistic narratives and explanations

---

[122] Croke (2012: 448).   [123] Oqubay (2016).

challenged in this chapter. The standard diagnoses are too often based on ignorance: a consultant arriving for the first time in Maputo to lead a team evaluating the impact of donor expenditure was asked what he knew of Mozambique. He replied to one of the authors of this book, 'oh, very little but it does not matter because we can use the Dominican model'. Much policy advice is dusted off the shelf and takes this form.

3

Varieties of Common Sense

3.1 Introduction: The Fog of Development Economics

The air that policymakers breathe is thick with the smog of conventional wisdom: with particles of ideas and assumptions that stick loosely together to form a miasma of apparently self-evident truth—of common sense. The effect is that assumptions and evidence are not always challenged. Common-sense works like the mental short-cuts that people make, relying on habits of thought and bias: the field studied by behavioural psychologists that has begun to influence economists and policy officials.[1]

In this chapter, we outline two archetypal forms of conventional wisdom that have come to hang over the atmosphere in which policy decisions are taken in Africa. First is the set of ideas associated with orthodox, neoclassical economics. Second is the bundle of arguments linked to anti-imperialist 'third worldist' development theory, as well as some forms of structuralist development economics. At first sight, these are very different, contradictory approaches. However, rather than tracing their origins and complex trajectories, which has been done many times elsewhere, our objective is to draw attention to what they have in common.[2] The ideas of these two supposedly contending approaches can often be seen to overlap in the views and statements of policy officials, advisors, and university economists. One example, discussed in Section 3.4, is reflected in widespread support for the African Continental Free Trade Area (AfCFTA).

If there are two different schools of thought influencing policymakers, neither is wholly self-contained. Rather, each has a range of variants, some more narrowly intolerant than others. Additionally, approaches from both schools often share one of two distinct attitudes: pessimism (and 'impossibilism'), or naive optimism. We will show how an attitude of 'impossibilism' is shared by development economists who otherwise would regard themselves as sharply at odds. This 'impossibilism' unites, for example, those who are pessimistic about gains from processing primary commodities in low-income countries with those who insist that such countries can never create firms capable of climbing higher than the

---

[1] Kahneman (2012); Lewis (2017). For a very different approach to how decisions are made, see Tuckett (2011); Chong and Tuckett (2015); Dow (2012).
[2] See, for example, Thirlwall and Pacheco-Lopez (2017); Meier and Seers (1984); Hirschman (1981b); Howard and King, (1992); Glyn (2007); King (2009).

African Economic Development: Evidence, Theory, Policy. Christopher Cramer, John Sender, and Arkebe Oqubay, Oxford University Press (2020). © Christopher Cramer, John Sender, and Arkebe Oqubay.
DOI: 10.1093/oso/9780198832331.001.0001

lowest rungs on the ladder of global value chains. On both sides of the rhetorical divide, impossibilists believe that rapid capitalist industrialization in poor economies will fail to create a sufficient number of jobs in factories.

We will then go on to look at a very different, but still commonly shared, attitude: naive optimism. In particular, we are sceptical about widespread programmes promoting bottom-up, micro-enterprise, and cooperative development. We argue that an analytical attitude of *possibilism* should not be confused with naive optimism, and, as elsewhere in the book, warn against prettifying capitalist development (or, indeed, African long-run history). The contradictions discussed in Chapter 2 are not a 'bolt-on' for economic analysis, but are front and centre of our analytical framework, and, we argue, ought to inform all analysis and policy design (and evaluation).

A glance at some of the evidence on economic growth over the past sixty-odd years, for example, suggests that common-sense stories about the preconditions of growth are misleading. The country that had the *least* exposure through colonial settlement to Western European 'inclusive institutions' (that Acemoglu, Johnson, and Robinson see as critical to long-run development) achieved more cumulative growth between 1960 and 2016 than almost every other African country (Figure 3.1).[3] What brief colonial settlement there was in Ethiopia took the form of fascist Italian occupation, during which some infrastructure was built and there

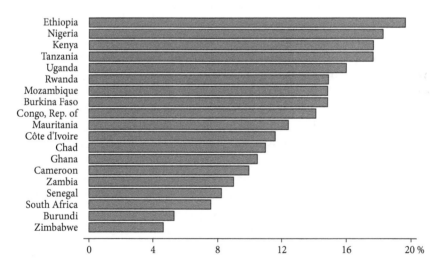

Figure 3.1 Cumulative growth in GDP (percentage growth 1960–2016, selected African economies)
Source: Maddison Project (2018).

---

[3] Acemoglu, Johnson, and Robinson (2002); see also Chapter 2.

was a spectacular massacre in Addis Ababa.[4] Ethiopia was not landlocked for all this period but became so after 1991, and was cut off even more from sea ports in the war with Eritrea in the late 1990s. The country is also clearly in what some economists classify as a 'bad neighbourhood'. It has been characterized for much of this period by what well-known orthodox economists call 'policy syndromes' (i.e. non-orthodox policies). And it has for most of the period clearly not been a liberal multi-party democracy. Some of those African countries with the weakest cumulative growth in this period—including South Africa and Zimbabwe—had, by contrast, far greater experience of Western settler colonialism and—especially in the case of South Africa—have adopted 'market-friendly' economic policies more resolutely than other countries. Not only does the evidence in Figure 3.1 highlight the *diversity* of economic experience in sub-Saharan Africa, it also challenges a number of common-sense assumptions about the 'drivers' of economic development.

3.2 Common Sense and the Reproduction of Powerful Ideas

Exercising power involves both force and consent.[5] Hegemony relies on acceptance. Getting people to regard a set of ideas and policies as 'natural' involves the deployment of 'rhetorical commonplaces': key phrases and ideas that are circulated, repeated, and insisted upon, until they come to shape the contours of legitimate debate.[6] We will highlight a number of rhetorical commonplaces in this book, including 'reforming the labour market' and 'getting prices right', which distil complex bodies of thought and argument into oversimplified forms.

Rhetorical commonplaces reinforce conventional wisdom: the 'popular conception of the world'. While common sense can mean 'good sense'—the type of things people say and do that are generally considered obvious and sensible—it can have more complex meanings and ambiguous political implications, as Antonio Gramsci has shown. For Gramsci, common sense involved the 'givenness' of a set of beliefs and ideas—their apparently self-evident quality. Common sense can be a barrier to political change as it helps cement the idea among poor and oppressed people that their circumstances are inevitable, or even for the best. However, if popular pressure can be creatively combined with a disciplined effort by intellectuals, it may be possible to reshape common sense to support political change.[7] In this chapter, we challenge conventional wisdom with a view to developing more convincing accounts of previous experiences, as well as more effective policies for the future.

---

[4] Campbell (2017).   [5] Anderson (2000); Purdy (2014).
[6] Jackson (2006); Krebs and Jackson (2007).   [7] Gramsci (1971: 422); Crehan (2011).

In the battleground of common sense and how it relates to processes of socio-economic transformation in Africa, ideas are weapons. They are used to disarm opposing views, and reflect, serve, and combine with material interests. As Keynes famously put it: 'Practical men who believe themselves to be quite exempt from any intellectual influence, are usually the slaves of some defunct economist. Madmen in authority, who hear voices in the air, are distilling their frenzy from some academic scribbler a few years back.'[8] Donald Trump's presidency draws on a number of such scribblers, not least Ayn Rand and Samuel Huntington. Meanwhile, economic policy in Julius Nyerere's Tanzania was heavily influenced by the ideas of the Fabian Society in the UK.[9]

There is never a straightforward causal relationship between ideas and policy implementation. It is facile to explain Pinochet's policies in Chile as merely the outcome of ideas put forward by the 'Chicago boys', or to account for deflationary policies introduced by the Central Bank of Uganda with reference only to the intellectual influence of the Washington financial institutions.[10] Even so, the market for ideas is rigged: a huge amount of resources continue to be invested in legitimizing a specific range of ideas about economic development in Africa and elsewhere. The World Bank and donor governments have invested heavily in 'capacity building'—a rhetorical commonplace that suggests obvious technical needs while neutralizing the politics of such support.[11] The International Food Policy Research Institute (IFPRI) represents a specific example of this. IFPRI's ideological and political priorities were clearly described by Washington aid insiders in a discussion of the sustained, influential, and well-funded 'support' programme in Ethiopia:

> [T]he great bulk of IFPRI research (and the training of its research staff) is rooted in neo-classical economics. The upshot is that a significant share of IFPRI's research in Ethiopia may be fairly characterized as seeking (second-best) solutions to problems created by market failures, while another large share is directed towards the creation and operation of institutions as a possible prelude to first-best solutions.[12]

One IFPRI-recommended solution was the strengthening of the Ethiopian Commodity Exchange, the results of which were disastrous for Ethiopia's most important export commodity—coffee.[13]

---

[8] Keynes (1936: 383).
[9] Smith (1985) on Nyerere; Marshall (2018) and Robin (2017) on Trump.
[10] A more nuanced, but still rather mechanical, account of the determinants of Central Bank policy in Africa has been provided by Dafe (2017).
[11] Van Waeyenberge, Fine, and Bayliss (2011).   [12] Slade and Renkow (2013: 11).
[13] Slade and Renkow (2013: 19); Cramer and Sender (2019).

Another example of international support for 'capacity building' is the African Economic Research Consortium (AERC), funded by a variety of major donors, including the United States Agency for International Development (USAID), the World Bank, the Bill and Melinda Gates Foundation, and the UK Department for International Development (DFID). Evaluations of the AERC have noted that its training has a 'narrow' focus on a technical and mainstream approach to economics and that a restricted set of macroeconomic issues linked the international financial institutions' views of stabilization policy. The emphasis is on 'rigour'—a persuasive rhetorical commonplace in itself, with Thandika Mkandawire describing the AERC as 'perhaps the most spectacular attempt to transform a discipline ever carried out in any continent'.[14] There have been close links between the AERC and the Harvard Institute for International Development, which has promoted a narrow neoclassical version of political analysis, as well as strongly influencing African policy debates by embedding staff in the Mozambican and Kenyan Ministries of Planning.[15] The AERC is just one part of a network of economists that helped to disseminate a single and exclusive neoclassical vision of economics within Africa from the 1980s onwards.[16] The broader phenomenon is not confined to Africa, as former foreign advisors to Eastern Europe 'seem to have acquired the same "educated incapacity" . . . in the same schools and universities, and to be applying in later life the same narrow, abstract and irrelevant methodology'.[17]

When the AERC did start engaging with 'political economy', it did so largely by appealing to public choice theory. The turn to public choice theory as a response to criticism that AERC research lacked political economy is a good example of the instinctive reaction of those working in the economics mainstream, which has:

a curious self-sealing capacity. Every breach that is made in it by criticism trying to let in some air from reality is somehow filled up by admitting the point but refusing to draw any consequences from it, so that the old doctrines can be repeated as before.[18]

It is not only orthodox economists, though, who are immune to the accumulation of contradictory evidence. Many of those firmly on the other side of the intellectual divide, with their emphasis on structural barriers to development and the dangers posed to poor countries by the capitalist world market, are also remarkably stubborn in the face of inconvenient evidence. One example, discussed in more detail in Chapter 5, involves their shifting theoretical explanations for the impossibility of achieving growth in export revenues, leading to the standard

---

[14] Mkandawire (2014: 186).   [15] Bates (2017).   [16] Mkandawire (2014: 186).
[17] Wiles (1995: 46).   [18] Robinson (1977: 22). See also King (2015).

policy conclusion—focus on production of manufactures for the domestic market, or on South–South trade.

3.3 Sources of Pessimism in Development Economics

Mission Impossible: Constrained by a Factor Endowment Straitjacket

Economists trained in neoclassical economics and many of those trained in more structuralist development economics, or in neo-Marxist political economy, often share the view that low-income countries have little realistic prospect of developing into industrial economies. This view taps into two streams of common sense, each of which distils complex economic thinking into simple home truths. One draws on the idea of comparative advantage, while the other draws on structuralist (and sometimes dependency theory) ideas about the inevitable consequences of trade between richer and poorer countries.

If ever there were a rhetorical commonplace in economics, it is the idea of comparative advantage, with the authoritative *New Palgrave Dictionary of Economics* proclaiming it 'the deepest and most beautiful result in all of economics'.[19] Comparative advantage is frequently deployed to deter governments from intervening to accelerate structural change, and even when economists enamoured of the idea recognize its limits, it still leads them to be extremely pessimistic about the prospects of government intervention successfully flouting the principle.[20]

The principle, deriving from David Ricardo's eighteenth-century insights,[21] suggests that a country should specialize in producing those things in which its production costs, relative to other countries, are cheapest, irrespective of whether it has an absolute cost and efficiency advantage in producing other things. This involves producing and trading in products generated by locally abundant (relatively cheap) inputs, with the least possible use of those inputs that are scarce (relatively more expensive than in other trading partner countries). As suggested by Chandra, Lin, and Wang:

> An industry is an economy's latent comparative advantage if, based on the factor costs of production which are determined by the economy's endowment structure, the economy could be competitive in this industry . . .[22]

---

[19] Findlay (1987: 514).   [20] Krugman (1987).
[21] King provides a very clear discussion of the intellectual influence on later economists of Ricardo's views on trade (King, 2013a: 81–106).
[22] Chandra, Lin, and Wang (2013).

One influential version of the factor endowment approach to understanding comparative advantage analyses differences between countries in the ratio of skills to cultivable land. According to this analysis, African countries—which are endowed with great expanses of cultivable land but relatively few people with high-level technical skills—ought to specialize in *unprocessed* primary commodities for international trade. Gradually, productivity in these African countries may rise and, eventually, the stock of skills may increase relative to the stock of cultivable land. Such an analysis is pessimistic about the scope for immediate government intervention to support, for example, primary commodity processing. The Chief Economist of DFID between 2000 and 2005 has underwritten this analysis, arguing that:

> The export share of primary products is consistently larger in the land-abundant regions than in the land-scarce regions, as [Heckscher–Ohlin] theory and common sense predict.[23]

It is easy to point to poor, labour-abundant countries that invested in capital- and skills-intensive production only for their factories to run aground, failing to come close to internationally competitive standards. Using comparative advantage as a cautionary tale when advocating a reduction in barriers to trade, however, is not the same as drawing policy conclusions from, say, a modified Heckscher–Ohlin model built on bizarre assumptions about full employment, capital, and skilled labour immobility. For some economists the non-realism of assumptions is a badge of scientific honour; but it *does* actually matter that the way the model is constructed does not in any way represent the world it is supposed to capture. 'When policy conclusions are drawn from such models, it is time to reach for one's gun', argued one mathematical economic theorist.[24] The trouble is, people do draw policy conclusions from such models, again and again.

Such policy conclusions should also be rejected because of the evidence on trade and economic growth. Even a generous interpretation of the regression literature concludes that 'the nature of the relationship between trade policy and economic growth remains very much an open question'.[25] Unfortunately, a great many economists were unwilling to await answers to this question, and 'The tendency to greatly overstate the systematic evidence in favor of trade openness has had a substantial influence on policy around the world.'[26]

It was this attitude of blind faith that, in the 1990s, prompted the World Bank to pressure Mozambique into implementing a radical trade liberalization policy. World Bank economists called for the removal of barriers to exporting

---

[23] Wood (2017: 6).   [24] Hahn (1984: 29); Lawson (2007).
[25] Rodriguez and Rodrik (2001: 338).
[26] Rodriguez and Rodrik (2001: 266 and 317). On the inadequacy of measures of 'openness' in the trade policy literature, see Fujii (2017).

unprocessed cashew kernels, as well as the lifting of state protection for local factories processing raw cashew nuts. Mozambique had been the largest cashew nut producer in the world and had a substantial processing industry. However, after years of warfare and the exodus of most of the business class, the cashew sector was, by 1992, in crisis. The government's continued protection of the processing industry, through a ban and then a high tariff on raw nut exports, had failed to generate a regular supply of high-quality processed cashew exports. To World Bank officials advocating trade liberalization, this was a classic case of the dangers of state support for factories in Africa, as well as of the costs of breaking the comparative advantage commandment.

If the government were to get rid of tariffs rapidly, what would happen next? While World Bank economists expected the domestic processing industry to suffer, they did not seem worried by the consequences for large numbers of female factory workers. Any short-run shock would, they believed, be outweighed by the large gains that were expected to flow later through 'getting prices right'.[27] The common-sense logic was that a tariff (or a physical ban on exports) distorts prices, sending the wrong signals about relative abundance and scarcity: in this case, processors in Mozambique could buy raw cashew kernels at an artificially low price.

Removing tariff protection would allow cashew traders acting for international buyers to 'find' the 'right' price for unprocessed, raw cashews. In a liberalized market, traders would compete to offer poor farmers a competitive price; farmers would respond with an increased supply; and about a million rural households would earn a substantial income by redirecting their unprocessed cashew output away from inefficient local processing factories to meet buoyant demand (mainly from India). This would tilt the economy back against the 'urban bias' that Paul Krugman argued had previously prevailed: the export tax 'almost certainly subtracts from, rather than adds to, the country's miserably low income'.[28] The suggestion that the 10,000 female employees in Mozambique's processing factories who lost their jobs had been the beneficiaries of an urban bias in policymaking is absurd. These women were not a privileged urban worker elite, isolated from rural households. Starting in the late colonial period, thousands of women had migrated from rural areas to the cities, out of desperation, in search of jobs sorting, shelling, and packing cashews. Once employed, they were commonly stigmatized, labelled as loose women, and they were paid below the minimum wage:

> They were suspect in the urban African community as a whole, in part because they were disproportionately divorced, widowed, separated or single. Factory work . . . was neither sought after nor prestigious.[29]

---

[27] Hilmarsson (1995).   [28] Krugman (2000).   [29] Penvenne (2015: 213).

But reforms invoking the common-sense commandments to 'get prices right', liberalize trade, and follow comparative advantage achieved very little. The Bank had not fully analysed the global cashew market or the political economy of a rapidly changing post-war Mozambique. The market was not a perfectly competitive level playing field: other, much more powerful countries were intervening in their own economies to support cashew processing and production; the market was dominated by Indian demand patterns rather than being spread globally; and simple price reforms cannot address the fundamental causes of low output and productivity in agriculture.

According to one assessment of the reforms, the benefits to cashew growing households amounted to an *average* $5. Margaret McMillan and Dani Rodrik argued that efficiency gains were 'puny'. If prices did rise and some rural incomes did grow a tiny bit, the overall gains were offset by losses: factory closures and protracted unemployment. They concluded that the 'aggregate static gains produced by the liberalization were a wash', that is, they came to nothing.[30] A more recent World Bank research paper reviewing the Mozambican cashew drama found that real producer prices by 2008 were about the same as before the reforms. Output per cashew tree remained generally very low, though higher among the larger-scale producers. The larger-scale capital-intensive processing factories went out of business. A number of smaller, more labour-intensive processing firms did slowly emerge in the 2000s, though they depend heavily on public and external support. The reforms also seem to be promoting a 're-cottagization' of cashew processing and there are claims that workers are paid below minimum wages.[31] The fundamental problem with the sector remains the low level of output, the poor quality of the cashews produced, and low productivity.[32] Unshelled cashew export volumes have never recovered from a post-war peak in 2001 (Figure 3.2) and revenues have been very volatile.[33]

Mission Impossible: Paralysed by the Prebisch–Singer Hypothesis

If comparative advantage incites pessimism among neoclassical economists, the pessimism of many other development economists springs from *critiques* of comparative advantage. The source for much of this pessimism lies in the work of structuralist economists, who nail a version of the Prebisch–Singer thesis to the door of neoclassical orthodoxy. The thesis, which claims there is a secular decline in the net barter terms of trade between primary commodities and manufactures,

[30] Macmillan, Rodrik, and Welch (2002).   [31] Penvenne (2015: 229).
[32] Aksoy and Yagci (2012).
[33] Food and Agriculture Organization Statistical Database (FAOSTAT).

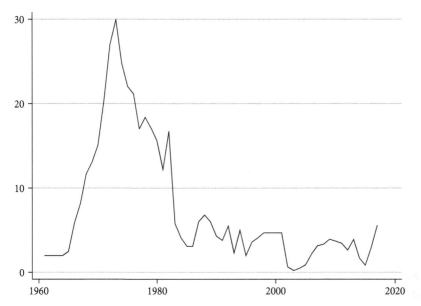

Figure 3.2 Volume of exports of unshelled cashews from Mozambique (in thousands of tonnes), 1960–2016
Source: FAOSTAT (2019).

is based on empirical claims about patterns of income, demand, and production globally. In 1949, Hans Singer (at the UN Department for Economic Affairs) and then Raúl Prebisch (at the UN Economic Commission for Latin America and the Caribbean) highlighted important trends in the world economy: poorer countries tended to specialize in the production of primary commodities; richer countries in manufacturing. As incomes rise, people typically spend a smaller share of their income on basic (food) goods. In a growing global economy, this means demand for manufactures tends to be strong, while the demand for primary commodities remains relatively weak. Put differently, there is a relatively high income elasticity of demand for manufactures, and a relatively low income-elasticity of demand for primary commodities. Consequently, there is upward pressure on the price of manufactures relative to commodity prices.

An excess supply of labour in poor countries, combined with the greater bargaining power of trade unions in richer societies, adds to this upward pressure. So, in another pessimistic account of the export prospects of developing countries, the power of trade unions in advanced capitalist countries means that most gains from productivity increases and trade will be distributed unevenly: the advanced capitalist country will exploit primary commodity-exporting countries by trading manufactured commodities (embodying small quantities of high-paid labour) for primary products (embodying much greater quantities of low-paid labour).[34] Additional explanations for declining primary commodity prices point to historic patterns of technological change—including the introduction of synthetic substitutes (for example, Madagascan and Ugandan vanilla beans, substituted in many confectionary factories by synthetic vanilla essence, or Tanzanian sisal, which was hit by the introduction of polypropylene substitutes in the 1970s)—as well as to declining prices received by primary commodity exporters caused by the growing power of oligopsonistic purchasers in these commodity markets.

Perhaps the most dramatic argument about the disadvantages of primary commodity exports claims that they are associated with declining domestic food grain availability. Distinguished Marxist scholars have argued that:

> The classic case in more recent years of production for the metropolitan market undermining food security relates to Africa. The integration of Africa as an agricultural exporter to the advanced capitalist countries was greatly strengthened under the diktat of the Bretton Woods institutions at the beginning of the 1980s . . . because of the adverse shift in the terms of trade for their primary commodity exports vis-à-vis manufactured goods . . . This thrust on exports of agriproducts meant a shift away from food crop production.[35]

Similar arguments have been used by scholars, political leaders, and non-governmental organizations (NGOs) to support a common-sense policy promoting food self-sufficiency. However, the African evidence on recent and historical trends in agricultural exports, food production for the domestic market, and nutritional status, provides little support for such policies (see Chapter 9).

Those pessimistic about the export prospects of developing countries also argue that

> in their eagerness to industrialize, for which foreign exchange was needed for importing machinery and other capital goods, each of the newly decolonized economies of the periphery competed with the others to push out as much of its traditional primary commodity exports as it could. The suppression of nominal prices of tropical commodities (and the adverse movement in the terms of trade) . . . continued even after decolonization for this reason.[36]

A similar argument goes that, since an increasing number of low-income economies have tried to emulate East Asian success in exporting labour-intensive or low-tech manufactured exports, the market prices of these manufactured goods have fallen relative to the high-tech manufactures produced in advanced capitalist

---

[34] Smith and Sender (1983) criticize this form of unequal exchange theory.
[35] Patnaik and Patnaik (2017: 109).   [36] ibid. (2017: 107).

economies.[37] The United Nations Conference on Trade and Development (UNCTAD) has for many years repeated the view that 'It is well-known that export-led growth strategies must sooner or later reach their limits when many countries pursue them simultaneously.'[38]

The policy implication of this dismal view of the external environment is that a greater proportion of production in developing countries should be geared towards domestic, rather than world, markets. UNCTAD theorists, like the dependency theorists in 1970s Tanzania, hope that this 'rebalancing' of production will also reduce imports and the balance of payments constraint on growth (discussed further in Chapters 4 and 5).[39]

Although 'few hypotheses in development economics have been studied more intensively' than the Prebisch–Singer suggestion that there is a long-run negative trend in the prices of internationally traded primary commodities relative to those of manufactured products, 'findings have varied to such an extent that there is still no consensus in the literature'.[40] There is also no clear consensus on the empirical case for greater diversification among primary commodity producers (this being a key policy response to anxieties about the terms of trade). International Monetary Fund (IMF) (and other) analysis of the evidence concludes that 'higher incomes are not typically associated with greater diversification for commodity exporters'.[41]

Mission Impossible: The Global Business Revolution

Some dependency theorists introduce yet another set of pessimistic arguments, highlighting the domination of research and development (R&D) by developed economies. As a consequence, developing economies in sub-Saharan Africa cannot produce the most globally competitive or innovative manufactures, as the leading corporations in developed countries have created unbreachable barriers to entry and 'captured rents'.[42] A less pessimistic view of the prospects for some developing countries describes 'the global business revolution'.[43]

This revolution, beginning in the 1980s, unleashed powerful forces of *concentration*, leading to cascading layers of suppliers being controlled by 'system integrator' firms. Supply relationships are structured in what are known as global value chains or global production networks, with the relevant literature often emphasizing how very difficult it is for firms in developing countries to climb the ladder of global production due to the barriers imposed by firms higher up.

[37] Chakraborty (2012).   [38] UNCTAD (2013: i).
[39] Mayer (2013: 1); UNCTAD (2014: 101–2).   [40] Cashin and Pattillo (2006: 845).
[41] IMF (2014: 10); Lectard and Rougier (2018).   [42] Kaplinsky and Morris (2008).
[43] Nolan, Zhang, and Liu (2008).

During an earlier period, a few national economies were able to achieve industrialization, using protectionism and state intervention; they then tried to 'kick away the ladder' of industrialization they had previously climbed. Now, first-mover 'system integrator' firms grease the rungs so that those lower down can rarely, if ever, get a purchase on the ladder's higher reaches.

The massive supermarkets at the head of 'buyer-driven' value chains, or the firms at the summit of producer-driven chains, have enormous power, often blurring the lines differentiating one firm from another. For example, it is not always clear to what extent a Kenyan farm enterprise growing ornamental plants for export to the Netherlands is independent from the Dutch corporation that controls much of the genetic R&D and input supply, and that buys almost all of the farm's output. There is, though, evidence of successful national firms within developing countries 'climbing the ladder',[44] including Thai firms like Thai Union Frozen Products (TUF) (tuna and other seafood) and Charoen Pokphand Foods (CPF) (poultry) that have become global leaders, or the Brazilian JBS (the largest meat-processing firm in the world).[45]

Dammed If You Do

Impossibilism appears in many guises in development economics. Two further forms it takes can be seen in the resource curse literature and in the injunction to avoid large-scale infrastructural 'mega-projects'. In Chapter 6 we address the gloomy argument that mega-projects—such as the proposed Grand Inga Dam on the Congo River—are 'over budget, over time, over and over again'.[46] As in the cases already mentioned, we argue that this stance creates a cast-iron law out of evidence that may not be universally relevant, and involves a partial view of the history of such projects. As regards the resource curse, much has been written on the subject, so we will make only brief comments here.

The resource curse argument, a version of primary commodity pessimism, itself has variants. One—the original—is a straightforwardly economic argument, which proposes that an abundance of natural resources leads to 'Dutch disease'. A resource boom leads to a foreign exchange bonanza, which pushes up the value of the exchange rate in the country in question. An appreciating currency then prices the country's other exports out of international markets and, because they are no longer competitive, these other exports collapse, together with their associated jobs, fiscal revenue, and potential for domestic linkages. Dutch disease

---

[44] Ponte et al. (2014).   [45] Kingkaew (2012).

[46] The best-known and most persistent academic critic of mega-projects is Flyvbjerg (2011). NGOs such as the Oakland Institute and International Rivers (https://www.internationalrivers.org/resources/the-new-great-walls-a-guide-to-china%E2%80%99s-overseas-dam-industry-3962) also publicize pessimistic views about the benefits of large-scale infrastructure projects in Africa.

is exacerbated if we acknowledge that many natural resources—oil being the classic example—may be 'niche' or 'enclave' activities. These are geographically concentrated (and may even be offshore); are hugely capital intensive; rely on highly specialized expatriate expertise; and generate little by way of domestic employment or linkages. Oil production in Nigeria is often regarded as a classic case of Dutch disease in Africa.

The other variant of the resource curse argument involves a slightly more complex political discussion. Here, natural resources offer 'easy money' to greedy governments, generating a large flow of royalties into the state budget from highly concentrated sources. A government in this position need not bother with the politically difficult and administratively challenging business of taxing the population and providing public goods in return. With less connection to the population and given the scope for resource rents to become something of a 'honey pot' attracting all manner of rival claimants, this is a potential recipe for corruption, extreme inequalities, and violent conflict.[47]

There is nothing particularly African about the resource curse: after all, the disease was first identified in studies of the booming price of wool in Australia in the first half of the nineteenth century and is named for the decline in manufacturing in the Netherlands after the discovery of natural gas in 1959. It is also worth noting that neither country's experience of the Dutch disease destroyed the longer-run capacity of their economies.[48] Routes to economic collapse take many strange turns and are not inevitable, even in Venezuela, which managed to combine oil production with diverse industrial output and gross domestic product (GDP) growth for rather a long time.[49]

Within Africa, South Africa's very rich resources of minerals and energy have been associated with an inadequate growth rate of an unusually import-intensive manufacturing sector; but manufacturing output did grow (and diversify) to some extent and in some periods, when encouraged by state intervention. The complex political economy of exchange rate and macroeconomic policy formulation in South Africa—and of investment in its state-owned enterprises (SOEs)—cannot be understood within a simple resource curse framework.[50]

Finally, Norway's history should give pause for thought to the geographical determinists who have written about Africa's poor and cursed prospects. Norway industrialized 'through the development of geographic features usually considered adverse' and on the basis of 'the country's greatest natural resource' (at the time): waterfalls. Hydropower fuelled the rapid development of a multitude of industries, from electrochemical and electro-metallurgical factories to pulp and cellulose plants.[51] Much later, Norway managed to develop a successful oil sector—albeit with strong upward pressure on the exchange rate—while preserving the country's

---

[47] Collier (2008: 38).   [48] Stapledon (2013).   [49] Di John (2009).
[50] Clark (1994); Fine and Rustomjee (1996); Marais (2013).   [51] Thomson (1938).

remarkably egalitarian governance of natural resources and supporting a wide array of technically sophisticated industries.[52]

3.4 Naive Optimism and Capitalism with a Human Face

Impossibilism often involves insisting that efforts to accelerate structural change will fail because of the binding constraints afflicting all late-late industrializers. A very different approach is the 'possibilism' of Albert Hirschman, who thought that the field of development was 'an exceptionally good hunting ground for exaggerated notions of absolute obstacles, imaginary dilemmas, and one-way sequences'. In Chapter 2, we showed how many econometricians have claimed to explain Africa's development 'failure' by referring to a miscellaneous mix of obstacles, encapsulated in the 'Africa dummy' variable.[53] The essence of the possibilist approach, by contrast, 'consists in figuring out avenues of escape from such straitjacketing constructs in any individual case that comes up'.[54]

Hirschman's possibilism is not, however, to be taken as a licence for naive optimism. Widening the limits of what may be thought possible comes at the cost, Hirschman accepted, of 'lowering our ability, real or imaginary, to discern the probable'.[55] There are clear indicators of when possibilism is in danger of spiralling into naive optimism. When the list of 'ifs'—of all the conditions that would need to be in place for a scheme to work—stretches too far, then the project or policy may be unrealistic.

This section highlights two strains of common sense that exemplify naive optimism. One has already been alluded to: the belief that reading the runes of current comparative advantage will unleash future economic development and structural change. The other is the belief that the best way to stimulate growth, expand employment, and reduce poverty is by promoting small farms, as well as small, or even micro, enterprises. Both are misleading forms of fantasy.

Although absolute advantage underpins most growth in world trade, African policy officials are misguidedly encouraged to commit to the principle of comparative advantage. Naive optimism characterizes the insistence of neoclassical economists that merely following the pointers of comparative advantage or 'latent' comparative advantage will unleash a smooth process of 'convergence', 'catching up', and development. Such naive optimism also characterizes the faith of other economists that policies such as additional South–South cooperation or a new development bank will magically allow poorer economies to catch up by trading among themselves.

---

[52] Ossowski and Halland (2016).
[53] For a much less critical discussion of regressions using the Africa dummy see Collier and Gunning (1999).
[54] Hirschman (1971: 28–9).   [55] Hirschman (1971: 28).

Additionally, at a time when global capitalism is increasingly dominated by massive corporations acting as 'systems integrators' for internationalized production chains, a great deal of policy advice (and resources) continues to push African policymakers towards strategies built around tiny enterprises. Advisors and economists who usually claim to be fiercely opposed are again united, this time in supporting 'bottom-up' approaches to structural transformation. One version promotes faith in decentralization (in the hope it will empower local people and increase responsiveness to the needs of local communities), alongside the belief that dynamic smallholder farmers, microfinance, and micro-credit will create a breeding ground for female and other entrepreneurs. Another version is influenced by the analytical presumption in neoclassical economics that everything can and should be rooted in individual choices—the so-called micro-foundations of macroeconomics. One of the most pervasive nuggets of conventional wisdom in political discourse around economics is the idea that an economy is similar to, and therefore should be run like, a household.

Bottom-up policy prescriptions are consistent with the widespread but naive notion that capitalism can be given a makeover by enlightened leaders committed to the liberal values of equality, solidarity, and citizenship—'capitalism with a human face'. In the late 1980s, influential development economists scoured the world in search of a country successfully pursuing macroeconomic policy that 'fully protects the human dimension'.[56] For these individuals, capitalism's 'human face' represented only good things; a social-democratic visage unscarred by conflict, crisis, or exploitation. In effect, it is 'photo-shopped' or Barbie doll capitalism: filtered, prettified, with the contradictions smoothed and airbrushed away.

To imagine a fully inclusive, appealing 'capitalism with a human face' is to be fooled by Oscar Wilde's protagonist Dorian Gray, whose features remain exquisitely beautiful, young, and pure. A painting of Dorian, hidden away in a locked attic, does change and age, unlike his human face; it bears the imprint of his betrayals and crimes. When Dorian finally stabs the portrait with a knife, his servants, hearing a scream, go up to the attic and find a painting of a beautiful young man, as well as their master—with a knife through his heart.

> He was withered, wrinkled, and loathsome of visage. It was not until they had examined the rings that they recognized who it was.[57]

We believe that understanding economic performance in Africa will be improved by visits to the attic, by studying both sitter and portrait.

---

[56] Stewart (1991: 1861).   [57] Wilde (2006: 188).

Global Free Trade or Pan-African Economic Integration? Shared Naive Optimism

Strains of gloom and optimism run parallel through much of the history of economic thought. What separates reflex pessimism and naive optimism is the mix of assumptions made. Assumptions are a set of conditions—'ifs'—that allow a model or theory to hold together logically and generate predictions. Despite often being counter-intuitive, these ifs are what underlie much of what is accepted as common sense. They require closer scrutiny by policy officials.

The formal models that take Ricardo's original insight about comparative advantage and insist it should inform contemporary policy are built on a string of ifs. Comparative advantage produces optimal outcomes and a 'theoretically harmonious world'[58] *if* there is no involuntary unemployment; *if* capital is immobile between countries; *if* prices adjust instantly, automatically, and painlessly following trade liberalization; *if* the only relevant gains from trade liberalization are static gains; *if* the flow of ideas and investment and economies of scale are irrelevant and there are constant returns to knowledge accumulation. Some models go further. One, for example, predicts universal gains from trade liberalization *if* knowledge is a non-rivalrous public good (that is, all technical knowledge is freely available to everyone), and *if* trade flows facilitate full diffusion of knowledge.

The ifs are like advertising small print—few people bother to examine them closely. These, however, are not minor details, but are at the very core of the models built around them. A substantial body of critical literature addresses these conditions, pointing out that, in reality, capital flows in ways that differ radically from the assumptions made by Ricardo.[59] The critical literature also argues that African policy officials should not be expected to sign up to a deal based on the fanciful supposition that knowledge is a non-rivalrous public good, or that payments adjustments are quick, automatic, and without costs. In a global economy in which many sectors are dominated by huge corporations with integrated systems of suppliers, knowledge is often jealously guarded within supply chains. A single Illy coffee capsule, for example, has seven patents in its design.

In a world economy where the ifs of comparative advantage theory are unfulfilled wishes, absolute advantage dominates. Relative prices are not enough to propel changes in the structure of output. The relative price of land, labour, and capital—the keys to the comparative advantage doctrine—matter less where rents from 'rivalrous' knowledge are protected, and where competitiveness owes as

---

[58] Milberg (2004).   [59] Milberg (2004: 17–18); (King, 2013a: 98).

much to state interventions creating the institutions determining productivity as to relative 'factor' costs.[60]

Meanwhile, many people nervous about global economic integration instead pin their hopes on South–South cooperation and regional economic communities (RECs). They expect trade among 'Southern' economies to cut the enduring bonds of colonial history, thereby allowing for greater self-reliance and policy autonomy. The swell of support for South–South cooperation and initiatives such as the AfCFTA is partly based on a pessimistic view of possible integration into the wider world economy. Such pessimism, however, quickly turns to optimism once the prospect of escape from the clutches of the West (or North) is clear. Strains of economic nationalism, pessimism about the prospects of wider global economic integration, pan-African and broader 'South–South' solidarity, and orthodox economics have been woven together to produce a blanket optimism about prioritizing African economic integration.

The AfCFTA is expected to 'boost intra-African trade, stimulate investment and innovation, foster structural transformation, improve food security, enhance economic growth and export diversification'.[61] Accelerating intra-African trade is regarded as especially beneficial because, while 'Africa exports mainly commodities to the rest of the world, intra-African trade displays high concentrations of value-added products (and services)'.[62] The AfCFTA is expected to 'leverage Africa's progress towards attaining several Sustainable Development Goals', such as poverty elimination and gender equality.[63] Specifically, the hope is that regional integration will allow for the exploitation of economies of scale, will encourage investment, and will stimulate productivity-enhancing competition. Regional value chains will emerge as a result. All these developments combined will, in turn, lead to poverty reduction.[64]

These visions of African economic integration rest on the same naive and unrealistic ifs underpinning comparative advantage doctrine. For example, while the case for integration may be made by spinning out predictions from a static computable general equilibrium model, these models often—as the authors of one such exercise note in a footnote—ignore 'missing' or 'inefficient' markets. (In other words, these models 'work' *if* there are complete and perfectly competitive markets.) Further ifs include: the AfCFTA will achieve all its goals *if* measures are taken to address regional inequalities, *if* governments implement the agreements they sign up for, *if* entrenched interests that have made it difficult for African RECs to succeed are set aside. The list goes on.

---

[60] Some of the forms of state intervention and the types of banking institutions that determine competitiveness are discussed in Mazzucato and Penna (2016).
[61] UNECA, African Union, and African Development Bank (2017: xi).   [62] Ibid.
[63] UNECA (2017: 11).   [64] Mold and Mukwaya (2016).

The push for greater regional integration in Africa attempts to make a virtue out of a weak performance in wider global international markets. Figure 3.3 illustrates this failure, showing that despite an increase in the value of exports from African countries since the early 2000s, their *share* in global exports has remained below 6 per cent. In fact, their share is now smaller than in the late 1990s. Even Africa's primary commodity exports (regardless of whether oil exports are included) have shrunk to less than 5 per cent of global primary commodity exports (see Figure 3.3b), meaning that other parts of the world became successful exporters of precisely the commodities regarded as unpromising by some advocates of intra-African trade. Such advocates optimistically believe that, unlike trade with the rest of the world, trade with other African

(a) Manufactured exports (% of world exports)

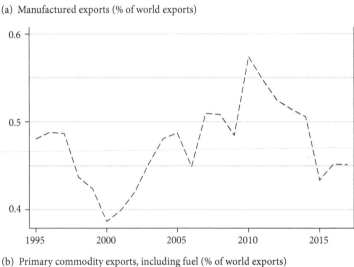

(b) Primary commodity exports, including fuel (% of world exports)

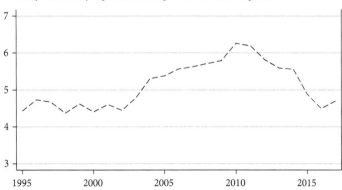

Figure 3.3 Sub-Saharan African exports as a share of global exports, 1995–2017
Source: UNCTAD (2018).

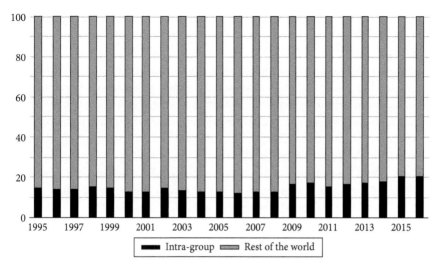

Figure 3.4 Intra-trade and extra-trade exports share by destination, sub-Saharan Africa

Note: Intra-group trade is defined as trade between all members of a group.
Source: UNCTAD (2018).

countries will avoid this gloomy prognosis, as new opportunities for trade in other commodities—including more processed exports—will emerge.

One reason to query high expectations for intra-African trade is the 'dismally poor implementation record' of regional integration agreements.[65] Despite decades of negotiations and agreements within subregions and RECs in Africa, intra-African trade remains a *tiny* proportion of the continent's overall trade. As Figure 3.4 shows, even taking into account some recent intra-trade growth, it still only accounts for a fifth of total trade.

In short, while African regional economic integration and greater intra-African trade may be rhetorically appealing on grounds of economic nationalism or South–South solidarity, as a blueprint for accelerated development it is a fantasy—based on exactly the same theories and conditional assumptions as a push for global free trade on comparative advantage grounds.

Small and Bottom Up is Beautiful: Micro-Finance, Entrepreneurship, and Cooperative Development

Another variety of common sense is the belief in the individual and the small-scale as wellsprings of development, technological dynamism, and structural change.

---

[65] Hartzenburg (2011).

Supposedly competing views converge here too, for example in arguments for financial inclusion and micro-credit, for entrepreneurialism, and for prioritizing small farmers.

Many politicians have made use of the idea that 'an economy is just like a household' in order to justify the economic policies they favour. Electorates are routinely told that just as households need to be careful not to spend beyond their means, so countries need to adopt the same attitude. This means national debt should be reduced, and public and private borrowing (and spending) reined in. This was at the heart of Margaret Thatcher's rhetoric about fiscal policy in the UK in the 1980s. Meanwhile, in the wake of the Global Financial Crash of 2008, German Chancellor Angela Merkel used the common-sense maxim that 'One should simply have asked the Swabian housewife.' This was because every house-wife 'knows that we cannot live beyond our means'.[66]

This is perhaps the most striking case of a 'common-sense' idea in economics: apparently obvious and sensible, easy to understand, powerfully influencing policy debates, while at the same time deeply ideological (in Marx's sense of ideology as an inversion of reality). An economy is not like a household. It is not even like a business firm. There are two main ways in which this Swabian housewife logic fails. First, compared to private households, governments have many more and effective tools at their disposal to manage debt. Furthermore, public sector debt can be key to sustaining and expanding economic activity (the returns to which can be used to make repayments). Second, the Swabian housewife logic runs into a fallacy of composition. As Keynes pointed out, calling it the 'paradox of thrift', an individual may increase saving by withholding spending, but if all individuals in an economy raise their saving simultaneously then there will be a decline in output and income, meaning aggregate saving will be unchanged (at best).

Methodologically, this logic is linked to the idea that macroeconomics is simply the aggregation of individual micro-economic choices. Together, these form the 'micro-foundations' of macroeconomics, with causation running *up* from these micro-foundations to the overall macro-economy. What is missing from this vision is the possibility of 'downward causation': the idea that the structural features of a society, including macroeconomic change, can exert a huge influence on individual behaviour (it also leaves out the possibility that 'macro' and 'micro' can be jointly affected by other factors).

In development economics, this emphasis on the individual as the foundation of the economy has wider implications, forming the backdrop for strongly held beliefs about how economic policies should be designed to support plucky indi-vidual development efforts in the smallest production units. African economies are, in fact, defined by the small scale of most of their productive units, being

[66] Bennhold (2010).

dominated (numerically) by tiny firms and very small farms. By one count, approximately 80 per cent of farms in Africa are small, with the conventional wisdom—discussed at length in Chapters 7 and 9 – being that 'with few exceptions, land resources are distributed in a relatively equitable manner'.[67] When we began fieldwork in Ethiopia in 2000, the internationally celebrated general manager of the country's most important coffee cooperative union spun us the same story he had offered to other useful idiots, that *all* farmers producing both Fairtrade and other coffee had one hectare.[68] It took 15 minutes of interviews with members of a showcase primary cooperative to establish how deeply misleading this claim was: there was very clearly a wide size distribution of farms among cooperative members—from less than 0.5 hectares to more than 35 hectares. Some members only had a few coffee bushes while others were hiring wage labour to cultivate their large coffee farms.

African businesses are predominantly very small, with small and medium enterprises (SMEs) said to account for 95 per cent of all African firms. In one sample of countries, the most common size category (the modal group) of formally registered enterprises comprised those employing between zero and nine people.[69] This understates the reality, however, as it ignores the proliferation of tiny micro-enterprises, most of which are not formally recorded in enterprise surveys and national accounts. The Rwandan economy, for example, 'remains dominated by a mass of single employee micro-enterprises'.[70] Many people interpret this as showing that these micro- and small farms have 'the greatest development potential'. African heads of state have pledged to introduce 'specific policies and strategies to assist traditional small farms in rural areas'.[71] Similarly, many people argue that 'SMEs are central to wealth creation by stimulating demand for goods, investment and trade' in Africa, through their contribution to job creation, discovery of new markets, and capacity for innovation.[72]

Such a 'pervasive belief in the importance of small businesses for growth and economic development' has encouraged wanton distribution of resources—by governments, donor agencies, and philanthrocapitalists—to SMEs or micro-, small, and medium-sized enterprises (MSMEs), including generous funding for training, financial access, and business development schemes.[73] This belief also lies behind the commitment to entrepreneurship programmes by some African leaders. For instance, Rwandan President Paul Kagame places responsibility for economic development squarely on the country's individuals (specifically, individual entrepreneurs), arguing that 'entrepreneurship is the surest way for a nation . . . to develop prosperity for the greatest number of people'.[74] The

---

[67] NEPAD (2013: 25).
[68] He has a starring role in an influential film promoting a prettier model of trade: https://blackgoldmovie.com/about-tadesse-meskela.   [69] Bloom et al. (2014: 16).
[70] Poole (2016).   [71] NEPAD (2013: 45).   [72] Muriithi (2017: 9).
[73] Naudé and Krugell (2002: 21).   [74] Kagame (2009: 12).

Hanga Umurimo strategy has encouraged the National University of Rwanda, the Private Sector Federation, the International Finance Corporation (IFC), and a selection of NGOs to back Kagame's enthusiasm.[75] The strategy aims to inculcate an entrepreneurial spirit among Rwandans, and exemplifies the assumption among many policy officials that changing attitudes and customs is a prerequisite to structural and economic change. It was precisely this view that Albert Hirschman challenged, arguing that often the direction of causality ran the other way round.[76]

Where it is clear that there are many obstacles preventing small farms and enterprises from succeeding, the next-best solution advocated by many is supporting the clubbing together of small producers to form associations, credit schemes, or producer cooperatives (or SME clusters). When economists argue for cooperatives and group credit, they often emphasize that this can help with pooling transaction costs and enabling economies of scale. Furthermore, economists in the 'information theoretics' tradition argue that peer monitoring in small lending groups can address the information problems (chiefly concerning creditworthiness) that beset rural finance and that often explain the high administrative costs of loan disbursement and steep interest rates charged to poor rural borrowers.[77] In such groups, borrowers collectively bear the burden of selection, monitoring, and enforcement that would otherwise be faced by the lender.

Other, often sweeping, claims are sometimes made in favour for cooperatives: that they are a bulwark against communist uprisings,[78] that they protect small producers against venal middlemen, that they are 'pro-poor', and that they are 'empowering', especially for women.[79] It has even been argued that rural cooperatives

> contribute in significant ways to ... ensuring environmental sustainability, tackling the HIV/AIDS and malaria pandemic, and mainstreaming gender.[80]

For some naive optimists, rural cooperatives are a haven for women living in a 'post-wage' society and signpost possibilities of a life 'outside of wage labour and production circuits'.[81] Bina Agarwal is perhaps the most prominent advocate of the potential benefits of group farming for women, though she does acknowledge that 'there has been no systematic study of the impact of group farming on women in developing countries, based on carefully collected quantitative and qualitative data'.[82]

---

[75] Poole (2016). *Hanga Umurimo* transliterates as 'Create Own Jobs' and was subtitled 'Start Small, Grow Big'.
[76] Hirschman (1971).   [77] For example, Hoff and Stiglitz (1993).   [78] Tooze (2014).
[79] Wedig and Wiegratz (2018: 349).   [80] Nannyonjo (2013: 3).   [81] Williams (2017a).
[82] Agarwal (2019: 3).

Our own research into the political economy of rural cooperatives in Africa suggests such grand hopes are ludicrously unrealistic. Ledgers from coffee cooperatives in Ethiopia and Uganda explode rural egalitarian myths.[83] These are producer organizations that serve the interests of a very small minority of members, namely the farmers with the largest plots of land, who can obtain the greatest benefits from access to cheaper fertilizer and higher priced market opportunities. Cooperatives of Ethiopian coffee producers and Ugandan tea and coffee producers—including those certified by Fairtrade—probably *increase* rural inequality. Because they draw additional resources (e.g. in the form of 'ethical' trade price premiums), these disproportionately swell the income of the minority of member-producers who sell the bulk of the cooperative's 'certified' output. These cooperatives also often fail to serve the interests of their poorest members, let alone those excluded from joining in the first place.

Powerful ideas about the virtues of cooperative and small-scale farming enterprises are sustained not on the basis of evidence, but on the breeze of modern economic theory and the idealism of many working in the NGO sector. Nowhere is this clearer than in the arguments promoting small family farms, which claim there is an inverse relationship between farm size and productivity: small farms are deemed more efficient (crucially, on a measure of productivity per hectare rather than labour productivity) than larger farms. One explanation for this concerns the difficulties larger farmers have in monitoring labour on great tracts of land.

We spend more time examining these arguments in Chapter 9, arguing that African policy officials ought not to design agricultural policies on the basis of such an empirically weak claim. Here, we stress how the faith placed in the efficiency of small farmers by conventional economists—many occupying senior positions in Washington institutions and the United Nations (UN)—fits surprisingly well with the claims and preferences of a much wider range of intellectuals. These include those in pro-peasant agrarian social movements and NGOs who lobby against 'big ag' from bases in university-based think tanks. The Oakland Institute, for example, has published not very rigorous research on large farms in the Democratic Republic of the Congo (DRC) (and Ethiopia), lamenting the devastating economic and social costs of 'land grabs' by agribusiness, while dispensing patronizing policy advice: 'Congolese farmers should be considered innovative and hard-working entrepreneurs.'[84]

For many very small-scale farmers in Africa, the hard work and 'efficiency' lauded by so many economists is that of eking out a limited existence while failing

---

[83] Cramer et al. (2014b).
[84] Mousseau (2019: 17). The empirical weaknesses of the 'land grab' literature are discussed in Cotula et al. (2014).

to avoid chronic undernutrition. It is a form of 'efficiency' that is irrelevant for structural change, long-run development, or reducing the exploitation of women. For example, a large proportion of Ethiopian coffee farmers cultivate probably less than a quarter of a hectare.[85] A rapid and complete overhaul of Ethiopia's ageing coffee plant stock is urgently required, but the cost and logistical demands of replanting on millions of dispersed, minuscule plots is prohibitive. Very poor, very small-scale farmers cannot even afford to introduce low-cost changes—for example, in planting density, mulching, weeding, and in how beans are harvested and cared for after picking—that are known to generate relatively *quick* gains in yield. Newly planted coffee takes a long time (about four years) to produce significant increase in yields—too long for those living hand to mouth.

Such tiny plots cannot be the basis for 'catching up' with the increasingly complex, high-productivity, capital-intensive production that dominates global agriculture (and the world coffee market). Colombia, for example, has been much more successful in coffee production than Ethiopia, achieving substantial yield increases and engineering a radical restocking of the national stock of coffee trees. But Colombia's success has *not* been achieved by 'micro' coffee farmers, whose prospects are regarded as 'bleak'. Farms growing less than one hectare accounted for only about 6 per cent of the total area producing coffee in Colombia in 2007.[86]

Small and micro-enterprises, as well as the urban self-employed, fare no better than very small farms, a situation not confined to African or other developing economies. In the UK, for example, self-employed people have lower median earnings than employees do, while employees in new small firms have jobs that are more volatile, less productive, and less well paid; huge state subsidies encouraging new firms have not succeeded in creating sustainable new jobs.[87] The UK incidence of self-employment is relatively high, but research finds no evidence that changes in self-employment rates over time have any bearing on shifts in real GDP.

Failure rates for small businesses are high internationally, with about half of new small businesses in the USA and the UK failing within five years of starting up. In Africa, about half of new small businesses fail within three years, with one study finding that five out of seven new businesses fail within a year. South Africa appears to have particularly high rates of failure for new small start-ups, with estimates ranging between 50 and 95 per cent, depending on the sample and sector.[88] Even if small firms in Africa do manage to survive (at least initially), they tend not to grow.

---

[85] Minten, Schäfer, and Worako (2019); Cramer and Sender (2019).
[86] García-Cardona (2016: table 5.1 and 183). [87] Nightingale and Coad (2013).
[88] Olawale and Garwe (2010: 730).

SMEs that do survive in Africa usually make only a modest contribution to the growth process. The value added of firms employing less than thirty workers in Kenya (where very few start-ups last even a year) is lower than in larger firms, with smaller firms found to be less effective in absorbing new technology.[89] Small firms in Africa export less than larger firms too, so it can be argued they are less useful for macroeconomic balance and sustained growth (see Chapter 4).[90] Furthermore, evidence from developing countries more broadly suggests that workers in small enterprises have less access to decent on-the-job training than employees of larger firms.[91] We will discuss other research on the contribution of small firms to sub-Saharan African employment in Chapter 8.

The policy response following the rapid demise of SMEs is often not to query this policy fad or make more strenuous efforts to resist the lobbyists for entrepreneurs. Instead, the same tired reform proposals are wheeled out, from improving the 'doing business' climate to throwing even more resources into business support services and training. This is despite substantial resources having already been poured into programmes supporting SMEs in low- and middle-income countries, with underwhelming results.[92]

The results of the *Hanga Umurimo* programme in Rwanda are typical. The idea was to identify people with the 'right aptitude' and expose them to IFC-backed entrepreneurship training, thereby nurturing 'good business ideas'. The reality was that hardly any wage employment was created. Many beneficiaries thought the loans were actually grants, resulting in low repayment rates. Also, the vast majority of micro-credit loans (84 per cent) intended to support entrepreneurial activity in Rwanda are actually taken to smooth consumption, which is in line with wider evidence internationally.[93]

What goes unnoticed are the 'top-down' policies that *have* made a difference to the success and wider role of SMEs in some countries. Successful state promotion of SMEs has not been merely facilitative, but has *introduced* red tape and violated market theory. SMEs (variously defined) in South Korea, Taiwan, and Japan have advanced fastest where they are in concert with larger firms through various forms of subcontracting. Between 1972 and 1981, the South Korean government prioritized the promotion of heavy and chemical industries, which involved support for very large firms. At the same time, the government did support the SMEs supplying these large industries; it increased this support through the liberalization of the 1990s and into the 2000s.[94]

[89] Muriithi (2017).   [90] Naudé and Krugell (2002).   [91] Bloom et al. (2014: 39).
[92] Among recent reviews see Bloom et al. (2014); White, Steel, and Larquemin (2017); Piza et al. (2016). On the consequences and risks of fiscal and political decentralization in Africa see: Green (2008) and Erk (2015).
[93] Poole (2016).   [94] Amsden (2013).

3.5 Conclusion: Clearing the Fog

Our conclusion is not that a new mix of top-down state interventions combined with the embrace of global markets and deals with large firms will promote development in all contexts. Nor is our main aim the exposure of sworn ideological enemies appearing to advocate shared 'common-sense' policies. Rather, we have sought to identify a problem: the fog of development economics.

In subsequent chapters we aim to cut through the murk and, above all, encourage policymakers to query the theory and evidence underpinning common-sense views, whether these are imposed by creditors, donors, and financial institutions, popularized by well-meaning (*bien pensant*) NGOs, or advocated by home-grown nationalists. Such views are particularly unhelpful to policymakers when underpinned by impossibilist assumptions and/or tinged with naive optimism.

PART II
STRATEGIES OF ECONOMIC DEVELOPMENT IN AFRICA

4

Investment, Wage Goods, and Industrial Policy

4.1 Introduction

What can African policy officials do to promote sustained improvements in output, productivity, wages, employment, and welfare (and how can they 'catch up' with the advanced capitalist economies)? If investment is crucial, then how can the investment rate be raised? And is investment in some economic activities more important to the broader economy than others? Put another way, what are the greatest constraints on growth, and are certain types of investment less effective than others in promoting wider development?

Raising the investment rate is a necessary but insufficient objective if a society is to accelerate the development of its productive forces: the tools, machinery, sources of energy, and premises used in production, as well as the productive capabilities of the labour force (skills and know-how). The 'efficiency' of investment—its productivity—matters too, though it is not the overriding factor some economists have argued it to be and their measures of productivity do not make sense. Also vitally important is that policy officials identify which activities investment incentives should encourage—specifically, those most clearly associated with increasing returns, spill-overs and linkages, direct and indirect generation of employment, and generating foreign exchange.

We further argue that while supply-side issues—and institutional issues that may facilitate or hold back the development of productive forces—do matter, they have been given excessive emphasis in most of the economics literature. Instead, we emphasize the overriding importance of demand.[1] This in turn involves a discussion of what forms of demand are important and how they influence investment. One of these forms is external to a national economy: export demand. The dynamics of structural change in low- and middle-income countries typically generate a 'balance of payments constraint' that holds back whatever growth rate it is possible to sustain. An important determinant of developing countries' ability to sustain high growth rates is how effectively their governments address this constraint: that is, whether they can sustain a rapid rate of increase in imports.

---

[1] For a rare emphasis on the demand side as the key influence on patterns of industrialization in Africa see Wolf (2018).

African Economic Development: Evidence, Theory, Policy. Christopher Cramer, John Sender, and Arkebe Oqubay, Oxford University Press (2020). © Christopher Cramer, John Sender, and Arkebe Oqubay. DOI: 10.1093/oso/9780198832331.001.0001

Chapter 5 takes up this issue. However, there is another type of demand that is important for welfare as well as being a powerful influence on investment levels: domestic demand for wage goods (especially food, but also other basic consumer goods).

We not only reject simple distinctions between macro and micro levels of the economy; we also reject the orthodox neoclassical economic argument that there are 'micro-foundations' of the macro-economy (i.e. that the macro-economy is just the aggregate of choices made by a large number of individual 'agents').[2] 'Society does not consist of individuals,' Marx argued, 'it expresses the sum of connections and relationships in which these individuals stand.'[3] Similarly, we argue that an economy is the expression of a huge array of relationships (both domestic and global). Investment drives savings more than the other way round, but investment itself is shaped by a range of factors, including the distribution of income nationally and internationally, the state of productive forces (including levels of education and skill formation), and the level of demand. While investment decisions themselves may be 'micro', they are determined by macroeconomic balances and trends, as well as by institutions and policies that affect relative profitability across different activities, how restrictive monetary and fiscal policy are, the ease of capital flight, and so on.

An oft-repeated view guiding many policy recommendations throughout Africa is that savings are a prerequisite for investment. That is, low- and middle-income countries will not be able to achieve more investment unless they build up a pool of domestic savings to add to whatever foreign financial flows can be attracted. The implications of this apparently common-sense statement are wide-reaching and contentious. We contrast the 'savings lead to investment' approach, which is rooted in neoclassical economics, with another and—we argue—clearer way of thinking about growth and development, based on the thinking of economists such as Kalecki, Kaldor, and Keynes. Naturally, a different way of understanding the dynamics of growth and accumulation leads to a different way of thinking about how countries can improve investment, productivity, wages, employment, and welfare. This in turn leads to very different policy implications.

One question is how important it is to generate a high savings rate *before and in order to* secure rising levels of investment. Another is whether it matters where that investment is directed. The answer that emerged from a great deal of neoclassical growth theory was that, given diminishing returns, it is irrelevant which sector investment flows into. Another common argument is that rather than focusing on manufacturing or industrialization, better gains can now be

[2] On the delusional dogma of micro-foundations of macroeconomics see King (2012).
[3] Marx (1993: 265).

made by supporting the service sector, particularly activities such as information and communications, as well as tourism. According to this view, low-income developing countries may be able to skip the long process of industrialization—which has historically been socially disruptive and highly exploitative, as well as environmentally damaging—altogether.

In reality, the evidence from many countries' experiences of rapid economic growth in the modern era suggests that the sectoral concentration of investment really does matter. Historically, there has been something 'special' about manufacturing, with a high rate of investment in the sector particularly important to overall growth and development. In short, manufacturing has been and is an 'engine of growth'. We explain why.

In recent years, many neoclassical economists have 'rediscovered' industrial policy, with the result that it now means different things to different people. We do not agree, as others might, that there is a 'convergence' of views among economists of different traditions regarding appropriate industrial policy. We clarify why there are differences: for some economists industrial policy is only sensible if implemented in ways that stick close to the principles of neoclassical theory, in order to fix or correct market failures. For others, any sufficiently ambitious industrial policy involves significant departures from the orthodoxy.

Just as industrial policy became fashionable again, however, a new fear arose that a twenty-first-century trend—premature deindustrialization—will render manufacturing irrelevant as an engine of growth, employment, and structural change. Premature deindustrialization happens when the share of manufacturing value added (MVA) in gross domestic product (GDP) begins to fall at levels of income per capita significantly below those at which this shrinkage started historically in the now industrialized economies. We discuss this issue in Section 4.3 and argue that such evidence is not a reason for governments to give up on industrial policy.

4.2 Investment, Savings, and the Wage Goods Constraint

Investment Matters: 'Even a Skilful Cook Cannot Make a Meal Out of Nothing'

It is not possible to generate sustained growth, structural change, wage and employment growth, and welfare improvements without raising the level of investment relative to national income (the investment ratio). Of course, there can be wasteful, ineffective investments: capital sunk in wayward schemes or frustrated by demoralized management lacking adequate technical know-how. Also, economic development and structural change involves a progressive shift of resources into a diverse range of higher-productivity activities. Even so, it remains the case that long-run growth and structural change require substantial and sustained levels of 'capital deepening'.

This point can get lost amid the complex debates economists have about growth. An influential but implausible idea was that the historically unprecedented East Asian economic growth surge in the 1960s and 1970s could have been even faster if fewer inputs (including capital) had been used, less wastefully. Some argued that growth was a function of the accumulation of capital and not in any significant way a reflection of productivity gains. Assuming diminishing returns, growth in Singapore, South Korea, Taiwan, and elsewhere would, supposedly, fizzle out, a victim of inefficient over-accumulation, rather like what had been observed in the Soviet Union. Others argued the opposite: that East Asian growth was the result of assimilating improved technologies from overseas and closing the 'ideas gap'. However, these critics used essentially the *same* kind of model, just using different estimates of variables. Both sides kept faith with the idea that free markets played a leading role in the countries' 'miraculous' growth.[4]

Behind this debate lay the history of growth theory. Thinking about what determines rates of growth and why they differ over time and between countries has long been a source of controversy. For many decades, perhaps the most influential approach among orthodox economists was the neoclassical production function. In an aggregate production function, output is a product of the factors of production (essentially capital and labour) and an estimate of their overall productivity, or 'total factor productivity' (TFP).

TFP estimates play a significant role in many analyses of growth in Africa. For example, a simple production function, with a 'productivity growth residual', lay beneath a major growth accounting exercise applied to 18 African countries in the mid- 2000s.[5] If capital and labour inputs are accounted for, then any growth over time not accounted for by changes in these factor inputs is a 'residual', taken to represent TFP. Contributors to an African Economic Research Consortium (AERC) project on growth argued that TFP growth had been very slow in Africa, and that this could be addressed if more African countries adopted 'syndrome-free' policy regimes. This meant not only avoiding the syndrome of state failure, but also other syndromes, such as splurging natural resource windfalls on infrastructure or introducing 'state controls', which involved intervening in markets and 'distorting' prices.[6]

The many difficulties in collecting, say, reliable demographic data or working out the level and rate of growth of output, pale beside the problems associated with TFP data. Growth accounting exercises that focus on estimating TFP rest on assumptions that are at the core of neoclassical economics in its purer forms:

---

[4] Birdsall et al (1993); Krugman (1994a); Romer (1992); Young (1992).
[5] Ndulu and O'Connell (2008: 19).   [6] Fosu (2012: 183).

perfect competition, full employment, constant returns to scale and diminishing returns to individual inputs, and perfect, easy substitution between capital and labour. Aggregate production functions imagine a whole economy as a single sector. But even if trying to work out TFP in terms of a single output—say, wheat production in the Punjab, coal in South Africa, or steel in South Korea—this is an exercise that will produce meaningless results, given the extremely varied outputs and qualities of each product.[7]

Typically, explanations for perceived patterns of TFP have nothing to do with the underlying model, and, in fact, often violate the very assumptions on which the estimates are made. In some cases, wildly unrealistic explanations are given. The debate about East Asian economies was kicked off in the 1990s by a paper suggesting that Singapore was a free market economy (conforming to the model's assumption of perfect competition). We know this is far from true. A TFP account of South Korean steel is 'riddled with insoluble theoretical and empirical problems that conceal rather than reveal the nature of the South Korean steel industry'.[8] Estimates of TFP trends in the South African coal sector are similarly misleading, constructed out of an imaginary model that, rather than being a technical simplification, is a complete misunderstanding of the sector. The market for coal in South Africa historically has *not* been perfectly competitive, but instead highly concentrated. One reason this matters is that the structure of the coal sector and its political links have shaped trends in investment over time. A tight coordination between a very limited number of mining (and energy) firms and the state, and the apartheid state's institutional exploitation of labour, underpinned the expansion of the coal sector before political uncertainties and foreign disinvestment broke apart the 'political settlement' in the 1980s.[9] At the aggregate level, it is fairly easily shown that the history of the modern Zambian economy cannot be understood in terms of the perfect competition, constant returns, and full employment assumptions deployed in growth accounting models. In cases where these conditions do not hold (and they have never held in Zambia), then it becomes unclear what it is that estimates of TFP are actually supposed to be measuring (and this not even mentioning problems with the underlying data).[10]

Although many well-known economists promoted efforts to quantify the sources of East Asian growth using measures of TFP, they paid no attention to the profound conceptual and empirical problems with aggregate production functions.[11] A review of their work concludes that aggregate production functions 'are a dead end because they ask the wrong question, which they try to answer with the wrong data and because the model that underlies these approaches can never be refuted empirically'.[12] Unfortunately, there is a huge amount of research on

[7] Bharadwaj (1974); Fine (1992); Sato (2005).   [8] Sato (2005: 636).   [9] Fine (1992).
[10] See Pollen (2018), critically assessing Mwanawina and Mulungushi (2008).
[11] Krugman (1994); Pasinetti (2000); Reati (2001).   [12] Felipe and McCombie (2017: 2).

African economies that follows these East Asian examples, ignoring inconvenient methodological difficulties when attempting to explain growth.

Orthodox growth thinking later followed two different, if related, tracks. One of these built up the growth accounting approach used in earlier models, but sought to include an ever-increasing number of variables to 'explain' the remaining residual (i.e. the portion of growth outcomes not easily explained by the shorter list of variables). In Africa, this took the form of a flurry of growth regressions seeking to explain the difference between average growth rates over time in Africa compared to the rest of the world, as captured in a dependent variable (the variable to be explained) known as the 'Africa dummy'. This voluminous literature also reached a dead end,[13] with a key figure in neoclassical growth theory remarking that this growth regression literature was 'statistically unprepossessing'.[14]

The other track was the development of 'new' or endogenous growth theory. This theory recognized that increasing returns do exist and are significant. In reality, economists had really known this but found it difficult to deal with technically. One of the key figures in neoclassical economics, Alfred Marshall, explained that there was both a Law of Diminishing Returns and a Law of Increasing Returns: 'while the part which nature plays in production shows a tendency to diminishing return, the part which man plays shows a tendency to increasing return'. But the latter tendency faded into relative insignificance through successive editions of his *Principles of Economics*.[15] Much earlier, Adam Smith also recognized the importance of increasing returns, but he too had turned away from them, to the point that Nicholas Kaldor would later quip that economics went wrong after Book 1, Chapter 4 of the *Wealth of Nations*, when Smith dropped the assumption of increasing returns.[16]

Thus, having for many years evaporated from economics, increasing returns made a comeback in 'new' growth theory models, which attempted to account for the origins and persistence of imperfect competition and make analytical sense of sustained divergence between economies. If increasing returns matter, and are a source of imperfect competition (because, for example, 'first-mover' firms build a competitive edge through reaching a scale that competitors may take a long time to achieve, if at all), then investment in economic activities with scope for increasing returns matters more than it does in models assuming constant or diminishing returns. Furthermore, states may play an important role in nurturing such investment in larger-scale innovative production.

Unsurprisingly, there is huge debate about the usefulness of new growth theory, with the most obvious critique being that it is not really new at all but is 'old wine in new bottles'. After all, economists outside the neoclassical orthodoxy had long

---

[13] Jerven (2011).   [14] Solow (1994: 51).   [15] Marshall (1920: 196).
[16] Thirlwall (2003: 7).

argued for the importance of increasing returns in economic growth. Furthermore, critics argued that these non-orthodox economists—such as Kaldor—were more realistic in their ideas about growth as a process of cumulative causation, proceeding through tensions and disequilibria, rather than a matter of markets working themselves out through constant adjustments to a state of equilibrium (see Chapter 6 for a discussion of equilibrium and balance in development economics). Heterodox economists charge that 'new' growth theorists grafted a *partial* recognition of reality (increasing returns, imperfect competition) onto a core model still rooted in the same infertile soil, that is, the methodologically individualist, equilibrium-based theory of neoclassical economics.

By the 2000s, some of the protagonists of orthodox economic growth theory finally began accepting the obvious: that it is extremely difficult to understand the finer processes of economic growth. William Easterly, for example, who had previously argued that high scores on an index of ethno-linguistic fractionalization was a key reason behind 'Africa's growth tragedy' wrote: 'in reality, high-growth countries follow a bewildering array of paths to development'.[17] Other economists aimed 'to be comprehensive in including potential explanatory variables: firm characteristics, geography, infrastructure, access to finance . . . We offer a menu of facts and explanations' in the hope of explaining 'Africa's disadvantage'.[18] Growth, then, becomes something of a hodgepodge recipe; a bit of market openness with a dash of good governance thrown in along with various other ingredients. This approach does at least accept the importance of investment, with a recent analysis by International Monetary Fund (IMF) economists of the long-run data for sub-Saharan Africa stating that 'investment seems to play a strong role in warding off growth stops and sustaining growth spells, as it not only supports aggregate demand but also expands productive capacity'.[19]

Growth is about 'accumulation and innovation', with innovation—technical change—itself embodied in the capital stock (for example, investment and innovation combine in a new and faster pattern-cutting machinery in the textile industry). The long-run evidence analysed by Maddison shows an 'impressive growth of non-residential gross capital stock per person employed' in France, Germany, Japan, the Netherlands, the UK, and the USA between 1890 and 1987.[20] What is especially striking in his historical data is how the 'followers'—those countries, above all Japan, who were catching up to the UK (the first economic leader of the modern capitalist era)—had the fastest growth over time in capital

---

[17] Easterly (2009); Easterly and Levine (1997).

[18] Harrison, Lin, and Xu (2014). See also Commission on Growth and Development (2008).

[19] Arizala et al. (2017: 17); see also Ghazanchyan and Stotsky (2013: 3). Earlier cross-country regressions produced fragile results on the determinants of growth. But Levine and Renelt (1992) did find that across many different statistical studies the clouds parted to reveal a clear and strong relationship between the investment ratio and growth.

[20] Maddison (1991: 65).

stock per employee. Such historical experience itself embodies what is called 'the advantages of backwardness'.[21]

Maddison focused on the proximate causes of growth experiences, which he distinguished from the less easily quantifiable and generally more debatable ultimate causes (including institutions, ideologies, pressures from interest groups, historical accidents, and variations in national policy). His explanation of episodes of growth, convergence on the leader, and slow-down across these advanced capitalist economies from the late nineteenth to the late twentieth centuries emphasizes that 'the movement of capital stock provides a much more powerful degree of explanation for growth acceleration and slow-down than . . . the analysis of labour input'.[22]

The post-Second World War history of 'catching up' development confirms the point. A comprehensive review of the most rapid experiences of economic development found: 'Capital accumulation holds the central place in East Asia's virtuous growth regime.'[23] Accumulation—the share of investment in GDP—rose from 10 per cent in Korea and from 16 per cent in Taiwan in the 1950s to more than 30 per cent in the 1980s; Southeast Asian economies such as Indonesia, Malaysia, and Thailand began to raise their investment-to-GDP ratios in the 1970s and kept them high; while China sustained a rise from an already significant 25 per cent ratio in the early 1970s to more than 35 per cent in 1995–2000.

One argument in favour of pushing for a high investment rate is that 'even a skilful cook cannot make food out of nothing'.[24] All too often, however—in many Latin American and African countries, for example—investment has either tailed off too soon or gone into speculative urban construction (rather than productive infrastructure). Furthermore, in a context characterized by an acute balance of payments constraint, investment has often failed to promote a sufficiently fast rate of growth of export earnings. Thus, a fundamental issue is what alternative returns are available to those allocating investment finance—whether it be in tax havens abroad, real estate, the financial sector, or in manufacturing—and how policy affects these relative returns.

Savings and Investment: The Mainstream View and the Fate of Financial Liberalization

How, though, are low- and middle-income countries to raise and sustain a high rate of investment? How are they to finance investment? In this section, we argue

---

[21] Research on these advantages was pioneered by Gerschenkron (1962) and has been discussed more recently by Shin (2013).
[22] Maddison (1991: 139).   [23] Storm and Naastepad (2005: 1073).
[24] Yongzhi and Kun (2020).

that demand is a far more important driver of *sustained* investment than is often acknowledged, and that levels and patterns of demand are shaped by institutions, as well as historically specific social relations and politics. This is contrary to the typical emphasis of economics texts, which emphasize supply-side sources of investment and growth.

Given the assumptions underpinning growth accounting exercises and the measurement of TFP (discussed earlier in this section), it is unsurprising that the standard policy recommendations are designed to: bring economies ever closer to the ideal of perfect competition (market deregulation, privatization); encourage a proliferation of small and medium-sized, price-taking enterprises (entrepreneurship programmes, access to finance schemes, micro-credit facilities); and encourage frictionless switching between capital-intensive and labour-intensive production in moves towards full employment (greater 'flexibility' of labour markets without minimum wages, legal constraints on hiring and firing, and/or powerful trade unions). A key market that, if sufficiently liberalized, is supposed to funnel household savings into investible funds is the market for finance.

Mainstream economists argue that economies need to build up both public and private sector savings in order to create a pool of investible surpluses available to private enterprises through the financial system. If the banking system lends these savings at interest rates set by market transactions and conditions, this will help to weed out unproductive borrowers incapable of generating high enough returns to meet repayment obligations. In other words, market-determined interest rates will lead to efficient investment, while institutionally regulated (or repressed) interest rates may lead to indiscriminate and wasteful investment. According to this view, it is best to let market prices determine interest rates and stimulate a gradual increase in savings, which will in turn lead to a gradual rise in efficient investment. As one summary of the influential McKinnon–Shaw argument for financial liberalization claims:

> introducing market principles and competition in the banking sector increases
> *interest rates on deposits. These higher interest rates lead to higher saving and
> investment rates, ultimately contributing to higher* growth rates . . . increasing
> competition puts pressure on the profit margins of banks, in particular on the
> interest rates demanded for loans. This reduces the cost of debt, leading to a rise
> in investment and growth.[25]

The empirical evidence does *not* confirm a causal relationship between financial liberalization and growth.[26] Rather, data on GDP per capita growth rates in sub-Saharan African countries from 1950 to 2016 show that financial liberalization is

---

[25] Hermes and Lensink (2014: 5).   [26] Ibid.

linked to episodes of growth *deceleration*. Neither is there any evidence linking fewer financial restrictions with growth acceleration elsewhere in the world,[27] with financial liberalization in several Latin American countries, for example, followed by a string of domestic financial crises, including the Mexican 'Tequila Crisis' of 1994–5.[28] Additional costs associated with financial liberalization include a higher frequency of financial crises, more volatile flows of capital, and the social costs associated with 'financialization'.[29]

In the wake of the global financial crisis, some of the problems of overenthusiastic 'financial globalization' were reluctantly recognized even by economists employed by the IMF.[30] As a result, a new literature developed in largely mainstream quarters, arguing that while the direct benefits of financial globalization were 'elusive', there were indirect benefits. However, these indirect benefits only tended to kick in when economies had passed certain 'thresholds' of financial depth, institutional preconditions, and level of per capita income.

Investment and Savings: A More Keynesian/Kaleckian View

There is another view, usually associated with Keynes and Kalecki, that investment generates the savings needed to cover its financing over time.[31] Productive investment creates wage incomes and profits, some of which are saved—by employees depositing savings in banks, by firms retaining profits or banking surpluses.

Again, the East Asian experience, where a high and rising investment-to-GDP ratio *preceded* rising savings rates, is instructive. In terms of macroeconomic balances, there was an '*ex ante* excess of investment over savings'.[32] That investment was anything but gradual and market-led, instead being the product of determined state intervention that amounted almost to 'forced investment'. East Asia may be exceptional in many ways, but in the basic fact of investment surges driving rising savings there is nothing unusual about the region's experience. Elsewhere, for example in Mexico between the 1940s and late 1970s, firms made investment decisions based on judgements of expanding market size and 'independently of the availability of finance'.[33]

Even if there *are* investible savings generated domestically, they are often not invested, becoming what Albert Hirschman called 'frustrated savings'.[34] After

---

[27] Arizala et al. (2017). See also Arestis (2005) and Loizos (2018) on the theoretical flaws of the financial liberalization thesis and the lack of convincing evidence for it.
[28] Ros (2012: 9).   [29] Karwowski, Shabani, and Stockhammer (2017); Sawyer (2017).
[30] Kose, Prasad, and Taylor (2009: 1).
[31] For an introduction to Keynes's economics see Skidelsky (2010).
[32] Storm and Naastepad (2005: 1084). See also Vos (1982).
[33] Fitzgerald (1980). Between 1950 and 1981, real GDP in Mexico grew by 6.5 per cent per year (Kehoe and Meza, 2011).
[34] Hirschman (1958: 35).

financial markets and the capital account were deregulated in South Africa, for example, there was a dramatic acceleration of purchases of short-term financial assets (by both domestic and foreign speculators) to achieve quick capital gains, while flows into productive investments dwindled.[35] Enormous sums of African savings have been squirreled away abroad and in tax havens, or held by large corporations but not invested productively within African economies. Between 1970 and 2015, capital flight from 30 sub-Saharan African economies reached huge proportions, according to one reckoning much larger than the capital inflows of official development assistance and foreign direct investment; and capital flight has been accelerating.[36] These authors suggest that the main motive for capital flight from Africa was to evade taxation or the seizure of illicitly acquired assets; but this suggestion risks underestimating the significance of demand. If savings are to be invested—and corporate profits reinvested in Africa—there must be confidence in expanding demand.

Angola and Ethiopia provide examples of this dynamic. In Angola, following the end of the country's war in the early 2000s, rising oil prices and Chinese demand did create opportunities for illicit asset accumulation and capital flight.[37] But there were also incentives to invest domestically because of oil-fuelled expectations of rising middle-income consumption; and high oil prices also sustained the government's ability to spend on urban housing and infra-structure projects as part of its strategy for post-war reconstruction and political consolidation. The infrastructure and housing boom had clear linkage effects, leading to the emergence of a building materials and cement production indus-try (and associated employment) within Angola. Rising Angolan middle-class incomes in the wake of rising export earnings prompted investment in, for example, the brewing and beverages sector. This in turn led to linkages to bottling and canning facilities in Angola, some of which grew large enough to export to other African economies.[38] In Ethiopia, a large-scale government programme to construct middle-income urban housing was the demand spur that led to a domestic cement industry (and then later expansion of foreign-owned cement production as well) and to the proliferation of domestic building materials and services firms.[39]

These experiences confirm the views of economists working in the tradition of Keynes and Kalecki. One of these, King, for example, highlights the proposition that:

> The relationship between aggregate investment and aggregate savings is funda-mental to macroeconomic theory, and causation runs from investment to saving, and not vice versa.[40]

---

[35] Isaacs and Kaltenbrunner (2018).   [36] Ndikumana and Boyce (2018).
[37] Ferreira and Soares de Oliveira (2018: 17–18).   [38] Wolf (2017; 2018: 211–91).
[39] Oqubay (2016: 105–48).   [40] King (2013b: 486).

It bears repeating that there is a great rift between those who think savings 'lead to' investment and those who think investment can lead to and be matched by savings. Most policy advice to developing countries is based on the former (neoclassical) view and ignores the intellectual revolution in economics during the 1930s:

> Keynes's intellectual revolution was to shift economists from thinking normally in terms of a model of reality in which a dog called savings wagged his tail called investment to thinking in terms of a model in which a dog called investment wagged his tail labelled savings.[41]

However, the econometric evidence on the relationship between savings and investment in 10 African economies suggests that this is complex, varying from country to country.[42] It may be difficult to make simple and universal statements about causation for several reasons: first, there is a 'chicken and egg' problem: a virtuous cycle of investment generating and being matched by savings (in macro-economic accounting, savings must equal investment), which in turn allows for more investment, has to start somewhere. This often requires high borrowing (including borrowing abroad), directed credit, and government spending, and can involve rapidly creating surpluses out of exploitation, wage repression, and forced or deferred savings. Second, savings do not instantly and automatically appear to rescue macroeconomic balances and match investment. Policy measures are important in mediating this. And, third, the impetus to sustain investment can peter out. Initial sources of financing may evaporate if the balance of political forces changes such that profits are squeezed by high wages and demand for more consumer goods is asphyxiated by high costs of living, or if broad consumer demand fails to grow because of extreme income inequality, as has been argued is the case with regard to sluggish manufacturing growth in Angola.[43] Flows of concessional finance from abroad are often volatile and driven by geostrategic and political forces.[44] The animal spirits (as Keynes called them) of both African and foreign investors flicker and fade for various (licit and illicit) reasons, but often result in massive shifts in the volume of capital flight. This third issue is obviously political, involving struggles over the distribution of surpluses between profits and wages.

The State and Uncertainty

How, then, does it come about that the investment ratio is raised, increasing aggregate demand and setting off a cumulative process of growth? Firms, both

---

[41] Meade (1975: 82).   [42] Adam, Musah, and Ibrahim (2017: 104).

[43] Wolf (2017). The theoretical and empirical difficulties of assessing the impact on economic growth of inequality in the distribution of income are discussed by Hein and Vogel (2007).

[44] Broich (2017); Lang and Presbitero (2018).

domestic and foreign, will be eager to invest if they can identify opportunities in a large and growing market: demand propels investment. In the prevailing uncertainty of capitalism, strong evidence of demand and an expanding market helps create 'animal spirits'—the herd-like behaviour characteristic of investors, expressed in this case in the confident expectation that market demand will be buoyant. Keynes emphasized the role that hunches, anxiety about the actions of others, and emotions play in investment decisions. More recent and fashionable work in 'behavioural' economics explores bounded rationality and systematic 'biases' and heuristics (what earlier economists might have called rules of thumb) in economic behaviour, but much of this work effectively makes modest tweaks for 'irrationality' on largely unaltered neoclassical models and principles.[45]

However, the whole point about low-income economies is not only that the supply of factories and new machines is low, but also that the absolute level of aggregate demand is low. Furthermore, growth in demand is often faltering. In middle-income countries the market for many goods and services might be larger, but all too often the momentum of growth in aggregate demand stalls. Investment decisions in developing countries rely not only on the choices of individual capitalists or firms, but also a on a number of other factors, such as how liberalized capital markets are, the pattern of income distribution, and how institutions and infrastructure function. Additionally, how societies are structured—for example, marked spatial, racial/ethnic, or gendered inequalities and the strength of trade unions—shapes patterns of effective demand that has consequences for investment.[46] In these circumstances, sustaining high investment ratios has typically involved a leading role for the state.

States can also have a powerful role in sustaining investment in order to avoid the sudden collapses in growth that some economists have come to emphasize as being a critical threat to sustained structural change. Economic historians argue that

> The improvement of economic performance over the long run has occurred primarily because the frequency and rate of shrinking have both declined, rather than because the growing rate has increased.[47]

If public sector investment fails to grow, as in Latin American economies after the 1982 debt crisis, then both investment-to-GDP ratios and growth will stagnate.[48] In several East African economies, policy-induced declines in demand between the 1980s and mid-1990s, signalled by massive reductions in real wages in the public sector, were also associated with collapses in growth. Across a wider group

---

[45] On the difficulties of grafting behavioural twigs onto the root stock of Keynesian theory see King (2013b: 505).

[46] Tilly (1999) outlines four mechanisms, of which the most important is exploitation, that sustain 'categorical inequalities' which prove extremely durable.

[47] Broadberry and Wallis (2017: 3–4).   [48] Ros (2012, 13–14).

of sub-Saharan African countries it has been argued that lower government expenditures (after signing agreements with the IMF) had the effect of reducing growth and employment while widening inequality. Where policies were introduced to restrain domestic demand *without* the direct intervention of the IMF, as in South Africa since the mid-1990s, the economy remained 'stuck in low gear'.[49]

If the state is the central economic actor in the drama of late development, even more so than in advanced economies, one important role it must play is in stimulating and coordinating investment.[50] Aside from the issue of using state-owned enterprises to achieve these ends, this includes managing monetary policy, fiscal policy, and development finance: that is, organizing macroeconomic policies and a financial system around the goals of sustained long-run economic growth and structural change. These goals have to be defined in terms of growth, productivity, employment, and the balance of payments. That, however, is completely contrary to the advice that has been meted out to the central banks and governments of developing countries since the late 1970s or so. African governments who wish to avoid growth collapses are still subjected to conventional policy exhortations—made to adopt monetary policy geared towards low inflation, reduce market distortions, and improve the business climate—by some IMF economists.[51] Such economists appear to shrug off the doubts that the IMF's own Chief Economist expressed in 2011 about this skewed advice, that mainstream economists and policymakers had 'convinced [themselves] that there was one target, inflation. There was one instrument, the [interest] policy rate. And that was basically enough to get things done.'[52]

Development Finance: Central Banks, Development Banks, and Government Spending

The common-sense view dismissing development banks has been so powerful that it can easily seem as if such banks are an historical oddity, a diversion from the norm of prudent and sensible banking. A review of the history of debates on financial systems from the early twentieth century onwards finds that the neoliberal way of thinking about banking, central banks, and monetary policy is actually the exception.[53] A sensible approach is now said to involve keeping central banks out of a government's hands ('independent') so that the former can focus on holding inflation as low as possible, and this approach is part and parcel of a belief in the virtues of austerity and a commitment to curbing demand. It also involves deregulating capital markets, making it harder for governments to kick-start a higher investment ratio thanks to the increased difficulty of financing investment

---

[49] Simson (2017); Weeks (1999).   [50] See, e.g., Rodrik (1996) on South Korea.
[51] Arizala et al. (2017).   [52] Blanchard (2012: 1).   [53] Epstein (2013).

projects through central bank policy. In this scenario, there is no incentive for central banks to limit the flow of investment into shopping malls and luxury condominiums and instead promote investments targeting structural change, increased employment, and rising productivity.

The range of instruments that central banks can use, and have often used, is in fact far wider than simply tinkering with short-term interest rates in the service of low inflation. Rather, central banks can play many other roles, both through their links to development banks and through their own policies and practices. Many developing countries, and in the earlier part of the twentieth century also the UK, US, and European governments, took a very different view of central—and development—banks. Particularly after the Great Depression, central banks came to be major agents of economic development, and there is a long and richly varied history of state-owned 'development' banks. This evidence largely dispels more recent myths claiming that state-owned banks are inevitably inefficient.[54]

There are examples of lax and corrupt central bank regulation of the banking sector that have undermined investment efficiency and political stability, including in countries where reforms have been introduced to make the central bank more independent.[55] On the other hand, central banks in many countries have, among other things, successfully introduced capital controls to reduce exposure to volatile surges in inflows and outflows of capital; made low-cost capital available to specific development institutions; used differential discount rates to allocate credit to large, priority capital projects; and imposed reserve requirements that fund government bonds. Development banks, meanwhile, have been used to provide concessionary loans, often with lengthy repayment schemes, to stimulate investment in new manufacturing activities.[56]

Central banks have also frequently got prices wrong—anathema to the neoclassical economist—by engineering negative real interest rates, again to stimulate borrowing for investment and to make it easier for governments to use deficit financing to push for higher investment rates.[57] Governments often have to spend more than they receive in tax revenue in order to bring about higher investment rates, the aim being to sustain a high level of demand rather than restrict it. To re-emphasize a key point: what might make sound economic sense for a household does not make sense for an entire economy (see Chapter 3).

Of course, government deficit funding can also result in wanton spending and wasteful use of extremely scarce resources, for example in accommodating military adventures or providing for handouts to special interest groups in order to

---

[54] Marois (2016).   [55] Nyambura-Mwaura and Genga (2016) on Kenya.
[56] Lazzarini et al. (2015). On BNDES (Banco Nacional de Desenvolvimento Económico e Social) see: Tavares de Araujo Jr. (2013) de Aghion (1999); UNCTAD (2016); Di John (2016). Weiss (2015) emphasizes the role development banks can play in counter-cyclical spending, boosting demand at critical points in the economic cycle.
[57] Epstein (2013); Amsden (2001).

preserve political power. An obvious example is the post-independence history of Zimbabwe, a country whose sizeable formal sector, well-developed civil service, and initially successful record of post-independence service delivery seemed to mark it out from hyperbolic generalizations about weak states in Africa.[58] Ultimately, though, it suffered catastrophic economic decline, rapid deindustrialization, shrinking agricultural output and exports, currency collapse, and periods of hyperinflation.

There have been different phases of the Zimbabwean crisis but what unites them is a *political* dynamic: the 'violent intolerance' of the leadership of the ruling Zimbabwe African National Union—Patriotic Front (ZANU–PF) in attempting to remain in power.[59] This commitment was pursued through institutional and policy measures that made large numbers of people with access to (but not title over) land, minimum-wage protected jobs, and civil service positions dependent on the central state. Institutions were increasingly politicized and in many cases militarized.[60] Meanwhile, an increasingly dominant group of rentiers accumulated private wealth through the state while failing to play the role expected of a productive capitalist class.[61] In the 1990s, a poorly designed and implemented enhanced structural adjustment programme (ESAP) was championed by domestic elites (*not* imposed by the IMF and World Bank, which, whatever their failings, insisted on the inclusion of a social programme, against the instincts of the government). This paved the way for even faster deindustrialization and further opportunities for personal wealth and rent accumulation. By the end of the 1990s it had become obvious the government could or would not control its deficits and confidence in the economy plummeted, with the currency collapsing in late 1997. Further economic mayhem continued throughout the 2000s, encapsulated by, among other things, unbudgeted pay-outs to war veterans, an economically misjudged land reform, and a military excursion into the conflicts of the Democratic Republic of the Congo (DRC).[62]

But if—by contrast with the Zimbabwean experience—'excess' demand represents investments in activities and capital equipment that raises productivity (and foreign exchange earnings), then it makes no sense to rein in demand. A striking example of a government refusing to repress demand and presiding over a sharp increase in net borrowing from the rest of the world is Norway in the 1970s. Norway encouraged a rapid surge in investments in capital equipment to facilitate increased productivity in the country's new oil sector. Thus, policy officials can choose either to follow Norway's example by provoking a supply response when

---

[58] Alexander and McGregor (2013).
[59] Raftopoulos and Mlambo (2009); Davies (2004); Alexander and McGregor (2013).
[60] Verheul (2013); Alexander (2013).   [61] Davies (2004); Dashwood (1996).
[62] Towriss (2013).

macroeconomic deficits develop; or they can react how the orthodoxy of the past forty years advises, by repressing demand.[63]

The most important point here is how policy officials can bring about a rapid increase in investment levels. One view is that positive high real interest rates will make it possible for the more efficient private sector investors to borrow and invest. If this leads to an external imbalance (because undirected new investment may lead to imports rising faster than export earnings), then foreign investment should be encouraged to cover the external gap or exchange rate adjustments should be made to send more appropriate signals to investors. That is largely the approach the South African government embarked on after the first post-apartheid elections, when it set out to (and for a while managed to) reduce the fiscal deficit, meaning the government no longer competed for savings with the private sector and inflation could slow down. However, real interest rates remained very high, growth was slow, and private investment—both domestic and foreign—dismally failed to respond in the manner predicted by a large chorus of mainstream economists.

The alternative is to argue that government deficit spending is central to boosting the investment ratio, especially because private sector enterprises are so reluctant to invest in low-income and slow-growing economies. Their reluctance is perfectly reasonable. The market is relatively small and often stagnant, and, while growth episodes happen, they are typically short-lived. Uncertainty is pervasive and the risks investors face are very high. Additionally, the costs of investment are high as it is difficult to get inputs and costly to install equipment; infrastructure is either absent or creaky; and there are insufficient skills and technical know-how in the economy. Particularly in more open economies, it is likely to take some time before domestic enterprises can compete effectively in international markets, and in some situations private investors may be wary of bearing the cost of making production more profitable if others can cash in on their efforts without absorbing some of the cost, for example, when providing irrigation or graded roads. Thus, infrastructure becomes a critical issue: transport and power infrastructure short-comings undermine investor confidence, but the large financing commitments required to improve them are usually off-putting for private investors.

While the private sector makes only a small contribution to financing investment in African transport infrastructure, investment expenditures on road transport absorb a relatively high proportion of total public sector investment in low-income African economies.[64] Road construction costs per kilometre for activities undertaken between 2005 and 2007 are said to have been have been two or three times higher in some African economies than in other developing areas. Unfortunately, the costs of irrigation investments in sub-Saharan Africa are also

---

[63] Sandbu (2017).   [64] Gurara et al. (2017).

high compared to costs in South Asia and South East Asia.[65] In such circumstances, political risks loom larger too, with governments having to absorb a great deal of the risk in order to provide collectively enjoyed goods such as rural electrification and irrigation.

An example of these dynamics can be seen in Ethiopia's Upper Awash Valley, in which there is an ungraded road strung with sizeable farms on privatized land capable of extremely high-value output: fruits, flowers, and wine grapes. None of these enterprises has been able (or willing) to finance expenditures to improve the road, and despite repeated pledges by the regional government, nothing was done for years. This directly hits profitability and earnings, with a farm manager for a very large fruit growing and processing enterprise estimating that this business loses 12 per cent of the export value of packaged passion fruit puree because of damage done when the cartons are shaken up on the bad road.[66]

Investment, Savings, and the Question of 'Crowding Out'

Governments do *not* compete against the private sector, shrinking a pool of savings that would otherwise be used to fund efficient private sector investments. Rather, the government may build up deficits through productivity-enhancing expenditures that generate incomes (and savings), raising profitability across all sectors and creating further scope for private sector investment, as well as incomes and savings, to rise. The World Bank's most recent discussion of the relationship between public and private investment in Africa may be rather unsophisticated—based on crude cross-country statistical evidence, but they conclude that there is a significant positive association across the 26 countries studied—that is, public investment *crowds in* private investment.[67]

The same grudging acceptance that large-scale public expenditure can drive growth in low-income countries characterizes an assessment of the recent record in Ethiopia. Assuming unquestioningly that Ethiopia's heterodox macroeconomic policies must have perverse, growth-reducing effects, a standard neoclassical growth accounting model reveals that 'the negative growth effects of heterodox macro policies were quantitatively much less important than the positive growth drivers they helped to achieve'.[68] It is tempting to rewrite this statement: the evidence suggests that heterodox macro policies have driven rapid growth in Ethiopia. Critics of a dominant role for the public sector, such as Western donors of development assistance, have responded to Ethiopia's recent growth record

---

[65] Collier, Kirchberger, and Söderbom (2015: 31); Inocencio et al. (2007).
[66] Cramer and Sender (2019).   [67] Chuhan-Pole et al. (2017: 79–81).
[68] Moller and Wacker (2017: 199).

with an implausible counterfactual assertion: privatization, more foreign direct investment, and a smaller state 'would have' resulted in even faster growth.[69]

Ethiopia's heterodox policies have included financial repression, directing credit at negative real interest rates towards public investment in infrastructure, inflationary finance, and an overvalued exchange rate. These policies, combined with a fiscal revenue-raising effort and public consumption restraint in the wake of the Ethiopian–Eritrean War (1998–2000), enabled dramatic public investment in areas such as roads and rail, energy, education, and health. These types of public infrastructure investment (rising to 18.6 per cent of GDP by 2011) were the main factor in Ethiopia's growth acceleration, with real per capita GDP growth of 8.3 per cent per year between 2004 and 2014 higher than had historically been the case in the country, and higher than regional and low-income averages in the same period. However, despite noting the increasing consensus that infrastructure is central to growth and development, World Bank economists have insisted on the short-term view that Ethiopia's public sector-led strategy has 'led to a crowding out of many private investment projects owing to a lack of financing'.[70] They also believe that whatever the possible short-run contribution of heterodox economic policies, these are unsustainable:

> [W]e anticipate that macroeconomic policies face increasing trade-offs between public infrastructure improvements, private sector access to credit, and limits to restraining government consumption . . . Ethiopia's growth rate is likely to decelerate in the future . . .[71]

A still cautious but rather different and more convincing assessment of Ethiopia's macroeconomic balances suggests that the core approach may well be sustainable, as long as there is a greater commitment to generating rapid export growth.[72]

Mobilizing Savings, Managing the Growth of Consumption

If an investment push evaporates without generating incomes, profits, and savings, the balancing act will then have to involve contractions elsewhere or sharp increases in foreign borrowing (with strings attached). Thus, a government engineering a sharp increase in the investment level has to adopt policies which simultaneously ensure that investments are productive and that they result in rising real wages (as a source of savings as well as a source of demand). This may involve intervening to reduce some forms of consumption (for example, on luxury

---

[69] Wilson (2019a).   [70] Wilson Moller and Wacker (2017: 198).   [71] ibid (209).
[72] Coutts and Laskaridis (2019).

goods or foreign holidays by the elite and their children) and/or introducing incentives to save.

Restricting consumption (and domestic production) of luxury goods may be more difficult to do today than it was, say, in South Korea or Taiwan in the 1960s and 1970s. There is, for example, a sharp contrast between levels of car ownership in South Korea and Japan, on the one hand, and South Africa on the other (Figure 4.1).[73] At a per capita income level of around $3,000, car ownership in South Korea and Japan was about 5 per 1,000 people; at a similar level of income per capita in South Africa, car ownership is very much higher, about 65 per 1,000 people. Nonetheless, just as capital controls and development banking were anathema in international development circles for many years but have become more acceptable in the wake of the global financial crisis, so direct controls on consumption may yet come to play some role. These need not involve outright bans, but could include steep duties on luxury consumption as part of a broader effort to promote a national developmentalist ethos.

Other policies that would encourage savings to catch up with rising invest-ment levels include, among other things, post office savings schemes, keeping import duties low on investment goods, using tax breaks judiciously to encour-age investment, and directing the banking system to increase some forms of long-term credit on favourable terms. The key to many of these incentives to profitability is tying them to performance. This is what Alice Amsden called the 'reciprocal control mechanism' and is what has typically distinguished countries that have succeeded with state-led development strategies from those which

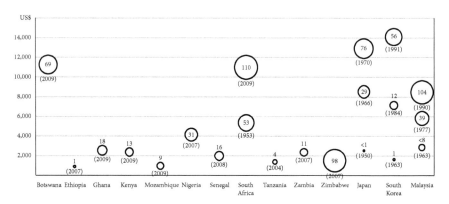

Figure 4.1 Passenger cars (per 1,000 population) in selected countries at different levels of GDP per capita

Source: Maddison Project Database for real GDP per capita (constant 2011 US dollars), data on passenger cars from African Development Indicators (2018) and Chang (2013).

[73] On Korea and Japan, see Chang (2006: 25).

have had a similar array of incentives but have failed to sustain the momentum of structural change.[74]

The history of Mozambique since late 1992, to take just one African example, illustrates a failure to monitor and control state resources. Carlos Cardoso, an investigative journalist, was assassinated in Maputo in 2000 while investigating corruption in a bank controlled by the state.[75] More recently, the travesty that is industrial policy in Mozambique reached astonishing proportions with revelations of a scandal involving loans contracted to support the development of a national fishing fleet and maritime industry: three privately incorporated but effectively state-owned enterprises failed to account for at least a quarter of the $2 billion they had received in loans, as well as paying millions more for purchased equipment than it was worth. The loans had been hidden from donors and, once revealed, pitched Mozambique into a protracted conflict with the IMF and other donors.[76]

There is a different—less overtly corrupt and unpleasant—method of financing investment. Many governments have financed a deficit-led investment programme through inflationary finance (and the forced savings it generates, as rising prices erode people's spending power and reduce consumption). When governments spend more than they receive in revenue, they usually have to secure the funds to do this from the central bank, which has to print money with potentially inflationary implications for the overall economy. The resulting dynamic takes the form of distributional (class) conflicts: inflation reduces real wages and raises profits, at least in the short term. This shift of resources from wage workers to capitalists releases resources for investment, given that capitalists are more likely to save out of profits than workers are out of wages.[77] It can also shift resources from wage workers to the state.

At the heart of many of the dynamics of investment, demand, government spending, and related policies, is one issue that gets very little attention in most economic texts and in advice to policy officials: what happens to the prices of basic wage goods.

Wage Goods: The Fundamental Constraint on Financing Investment

The most serious constraint on financing a cumulative dynamic of investment, productivity growth, employment, and savings, stems from the price inflation of

---

[74] Amsden (2001).   [75] Fauvet and Mosse (2003).
[76] Kroll (2017). See also Cotterill (2017).
[77] Joan Robinson (1964: 341) attributed to Kalecki the pithy formulation that in a capitalist economy 'workers spend what they get, capitalists get what they spend', though Kalecki's writings do not contain this direct statement.

basic wage goods. This compromises both savings by workers and the profitability of investment, and can also threaten political stability. This is the insight of Michał Kalecki's development economics.

African wage workers, especially relatively unskilled workers in elementary occupations—such as domestic servants, cleaners, and construction workers—spend a large proportion of what they earn on a limited range of basic goods and services. Spending on food takes up a large share (about 75 per cent) of their disposable income, together with basic wage goods such as clothing, kerosene, transport, and rent.[78] If the prices of these necessities rise relative to nominal wages, there are a number of implications. Employers can face pressure to raise wages in order that their employees stay in work and can work productively. This is a very real issue and if the pressure does not come through organized labour in the form of trade unions it may come through other mechanisms, including a wastefully high turnover of labour.[79] The increasing cost of wage goods has been one of the main reasons why flower firms and textile exporters in Ethiopia have found it difficult to retain workers; the result being not only that employers face recurring training costs, but also that labour productivity in Ethiopian floriculture remains low compared to levels achieved on farms in other countries.[80] If firms have to raise wages then their profit rate may be hit, negatively affecting the momentum of new investment. Even if firms avoid this pressure and protect profits, they may face insufficient domestic demand for the goods they produce, and wage workers will find it difficult to sustain, let alone expand, their rate of saving. Finally, sustained wage goods inflation may lead to a *political* reaction, frightening existing and potential investors.

While inflationary financing of government deficit spending is one possible source of wage goods inflation, the broader problem is one of how to finance economic development, with the core challenge for policymakers in developing countries being how to ensure an adequate, non-inflationary supply of these goods. Kalecki realized there were often rigidities (social and economic) that held back supply of agricultural commodities, leading to inflationary pressure as the number of urban industrial workers expanded. These supply rigidities lead not only to higher costs for wage workers, but also higher costs of intermediate goods such as sugar or cereals used by manufacturing firms in agro-processing industries. So, for industrialization and structural change to proceed, 'there must be no inflationary price increase of necessities'.[81] This is one reason why policies targeting investment to raise agricultural productivity are not an alternative to industrial policy, but are integral to it (see Chapter 9).

---

[78] Ivanic, Martin, and Zaman (2012) and Headey and Martin (2016) assess the impact of food prices and food price spikes, such as that in 2009, on poverty.
[79] Hardy and Hauge (2019).   [80] Schaefer and Abebe (2015); Melese (2015).
[81] Kalecki (1976: 78).

The domestic food supply may be a less binding constraint in a world of rising food productivity and, often, internationally available cheap foods. Even so, the volatility of global food prices means that carefully designed government interventions to protect the real wages of poor wage workers remain a priority. Additionally, the broader point that structural change and growth are constrained by the non-inflationary availability of basic wage goods holds. It is therefore surprising that Kalecki's insights have been largely 'forgotten or discarded'.[82]

Policy officials need to understand the importance of monitoring food prices and money wages much more closely. If financing investment ignores basic wage good inflation, then the distributional consequences may constrain the further growth of investment. Such a strategy is not economically or politically feasible over a long period of time, as it hits the lowest-paid worst, who have the least bargaining power to increase their money wages rapidly in response to food price spikes. And it is not—as some may think—a good thing for the rural population. Most people in rural Africa—and most definitely the poorest, who as we show in Chapter 8 depend on wage employment opportunities—are *net food purchasers*, and thus food price inflation may hit them harder than urban workers. In fact, food prices in difficult-to-reach rural areas and areas affected by violent conflict are often even higher than in large towns.[83]

Inflationary shocks may be unavoidable. Violent conflicts, global commodity speculation, and climatic shocks can provoke or accelerate wage good scarcity, as well as sharp price increases. In such circumstances, it becomes important to address price fluctuations with appropriate policies. Another 'lesson' from the historical record in East (and South East) Asia is that governments intervened to manage basic goods prices and got them 'wrong'. Two conclusions arise. First, long-term success in addressing rural poverty and reducing vulnerability to fluctuations in food prices requires public investment in rural infrastructure, above all in irrigation—an argument made in more detail in Chapter 9. The key to a secure non-inflationary supply of food is rising agricultural labour productivity. Agricultural growth also makes it possible for rural wages to rise, without which poverty cannot fall. Second, protecting low-income classes from periodic food price spikes requires state intervention to stabilize prices. The very mention of this is enough to alarm most economists, going as it does against established 'best practice', and raising the spectre of ineffective and long-lasting subsidies that distort key price signals in agricultural markets.

That said, policymakers would be remiss not to pay some attention to these warnings. There have been plenty of examples—in Africa, Latin America, and

[82] Wuyts (2011: 5).
[83] For instance, prices of maize are often much higher in rural than in urban South Africa, according to data in the National Agricultural Marketing Council's regular Food Price Monitor (http://www. namc.co.za). On the impact of violent conflict on food prices see Raleigh (2015).

elsewhere—of disastrous state management and control of agricultural markets that has resulted in the transfer of income from farmers to predatory bureaucrats.[84] However, as the relative success of state intervention in cotton marketing in some West African countries shows very clearly, such outcomes are far from inevitable.[85] It is important not to ignore the fact that it has been possible for other countries to successfully intervene to stabilize food prices against volatility on world and domestic markets. Food price stabilization in Indonesia and the Philippines, for example, has been expensive, but the benefits have outweighed the costs. What marks out rice price stabilization in Indonesia and some other East and Southeast Asian countries has been limited but sufficient government intervention in markets to ensure adequate stocks, as well as a government monopoly on importing rice to protect against huge swings in international prices.[86]

4.3 Sectoral Policies and Structural Change

In the first part of this chapter we discussed the challenge of raising investment levels, emphasizing how investment is constrained by the supply of food and other basic wage goods. The productivity of wage good production, in other words, sets a limit on an economy's ability to push investment to high levels and keep it there, in order to sustain the long-run capital accumulation that has historically been at the heart of growth, development, and catching up. Should resource allocation to agriculture, then, be the major priority? More broadly, if raising investment levels is key, does it matter which sectors attract investment?

The history of modern economic growth shows that contributions made by particular sectors to output growth matter a great deal. Specifically, what matters most is investment in manufacturing. However, a narrow, 'traditional' notion of manufacturing would be misleading, and could lead to a strategy that ignores gains from a range of activities that have not previously fitted neatly into this category. Later in this section, we discuss an expanded and policy-relevant definition of manufacturing.

Kaldor's Growth Laws and Structural Change

Economic development involves shifting resources out of low-productivity activities into higher-productivity economic activities. This is what we mean when we talk about 'structural change'. Structural change can also mean, broadly, a shift in

---

[84] For example see Williams (2009). [85] Gray, Dowd-Uribe, and Kaminski (2018).
[86] Timmer and Dawe (2007: 11).

the relative weight of different sectors. So, for example, many advanced capitalist economies have gone through phases during which they changed from predominantly agricultural economies to industrial economies; then, in a process known as 'deindustrialization', have become dominated by service sector activities. Sectoral shifts are central to our sense of structural change, but their relevance lies in what they imply for changes in productivity across the economy, as well as the growth of employment and export revenue.

In low-income countries, large numbers of people languish in low-productivity agricultural (and related rural) activities. They live and labour on small farms, and however hard they work, grind out only modest outputs, often of low value and for little material reward. Many live and work far from graded roads or railway links, walking for hours to weekly markets, weighed down by bananas or tomatoes, only to trudge back to farmsteads that are not irrigated and do not have any fertilizers to increase yields. In the dry terms of economics, the returns to labour are low. Their children often get insufficient nutritious food, no or at best poor-quality schooling, and are poorly served by health posts and safe drinking water.

Arthur Lewis provided the classic way of thinking about changes in the structure of employment during the process of development. It is frequently alleged that he focused on the importance of rural–urban migration or the shift out of agriculture into industry, but this is a misinterpretation—his point was always more about the shift into higher-productivity activities than specifically migration to cities. In his model of how accumulation might take place in a poor economy, more and more people begin to work in activities with dramatically higher productivity and returns to labour.[87] More capitalist enterprises are established in the economy and more people work for larger employers, earning higher wages. Historically, this takes the form of both a rising share of manufacturing industry in GDP and a rising share of total employment in manufacturing. Higher labour productivity comes about from a new combination of human labour and other inputs, such as machines, the organization of farms and firms, and logistical services.[88]

There is a fundamental process by which the more people focus on specific activities, the better they become at doing them, and then the higher the returns they typically earn. This is the terrain of Adam Smith's seminal discussion of how the 'extent of the market' (i.e. market size) and 'specialization' play off and support each other. The larger the market, the greater the scope for people specializing in particular parts of a production process; the more people are employed in these specialized roles, and the cheaper these efficiently produced products become, the further the market for them expands. When this is

---

[87] Lewis (1954).
[88] Differences in labour productivity (and in the growth of labour productivity) between low-income and advanced capitalist countries are discussed in Schaffner (2001).

repeated across different goods, a cumulative causation process will kick in and underpin sustained economic growth.

A corollary of the cumulative causation process is new opportunities for production to benefit from economies of scale and scope. One reason that the unit cost of producing outputs falls as more and more of them are produced is precisely that the firm, and its workers, become increasingly efficient in producing them: there is 'learning by doing'. Adam Smith naturally saw this too, with economies of scale playing a significant role in the early chapters of *An Inquiry into the Wealth of Nations*. Increasing returns, however, faded from economic view for a long time.

If the assumption of diminishing returns is a founding axiom of neoclassical economists, for other economists, identifying where there is scope for increasing returns is a key principle of analysis and policy design. What has become clear to many is that the scope for increasing returns is significantly greater in manufacturing than in either agricultural or service activities (there is also a relatively high scope for economies of scale in some other industrial activities, such as mining, utilities, and construction).

Manufacturing seems also to be associated with higher productivity and swifter improvements in productivity than other sectoral activities, with evidence showing that 'value added per worker is much higher in manufacturing than in agriculture'. Shifting resources from agriculture to manufacturing, in line with this evidence, results in a one-off economic gain. There may be more dynamic gains too, if the rate of growth of productivity is faster in manufacturing than in other sectors. In most developing countries, the historical as well as the most up-to-date evidence shows this to be the case.[89]

It was this kind of evidence that led Kaldor to craft his three 'growth laws', though, as we show, these need to be expanded to four in order to take account of the balance of payments constraint on growth. Kaldor's original propositions are as follows. First, there is a strong positive relationship between the rate of growth of output in manufacturing and the rate of growth of GDP. This is not just an 'association' but a causal relationship, for which there is a huge amount of evidence.[90] It is this evidence that is behind the rediscovery of industrial policy—active interventions by governments to accelerate and promote manufacturing expansion—among many mainstream economists, and that has led to rather misleading claims of a new consensus among economists. Unusually, a recent contribution by IMF economists expressly referenced some of the well-known and previously ignored heterodox work on industrial policy.[91] Actually, there is no such consensus; the mainstream case for industrial policy only justifies very

---

[89] Szirmai (2013).   [90] For a summary see Storm (2015).   [91] Cherif and Hasanov (2019).

limited forms of policy 'correcting' market failures rather than creating new markets.[92]

Kaldor's second proposition is that there is a strong positive relationship between the rate of growth of manufacturing output and the growth of manufacturing labour productivity. This is also known as Verdoorn's Law and captures dynamic economies of scale. It flows from the greater scope for learning by doing, specialization, and economies of scale in manufacturing; as well as from rising investment in industrial equipment and machinery that itself embodies productivity-raising technical change.

There are implications for what happens to employment. If a firm can produce the same output with fewer workers, or if firms are increasing output faster than they take on new employees, then the employment elasticity of manufacturing will decline. Tregenna finds that industrial upgrading and new labour-dislodging machinery were associated in South Africa, between 1980 and 2005, with a falling employment multiplier in manufacturing. Manufacturing is still the engine of growth but it may not always carry quite so many people with it (at least, not *directly*).[93]

Policy officials in Africa might see a dilemma: why should they promote manufacturing if it is not helping to address the fundamental challenge of creating sufficient employment to absorb the (rapidly growing) number of new entrants to the labour force? But there is no dilemma. Even within manufacturing, many kinds of production generate large amounts of new employment, and even if manufacturing has directly a low employment elasticity of output, it is hugely important *indirectly* to the employment-creation capacity of the economy as a whole. Evidence suggests that for every manufacturing job created two or three jobs are also created outside the sector as a result of manufacturing expansion.[94] The contribution of manufacturing to employment is even stronger once we accept a broader definition of manufacturing that takes account of agricultural production, which is, on closer inspection, clearly industrial (see later in this section). However, the most appropriate distinctions are not those between manufacturing and other activities, but between those activities with a high potential for increasing returns and employment multipliers, and those without such potential.

Kaldor's third proposition is that there is a strong positive relationship between the growth of manufacturing productivity and productivity in the rest of the economy. This is partly because, as manufacturing draws labour out of, say, agriculture, it leaves behind a smaller agricultural labour force *without* shrinking

[92] Cramer and Tregenna (2020).
[93] Tregenna (2012). This kind of engine without an employment chassis was dubbed, in one view of economic performance in India, 'growth sans employment' (Kannan and Raveendran, 2009).
[94] Lavopa and Szirmai (2012).

overall agricultural output. But it is also the outcome of a richer process, whereby productivity gains in manufacturing are diffused to other sectors through the supply of cheaper equipment and inputs to agricultural producers—for example, agro-chemicals and irrigation pumps. They are also spread through industrial demand for agricultural inputs—for cotton inputs into in textile production, for example—and propagated by the spread of organizational know-how, though this too is a matter for policy rather than just an automatic process.

Empirical work has largely confirmed the significance of these propositions. For example, Wells and Thirlwall tested for and found clear evidence of Kaldor's growth laws across a number of African economies.[95] Elsewhere, another recent study found support for Kaldor's first and second laws in a group of 63 middle- and upper-income countries.[96]

The implication is that there is a very strong case for governments designing and implementing industrial policy to promote manufacturing investment, as this results in *general* economy-wide benefits. Later in this section we show how important it is to think carefully about what kinds of activity to include within the range of industrial policy, as well as highlighting some of its key features. Before we do that, though, we focus on the significance of the balance of payments constraint.

The Balance of Payments Constraint

One thing that can bring momentum to a standstill is, as previously discussed, inflation in the prices of food and other necessity wage goods. Another equally important factor is a shortage of foreign exchange. Developing countries have a thirst for imports. Partly this is a function of rising incomes: as the demand for basic goods starts to take up less of people's incomes, there is rising demand for a range of imported consumer goods, whether this be globally fashionable second-hand jeans and T-shirts, or smartphone apps. Even more importantly, almost by definition an expanding economy must invest in technology-embodying machines and inputs, which creates a powerful need for imports. A developing economy does not have to reinvent the wheel of industry—rather, one of the advantages of backwardness is that expertly designed wheels can be imported. To some extent, it may be possible to limit the rate of growth of luxury consumer good imports, but it is impossible to successfully sustain rapid development if imported capital and intermediate goods dry up. The building of the Grand Ethiopian Renaissance Dam, the Kandadji Dam in Niger, and the infrastructure renewal programme in Côte d'Ivoire are all associated with sharp spikes in

---

[95] Wells and Thirlwall (2003).　　[96] Marconi, Reis, and Araújo (2016).

imports.[97] Across sub-Saharan Africa, electric and non-electric generating equipment imports increased from $2.3 billion in 2000–3 to $11.6 billion in 2008–11.[98]

The greater the demand for imports, the greater the challenge of securing enough foreign exchange to cover the import bill. It is very difficult for an economy to sustain a growing balance of payments deficit indefinitely. If the size of the deficit is accelerating and will have to be financed from additional foreign sources, then there is a real danger that a government may be forced to abandon any kind of independent policy initiatives: arguably, this has sometimes affected policy direction in countries such as Ghana and Mozambique.

An economy can acquire the foreign exchange needed to finance its import bill by attempting to attract foreign capital flows, including concessional loans and grants (i.e. foreign aid or overseas development assistance); or by earning foreign exchange through exporting goods and services. All these sources of foreign exchange involve costs and uncertainties. Commercial capital flows are regarded as more beneficial to Africa than aid, especially by employees of Goldman Sachs, such as economist Dambisa Moyo.[99] But 'hot money' funds shifted into African emerging market bonds and stock exchanges, as opposed to foreign direct investment in farms and factories, are fickle, responding unpredictably to international changes in interest rates, policy environments, and bandwagon hunches about the next global bonanza or calamity. Those directing these flows to emerging markets are said to be involved in 'stampedes by intrinsically restless (and often underinformed) fund-managers—so prone to oscillating between manias and panics'.[100] Additionally, lines of credit from China (secured by export commodities or escrow accounts) are now an extremely important, but often poorly recorded and administratively opaque, source of finance for new energy infrastructure projects in several African countries.[101] At the same time, it has been the vogue in recent years to use public–private partnerships (PPPs) as a means of financing infrastructure investment across the world. PPPs have been promoted in Africa by the African Development Bank, United Nations Economic Commission for Africa (UNECA), and the African Union, with the support of the World Bank and Organisation for Economic Co-operation and Development (OECD) among others.[102] Supporters argue that risk is transferred to the private sector and that PPPs are good value for public money. But their record globally, including in the UK, which was one of the pioneers of PPPs, has been unimpressive.[103] Many people, including research staff at the IMF, warn how difficult it is to put in place effective institutional mechanisms to protect public finances against spiralling costs and fiscal unsustainability,

---

[97] See, e.g., World Bank (2013).   [98] Co (2014: 11–12).   [99] Moyo (2009).
[100] Palma (2012: 3).
[101] Tang and Shen (2020); Brautigam and Hwang (2016). On the lack of transparency or effective monitoring of a Chinese financing agreement for a mining project, see Landry (2018).
[102] Loxley (2013).
[103] Boardman, Siemiatycki, and Vining (2016); Booth and Starodubtseva (2015); NAO (2018).

'particularly when governments ignore or are unaware of their deferred costs and associated fiscal risks'.[104]

The volatility of foreign aid flows has created very serious problems for policymakers and economic performance in Africa. Donor agencies can swiftly change the activities to which they commit resources depending on the latest ideas in vogue.[105] The administrative costs of experienced public officials having to deal with a proliferating number of donors, donor fads, and demands are high.[106] Foreign aid also comes with strings and narrows economic policy debates, providing material and intellectual support for African elites arguing for demand restriction and market liberalization, and reinforcing flawed ideas through repetition of rhetorical commonplaces. As has been pointed out, IMF programmes

> still incorporate a considerable number of structural conditions, and the total number of such conditions still far exceeds that observed in the pre-1994 period. The emphatic return of structural conditionality in recent years calls into question the IMF's 'we won't do that any more' rhetoric.[107]

It is possible to negotiate important improvements in the terms by which foreign investment and foreign aid inflows become available, as shown by the variety of outcomes and negotiating strategies across African countries. Foreign aid 'essentially means an improvement of external conditions of growth' and may be compared to 'a positive shift in terms of trade to the extent which both increase the capacity to import'.[108] However, negotiations over concessional and non-concessional flows might not always be successful—or even be conducted in the national interest—so an over-reliance on these sources of foreign exchange is unwise. Under the pressure of demand for imports, it may be a far more effective strategy for sustaining growth to promote a rapid expansion in foreign exchange earnings through exports. Thirlwall's Law, capturing this insight, states that a country's growth rate over the long run is set by the ratio of the rate of export revenue growth to the income elasticity of demand. The faster imports expand as an economy grows, the faster export earnings have to rise if growth is to be sustained.[109]

There are two dimensions to why exports have to be at the heart of a development strategy. One is that, as explained, the momentum of accumulation and structural change cannot be sustained without a swift rise in export revenue. The other is that exports—especially manufactured exports—are at the heart of the dynamics captured in Kaldor's propositions. Exploiting the economies of scale

---

[104] Irwin, Mazraani, and Saxena (2018: 1).
[105] On the impact of aid volatility on growth see Museru, Toerien, and Gossel (2014) and Hudson and Mosley (2008); on aid uncertainty see Lensink and Morrissey (2000).
[106] Presbitero (2016: 18).   [107] Kentikelenis, Stubbs, and King (2016: 14).
[108] Kalecki and Sachs (1966: 44, 24).   [109] McCombie (1989).

that manufacturing has a special propensity for depends, just as Adam Smith claimed, on the 'extent of the market'. Given the extent of the market (i.e. demand) is limited in developing countries and within the African region, the rest of the world must *ergo* be the major source of demand. This is just one of the ways in which manufactured exports matter to industrialization-led development. More formally, there are two linked relationships that have been observed internationally. First, growth in manufacturing raises the rate of growth of export earnings. Second, the faster export earnings grow, the higher the overall growth rate of the economy.

What Counts as Manufacturing?

Auto assembly plants, furniture workshops, a tomato canning facility, industrial parks exporting garments, a blueberry producer: all except one are classified in standard statistics as manufacturing. The obvious exception is the blueberry producer, but arguably blueberry producers and exporters ought to be regarded as industrial producers. If a blueberry producer in South Africa is highly capitalized and has invested in a range of physical components, inputs, and processes, and if that producer has organized the production process into a long string of distinct and specialized operations, are they merely a large farmer? Expanding the idea of what is included in industrial production has important policy implications.

If policy officials want to take seriously the dynamics of structural change and promote investment, they need to recognize the shifting boundaries around the 'industrial', classifying economic activities according to their role in an economy: above all, their potential to generate increasing returns of scale and scope; accelerate productivity gains; lead directly and indirectly to employment growth; and produce foreign exchange earnings.

Changing the understanding of what constitutes manufacturing is even more important when we consider that much agro-industry is in fact more labour-intensive than a great deal of the manufacturing industry located in export-processing zones or industrial parks. In Ethiopia, for example, the total number of workers employed by agribusiness in floriculture was, by 2012, already considerably larger than total employment in the manufacture of textiles or in the basic metal and engineering industries. In Kenya, meanwhile, 125,000 workers were employed in the cut-flower sector in 2015, which was about 3 times the number of people employed in textiles, and 20 times larger than the number of people employed in the motor vehicles subsector.[110]

---

[110] See www.unido.org/statistics; Ethiopian Horticulture Development Agency (2012: 16); Gebreeyesus (2014); Mitullah, Kamau, and Kivuva (2017: 30).

Farms nowadays increasingly require massive investment in complex technology and equipment, and employ highly trained and productive workers. People may (and do) migrate in search of employment opportunities with higher returns, not simply from rural areas to towns and cities, but also from one rural area to another. A development strategy designed to raise investment levels and increase profitability in the economy has to take into account the huge scope for productivity increases (and employment growth) *within* rural areas, as well as in urban and peri-urban factories.

Premature Deindustrialization: The Latest Version of *Fracasomanía*?

Rumours of the demise of industrialization as the engine of development are greatly exaggerated. Many neoclassical economists traditionally argue that it matters little which sector economic activities take place in, and that therefore it is market 'distorting' to try and encourage manufacturing specifically. Additionally, there are old populist arguments that it is possible to raise income per capita without having to 'pass through' an (unhappy) industrial stage.[111] A similar tradition of pessimism about the feasibility of industrial policy in Latin America led Albert Hirschman to coin the phrase *fracasomanía*—an obsessional fascination with failure.

More recently another theory of failure has gained currency: the risk of 'premature deindustrialization', which has shown that there is a global trend for economies to experience, for structural reasons, a shrinking share of manufacturing in GDP at much lower income per capita levels than has historically been the case. An optimistic slant on this issue, tinged with the enduring appeal of economic populism, is that services are nowadays more productive than manufacturing, and therefore it may be possible to have a service-driven development strategy without having to grind through the socially, environmentally, and technically challenging process of industrialization.[112]

However, the evidence across developing countries suggests a far more positive interpretation of the 'premature deindustrialization' narrative, even taking into account a traditional classification system that—we and others argue—is increasingly unfit for purpose. In real terms, global MVA increased in every year between 1995 and 2015.[113] In the developing countries as a group, *aggregate* MVA/GDP has in fact risen rather rapidly since about 2002, as shown in Figure 4.2. Disappointing shares of MVA in GDP and weak manufacturing employment,

---

[111] Kitching (1989) remains a classic critique of this populist tradition in development economics.
[112] Ggombe and Newfarmer (2018).   [113] Hallward-Driemeier and Nayyar (2017: figure 0.5).

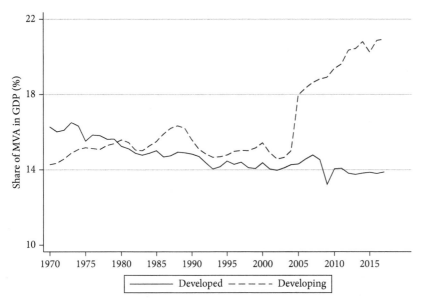

Figure 4.2 Aggregate share of MVA in GDP by development group, 1970–2017
Source: UN Statistics Division (2019), Income Classification: World Bank GNI per capita, Atlas methodology (2019).

with the UK economy as an extreme example of the latter, are attributable to *policy failure* in some countries rather than the structural impossibility of industrialization.[114] The growth of MVA has been especially impressive in East Asia, where China in particular has shown the enduring scope for manufacturing expansion and manufacturing employment growth.

4.4 Conclusions: Criteria for Policy Priorities

We have argued in Section 4.3 of this chapter that manufacturing, suitably (re) defined, plays a leading role in economic development. There are good reasons for this, which are captured by Kaldor's growth laws and supported by consistent evidence internationally. Despite claims that 'premature deindustrialization' means that manufacturing is no longer an effective engine of growth and employment generation, the evidence demonstrates this is not true. What has been the case in many countries in the recent past is not a guide to what governments can and ought to do to promote economic development in the future. Industrialization

---

[114] Haraguchi, Cheng, and Smeets (2017: 307). On the dismal performance of employment in the UK manufacturing sector, see Rowthorn and Coutts (2013).

remains central to economic development, and industrial policy remains central to making industrialization happen.

The scope of industrial policy is wider than before. Manufacturing has become increasingly imbricated with other activities traditionally labelled as services or agriculture. This has resulted in the servicification of manufacturing and the industrialization of freshness, meaning industrial policy has to address these trends. The instruments of industrial policy have, for example, been shown to be useful in supporting the expansion and competitiveness of high-value agricultural production in some African economies.

Finally, industrial policy must focus on manufactured exports. The association between manufactured exports and sustained higher rates of growth is a strong one. Just as more diversified and higher-productivity manufacturing is likely to help protect against the frequency and intensity of growth collapses, so too is an effective manufacturing export sector. This is because, among other benefits, it can help overcome the balance of payments constraint that is often a cause of stalled growth.

Both industrial policy and linked policies promoting agribusiness should follow four criteria guiding the allocation of all government support (other chapters pick up on these criteria, so we will highlight them only briefly here). First, does an activity or sector generate foreign exchange earnings (i.e. will it help relax the balance of payments constraint on growth)? Second, is it characterized by scope for rising labour productivity vis-à-vis other sectors and activities? Note that this is not the same as asking whether or not it is manufacturing in the traditional sense. Third, will it create employment (directly and indirectly), especially for women? In particular, will it generate an increase in higher-productivity job opportunities relative to other projects that might benefit from state support? Fourth, will it help address the need for a non-inflationary supply of basic wage goods? Even if resource allocation addresses these criteria, investment or investment support can only work if it is supported by other policies, for example reducing the risk of export revenues flowing into tax havens abroad.

These criteria need to be combined with policy design that takes sequencing into account. The question that should be asked when considering a potential incentive or infrastructure investment is: how *fast* will this or that activity bring foreign exchange earnings onstream? In some circumstances, there may be a case for supporting an activity that does not meet all the criteria set out, but that does promise to relax one binding constraint (e.g. foreign exchange or wage goods supply) particularly quickly, creating greater room to pursue longer-term objectives. This is relevant for debates about the role of primary commodity exports, with many governments and development economists having neglected investment in this area. In neglecting these activities for fear of, for example, declining terms of trade, governments may miss out on high international prices for particular commodities, thereby foregoing short-run foreign exchange earning opportunities that could be fundamental to deeper prospects for structural change.

To conclude this chapter with an example, a large-scale investment in Ethiopia promoting a rapid expansion in high-quality, premium-priced, wet-processed coffee production capacity may address several of our key criteria for selective intervention by government. It would involve a large 'lumpy' investment in infrastructure (e.g. rural roads and electrification) that without government spending would not happen nearly fast enough. It would generate additional foreign exchange, without a long lead time to develop international competitiveness. It would also generate a substantial increase in rural wage employment for women. The output of each of these workers will be lower than the output per worker in, say, factories producing sports shoes, but their labour productivity would nevertheless be much higher than that of most workers in rural Ethiopia.[115] An effective policy promoting the rapid expansion of high-yield, higher-quality coffee would require exactly the kind of 'reciprocal control mechanism' characteristic of effective industrial policy and for the same reasons; namely, the need to provide selective incentives to those with a demonstrated capacity for and track record of generating foreign exchange and employment in a sector with the potential for generating linkages to other activities, which are also likely to be producers with scope for scale economies. It would make industrial policy for other activities—for example, packaging, cement, and machine tools—much more feasible due to its contribution to the balance of payments.

These kinds of criteria for policy design, as well as the broader significance of setting export growth as a high priority, are developed in Chapter 5 on trade.

---

[115] Cramer and Sender (2017) developed a strategy for priorities in the complex Ethiopian coffee sector.

5

The Trade Imperative

5.1 Introduction

In mainstream development economics, the pursuit of macroeconomic stability is elevated above all other objectives, including growth in production or employment. Macroeconomic stability is regarded as the fundamental prerequisite that unlocks growth in output and then, if markets are suitably flexible, other positive outcomes like employment expansion. This mainstream view also determines trade and exchange rate policy: balancing the external account is the primary objective of policy, rather than the level of output at which these accounts (have to) balance. The key to both stability in the balance of payments and broader macroeconomic stability, from this perspective, is restraining aggregate demand. This, as we will explain, typically leads to policy advice designed to ensure low- and middle-income economies rein in import growth. Rapid import growth may signal 'easy' credit—representing excess demand—thereby upsetting the balance of payments applecart. The two main ways of curbing excess demand in an open economy are, first, to restrict 'excess' credit to the economy, and, second, to raise the relative cost of imports through exchange rate devaluation.

Non-mainstream development economists also often warn against rapid import growth, albeit for different reasons. The main reason for their anxiety is a pessimistic outlook on the possibility of financing imports. Export pessimism has long been entrenched in much of the advice emanating from, for example, United Nations Conference on Trade and Development (UNCTAD). In some versions, this pessimistic reflex reflects a broader anxiety about the dangers of integrating into the world economy. The implications for exchange rate policy are not always clear, although some economists taking this stance criticize International Monetary Fund (IMF) calls for devaluation: they argue that there is little point attempting to boost export revenues through reducing the price offered to international buyers by devaluing; they also berate IMF policy proposals because devaluation has inflationary consequences that hit the poor particularly hard.

African policymakers are surrounded by economists who espouse trade and exchange rate policy arguments derived from these (and similar) traditions. It is, therefore, not surprising that they often feel the case against rapid import growth being pressed upon them—by visiting consultants, or economists installed within government ministries, departments, and prime ministers' offices. Warnings about rising and 'unnecessary' imports seem, at first sight, to be eminently reasonable.

African Economic Development: Evidence, Theory, Policy. Christopher Cramer, John Sender, and Arkebe Oqubay, Oxford University Press (2020). © Christopher Cramer, John Sender, and Arkebe Oqubay.
DOI: 10.1093/oso/9780198832331.001.0001

In this chapter, we advocate a different approach. We insist that production, technological change, and employment growth should be primary policy objectives, and that macroeconomic policy should *serve* them. Furthermore, we argue that what matters is the *level of activity* at which the external accounts balance out, rather than a myopic focus on balance for balance's sake (see Chapter 6). Finally, we argue that African governments have to find ways to benefit from integration into the global economy, rather than making a virtue out of retreat (into relying overly on the domestic market or on regional intra-trade).

To accelerate growth and structural change, governments need to stimulate a rapid rate of growth of imports—especially of producer inputs and capital goods. For example, imports of capital and intermediate goods—embodying foreign technology and contributing to domestic technological change—accounted for more than 80 per cent of all imports by China between 1965 and 2007. Even as China's economy has evolved and its rate of innovation accelerated, imported inputs have remained very important; although the share of imported inputs in the value of manufactured exports has declined, it remains higher than 40 per cent. Furthermore, the total value of these imported inputs has continued to rise sharply since the late 1990s or so (see Figure 5.1). More generally, as soon as the East Asian 'tiger economies' began to grow rapidly, their 'investment boom required an increase in imports'.[1]

But—as we set out in Chapter 3—the thirst for imports characteristic of rapidly developing economies can easily threaten the sustainability of growth. This in turn means any strategy for growth and structural change cannot ignore the need for a rapid rate of growth of export volumes and earnings.

The evidence presented in this chapter shows that, historically, all experiences of sustained economic development and structural change have involved *rapid and sustained import growth rates*. Rising incomes, higher labour productivity, and higher wages in Africa lead to a thirst for both imported consumer goods and for the intermediate and capital goods needed to produce, for example, electricity. In many countries, growth and structural change have historically required policies encouraging a fast increase in imports, especially of producer goods, though also of consumer wage goods including food. The experience of these countries highlights the importance of the balance of payments constraint and leads to the policy conclusion that, in order to sustain import growth, African economies (even oil exporters flush with revenues) will need to allocate resources so as to ensure a *dramatic increase in the growth rate of their export earnings*.

It is not sufficient to recognize a general need to expand exports. It is also important to identify the specific types of economic activity and subsectors where investment may yield the fastest and largest gains in productivity and in exports,

---

[1] Herrerias and Orts (2013: 783).

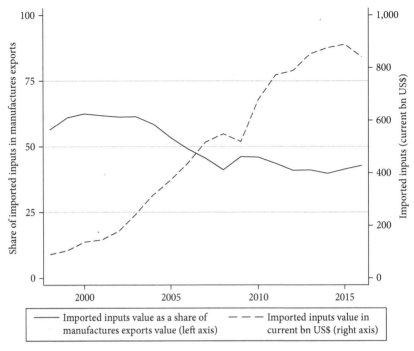

Figure 5.1 Imported inputs required to produce China's manufactured exports, 1998–2017

Source: UN Comtrade.

as well as the accompanying policies required to achieve expansion of output. These priorities, and the need to target investment, have been ignored in 'common-sense' policy advice to create an economy-wide 'enabling environment' and to avoid overambitious interventions that 'pick winners'. We argue that it would be a mistake to follow other 'common-sense' policy advice too, especially warnings not to invest to expand primary commodity exports because of a 'fallacy of composition'. This misguided policy advice is based on the assumption that these investments, if undertaken by a number of low-income countries, will cause the market to become flooded, and therefore fail to increase export revenues. If such warnings have been taken seriously by African policymakers, this may go some way to explaining the region's declining share in the world market for so many primary commodities.

A better theoretical guide to these issues would be based on Thirlwall's adaptation of Kaldor's Growth Laws, which emphasize the centrality of manufacturing. We broaden this, by also arguing for investment in higher-productivity, export-oriented agriculture. This is partly on the grounds that Kaldor-type growth effects increasingly operate in agribusiness enterprises, meaning they should be considered an integral part of Africa's industrial production (see Chapter 3).

We also argue that the labour intensity of many African agricultural exports makes it possible to accelerate the shift of (especially female) labour from low-productivity to high-productivity rural employment. In developing this argument, we propose that policy officials redefine what is understood by structural change.

Any investment strategy designed to facilitate a rapid rate of growth of imports must incorporate an effective exchange rate policy. This chapter discusses the consequences of over- and undervaluing exchange rates in Africa, as well as the difficulties of achieving (and defining) an appropriate exchange rate for any particular country and time. We set out some of the main arguments used in mainstream economics to address exchange rate questions, and we introduce some criticisms of these arguments. Overall, we argue that African governments should aim at competitive (i.e. undervalued) exchange rates—not in the vain hope that market prices are sufficient to balance the books and unleash entrepreneurial spirits, but as part of a set of policies designed to promote faster growth and accelerated structural change.

The accumulation strategy presented here differs markedly from that proposed by neoclassical economists. It also differs sharply, perhaps even more, from that proposed by many heterodox economists. Our argument in this chapter, as throughout the book, favours 'possibilism' (see Chapter 3) about import growth over the impossibilist lament of many structuralist development economists. We also query the views of economists who ignore the limits and costs of South–South trade, and who believe that foreign direct investment by developing country firms offers greater potential benefit to Africans than investment by other corporations.

5.2 The IMF and Macroeconomic Management

Many lower- and middle-income countries, faced with a rapid shift in the balance of payments leading to an immediate problem in paying for vital imported inputs, have to approach the IMF. The problem may have been caused by: a surge in import costs (as a result, for example, of a spurt of productive infrastructure investment); a terms-of-trade shock; or a spike in debt service obligations (if, for example, dollar-denominated debt obligations jump on the back of US interest rate hikes). Whatever the cause, the IMF tends to respond by looking for profligacy and policy mistakes in deficit countries. The burden of international payment adjustments must, as agreed at Bretton Woods after the Second World War, always be shouldered by deficit countries.[2]

Frequently, the negotiation of a Fund programme is an act of desperation. There may be few alternatives, as an IMF seal of approval is often necessary to

[2] Magalhães Prates and Farhi (2015).

unlock other concessionary finance, and it is also believed to calm the nerves of commercial lenders and investors. So it is important to understand the core principles and practice of IMF programmes, which tend to emphasize three things: first, 'adopting demand-restraining measures consistent with available financing'; second, securing 'available financing'; and, third, putting in place reforms supposedly promoting 'adjustment' and growth.[3]

We will discuss how the Fund has made subjective assessments of 'available financing' later in this section. Here, we emphasize the central policy prescription of IMF programmes: a rapid cut in the trade deficit achieved by reducing the demand for and the volume of imports.[4] At the heart of the Fund's thinking since the late 1950s lies the Polak model, which can be used to show that a fall in a country's reserves—a balance of payments deficit—happens when domestic credit increases beyond the demand for and supply of money. The model can also be used to disaggregate an increase in the stock of money into private and public credit creation, pinpointing government borrowing and fiscal expansion as the culprits for balance of payments deficits.

The model sees output as determined by the level of available finance and the propensity to import.[5] IMF staff have to assess the likely availability of external finance. If, for example, they think bilateral donors will not provide additional concessional finance to a government proposing a particular set of policies, they will insist more firmly on sharp changes to those policies. However, assessing 'likely availability of external finance' is a matter of judgement, and such judgements are open to dispute.[6] For example, in 1997, a former World Bank Chief Economist lashed out at the IMF's (in his view) baseless assessment that Ethiopia was unlikely to secure further international finance without a severe contraction of economic activity. The IMF had suspended its programme support and was insisting on drastic policy reforms, including financial sector liberalization, but the Ethiopian government resisted.[7] Despite IMF claims, there was little evidence that major donors were prepared to abandon Ethiopia—their military ally in a sensitive geostrategic zone. In fact, they seemed (confirmed by later experience) to be increasingly confident about Ethiopia's economic performance.

Some argue that Fund lending programmes can be quite flexible, and that the emphasis on demand repression is greater where fiscal imbalances (governments spending more than they receive in taxes) are the source of crisis, than where balance of payments difficulties are brought about by terms-of-trade shocks. Again, this raises the question of how to determine if budget deficits are 'unsustainable'—the Fund's record in forecasting key macroeconomic variables is unimpressive.[8] Fund programmes may also include some commitment to supporting growth, typically taking the form of ad hoc adjustments to balance of payments

[3] Mussa and Savastano (2000: 81).   [4] Taylor (1997: 147).   [5] Fine (2006).   [6] Ibid.
[7] On this controversy see Stiglitz (2002).   [8] An, Jalles, and Loungani (2018).

targets that allow for a slightly faster import growth rate than the model's core equations model would accept. One problem is that the Fund's opaque decision-making processes make it difficult to ascertain the relative importance of this element of flexibility in negotiating positions (compared, for instance, to the influence of the most powerful members of the IMF's Board) on the outcomes of negotiations.[9]

The global financial crisis of 2008 and its aftermath led to some soul-searching statements about the limitations of the traditional Fund analysis and policy stance. But the evidence—from crisis packages negotiated with European countries in particular, as well as from recent programmes in Africa—suggests that hopes for a less deflationary and more flexible IMF approach to balance of payments difficulties may have been overblown.[10]

5.3 Structuralist Fear of Imports

UNCTAD And IDEAs

The logic of many UNCTAD reports runs as follows. The import elasticity of growth in advanced economies has shrunk. As they continue to grow—slowly—they spend less of any additional income on imports. This makes it even more difficult for developing countries to grow, and to manage balance of payments challenges, by exporting to such economies. And when, as of late, the advanced economies are growing slowly, developing countries can only expand their exports by eating into other countries' share of world exports. Given these global economic conditions, developing countries should give 'greater attention to domestic and regional demand' and 'align their production structure more closely with their demand structure'.[11]

Others, for example, members of the International Development Economics Associates (IDEAs) network, talk of a 'collapse in developing country exports' following the 2008 global financial crisis—though admitting this is a price phenomenon, given that the growth rate of trade in terms of volume was barely any different in 2010–17 compared to 2000–9.[12] This message is driven home with claims of the 'exhaustion of advanced capitalism'.[13] Consequently, the 'export obsession that formed the basis of macroeconomic and development strategies is no longer useful'.[14] Against these pessimistic prognoses, it is worth noting that global import contractions have, thus far, occurred only rarely in the capitalist era.

---

[9] Killick (1993).   [10] Kentikelenis, Stubbs, and King (2016).   [11] UNCTAD (2014: 102).
[12] Chandresekhar and Ghosh (2018): http://www.networkideas.org/featured-articles/2018/04/the-collapse-in-developing-country-exports/.
[13] Ghosh (2018: 195).   [14] Ghosh (2018: 204).

In fact, between 1880 and 2010, global trade has contracted in just 12 per cent of years. Furthermore, the idea of a worldwide collapse in imports masks the actual heterogeneity of experience. Imports fell by far less in some countries than others; and overall they fell by significantly less in 2008/9 compared to the previous major episode of world trade shrinkage, the 1929 crash.[15]

There are other arguments advanced for focusing on domestic markets, or at least prioritizing trade with other 'Southern' or neighbouring countries at (presumably) similar levels of development. A fast rate of growth of imports may be dangerous because the dynamics of increasing returns give a competitive advantage to those already established in particular activities: 'when countries are open to external trade in a world in which increasing returns activities are significant, the chances are greater that such trade will cement existing divisions of labour between countries'.[16]

A Secular Decline in the Net Barter Terms of Trade?

Although trade pessimism has taken different forms over the decades, at its core is the idea that there is a structural ('secular') decline in the terms of trade—average export prices relative to import prices or the net barter terms of trade—faced by developing countries trading with richer economies. In its original form, as set out by Prebisch and Singer, this identified a trend in the export prices fetched by primary commodity exports relative to the price of imported manufactured goods.

The original Prebisch–Singer hypothesis laid the basis for import substitution strategies, as well as strengthening pessimistic views on whether developing countries could successfully pursue development through primary commodity exports. Combined with observations on the greater price volatility of unprocessed primary commodities, it inspired recommendations (by UNCTAD for example) that developing economies should diversify the number and type of their exports and that, prior to exporting, they should invest to process primary commodity domestically.[17] Later iterations of the pessimistic terms-of-trade argument suggest that even developing countries that achieve success in building up light manufacturing export sectors will soon suffer from falling terms of trade. One reason for this decline in the relative prices of manufactured exports from poor countries is that the world market is becoming flooded with such exports. Meanwhile, poor countries continue to expand their imports of more sophisticated manufactured goods from higher-income economies.

An adverse movement in the terms of trade, especially if it persists, can reduce growth rates. Even so, it is rash to take the Prebisch–Singer hypothesis as

---

[15] Van Bergeijk (2018).   [16] Ghosh (2019: 386).
[17] Osakwe, Santos-Paulino, and Dogan (2018).

reason to neglect investment in primary commodity exports, or to neglect export opportunities more generally in favour of national or regional self-sufficiency. First, the evidence for a secular decline in the net barter terms of trade remains unclear, despite a torrent of research studies.[18]

Second, there is no doubt that primary commodity prices are volatile, just as liable to undergo protracted surges as to tumble. While this is often taken to mean governments should not over-rely on commodity exports, it also opens up the opportunity to take advantage of price booms. The differences—for example—between Chile's long-term investment in copper mining and Zambia's poor long-term record in global copper production, are stark.[19]

Third, the Prebisch–Singer hypothesis has had an influence on academic debate and policy for more than fifty years; but in that period there have been lengthy periods of very strong prices for many commodities. The growth of China and a number of other economies—including Brazil, Mexico, India, Indonesia, Russia, and Turkey—led to a sustained increase in consumption and prices of energy, metal, and even some foods. Recently, these countries have together accounted for a larger share of consumption of coal, base and precious metals, and most foods, than the G7 economies.[20] Furthermore, over the long-term history of modern globalized capitalism, there can be no great confidence in the idea of a secular decline in Africa's terms of trade. A new long-run dataset of African commodities shows there was a prolonged rise in the terms of trade for African countries between 1820 and the 1880s, and that this terms-of-trade boom was larger in Africa than it was elsewhere.[21]

Fourth, primary commodity prices do *not* all move together, as is clear, for example, in Figure 5.2. It is misleading to take policy inspiration from an average commodity terms of trade. Income elasticities of demand for different foods vary hugely. While elasticities of demand for grains are typically less than one (i.e. growth in demand is slower than growth in incomes), they are higher for foods with a greater fat and protein content—as people get better off they can afford more of these. Furthermore, as discussed in Section 5.5, there is increasing scope within food production (and related commodities such as flowers) for branding and product differentiation, which is one of the factors distinguishing 'non-commodities' from commodities in trade. Indeed, income elasticities of demand (and price trends) for macadamia nuts, avocados, specialty arabica coffees, and other crops are extremely high. It is clearly important, when designing investment, trade, and diversification strategies, to disaggregate the terms of trade. While the wider group of 'emerging' economies account for much of the global consumption of metals, energy, and foods, the higher-income economies—especially the

---

[18] Spraos (1980); Cuddington and Urzua (1989); Pfaffenzeller (2018).
[19] For further examples, see Cramer and Sender (2019).   [20] Baffes et al. (2018).
[21] Frankema et al. (2018).

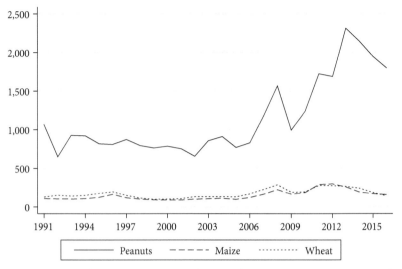

Figure 5.2 Commodity prices: peanuts, wheat, and maize (US$ per metric tonne)
Source: IMF Commodity Prices (2018).

European Union (EU)—are the most important market for 'processed agricultural' products. Despite this, some African countries have, in recent years, experienced a fall in the share of such high-value processed agricultural products sent to the EU.[22]

Fifth, African terms of trade held up well from the 1950s to 2000, even holding steady after the oil price hike of the early 1970s when overall commodity terms of trade fell. But whatever the trend in the net barter terms of trade for commodities over a given period, this is absolutely no guide to the net barter terms of trade for any *individual* country, or even group of countries. Thus, 'there is little evidence of a stable, long-run relationship between the commodity terms of trade and the national net barter terms of trade for the majority of the countries of Sub-Saharan Africa'.[23]

There is no convincing reason that African governments should neglect investment efforts to expand primary commodity exports. Instead, they should design policies maximizing their command over imports. This requires an investment strategy targeting those exports where the greatest medium-term gains—in foreign exchange, but if possible also in employment—are likely. It also means overcoming—rather than caving in to—difficulties that are sometimes used as excuses to shy away from participating in global trade. For example, some African government officials wring their hands at the strict phyto-sanitary standards necessary to thrive in global agricultural commodity trade, although Kenya's

---

[22] Partridge and Pienaar (2015).　　[23] Cashin and Patillo (2006: 856).

exporters have invested to meet many of these standards. In South Africa, complaints about the imposition of these standards justify a strategy of making a virtue out of investment failure—a claim that it is too difficult to succeed in international markets helps turn trading with other African economies into a rhetorical campaign of solidarity.

If the Prices Don't Get You, the Rules Will

While there has been a proliferation of non-tariff barriers (NTBs) in the wake of formal trade liberalization (the reduction in tariffs and quotas),[24] this is often only a partial reason at best for weak export performance. Again, South Africa's experience provides more convincing reasons for lacklustre export performance. Access to large markets for apples, pears, and other fruits in China and Thailand has been blocked, not by overly zealous phyto-sanitary rules, but by the South African government's failure to take the required action. Government officials took years to provide basic information required by the Chinese authorities on the amounts of pesticides used in apple orchards, while 'South Africa's fruit exporters have been denied access to Thailand since 2008 because the South African government has failed to update the phyto-sanitary rules applicable to the sector, thus hindering the certification process'.[25]

Prior to 2015, South Africa had not exported any plums to China for 10 years. Trade pessimists and some South African officials might complain of 'market access' problems. But Chile had managed to export large quantities of plums to China during the same period. Chile invested in a massive trade negotiation effort and succeeded in gaining access to the growing East Asian markets; South Africa did not make this effort and access remains very limited. Similarly, Peru managed to export avocados to US and Japanese markets, while South Africa failed. Thus, behind the nationalistic stress on market access difficulties, there is often a weakness in trade negotiation.

The WTO and 'Policy Space': Rules and Ruses

Similar weaknesses undermine the ability of many governments to make the best of prevailing World Trade Organization (WTO) rules, although much of the literature emphasizes that the governments of low-income countries have very limited opportunities to evade the strict requirements of WTO membership. For example, some critics fear that the WTO is little more than a crowbar wielded by

---

[24] UNCTAD (2013).   [25] Viviers et al. (2014).

the richest economies to force open developing country markets while continuing to protect their own competitive edge. The key argument here is that the WTO has, since its inauguration in 1995, reduced developing country 'policy space', making it virtually impossible for such countries to adopt industrial policies of the type used in earlier developing economies (in East and South East Asia especially). As Robert Wade argues:

> the main international agreements from the Uruguay Round—TRIPS, TRIMS and GATS—systematically tip the playing field against developing countries [. . .] Taken together, the three agreements greatly restrict the right of a government to carry though policies that favour the growth and technological upgrading of domestic industries and firms.[26]

Without doubt, the rules of the trading game have changed over recent decades. There are now bans on quotas for manufactured imports (making infant industry protection more difficult); limits on subsidies (making it more difficult for states to back national exporting champions); bans on local content requirements, as well as other trade-related investment measures (TRIMS), that might be used to direct the behaviour of foreign direct investors; and demands for a dramatic reduction in import tariffs. Tariffs are generally 'bound' at an upper limit, though they are often 'applied' at a different, lower rate. The Trade-Related Aspects of Intellectual Property Rights (TRIPS) agreement makes it harder for developing countries to secure technology transfer in time-honoured (piratical) ways, and is said to have facilitated a large flow of patent-related profits from 'Southern' to 'Northern' countries. Additionally, using the WTO Dispute Settlement Understanding (DSU) is costly for resource-constrained developing countries.

In parallel with the WTO, there are many preferential trade agreements (PTAs) and regional trade agreements (RTAs) that also often impose restrictions on developing countries. Thus, while a PTA such as the African Growth and Opportunity Act (AGOA) might give preferential access to the US market for some African exports, this comes at a price. Conditions imposed by the preference-giving country might include general commitments—to privatization or market liberalization—and/or more specific commitments, for example, regarding the relaxation of environmental standards or government procurement policy. Sometimes, these rules and conditions are more restrictive than the WTO, as the preference-giving country is able to negotiate better terms than they would have been able to achieve faced with stronger collective action among a larger number of developing countries.[27] Critics have also argued there may be quite

---

[26] Wade (2003: 622, 630). See also Weiss (2005).
[27] Aggarwal and Evenett (2014); UNECA (2016).

high costs and limited benefits as a result of economic partnership agreements (EPAs), negotiated between the EU and a number of African regional blocs.[28]

The rules of trade can be tough. But these rules and constraints do not eliminate the scope for policy initiatives: African policy officials do have room for movement—'policy space'. The rules themselves allow for a range of government interventions that can support industrial expansion and exports. Furthermore, the evidence is clear that governments can stretch these rules to expand the range of interventions in support of exports. Besides, policy officials can and should promote exports by adopting many other types of intervention not covered or prohibited in WTO rules. For example, targeted infrastructure investments—railways, ports, roads, and dams serving areas with a high capacity for foreign exchange and job creation—are fine, as are targeted and subsidized investment in skills formation. African states can intervene to provide marketing services to domestic champions, as well as tax concessions to selected foreign firms.[29] State financial institutions in search of economies of scale can adopt measures to bring about mergers of firms in strategic activities. Governments can set up public research and development (R&D) centres designed to generate and transfer technology to firms at 'competitive' prices (rather than at prices set to extract patent rents). States can use public procurement policy—especially in developing countries that are not signatories to the current agreements among only some WTO members—to foster domestic firms that may later go on to build export capacity.

The WTO has 'green light' exemptions that allow for state subsidies: to support R&D; to support disadvantaged regions of a country; and to help existing facilities switch to environmentally cleaner technology. A country can introduce 'trade restrictive' protection to encourage infant industries where the rate of aggregate import growth threatens to provoke balance of payments difficulties (under Article XVIII). It can also do this to protect a specific industry against an import surge (Article XIX), as well as to protect an industry against unfair trading practices (dumping, etc.) by other countries. Additionally, export taxes, for example, can be imposed to discourage exports of unprocessed commodities. There will, of course, be overt and covert attempts to interfere with the design and implementation of policies such as these. There is substantial variation in how WTO rules are agreed and applied. For example, rather than having tariff rates forced down by WTO *diktat*, the governments of some countries have willingly reduced them below what is agreed through their WTO commitments.[30] United Nations Economic Commission for Africa (UNECA) deserves credit for acknowledging the degree of variation and what is possible:

[I]n carrying out such policy measures, the real test becomes that of the policymakers' commitment to maintaining emphasis on industrial policy efforts. The

---

[28] UNECA (2016).   [29] Gallagher (2007: 82).   [30] Aggarwal and Evenett (2014).

situation is challenging, but if policymakers are swayed by the prevailing orthodoxy from the outset [or, we would add, by those who gain from that orthodoxy], the lack of policy space will only be accentuated.[31]

Since the creation of the WTO, developing countries have been able to 'game' the system effectively. Amrita Bahri's research has shown that 'With better bargaining and litigation strategies, and with the consequentially enhanced capacity to raise credible litigation threats, Member States can improve their "terms-of-trade".'[32] This may involve both knowing the rules, and stretching, interpreting, testing, and adjusting favourably to them: 'strategic lawyering'.[33]

Brazil, for example, has used the WTO's dispute resolution system in a variety of ways to protect domestic firms and support exporters, such as the formerly state-owned aircraft manufacturer Embraer. Not only were Embraer's export markets successfully defended against Canadian aerospace interests, careful preparation for litigation stimulated deeper productive relations between the Brazilian state and private sector. The Brazilian experience suggests that developing countries seeking to make the international trading system work for them need the services of experienced trade lawyers (and plenty of them); politicians with the nous to decide which cases to litigate and which to leave alone; and officials who can monitor trade practices in other countries.

African policy officials may be encouraged by another, even more dramatic, example of how to use the WTO system to promote and protect domestic industry:

> Despite expectations that China would abandon its more protective industrial policies after entering the WTO, during the past decade the Chinese government has increased its reliance on WTO-inconsistent measures as a key tool for managing the country's economy.[34]

China's officials have been astute in adopting policies, then holding out until they are challenged in the WTO. They then continue with the policies through what is typically a long, drawn-out period of negotiation and WTO procedures, before finally, if they are ruled against, scaling back protective or 'trade restrictive' measures. By the time this stage is reached, the policies have often already done much of the work needed to support a new domestic industry.

Foreign firms are pressed to operate through joint ventures with Chinese firms, pushed to transfer technology in key sectors, and persuaded to meet local content requirements. Meanwhile, the Chinese state promotes new sets of activity through state-owned enterprises, many of which are incompletely privatized, and sponsored through measures such as subsidies and cheap, targeted credit. This kind of approach was adopted in sectors such as wind power, high-speed railways, and

---

[31] UNECA (2016: 117). See also Aggarwal and Evenett (2014); Amsden and Hikino (2000).
[32] Bahri (2016: 642).   [33] Santos (2011: 594).   [34] Oh (2015: 1125).

solar power. When China was challenged in the WTO, the resultant negotiations took years. One tactic that drew the negotiation process out even longer was the neglect, by the Chinese negotiating team, to translate key documents into English, French, or Spanish (the three official WTO languages).[35]

A concerted attempt to adopt at least some elements of China's approach and tactics could begin to halt Africa's declining share of world markets, allowing faster growth in the imports required for accumulation.

5.4 Exchange Rates as Development Policy

Exchange rates can, along with other prices, be manipulated or 'got wrong' for productive, transformative, and competitive purposes. The standard economics textbook approach to exchange rates treats them as relative prices that balance or can create a tendency to equilibrium in the external account. But exchange rates are, rather, about the pace of change in an economy; they are key to the level and rate of growth of economic activity at which external accounts balance.

There are two main reasons why some economists are wary of government intervention to make exchange rates 'competitive' or 'undervalued'. The first is simply the belief that any intervention in markets is distortionary, leading to perverse economic outcomes. This follows from the approach noted in Section 5.2, in which the exchange rate is key to maintaining balance in external accounts (irrespective of the level of activity); and this approach prioritizes macroeconomic balance and equilibrium above production, growth, structural change, and, frankly, human welfare. These economists emphasize the possible costs of competitive devaluations, arguing, for example, that large deviations from 'equilibrium' prices can be harmful for growth.

This goes for both large undervaluations and large overvaluations. If the exchange rate is undervalued for any length of time, the consequences may include: an inefficient build-up of low-yielding foreign reserves; inflation and macroeconomic instability, especially if there are no countervailing measures to restrain wage growth; a reduction in the scope for using monetary policy to manage efficient levels of investment; and reductions in consumer welfare and overall demand, because undervaluation can act as a tax on consumption spending—though this ignores the scope for dynamic effects of an undervaluation, as discussed later in this section.[36] From this perspective, the role of central banks is limited, intervening in currency markets only to minimize large short-term swings in the real exchange rate; otherwise, they should use the exchange rate as a price helping to secure low inflation.[37]

---

[35] Oh (2015).   [36] Haddad and Pancaro (2010).   [37] Frenkel and Rapetti (2014).

The second source of anxiety about exchange rate undervaluation derives from different theoretical and political concerns. Partly, it is based on very reasonable fears about the impact devaluation might have on the price of wage goods and aggregate demand, and hence on growth. Economists within a Kaldorian or structuralist tradition—including staunch supporters of Tanzania's efforts in the early 1980s to resist IMF demands for devaluation—anticipate a redistribution of income away from wage earners, largely because workers' wages are unlikely in the short term to increase in step with the prices of already scarce imported goods.[38] This may increase political instability and encourage capital flight, as well reducing overall demand because wage workers—who have a relatively high propensity to spend their income—are experiencing falls in their real wages. With overall demand declining as a result of the devaluation, growth may slow. Another risk is that if external debts have been contracted in foreign currencies, then devaluation exposes an economy to deeper debt-servicing difficulties.

Furthermore, when exchange rates become undervalued, elasticities of supply and demand for African exports may scupper the benefits some economists anticipate. On the supply side, it is not clear that the volume of Africa's exports responded very positively or rapidly to price increases enjoyed during the post-2001 commodity boom.[39] Demand-induced responses may be weakened because much global trade now flows through supply chain links between firms spread across different countries. A country may export goods that are then intermediate inputs in long chains assembling final consumer products. A devaluation in one such exporting country may have only a modest impact on overall global demand for the final product, given the complexity and the number of economies contributing to production of that good. This effect may well vary depending on how significant a given country's contribution is to the final value chain product.[40]

It is also difficult to make confident predictions about the results of exchange rate changes for other reasons: a depreciation may make exports more competitively priced internationally, but at the same time it raises the cost of imports and hence of production, which in turn will be reflected in profitability and/or export prices. Thus, where the import content of exports is high—as is the case in many African economies—depreciation may be less effective in promoting export growth.[41] In addition, a devaluation designed to stimulate growth in the volume of exports may fail if capitalists prefer to concentrate their investment efforts on high-profit niche opportunities in the domestic market, such as urban property speculation. It may also fail because, as is common in many African countries, there are supply-side rigidities blocking a rapid commodity response to demand signals. Transport infrastructure may be weak or have collapsed, there may be

---

[38] Singh (1986).   [39] Mold and Prizzon (2010: 3).
[40] Ahmed, Appendino, and Ruta (2015: 17); Cheng et al. (2016).
[41] Ahmed, Appendino, and Ruta (2015: 17).

frequent power cuts and insufficient R&D to support production and increases in productivity—the price signal of a devaluation may be a faint blinking torch in an empty desert.

So there are reasons why some economic advisors to African policymakers (as well as African leaders such as Julius Nyerere) have argued vehemently against devaluation. But this opposition is usually eventually crushed, and it may be misguided. Exchange rate policy is too important to be guided by gestural opposition to Washington bullies, and insisting on maintaining an overvalued exchange rate can be a way of giving up policy responsibility. The evidence shows that growth episodes are clearly linked to competitive exchange rates, and there are clear mechanisms that help explain why this is so.

This empirical claim is linked to the analytical idea that exchange rate movements help determine the level and the rate of change of economic activity—at which, necessarily, the balance of payments account balances. The link between a competitive and stable real exchange rate and higher gross domestic product (GDP) growth rates is evident in a variety of regression analyses that use a range of datasets for GDP growth rates, as well as in historical case studies of growth episodes. There is evidence, too, that the effect is especially marked in developing countries, although the effect may be strong both in low- and high-income countries, but weaker in between.[42] Nonetheless, there is a plenty of evidence suggesting that targeting a competitive exchange rate is an effective growth-enhancing policy for developing countries.

Exchange rates have complex links to the rest of the economy, but some of the dynamics explaining how competitive undervaluations can generate faster GDP growth are beginning to be understood. Policies that shift resources away from non-tradeables towards tradeables can help accelerate structural change and growth, as this shift will often involve transferring resources from low- to high-productivity activities. Not all high-productivity activities fall into the sector conventionally defined as 'manufacturing', but many do, and it has long been argued that manufacturing is central to long-run growth and development (see Chapter 3), and that manufactured exports in particular are associated with sustained growth and development.

An undervalued exchange rate can signal profitability and provoke a shift of resources to tradeable activities. In low-income African economies, however, the incentive to invest in higher-productivity activities may have been dulled by the small size of domestic markets, meaning that potential economies of scale cannot be captured. Firms in these economies might be more confident about increasing their profits if a depreciation of the real exchange rate opens up larger international market demand, making it possible for them to benefit from economies

---

[42] Rodrik (2008); Rapetti et al. (2012).

of scale. This in turn may help unleash the cumulative efficiencies that evolve from spill-overs, linkages, and 'intimate connections' among firms within the country. In short, a competitive real exchange rate can set off a virtuous cycle of productivity improvements.

A currency undervaluation—changing relative prices with a view to promoting particular kinds of production—can work like a subsidy, increasing investors' profits and effectively acting as an 'infant industry' protection policy. It 'gets prices wrong' in order to create a profitable environment within which developing countries can generate competitive know-how, exploit scale economies, and accelerate 'learning'. It then works like one of Hirschman's linkages (Chapter 6), by providing a compelling signal of profitability and calling forth new investments. In one study, 92 episodes of manufacturing export growth were preceded by currency devaluations (facilitating both growth into new export markets and the growth of new export products). Other work confirms the structural change-promoting effect of currency undervaluation.[43]

Exchange rate policy is one (blunt) instrument, the effectiveness of which is likely to be greater when combined with other policies. These include public R&D; investment in education; and large investments in infrastructure, targeting especially those areas and activities with scope for foreign exchange earnings and employment growth that are also likely to stimulate dynamic increasing returns. There may also be a case for targeting how the subsidy that is an undervalued real exchange rate works—combining fiscal and exchange rate policy as a kind of selective industrial policy. One way to reroute the subsidy away from those tradeables less associated with structural change gains is to tax exports of products with little scope for dynamic increasing returns, productivity increases, or employment.[44]

In practice, it is difficult to determine the outcomes of exchange rate policy. If the key objective is to sustain a moderate, stable, and credible undervaluation, policy officials will need to agree on how best to assess the current level of under- or overvaluation of the real exchange rate. The importance of monitoring trends in the real exchange rate lies in the information it gives about relative profitability across economies. Most mainstream economists do not focus on this information, believing the main purpose of real exchange rate calculations is to highlight variations in rates of consumer price inflation between countries. However, these variations are not always a clear guide to relative profitability, and an undervalued exchange rate can lower the time preference for saving (increasing the willingness to save). It can also make investment more 'efficient', raising the marginal product of capital. Uncertainties about profitability and future flows of investment will continue to confront policymakers, but they can take comfort in

---

[43] Frenkel and Rapetti (2014); McMillan and Rodrik (2011); Freund and Pierola (2012).
[44] Guzman, Ocampo, and Stiglitz (2017).

the finding that investment is more likely to be sustained if there is an expectation that the exchange rate policy will not be subject to big swings.

Advocates of devaluation hope that a cut in domestic purchasing power (among wage earners and local material suppliers) will be offset by a rise in foreign demand for the country's output. This includes both demand for goods and services exported *and* demand to invest in assets in the country. If this is the case, then the effect of the currency depreciation will be to raise investment and output in the economy as a whole. As a result, wages may start to rise alongside sustained growth and productivity increases. It is important to emphasize that the positive effects of devaluation/undervaluation may be the result of attracting new flows of foreign investment, just as much (perhaps even more) as through the volume of trade.

It is clear from the discussion here that exchange rate policy is deeply political, involving judgements well beyond the remit (or the competence) of IMF techno-crats. Where wages are already very low and the cost of living is rising, will it be possible to persuade people to accept a rise in the general price level? It is well known that the inflationary effects of devaluations can be 'politically disruptive enough to derail' IMF programmes.[45] As Kalecki noted (see Chapter 4), acceler-ating wage goods price inflation may lead either to reduced investment, if it has to be accommodated in higher wages and lower profits, or to rising political conflict around falling real wages. An exchange rate devaluation risks something similar. It needs very careful political management (e.g. in the form of a 'deal' to secure the temporary acceptance of lower real wages, against the promise of faster growth, rising productivity, and longer-term rising real wages). This needs to be combined with an investment strategy to increase the non-inflationary supply of basic wage goods, as well as short-term market interventions to ensure that the prices of food staples do not rise above a certain threshold.

Finally, policy officials need to be aware of the complexities of judging exactly how much an exchange rate is over- or undervalued. They will in all likelihood find themselves in negotiations with the IMF, whose staff use a variety of methods (some more transparent than others) to make a judgement. How far a particular country's real exchange rate and current account deviate from the 'norm' observed in selected comparator countries will determine the Fund's estimate of (typically) overvaluation. Sometimes the IMF simply draws a regression line, roughly linking levels of per capita income to the real exchange rate across economies. How far a given country's real exchange rate veers away from the line of best fit ('the norm') shows the degree of overvaluation. For example, this method calculated the Ethiopian birr as being overvalued by 36 per cent in 2017.[46]

[45] Taylor (1997: 148).
[46] If the sample of comparator countries had been expanded to include commodity producers, the extent of overvaluation would have fallen to the less extreme figure of 22 per cent. IMF (2016: 32).

Any attempt to achieve a real devaluation of more than 30 per cent would almost certainly have had dramatic and unforeseeable consequences for the Ethiopian economy.

Many would agree that in recent years the birr was not set at an appropriate rate, despite nominal depreciations. Even so, the IMF assessment was probably an exaggeration, and it is hard to make sense of the method used to arrive at this extreme and risky assessment. We argue that because exchange rates really point to differences across countries in profitability, it would be better to gather data from several countries on unit production costs (wages and material/input costs per physical unit of output) for a comparable sample of tradeable and non-tradeable outputs. There is not good data on these for Ethiopia, or for many other African economies.

5.5 Narrow Definitions of Industrial Policy and Manufacturing: Assembly Plants or Plant Assembly?

In the past, economists and policymakers set priorities based on distinctions between broad economic sectors: agriculture or primary commodity production; manufacturing industry; and services. Non-mainstream development economists have emphasized the distinctive features of manufacturing: the link between manufacturing output and overall GDP growth; the link between manufacturing output and productivity in manufacturing; and the link between manufacturing output and productivity in the rest of the economy. Where neoclassical economists saw *no* distinctive features separating one sector from another, arguing for 'horizontal' policies that would affect efficiency across any sector, structuralist economists argued for more 'vertical' interventions that would accelerate investment specifically in manufacturing.

Evidence supporting Kaldor's views about the manufacturing sector's unique contribution to growth has been accumulating for several decades. The evidence also supports an industrial policy that involves selective interventions in support of particular industries, as well as the wielding of a 'reciprocal control mechanism'—a disciplining mechanism that ensures support for firms or industries is conditional on performance against specific criteria. In recent years, some neoclassically trained economists claim to recognize the role of industrial policy in economic growth and structural change. Two influences on this change of heart have been, first, advances in technique that have enabled better modelling of increasing returns—in the past, despite awareness of increasing returns, economists were unable to incorporate these returns in mathematical models. The second influence has been the increasing popularity of the 'market failure' and 'information theoretic' strain of neoclassical economics. These developments have helped foster a belated enthusiasm within the mainstream for industrial policy.[47] In late 2018, for example, an International Finance Corporation (IFC) official pronounced at a workshop on industrialization in Africa that industrialization was 'the dominant paradigm' for development. The only eyebrows raised were those of the few non-mainstream economists around the table not used to hearing any enthusiastic orthodox pronouncements about industrial policy. The same developments lie behind support for specific interventions in industries with a particular proclivity for 'learning externalities' and facing other market failures.[48] These are contrasted with primary commodity exports. This rediscovery of industrial policy is usually limited in two important ways.

First, the market failure underpinnings of some new advocates of industrial policy leads to a narrow set of policies. This approach is exemplified in the work of Justin Lin and the idea that industrial policy must be restricted to state interventions that 'facilitate comparative advantage' in Africa, typically focusing on light manufacturing and on removing red tape, improving the 'doing business' climate, and investing in infrastructure. Arguments along these lines do at least acknowledge that some form of industrial policy might be possible in Africa. But we argue that Lin's restricted view—imagine a car with huge blind spots curbing the view behind and a windscreen so fogged up that only part of the road ahead is visible—unnecessarily limits the possibilities for intervention. It represents a very partial understanding of the evidence on and history of thought about industrial policy.[49]

Second, while some acknowledge the significance of industrial policy in past experiences of 'catch-up' development, they also argue that the policies used (in countries such as Korea or Taiwan) can no longer be deployed effectively. This is partly because the rules of the game (WTO and other regulations) are misleadingly said to prohibit their use, and partly because it is thought that structural changes in the global economy mean that manufacturing is now less central to development: low- and middle-income economies are said to be in the grip of premature deindustrialization. We have already argued (in Chapter 4) that premature industrialization should not be considered an iron law preventing African governments from adopting effective industrial policies. Here, we criticize pessimists' understanding of the role of manufacturing—and their policy conclusions—in a little more detail.

Arguments about premature deindustrialization rest on a standard classification of sectors that is increasingly outdated and unhelpful for economic analysis and policy design. The irony is that the traditional three-sector classification is becoming irrelevant just as neoclassical economists are discovering there really are differences between sectors. The special characteristics that in the past were associated with manufacturing have become detached from broadly defined

---

[47] Cherif and Hasanov (2019).   [48] Guzman, Ocampo, and Stiglitz (2017).
[49] For a critique of Lin's new structural economics see Fine and van Waeyenberge (2013).

'sectors' and attached instead to specific 'activities'. The categorical boundaries between sectors have become blurred by global technical and economic changes. These have taken two forms in particular. First, there is 'servicification', meaning that an increasing share of the final value of many products is derived from services such as logistics or branding.[50] Second, there is the 'industrialization of freshness': the production of high-value fresh fruit, vegetables, herbs, and flowers is increasingly complex, sophisticated, and—by any reasonable definition— industrial. For example, a fresh orange produced for export from, say, South Africa to the UK, is technically more sophisticated, and industrially more com- plex, than an apparently more 'processed' product such as a carton of orange juice. Producing a consistent flow of top-quality oranges—meeting strict phyto-sanitary rules of market access for the EU, ensuring the oranges are perfectly ripe and juicy, and look the part—is an extremely difficult task. It involves an 'intricate nexus' that makes for a 'roundabout' production process—exactly the ingredients that make something 'industrial'.[51] Much of this activity is not captured in standard data on industrial output and is therefore missing from the literature on 'prema- ture deindustrialization'.

This blurring of categorical boundaries, and the resulting need to focus policy not on 'sectors' but 'activities', should inform the design of structural change policies. The two most important criteria to be applied before allocating resources are, first, what scope an activity has to generate a rapid increase in export earnings; and, second, what scope it has for generating employment (directly and indir- ectly). Other criteria—the scope for technical learning, for economies of scale, for generating 'intimate connections' between firms—may also be considered.

Policymakers need to know if these key criteria are satisfied more fully by, for instance, promoting turnkey garment assembly sheds or supporting the expansion of high-value horticulture and floriculture. Policymakers should also be prepared to ask other detailed and politically difficult questions: for example, whether it is appropriate to subsidize domestic food production when long-term price declines on international markets imply favourable terms of trade for African cereal importers; or whether subsidies should be directed towards the domestic produc- tion of food types that make little or no contribution to improving the nutrition of the poorest people.

5.6 Conclusions

We have argued that many policies are available for African governments to use in influencing outcomes from international economic integration. The arguments of

---

[50] Lodefalk (2017).   [51] Cramer, Di John, and Sender (2018).

the trade pessimists are misleading. There are, of course, considerable difficulties in trading with more powerful and wealthy partners, but there are many areas where policy can overcome some of these difficulties. Securing these gains is fundamental to successful structural change.

We have insisted that no simple magic trick policies are available: for example, effective management of an undervalued exchange rate involves many complementary policies, including achieving a non-inflationary increase in the supply of food and other basic wage goods. Above all, though, the argument presented in this chapter is that African governments need to design public investment strategies to achieve a rapid increase in the rate of growth of exports, so that they can relax the balance of payments constraint on growth and allow a sustained rise in imports—of capital goods, intermediate inputs, and consumer goods. Finally, we have raised questions about which economic activities should be the main beneficiaries of public interventions. If governments do not develop clear priorities when designing policy, they may end up at the mercy of individual fancies or the relative power of particular lobbying interests—all claiming to contribute to the people's welfare, the empowerment of women and the elimination of undernutrition.

Acknowledgements

Besides the references cited, Section 5.4 owes a debt to conversations with Michael Kuczynski and to presentations he made to a group of high-level policy officials from Ethiopia in June 2016.

6

Unbalanced Development

6.1 Introduction

Balance matters greatly to development economists from one end of the (ideological, methodological) scale to the other. For some, economies develop through the continuous balancing out of market exchanges, with a high-wire act of constant small adjustments facilitated by flexible prices, nudging the process onward one step at a time. For others, markets left to themselves may hang in a hopeless low-income equilibrium 'trap', snared by a series of 'gaps' (the savings gap, the skills gap, the technology gap, the capital gap). These different sets of ideas, converging on the importance of balance, lie behind a great deal of policy advice meted out to officials in African (and other) governments.

In this chapter, we argue that these visions of balance are blind to the history and dynamics of capitalism. They project fantasies of orderly and largely predictable processes onto fundamentally uncertain, contradictory, and frequently unstable realities. We contrast these illusions with a view of economic development that positively embraces imbalance, contingency, productive mistakes, and unexpected chain reactions.

> If the economy is to be kept moving ahead, the task of development policy is to maintain tensions, disproportions and disequilibria.[1]

In doing so, we resist the danger of replacing one fantasy with another by emphasizing the difficulties that come with fundamental uncertainty and detailing some grandiose development calamities. However, we also remind devotees of the steady and balanced that there have often been overlooked developmental benefits generated by supposed 'development disasters', like the infamous groundnut scheme in British colonial Tanganyika.

The ideas of Albert Hirschman are at the heart of this chapter. We summarize some of Hirschman's ideas in Section 6.3, highlighting not only his arguments about unbalanced growth but also his ideas about the 'hiding hand' (as opposed to the 'invisible hand'), as well as his broader 'bias for hope'. Hirschman's ideas have always garnered wary respect from many mainstream economists, but, unable for

[1] Hirschman (1958: 66).

African Economic Development: Evidence, Theory, Policy. Christopher Cramer, John Sender, and Arkebe Oqubay, Oxford University Press (2020). © Christopher Cramer, John Sender, and Arkebe Oqubay. DOI: 10.1093/oso/9780198832331.001.0001

the most part to absorb them into neoclassical models, they have nonetheless largely dismissed them.[2]

Before discussing Hirschman, the chapter sets out balanced growth models, assumptions, and strategies. We summarize the original 'balanced growth' strategy as well as more recent variants, such as the big push strategy. The latter include both structural adjustment programmes designed by the World Bank, and strategies for sustainable and inclusive development put forward by United Nations Conference on Trade and Development (UNCTAD). In arguing for productive imbalance, this chapter complements what we have already set out in Chapters 4 and 5 (on the economics of growth and trade), but here we focus on particular examples of firms and very ambitious projects, including Sasol in South Africa and Ethiopian Airlines, and large dams in Mozambique and elsewhere. The chapter also discusses the considerable risks involved in pursuing an unbalanced growth strategy (whether it is labelled that or not).

6.2 Ideas of Balance in Economics and Development

The idea of balance runs as a powerful current through much economic thinking and development strategy. It is not one idea, however. Rather, balance plays *different* roles in varying approaches to economic analysis. This section introduces some of these ideas.

Accounting Identities and Macroeconomic Balances

Balance is semantically slippery and can mean many things. One of the main usages involves balanced growth as a deliberate strategy for low-income economies to escape persistent low demand and low investment. However, there are also other, and in a sense deeper, notions of balance. The conventions of accounting (one person's liabilities are another's assets) lie at the heart of a national accounts system that, before and during the Second World War, was developed into the foundations of modern macroeconomics.[3] Analysing the interactions among three related balances in the economy—public (spending and revenue in the public sector); private (income, expenditure, and borrowing by private firms and individuals); and external (the balance of import spending and export earnings, plus capital account movements, and external borrowing)—is a fruitful way

---

[2] 'Mr Hirschman was never awarded the Nobel Prize in economics he so richly deserved, perhaps because his writing was hard to classify' (*The Economist*, 2012).
[3] On the history of the national accounts system in the UK see Tily (2009) and in Africa, Deane (2011).

of identifying trends in an economy, as well as spotting any alarming tendencies.[4] An Ethiopian application of this approach in 2017 was probably the first time it had been applied in sub-Saharan Africa. It confirmed the importance of the public sector in leading growth in recent years; made it more obvious than is normally acknowledged how important private sector investment has been, especially after 2012; and suggested that although external spending was sufficiently above earning to cause concern, there was no immediate danger of a 'debt crisis'.[5]

While macroeconomic imbalances may be a source of crisis, some of the focus on achieving macroeconomic balances is misleading, fetishistic, and obsessional. In Chapter 5, for example, we argued that the key is not *whether* payments balance out neatly, but what the *level of economic activity* (investment, employment, etc.) at which the external sector balances is.

Equilibrium Thinking

Deeper in economic ideas and methodologies lies the notion of balance that is equilibrium. Neoclassical economics considers that economies, especially if markets are left largely to their own devices, tend to equilibrium. Alfred Marshall, a pioneer of modern economics, wrote:

> As, in spite of the great differences in form between birds and quadrupeds, there is one Fundamental Idea running through all their frames, so the general theory of the equilibrium of demand and supply is a Fundamental Idea running through the frames of all the various parts of the central problem of Distribution and Exchange.[6]

In general equilibrium models, this complex balancing act is achieved through myriad adjustments of wants and offers—supply and demand—among buyers and sellers, reflected in continuous movements in relative prices. Flexible prices allow markets to 'clear' at an equilibrium price at which there is no excess of supply over demand or of demand over supply. This powerful idea may be used to analyse any manner of social phenomena beyond merely markets for goods and services. In a trend that became known as 'economics imperialism', many economists took to claiming they could explain an ever wider set of social phenomena by using the core precepts of neoclassical equilibrium economics.[7] Equilibrium became fundamental to the work of most economists during the twentieth century. As a result, key aspects of industrial reality—acknowledged early on in Adam Smith's *Wealth of Nations* and in Marshall's analysis of diminishing and increasing returns—were sacrificed on the altar of mathematical tractability. Mainstream

---

[4] Godley (1999).   [5] Coutts and Laskaridis (2019).   [6] Marshall (1920/1997: 8).
[7] Fine and Milonakis (2009), Cramer (2010).

economics can be defined as the formal modelling of how maximizing individuals with unbounded rationality behave, operating in markets with strong tendencies towards equilibrium. Robert Solow summarized it in three words: 'greed, rationality, and equilibrium'.[8]

While such methodological constraints have shaped much of modern economics, some within the neoclassical mainstream have sought to escape them. Kenneth Arrow showed how absurdly restrictive the conditions necessary to make general equilibrium possible were; many others took their cue from his and related work to explore the implications of more realistic departures from perfect competition, price-taking by all economic 'agents', and perfect information. Endogenous growth theorists attempted to incorporate at least some forms of increasing returns into formal models,[9] while others explored the manifold implications of imperfect and asymmetric (i.e. decidedly imbalanced) information.

Even these economists, though, were nervous of policy officials taking the hint and doing things 'out of step'. Trade theorists such as Paul Krugman, who at least for a while acknowledged how actually existing increasing returns placed limits on comparative advantage theory, made a point of counselling developing country governments not to abandon free trade. Economists who noted the ambitious, *unbalanced* interventions promoting rapid industrialization in countries such as South Korea and Taiwan, nonetheless advised African governments not to emulate such policies.[10] Joseph Stiglitz, for example, argued that a government ought to match its interventions to its current administrative capacity. Meanwhile, trade economists such as Adrian Wood have argued the importance of waiting for the stock of skills to rise relative to the extent of cultivable land until a shift in relative prices indicates changing comparative advantage. Wood believed that, for most African countries, this was 'bound to be a slow process'.[11]

Generally, policy advice emanating from those trained in neoclassical economics is doctrinally attached to what Alfred Marshall called the 'Principle of Continuity', summed up in the epigraph to his major work: *'natura non facit saltum'* (nature does not advance by leaps).

Not all economists have been seduced by equilibrium economics, with one of its most trenchant critics being Kaldor:

> I should go further and say that the powerful attraction of the habits of thought engendered by 'equilibrium economics' has become a major obstacle to the development of economics as a science.[12]

---

[8] Cited in King (2013c: 19).   [9] Romer (1994, 1996); Ruttan (1998).
[10] Krugman (1987, 1993). Rodrik (2016: 15) argues that other countries that built up a head start in industrialization behind protective walls and through the use of import substitution and manufactured exports 'make it difficult for Africa to carve a space for itself'.
[11] Owens and Wood (1997: 1468). See also Lin in Lin and Chang (2009) on the 'high costs' of defying comparative advantage.
[12] Kaldor (1972: 1237), cited in King (2009b: 162).

Kaldor's critique was partly methodological: neoclassical economics typically proceeded from assumptions that were either unverifiable ('maximizing' consumers or businesses, for example) or observably false (perfect competition and information, linear and homogeneous production functions), where it ought to proceed from 'stylized facts'. But his critique was also a substantive one, stressing, among other things, the significance of increasing returns. Combining capitalism's competitive logic with the widespread role of increasing returns made for a self-sustaining growth process (that nonetheless required government intervention to keep rolling). In this process, the most important influences are endogenous, not exogenous as neoclassical economics assumes them to be.[13] Endogeneity—when variables are not fully 'independent' of each either, meaning that a variable that is a possible explanatory factor for an outcome may itself be influenced by changes in that outcome—makes for what Myrdal called 'cumulative causation'. Allyn Young had earlier had the same powerful insight, arguing that economic growth is 'progressive and propagates itself in a cumulative way'.[14]

Balanced Growth Big Push Strategies

Development economists have used other versions of balance, drawing implicitly or explicitly on the ideas of post-Second World War figures such as Rosenstein-Rodan and Nurkse, which advocated a purposive strategy of balanced growth.[15] These proposals built on the observation that economies could become stuck in a low-employment, low-income, low-investment equilibrium. Something was required to provoke investments that would pull a developing economy out of such a swamp of inactivity and low productivity. Given the low level of demand, individual investors are unlikely to act alone, while the size of the market is too small to generate demand for outputs from a new firm and thereby provoke a cumulative process of specialization. These doubts about the behaviour of individual investors in poor economies are a manifestation of Keynes' insight that, in conditions of fundamental uncertainty, private investors in richer countries will not easily commit to investing. Something, then, is required to help investors overcome their rational aversion to investing. For proponents of balanced growth, what was required in a low-income economy was a concerted 'big push' by the state—across a wide range of complementary activities.

The principle determining 'big push' resource allocation was the income elasticity of demand across specific activities. For example, industrial expansion should grow in step with food production and agricultural growth, while capital

---

[13] King (2009b: 163–6).
[14] Myrdal (1957); Young (1928: 533). On endogeneity and the challenge it poses to econometrics, for example, see Esping-Andersen and Przeworski (2001).
[15] Nurkse (1966); Rosenstein Rodan (1943, 1961).

goods production should grow in step with consumer goods output. Here, 'in step' does not mean at precisely the same rate, but at rates in harmony with relative elasticities of demand for capital and consumer goods, manufactures and food and agricultural inputs, and so on.

Early balanced growth strategies usually had in mind closed economies and, perhaps for that reason, remain attractive to those sympathetic to the views of 'export pessimists' (see Chapter 5). If there is scope for low-income economies to take advantage of 'autonomous' external demand (for exports), as well as scope for managing trade policy, then some of the demand and profitability concerns motivating big push arguments fall away.

UNCTAD and Other Modern Forms of Balanced Growth Strategy

UNCTAD's advocacy of a 'comprehensive policy approach' is the most sophisti-cated recent development strategy stamped with the imprint of earlier balanced growth ideas. This influence is explicit in UNCTAD's explanation for stalled industrialization in many countries, where 'investment levels . . . may still be too low to provide the big push required to trigger a self-sustaining process of expanding production capacities and domestic demand'.[16]

The UNCTAD policy proposals are ambitious, envisaging a development strategy where states effectively balance trade policy with industrial policy, design interventions to stimulate mutually supportive linkages, and at the same time put in place growth-enhancing institutions (the implication being that these institu-tions are *prerequisites* for development).[17] In the light of the instabilities and waste revealed by the 2008 global financial crisis, developing countries are also advised to 'rebalance' their economies away from financial sector dependence.

Given UNCTAD's (and many other economists') misgivings about relying on global demand, these countries are advised to rebalance towards home market supply and demand. Overall, 'attention is focused on the challenge of building linkages across various dimensions, the integrated policy approach this implies, and the institutional geometry that has been found in all the successful indus-trializers, irrespective of context, to meet this challenge'. They not only recom-mend an integrated policy approach involving an alignment of trade, competition, labour, and macroeconomic policies, but also argue that the initial 'push' may now (in the twenty-first century) need to be bigger than ever, because 'the pace of capital formation needed to kick-start and sustain a period of successful catch-up growth has been rising'.[18]

This precarious balancing act places demands on states and societies that trigger the same criticisms made about previous balanced growth strategies.

---

[16] UNCTAD (2016: 78).   [17] UNCTAD (2016: 179).   [18] UNCTAD (2016: 175–6).

UNCTAD's strategy seems to imagine that low-income economies have no debilitating scarcities—of resources, people, inputs, decision-making capabilities, skills, or investible funds—that may constrain simultaneous resource allocation across a wide range of activities. If there were no (or very few) such constraints, then it is unclear why a big push would be required in the first place. Furthermore, a balanced growth strategy assumes that different activities interlock seamlessly in ways that are readily calculable—assuming, for example, that income elasticities of demand can accurately be predicted for different goods.[19] There is no room in such a strategy for lack of data or unreliable estimates of future patterns of demand, nor indeed for fundamental uncertainty about whether severe weather events, domestic political struggles, or other disruptive events might clog the integrating mechanisms.

There is a further, less discussed, problem with these strategies of balance. An UNCTAD blueprint for sustainable economic growth indicates that many different things are *all* desirable. In this it resembles consultancy reports and government 'vision strategies' that set out lengthy lists of reforms, projects, interventions, and institutional designs, without pausing to make a reasoned case for which should be prioritized. Elsewhere we have given the example of international reports and national research institute documents stating what needs to change to improve Ethiopian coffee production and exports. These reports, whatever their assumptions, evidence, and logic, usually set out a bewildering array of wish-list changes.[20]

Far from being the exclusive preserve of UNCTAD, such policy and blueprint 'packages' are widespread. The World Bank's *World Development Report 2005*, for instance, 'contained a long list of reforms to systems of economic governance that countries would need to undertake in order to achieve significant progress in transformation'.[21] Another lengthy shopping list of reforms is the outcome of a recent attempt to put Africa's industrialization prospects into historical perspective: some economic historians argue that the potential for a manufacturing export boom in Africa—along the lines of what the UK and Japan achieved—is very limited. This is because 'Current wage gaps between African economies and late industrializing countries in Asia such as Vietnam and Bangladesh, or even China, are not nearly as large as the gap between Britain and Japan around 1900.'[22] Instead, they propose a development strategy that involves promoting growth *within* Africa's domestic markets, and requires the implementation of an extremely long list of 'priority' policies and mutually supportive, conventional preconditions: macroeconomic stability to enhance investor and consumer confidence; institutional improvements in property rights protection and bureaucratic processes, and the support of credit facilities and financial services; targeted technology transfer programmes and a limited, cautious use of protection to

---

[19] See Thirlwall (2005: 235) and Sutcliffe (1964).   [20] Cramer and Sender (2019).
[21] Balchin, Booth, and te Velde (2019: 12).   [22] Frankema and van Waijenburg (2018: 547).

pursue import substitution industrialization; social security for the poor; and reform of fiscal policy to raise revenue on domestic transactions.[23]

'Structural adjustment' programmes—designed by the World Bank for African economies with balance of payments difficulties—also had echoes of the big push idea. Programme funds came with 'conditionalities' that states were required to sign up to if they were to secure the Bank's support. Conditionalities flowed from a 'Washington Consensus' that economic stabilization and subsequent growth could only come about through adopting fiscal discipline; ensuring positive real interest rates; aiming at a competitive, 'fundamental equilibrium exchange rate'; liberalizing imports and foreign direct investment; privatization and deregulation; and establishing secure private property rights.[24] The heyday of the Washington Consensus passed, but in its wake came a variety of approaches—including Poverty Reduction Strategy Papers (PRSPs) and the 'good governance agenda'— which some have argued led to a further proliferation of conditionalities.

The 'good governance' agenda also bears the imprint of big push thinking. With weak or 'bad' governance identified as the key obstacle to economic development (once structural adjustment programmes had clearly failed), proponents of good governance argued for ambitious accountability and transparency reforms across a wide range of institutions, from revenue authorities to judiciaries and security institutions. Their argument had two key features: first, putting in place governance reforms was a fundamental *precondition* to sustained economic development; and, second, the reforms involved a sweeping range of simultaneous, 'big push', reforms. Governance reforms aimed at, for example, increasing public participation in policy decisions or making officials more accountable for their decisions, are widely agreed to be progressive.[25] This, though, is not the same as arguing that they are the first steps in a causal chain of economic development. Indeed, empirical evidence shows that the governance reforms proposed by international organizations and academics have *not*, historically, been necessary preconditions for development.[26] Instead, there is a more complex—or, as Hirschman put it when discussing the broader relationship between politics and economics, an 'on again, off again'—relationship between governance, growth, and development.[27]

Small Steps or Big Leaps

As a strategy, balanced growth may be attractive but unrealistic. Balance in the broader sense of a framework of economics and policy advice based on the idea of

---

[23] Frankema and van Waijenburg (2018).   [24] Williamson (1990).
[25] This is the basis for Mo Ibrahim Foundation campaigns: http://mo.ibrahim.foundation/.
[26] Khan (2012: 52).   [27] Hirschman (1994).

equilibrium provides a misleading conception of economic and structural change. Advocates of both balanced and unbalanced growth are 'united in their rejection of development by piecemeal marginalism'.[28] Alfred Marshall put great emphasis on the idea of continuity, and this was influenced by two huge advances of nineteenth-century thought: Darwin's insights into evolution and Cournot's development of differential calculus. In other words, the *natura non facit saltum* idea was very much an idea of its time. In economics, it underpins a very different image of change compared to, for example, Schumpeter's vision of capitalism as a 'perennial gale of creative destruction', or the brute force of (especially) the initial shift to and spread of capitalism described by Marx.[29] An intellectual apparatus held together by the rebar of marginal analysis and assumptions of diminishing or constant returns is not well suited to accounting for brutal real-world episodes of growth acceleration; shifts in industrial organization, foreign direct investment, and economic policy; or technical changes that have often come about during or in the wake of major wars. One such example can be seen in the dramatic growth rates experienced by Ethiopia (and Mozambique and Rwanda) since the early 2000s. Although some features of the past century may have helped lay the groundwork for recent economic changes in these African countries, it would be deluded to claim that such growth episodes reflect only a 'Principle of Continuity'.

6.3 Albert Hirschman's Development Economics

Pressures, Tensions, and Disequilibrium as the Motor of Change

It was exactly the problems that made a big push strategy unfeasible that promoted a response from Albert Hirschman, in what has been dubbed 'one of the most provocative books ever written on development strategy' (another, Paul Krugman, called it 'destructive').[30] Hirschman thought it more realistic to develop strategies that worked with the grain of shortage, using scarcity to bring other activities, capabilities, and investments into play. The idea at the heart of *The Strategy of Economic Development*, first published in 1958, was that the 'factor' in shortest supply in low-income economies was capitalist decision-making capability. Economizing on this scarce factor, by concentrating decision-making in specific kinds of activity, would, Hirschman argued, stimulate a chain of productive responses:[31]

From Hirschman's perspective there was a common problem: the view of development as a grandiose release of tension and blockages so that the economy

---

[28] Sutcliffe (1964: 630).   [29] Schumpeter (1942: 83); Marx (2010: 873).
[30] Thirlwall (2005: 237). Krugman (1994b).   [31] Hirschman (1958).

could put itself on a smooth path to a new, 'developed' equilibrium. This was pie-in-the-sky nonsense; the causality was the other way round. It was the very creation of 'pressures, tensions, and disequilibrium' that had to prime the motion and then unleash more frictions and tensions.[32]

This is as dramatic a divergence from conventional wisdom as Alice Amsden's argument that economic development is a process of 'getting prices wrong', rather than a gradual adjustment towards ever more 'correct' prices.[33]

Rather than limit ourselves to the well-rehearsed 'balanced versus unbalanced' growth debate,[34] we draw out some common themes from Hirschman's thinking over several decades, many of them refined years after *The Strategy of Economic Development* was first published. While Hirschman's ideas have never sat easily with orthodox neoclassical economists—nor, in fact, with many of their critics— they are practically relevant for governments. They are not especially formal (though some of them have been formalized to some extent);[35] nor especially programmatic; nor do they fit neatly into categorical 'frame views', whether neoclassical, structuralist, or neo-Marxist.

Models, Metaphors, and How to Be an Economist

Hirschman's way of doing economics was profoundly different to what became the global norm. He built from observation out to wider principles rather than insisting on an unchanging basis of behavioural axioms and deducing real-world patterns from them. He largely eschewed formal modelling. And he emphasized uncertainty: uncertainty irreducible to statistical risk. The distinction between calculable risk and fundamental uncertainty is one that goes back to Frank Knight,[36] and to Keynes, who said:

> The sense in which I am using the term [uncertainty] is that in which the prospect of a European war is uncertain or the price of copper and the rate of interest twenty years hence, or the obsolescence of a new invention . . . There is no scientific basis to form any calculable probability whatever. We simply do not know.[37]

Paul Krugman argues that Hirschman did not wait to be exiled from the economic mainstream but gathered up his followers and led them into the wilderness, where

---

[32] Adelman (2013: loc. 6153 of 16488).   [33] Amsden (1992).
[34] Thirlwall (2005); Sutcliffe (1964);
[35] One lasting formal legacy is the Herfindahl–Hirschman Index of Concentration, often used, for example by the US Department of Justice, in assessing levels of concentration and competition in markets.
[36] Knight (1921).   [37] Keynes (1937: 213–14).

they perished. Krugman argues that Hirschman's great error (along with some other 'high development' theorists) was that he favoured metaphors over models. This is a curious criticism given the heavy reliance of orthodox economics on metaphors, such as Adam Smith's 'invisible hand' (a 'mildly ironic' joke that Smith himself barely mentioned)[38] or the idea of a 'level playing field'. Metaphors are inescapable in economics, with some more conveniently converted into formal models than others.

Krugman misses the point.[39] First, what really obscured the insights of Hirschman and others was the growing influence—as Stiglitz points out—of ideas associated with Thatcherism (in the UK), Reaganomics (in the USA), and more broadly what Perry Anderson has called 'the single most successful ideology in human history': neoliberalism.[40] Second, it is not so much that Hirschman took himself off into the wilderness, but rather that orthodox economics banished as hopelessly maverick any analysis that did not fit with its highly particular, mathematical form of 'rigour'. In an age of 'economics imperialism', it was not just offbeat economists who bore the brunt of this hubris.[41]

Albert Hirschman was no economics imperialist—he preferred to consider himself a 'trespasser', venturing into other disciplines out of curiosity rather than to assert the economist's property rights or 'civilize' them with methodological individualism (let alone to set up the extractive institutions of randomized controlled trial experiments).[42] What he did commit to was 'immersion in the particular . . . essential for the capturing of anything general'.[43] In sharp contrast to the mainstream economic approach, Hirschman became 'increasingly aware that thorough historical reconstruction was the only way to unravel the mechanisms of development'.[44]

This approach allows for greater attention to the 'centrality of side effects' and to uncertainty than most economics is able to entertain. Hirschman argued that assuming away fundamental uncertainty and replacing it with probability calculations leads only to 'pseudo-insights'. Indeed, uncertainty in, for example, investment projects was not a mere nuisance factor but the very point: 'the element of the unknown, the uncertain, and the unexpected which deflects projects from the originally chartered course is considerable in all projects'.[45] Thus, what was methodologically required to assess projects and learn from them was a way of understanding what made the level of uncertainty greater in some projects than others. The World Bank should, he reasoned, avoid the 'pat air of certainty', and

---

[38] Rothschild (2002: 216). 　　[39] Stiglitz (1992).
[40] Anderson (2000: 13). On neoliberalism as a 'chaotic concept' see Jessop (2013); also King (2009a), Wade (2013), Saad-Filho and Johnston (2005).
[41] Fine (2002, 2009). 　　[42] Hirschman (1981).
[43] Hirschman (1967: 3) cited in Alacevich (2012: 7). 　　[44] Alacevich (2012: 5).
[45] Cited in Bianchi (2011: 9).

instead emphasize the role of uncertainty when designing and supporting projects. In effect, the Bank should explore the full range of possible outcomes (and accept that it could not map all of these out ahead of time). It is strange that some economists consider this approach backward, when there is increasing attention within the natural and physical sciences precisely to these issues. One Nobel laureate, in physics, for example, argues: 'Much of the real world is controlled as much by the tails of distributions as [by] means or averages . . . by the exceptional not the common place; by the catastrophe, not the steady drip . . . we need to free ourselves from "average thinking".'[46]

Hirschman wanted people to 'widen the lens when evaluating projects and look out for those unplanned hard to quantify dividends'.[47] Hirschman's alertness to the incidental benefits arising from projects, as well as to how social and political context informs project outcomes, stood in contrast to the then-emerging framework of cost–benefit analysis.[48] Sadly, his call to avoid a 'pat air of certainty' fell on deaf ears. A corollary of Hirschman's approach was the need to spend time 'in the field' and talk to as many people as possible. This was a trademark of his work that 'took shape in Colombian fields and factories. Getting to know the country meant getting near its people: lots of travel to talk to farmers, local bankers, industrialists, and artisans . . . '[49]

Perhaps because of how he approached economics, Hirschman came up with what is perhaps one of the most emphatic distinctions separating different economists and other development 'experts' from one another. Many, perhaps most, economists believe the secret to economic development lies in endowment, and to what extent a given country meets the necessary preconditions for development. Early in *Development Projects Observed*, Hirschman wrote that his own approach 'stresses the importance for development of what a country does and of what it becomes as a result of what it does, and thereby contests the primacy of what it is, that is, of its geography- and history-determined endowment with natural resources, values, institutions, social and political structure, etc.'.[50]

This rejection of the primacy of endowment is a radical departure from the views held by the various proponents of balanced growth; as well as from influential ideas that geography, climate, or a particular combination of geography and colonial history, determines outcomes.[51] It also runs contrary to the idea that societies have to put in place a particular set of institutions before any meaningful economic or social change can be attempted:

---

[46] Cited in Cherif and Hasanov (2019: 6).   [47] Adelman (2013: loc. 7143).
[48] Little and Mirrlees (1974, 1990); Dasgupta, Sen, and Marglin (1972); Squire and Van der Tak (1975).
[49] Adelman (2013: loc. 5408).   [50] Hirschman (1967: 5).
[51] Perhaps the most influential of the geography plus institutions literature is Acemoglu, Johnson, and Robinson (2001).

The custom was (and remains) to think of institutions as the precursors of projects; good institutions promote healthy ventures, bad ones produce disasters. As one might imagine, this often led to fatalistic thinking about the Third World, where institutions seemed so irrevocably bad . . . Hirschman considered this kind of fundamentalist storytelling . . . unhelpful.[52]

More recent work has confirmed Hirschman's suspicions about institutional pre-conditions. For example, Jaime Ros has examined the widespread institutional reforms implemented in Latin America after 1980, which sought to bring countries closer to the ideals of 'inclusive institutions'—the rule of law, protection of private property rights, democratic politics, market liberalization—favoured by many advisors. Since then, economic performance in Latin America has been *weaker* than it was in the heyday of state-led development between 1950 and 1980 (this is the case even if the 'lost decade' of the 1980s is ignored): the 'relative position of Latin America in the world economy went back in 2003 to the levels of 1900!'[53]

Other economists have shared his rejection of fundamentalist storytelling. An example is Alice Amsden, who emphasized the importance of 'experiment' in what she called 'the rise of the rest'—the convergence in incomes per capita of East and South East Asian economies with those of Organisation for Economic Co-operation and Development (OECD) economies.[54] While new constraints on 'policy space' were, as Amsden suggests, introduced during and since the late 1970s and early 1980s, it is important not to overemphasize the degree to which developing countries have been compelled to do it the 'Second American Empire' way. Despite the heavy hand of conditionality, governments of developing countries have had and still have room for policy manoeuvre (as shown with regard to trade in Chapter 5). Some have more room than others—for geopolitical reasons—while some have taken more effective advantage than others of the scope for experiment.[55] As the late Ethiopian Prime Minister put it:

[W]e determined that we would select what is most suitable for Ethiopia from different countries around the world: the U.S., Germany, China, Korea, wherever. I call it the 'Frank Sinatra' model: 'I did it my way'.[56]

Mechanisms I: Development of Institutions and Capabilities through Tension and Disequilibrium

Pressure, disequilibrium, tension: these, according to Hirschman, were the motors of developmental change and the source of his enduring 'bias for hope'. Much of

---

[52] Adelman (2013: loc. 7020 of 16488).   [53] Ros (2012: 12).   [54] Amsden (2009).
[55] Whitfield (2009); UNECA (2016).   [56] De Waal (2018: 2).

Hirschman's work concerned the mechanisms through which such changes came about; in particular, the idea of forward and backward linkages and the idea of the hiding hand. His notion of development *creating* institutional and other change has been echoed by recent critics of the 'good governance' agenda. For example, as Chang argues: 'Historically, behavioural and institutional structures that are considered to be pro-developmental have emerged and evolved as the consequence, rather than the cause, of economic development.'[57] Another contemporary version of this approach is to argue that markets and institutions 'co-evolve', and that productive activities—at least initially—often develop within institutional contexts that differ dramatically from those imagined in the 'good governance' agenda.[58]

One rapidly expanding industry in Nigeria has emerged in an institutional, social, and policy context far removed from the dream world of good governance, secure property rights, or 'inclusive' institutions: the Nollywood film industry. While some observers have rushed to romanticize a tale of informality and success,[59] there is still far too little known about the industry to make that a convincing account. Nollywood films proliferated in the early 1990s; they were pushed out fast through a network of distributors before producers' profits were wiped out by rampant piracy.[60] A macroeconomic stabilization programme had led to a sharp devaluation of the Naira that, combined with lack of enforcement of intellectual property rights laws and widespread physical insecurity (which meant the abandonment and disrepair of cinemas), created a domestic market opportunity for supplying entertainment to people's homes.[61] What evolved was a form of unplanned import substitution industrialization. Nigeria was 'unfit'—in Hirschman's term—for any such development, and was 'an unlikely locale for the development of a video film industry'.[62] Constraints included: 'informal distribution and marketing networks, extensive piracy, poor production quality, lack of production, distribution, and exhibition infrastructure, lack of film studios, insufficient funding sources and venture capital, inadequate skills and training, industry fragmentation, and a lack of data necessary for planning and industry decision making'.[63] As the Nollywood industry consolidated, attracting more finance and catching the eye of diaspora Nigerians, there were increasingly loud calls for the federal government to clamp down on piracy and enforce intellectual property rights. From 2013/14, Nollywood was included in the new (and rebased) national accounts, which made clear the film industry was a substantial contributor to national income. The state did eventually get more involved, but inconsistently and with only partial effects. There has continued to be a struggle between different interests within the industry (powerful financiers/distributors, pirates,

---

[57] Chang (2006).   [58] Ang (2016).   [59] Ang (2016: 232–7).   [60] Arewa (2012).
[61] Igwe (2018: 37).   [62] Arewa (2012: 13).   [63] Ibid.

producers, etc.), and what appears to be an increasing differentiation of the market as parts of it are subjected to 'gentrification'.[64]

What Hirschman identified as the core constraint—developmental decision-making capability—mirrors the more recent focus on productive capabilities by economists who take economic history and the history of economic thought seriously.[65] Hirschman's notion of how such capabilities develop has much in common with thinking about increasing returns—what in Kaldor's growth laws, for example, features as 'learning by doing':

> It could be argued that a country without much experience in solving techno-logical problems should stay away from projects requiring a large capability in this regard. But the opposite course can also be defended: how will the country ever learn about technology if it does not tackle technologically complex and problem-rich tasks? In this reasoning a certain 'unfitness' of the project for a country becomes an additional and strong argument for undertaking it; for the project, if it is successful, will be valuable not only because of its physical output but even more because of the social and human changes it will have wrought.[66]

Mechanism II: The Principle of the Hiding Hand

It is worth stressing how different Hirschman's approach is from the standard advice to match state interventions to current capacity.[67] Nowhere can this be more clearly seen than in his principle of the 'hiding hand'. The conventional view is that 'developing countries ought to stay away from bites bigger than they can chew'.[68] Flyvbjerg is an influential critic of big bites or so-called 'mega-projects', arguing that they are 'over budget, over time, over and over', and that they have regressive distributional effects to boot.[69] This critique argues that planning officials are misled into a 'planning fallacy' whereby they are systematically over-optimistic about costs, benefits, and timing, to the extent that it is 'difficult to disentangle deception from delusion'.[70] The planning fallacy appears to out-weigh the hiding hand in Flyvbjerg's statistical analysis of 2,000 development projects.

However, Flyvbjerg commits the very errors Hirschman sought to escape: his analysis favours 'the pat air of certainty', overlooking the full range of possible

---

[64] Igwe (2018).   [65] Cimoli, Dosi, and Stiglitz (2009); Best (2018).
[66] Hirschman (1967: 129).
[67] This was, for example, the main argument of the World Development Report 1997 (World Bank, 1997).
[68] Flyvbjerg and Ansar (2014): https://www.theguardian.com/sustainable-business/hydroelectric-dams-emerging-economies-oxford-research.
[69] Flyvbjerg (2014).   [70] Flyvbjerg (2016).

project outcomes. Instead, he treats projects as standalone, discrete 'interventions', the costs and benefits of which are estimated beforehand and accurately recorded upon completion, all within a self-contained model that is 'independent of any wider development calculus'.[71] In doing so, the analysis has no room for full project life-cycle outcomes or unintended consequences.

There is plenty to be wary of in Hirschman's *Development Projects Observed*: the sample of projects was very limited; there was not much probing of the role of governments; and it failed to provide the 'operational' tool that the World Bank officials who commissioned the work had hoped for. However, the essential insights of the book remain valuable. In contrast to Flyvbjerg's testing of an extremely restricted (mis)understanding of the hiding hand idea against a dataset of exclusively infrastructural projects, another statistical analysis by Ika sampled 161 projects across a range of sectors. Ika's findings were very different, with, for example, the hiding hand more common than the planning fallacy by a factor of four to one.[72] Examples within Ika's study included the World Bank-funded Ouagadougou Water Supply project in Burkina Faso. Despite suffering from cost overruns of about $60 million, the project exceeded expectations, connecting more than 90 per cent of the city's population to the water supply. A project that might appear superficially more successful was the Chad–Cameroon oil pipeline, which came in ahead of schedule and without huge expenses. However, rather than supporting poverty reduction, the revenues it has generated have largely been funnelled into arms purchases and private accounts.

Tanganyika's Infamous Groundnut Scheme

A 'possibilist' approach rejects any systematic pessimism about mega-projects. Instead, it looks for unpredicted and less well-measured side effects, as well as the scope for creative decision-making and the accelerated development of capabilities. Such an approach reveals there were, in fact, important and (to varying degrees) lasting social and economic effects that are absent from accounts of one of the most renowned development failures of all: the groundnut scheme in colonial Tanganyika. Driven by the UK's desperate need to reduce shortages and import costs of vegetable oils in the wake of the sudden US announcement—after the Second World War—that it was ending financial support to its allies, the project expressed 'a faith (or fantasy) that the scheme would generate a great leap forward of the productive forces in the area's agriculture'.[73] It failed, spectacularly, due to a host of misconceptions and errors:

> What happened in practice was, first, that the targets of the scheme were reduced year after year while, second, its cost was progressively adjusted upwards. When

[71] Room (2018: 368).   [72] Ika (2018).   [73] Rizzo (2006: 236).

it was finally shut down in 1951, over £36 million of British public money had been spent on a scheme that imported more groundnuts as seed than it actually harvested.[74]

Nevertheless, the groundnut scheme had multiple side effects, with very real local consequences in Tanganyika's Southern Province:

> The money it brought into circulation through wages and other expenditure— vast sums of money relative to conditions before the scheme—augmented the spending power and welfare of many local people, at least for a few years. For some, however, the scheme marked the beginning of a process of capital accumulation that lasted well beyond 'those days of great prosperity'.[75]

There was also a learning externality that affected a proposed railway linking East African and Rhodesian networks. Reacting directly to the failures of the groundnut scheme, consultants and planners for the railway shifted their focus away from export orientation towards African agricultural potential and welfare outcomes.[76] Though the railway itself was not built in the colonial era, it was eventually revised and built by China as the TAZARA Railway.

The TAZARA Railway as the Connective Tissue of a Rural Economy

The Tanzania-Zambia Railway Authority (TAZARA) Railway is itself a good example of how the more obvious forms of project evaluation can miss socio-economic dynamics. The railway was a profoundly political undertaking: in the late 1960s, the governments of recently independent Zambia and Tanzania wanted to build a railway connecting Zambia's Copperbelt with the port of Dar es Salaam, reducing Zambia's dependence on transport routes through what was then Rhodesia. The World Bank would not finance it, nor would the USA, the UK, Japan, or the Soviet Union. Finally, with China having agreed to finance and lead construction of the railway, the project began in 1969 and was completed—two years ahead of schedule—in 1975. Internationally, the railway was dismissed as the 'bamboo railway' and, in a number of ways, it did fail: engines and wagons frequently broke down; transhipment and offloading at key points in Tanzania and Zambia were slow; and cargo and passenger traffic were far below planned levels. There were intermittent programmes to resuscitate the railway,[77] the latest of which was a large-scale commitment, again by China, to support a TAZARA rehabilitation scheme to the tune of some $1.2 billion.[78]

---

[74] Rizzo (2006: 208).   [75] Rizzo (2006: 236).   [76] Bourbonniere (2013).

[77] Briggs (1992), Monson (2005).

[78] https://constructionreviewonline.com/2019/04/refurbishment-of-tazara-railway-line-to-receive-us-1-2bn-boost/.

Despite the headline disappointments of the railway, however, it has transformed lives along its route: 'local traders, farmers, and workers use the railway in many ways to improve their lives, and an analysis of these railway-platform markets suggests that the standard assessments overlook something real and important'.[79] The railway has made it possible for farmers to switch to the cultivation of higher-value crops, and made it easier for them to market their surpluses. Itinerant traders—*wamachinga*—help move products between the different agro-ecological zones along the railway's route, fostering an expansion of market size and refinement of specialization. They also bring important basic consumer goods—plastic buckets, used clothing, aluminium cooking pots—to remote rural villages. Casual and temporary wage workers, as well as those laid off during the privatization of the Kilombero Sugar Company, have used the railway to travel further when they cannot get access to land near the sugarcane company and its existing outgrower scheme area. The railway is, in short, the 'connective tissue' of a complex and dynamic rural economy.

Cahora Bassa: Dammed if You Do, Damned if You Don't

A possibilist perspective would also challenge critiques of Cahora Bassa Dam in Mozambique. Opposed to the naively optimistic 'high modernism' of the Portuguese colonial planners—and then the post-independence Frelimo government—Isaacman and Isaacman swing to the opposite, consistently pessimistic, extreme. While they do describe ecological changes and the experience of the people who most obviously lost out from the dam's construction,[80] they fail to capture the complex dynamics linked to its history.

Cahora Bassa was conceived at a challenging regional and international political moment, and one way the Portuguese succeeded in getting the project financed and built, towards the very end of their colonial rule, was to do a deal with the apartheid regime in South Africa. This involved selling electricity from the dam to Eskom, the South African electricity utility, at desperately low prices for decades to come. In 2018, Frelimo negotiated a 46 per cent increase in the price paid by South Africa for Cahora Bassa electricity (though this still left it below market rates).[81] While Mozambique's hydro-sovereignty was clipped for many years, exporting energy was nonetheless one way of mitigating the foreign exchange constraint. Further indirect effects, for example through employment in agriculture and the development of hydrologically related engineering and management capabilities later applied to other dam plans in Mozambique, are less well researched and are neglected in the Isaacmans' account. Others argue that 'electricity provision in Mozambique plays an important role in statecraft

---

[79] Monson (2005: 1).   [80] Isaacman and Isaacman (2013).
[81] https://mozambiqueminingpost.com/2018/08/31/mozambique-energy-hcb-announces-power-tariff-increase-for-eskom-verdade/.

and provides accumulation opportunities for governing elites'.[82] A hydraulic bureaucracy has indeed developed in Mozambique, sustaining a commitment to projects geared towards reducing economic dependence on South Africa, while increasing (especially southern Mozambican) agricultural productivity.[83]

As Hirschman put it, the hiding hand is a way of 'inducing action through error'.[84] It is a corollary of Keynes' argument that the rational investor, given fundamental uncertainty, would never invest.[85] The hiding hand involves under-estimating both the likely difficulties of setting up and running a project and the problem-solving abilities of those implementing it. Planners, having been over-optimistic prior to embarking on a big new infrastructure project—say, the Grand Ethiopian Renaissance Dam (GERD) or the Hoosac Tunnel in the USA—swiftly run into an array of difficulties and obstacles they had not anticipated. However, having committed considerable resources—and having used many rhetorical devices—to mobilize public support, it is difficult to back out. A crisis in the project may then provoke fresh and creative capabilities—technical, financial, and even political—in order to find solutions. In *Development Projects Observed*, Hirschman suggested that 'the only way in which we can bring our creative resources fully into play is by misjudging the nature of the task, by presenting it to ourselves as more routine, simple, undemanding of genuine creativity than it will turn out to be'.[86]

The Grand Ethiopian Renaissance Dam

The GERD is a particularly good example. The audacious idea of building a 5,250-megawatt hydroelectricity-generating dam on the Nile was, it appeared to many from the start, wildly overambitious. The plan seemed especially ill-conceived because the government could not secure World Bank or Chinese concessional funding, partly because of the very real risk of a political, even military, backlash from Egypt, which has always asserted 'hydro-hegemony' over the Nile.[87] The Ethiopian government then had to find alternative sources of finance for the dam—almost $5 billion was the original estimate—a major challenge for a low-income country. Over-optimism, overcommitment, and the identification of this project as the brainchild of Prime Minister Meles Zenawi meant there was no way out. The government then did manage to find *new* ways of solving the financial problem, partially at least, while also making more progress than many outside observers had thought possible to finesse the diplomatic problem. The financing measures they were forced to adopt could be described as 'fiscal linkages'; they included a new deferred savings scheme imposed on public sector employees; the

[82] Power and Kirshner (2019: 500).   [83] Rusca et al. (2018).   [84] Hirschman (1967: 29).
[85] On the psychology of investment see Keynes (1936: 147–64) and Tuckett (2011).
[86] Hirschman (1967: 13). On the Hoosac Tunnel in the USA see Ika (2018: 370).
[87] Cascão (2008).

creation of a diaspora bond whose marketing and results may have had complex social and political effects on the relationship between many diasporic Ethiopians (e.g. in the USA) and the Ethiopian government; and donations to the dam that many foreign investors were invited to make.

The GERD has—as Flyvbjerg and others predicted—suffered delays, thanks to political-technical difficulties and resource shortages. It remained unclear when, and for some even whether, the dam would be completed. The chief engineer was found shot dead in his car in Meskel Square in the heart of Addis Ababa. The military enterprise Metals and Engineering Corporation (METEC) lost its contract for much of the construction. The GERD is a good reminder that it would be naive to assume the mechanisms Hirschman identified work out automatically for the best. He argued, for example, that reducing one form of uncertainty could create new and worse uncertainty in other ways:

'a decrease in financial uncertainty may stimulate administrative uncertainty as the securely financed project becomes more attractive to parasitic appetites and is under less pressure to put up a good performance . . . The attempt to eliminate totally one particular kind of uncertainty may therefore not only be futile, but counterproductive.'[88]

During the course of construction of the GERD, financial uncertainty has never been wiped out, while 'administrative uncertainty' appears to have survived and it does seem the case that 'parasitic appetites' have nibbled at the project.[89] But parasitic appetites have not *overwhelmed* the project, in the way that they have in many abandoned dam projects in Nigeria (for example, the failed Chinese-backed Zamfara Hydropower Dam).[90]

It is far too soon, at the time of writing, to write off the GERD, which, despite cost and time overruns, may yet provide a huge boost to an economy that remains sorely constrained by unreliable power supplies. Partly because of security and political concerns, no research at all has been done and very little is known, beyond the anecdotal, about the possibly manifold 'side effects' that this giant construction project has had: we can only guess at the 'human and social changes' that it has wrought, from the many services and construction activities and input supplies spawned by a large-scale construction camp, to the possible spill-over effects (for example, on child nutrition or girls' schooling) in the distant village homes of the 8,000 or so migrant Ethiopian workers on the dam, to which they doubtless send some of their wages. Very little is known either about the development of Ethiopian decision-making capabilities either in engineering or in the

---

[88] Hirschman (1967: 84).   [89] Hirschman (1967: 52–5).
[90] Olorunfemi and Onwuemele (2017).

management of local conflicts over displacement and resettlement or about financial and fiscal capability development.

Mechanism III: Linkages

The better known of Hirschman's unbalanced growth mechanisms is linkages. A backward linkage occurs when a new activity makes viable or stimulates upstream activities that feed into it by supplying inputs. A forward linkage occurs when new activities emerge downstream as a result of a factory or facility coming into operation, with its output used to produce other goods. Take, for example, Bell Equipment in South Africa. The firm began as a backward linkage, responding to growing output from the agriculture and forestry sectors by investing in equipment-making for sugarcane and timber cutting. Bell then developed the capabilities to produce inputs for other, *non-agricultural* activities, and grew to become a major supplier of large earth-moving equipment for the global mining industry.[91]

Linkages spread beyond forward and backward to include employment, fiscal, and spatial linkages. Linkages, though, are not mechanistic or automatic, and are only likely to flourish where supported by government policies. There is scope, for example, for fiscal linkages from resource extraction to generate revenue that makes possible the funding of improved infrastructure, research and development (R&D) investment, education, and health. However, such linkages can only function if domestic conflicts over 'the politics of the belly'—in which power struggles are largely concerned with access to wealth—can be settled.[92] The International Monetary Fund (IMF) now advocates greater exploitation of fiscal linkages related to natural resource exploitation in, for example, Zambia. Elsewhere, many political economists agree that in Nigeria, Uganda, Zimbabwe, and Tanzania, the introduction of effective policies to monitor and regulate (let alone maximize) resource revenues has been delayed for decades.[93] One estimate suggests African governments tax only about 3 per cent of the value of mining output.[94]

Backward linkages may not be maximized unless a government insists on local content policies—that is, a commitment to source local inputs—in foreign investment project bids. Another possibility is to insist on R&D spending in-country. In Brazil, for example, impressive innovations followed the introduction of a

---

[91] Jourdan et al. (2012: 57).   [92] Bayart (1993), Clapham (1994).

[93] See http://www.mining.com/imf-favour-zambia-mining-tax-changes/ on Zambia's proposed tax hikes on copper mining in 2015, for example; Doro and Kufakurinani (2018); Hundsbæk Pedersen, and Bofin (2019).

[94] Extractive Industries Transparency Initiative (EITI): https://eiti.org/summary-data, cited in Moore, Prichard, and Fjeldstad (2018: 92).

contractual clause forcing oil companies to invest 1 per cent of gross revenues from large oilfields into R&D.[95] There are, though, also plenty of counter-examples, where inept policies have undermined linkage development. The neglect of R&D in South Africa's Chamber of Mines Research Organization (COMRO) and Zimbabwe's Institute of Mining Research, for instance, means that any development of the platinum seams in South Africa's Bushveld and Zimbabwe's Great Dyke will be pursued with imported rather than domestically produced equipment and machinery.

Opportunities for forward linkage promotion in South Africa were missed because the government prioritized fundamentalist market liberalization policies:

> An example would be Anglo American's divestment from its main platinum group metals downstream beneficiator and technology developer, Johnson Matthey Plc in the 1990s (when it was the major shareholder, at more than 40%), after investing heavily in it, especially in technology development, over the previous 40 years. This was probably due to its increasing focus on 'core competence' (mining) in preparation for its exit and London listing.[96]

Another example of weak or failing linkages can be seen in the 'destructive restructuring' of Scaw South Africa, a steel and engineering firm that, since the 1960s, had built up a range of sophisticated capabilities through linkages to mining, transport infrastructure, and construction. After 2007, however, the Anglo-American asset-striping strategy involved raising loans against Scaw's balance sheet, securing loan proceeds for the parent company, leaving Scaw to service the debt, before finally 'unbundling' and disposing of Scaw. Another factor that weakened Scaw's linkage momentum was the decline in domestic infrastructure investment after 2010.[97] More broadly, it has been argued that a lack of strategy to develop linkages and a broader manufacturing base, alongside trade liberalization, low public investment, an uncritical embrace of foreign ownership, and offshore listings by the major South African corporations 'contributed to a process of destructive restructuring and unbundling of engineering and the subordination of steel to the global strategies of new foreign owners'.[98]

The intricate dance of forward and backward linkages is well illustrated by the relationship between the floriculture sector and Ethiopian Airlines. Having a well-run, state-owned airline made it much more feasible for the government to promote expansion of the country's floriculture sector, based on favourable agro-climatic conditions and relative proximity to major European markets. It meant the government could fairly easily push for improvements in freight handling and airport cold storage, as well as offer competitive services to new

---

[95] Mancini and Paz (2018: 141).   [96] Jourdan et al. (2012: 61).   [97] Zalk (2017: 292–303).
[98] Zalk (2017: 318).

investors (Ethiopian and foreign). The rapid expansion and then consolidation of floriculture in turn provoked expansion and improvements in Ethiopian Airlines. The just-in-time demands of global floriculture meant the airline had to be able to provide higher-quality services, with its evolving capabilities in handling flower exports then giving it a base to develop larger logistics services for other activities in the economy.[99] Similarly, it was the severe balance of payments constraint that resulted from Ethiopia's unbalanced growth, as well as the big push of subsidized investments in new industrial parks and the construction of a new railway linking Addis Ababa with Djibouti's port, that revealed severe logistical bottlenecks, which in turn provoked massive new projects to overcome them. These included a £150 million World Bank-financed investment to improve trade logistics, particularly in the Modjo dry port.[100]

'Unfitness' and 'Exercises in Courage': Large-Scale Projects in Ethiopia and South Africa

Development through linkages, economic change propelled by disequilibria, and the hiding hand are all mechanisms that may operate in a variety of contexts. How effective they are, though, depends on a number of factors, the most important of which are policy related and political. We close this chapter with two very different examples—one from Ethiopia and one from South Africa—that highlight these and related Hirschmanian themes, including the 'narrow margin for failure' that is yet another possible influence on investment and project outcomes.

Ethiopian Airlines
Ethiopian Airlines is itself is a good case of 'unfitness'. Common-sense thinking and the vast majority of development economists would *not* recommend that one of the poorest countries in the world support a state-owned airline.[101] Ethiopian Airlines was inaugurated as a small domestic airline shortly after the end of the Second World War, at a time when 96 per cent of the population were illiterate. The British had just ended Italian occupation, reinstalled Haile Selassie, and plundered much of Ethiopia's manufacturing equipment, shifting it to their colonies elsewhere.[102] Over the following seventy years or so, the airline grew to be a 'fully integrated, technologically sophisticated, internationally competitive, and highly profitable 21st century aviation company'.[103] Ethiopian Airlines is the largest carrier in Africa and its growth in recent years—including a fourfold

---

[99] Balchin, Booth, and te Velde (2019, 15–18).
[100] http://projects.worldbank.org/P156590?lang=en.
[101] For a witty but offensively racist account of the state of Ethiopian transport not so long before the founding of Ethiopian Airlines see Waugh (2010).
[102] Pankhurst (1996); Wrong (2005).   [103] Oqubay and Tesfachew (2019).

increase in passenger traffic between 2010 and 2018 (up to 12 million in 2018)—is in marked contrast with the decline of (and allegations of corruption in) South African Airways (SAA) and in Nigeria Air.[104] All manner of capabilities have developed along the way, from the maintenance and technical facility to the Aviation Academy serving Ethiopian, African, and Middle Eastern airline companies, to the freight terminal and integrated airline catering facilities. While several other state-owned Ethiopian enterprises have floundered, there has been consistent support for Ethiopian Airlines as a 'national champion'. This has allowed the airline's management to weather periods of instability and resist intermittent interference from the government of the day.[105] Localization 'has been enforced by restrictive regulations governing foreign investment. These stipulate that only the Ethiopian government can provide air transport services on aircrafts with a capacity of more than 50 passengers, while only Ethiopian citizens can provide such services on aircrafts with lower capacity'.[106]

Both Ethiopian Airlines and the promotion of an Ethiopian floriculture sector—with substantial support from the Ethiopian and also Dutch states—highlight another Hirschman observation: that one of the determinants of whether economic endeavours in developing countries are successful or not is whether they have a 'narrow margin for failure'. This is something that very much characterizes the floriculture business: rose stems snipped and packed, for example, on a farm on the outskirts of Bishoftu need to be kept in precise temperature and humidity conditions while being transported (within a day) to European markets. Should they spoil, the financial costs would be huge. To get this right it has been necessary to: adapt techniques from 'role model' firms and sectors in the Netherlands and Kenya; mobilize the resources of Ethiopian Airlines; sharply improve the efficiency of the Ethiopian Investment Commission (EIC); and deploy the state's monopoly of legitimate force (every truckload of roses travelling from a flower farm to the airport cold storage depot is accompanied by a state-employed armed guard). The development of Ethiopia's flower sector has been propelled by bottlenecks, crises, and disequilibria, rather than by a fully planned and balanced growth package of across-the-board investments.

Sasol

Hands visible, hiding, throttling, and doubtless others, have long been at play moulding the history of Sasol, a formerly state-owned chemicals enterprise in South Africa that was privatized in the late 1970s, though it has since continued to benefit from state support. Sasol's history is full of ambitious leaps, political

---

[104] See, e.g., Cotterill (2018); Ifeanyi (2016). For trends in international capacity within Africa see https://www.anna.aero/2019/10/24/africa-has-1140-international-flights-within-the-continent-daily-ethiopian-is-1/.
[105] Oqubay and Taffere (2019).   [106] Balchin, Booth, and te Velde (2019: 16).

intrigue, imaginative leadership, 'privatization by panic', and technical linkages.[107] Despite there being nothing remotely balanced about its development, the company has somehow 'survived the obsolescence many critics predicted'. In the early years of Sasol's existence, the company's management felt badly let down by the technical inputs of an American management consultancy firm. The consultants responded by highlighting the uncertainty of the project and arguing they were 'groping with the unknowns of a developmental project'.[108]

Taking on a large-scale synthetic fuel production (oil-from-coal) scheme, in a country that had a shortage of skilled labour, was an 'exercise in courage'. Like Ethiopian Airlines, Sasol reacted to the pressure of a domestic skills bottleneck by setting up its own technical training college.[109] Formally created in 1950, the firm perpetually teetered on the brink of technical catastrophe and economic non-viability. However, its strategic significance became increasingly clear to the apartheid government, even as labour costs rose in the 1970s. The company only survived the technical problems it struggled with during the 1950s through direct state financial support, as well as the very low cost of labour that made the scheme viable in South Africa. The paradox is that while South Africa has created an important chemicals industry as a result of Sasol's creation and expansion (and it is difficult 'to imagine this as taking off historically without massive state intervention'), Sasol has *not* been the crucible of a diversified national chemicals industry.[110]

Through its early years Sasol developed technical and organizational capabilities that, in the 1960s, enabled it to push aggressively for diversification. One forward linkage was realizing the economic potential of methane generated in the oil-from-coal process, using a subsidiary that distributed this gas to industries through high-pressure pipelines. In fact, it became clear that the chemicals produced in the oil-from-gas process were actually *more* valuable than the petrol produced. Linkages fanned out backwards to mining; forwards to explosives, fertilizer, and polymers. Two oil price hikes in the 1970s, as well as increasing international hostility to—and sanctions against—apartheid, meant that Sasol's oil-from-gas capabilities suddenly seemed to make some economic sense. However, the costs of new plants played into the hands of those keen to seek private finance. Once privatized at an undervalued price, the new-look Sasol continued to benefit from considerable state support through tariffs and price regulations. This helped line the pockets of the previous management, though this was by no means an unusual example of the effects of privatizing state-owned enterprises in the 1980s.[111]

Sasol's history is a complex one, of rapid technical capability development, state support, and both the development and thwarting of linkages. The absence of

---

[107] Sparks (2016).   [108] Sparks (2012: 57).   [109] Sparks (2012).
[110] Freund (2019: 121).   [111] Meek (2014).

forward linkages is particularly striking in South Africa, where the plastic industry has effectively been prevented from taking advantage of low-cost polypropylene feedstock. Linkages have been thwarted in Mozambique too, where Sasol engaged in a project to extract and pipe natural gas to South Africa. It was Mozambique's first big natural resource project and the evidence suggests that the country was badly disadvantaged by the deal (undermining fiscal linkages). Furthermore, the potential of cheap natural gas to help promote social welfare benefits and industrialization linkages within Mozambique and Southern Africa was not realized. Instead, Sasol derived huge profits from buying natural Mozambican gas very cheaply and selling to industries in South Africa at high prices.[112]

6.4 Conclusion: Exit Balance

Balance, as an organizing principle, runs through much thinking on economic development, both from orthodox and more heterodox viewpoints. Balance is fetishized above growth and development in IMF advice; is the defining feature of neoclassical economic theory and modelling; and is the anxious concern of UNCTAD advice to governments pushing for mutually supportive changes across a huge range of sectoral and institutional activities.

We have argued that policy officials should reject this obsession with balance— it creates unrealistic expectations, is analytically misleading, and can throw development strategies off course. By contrast, we have argued for greater commitment among policy officials to a strategy of unbalanced growth, using this as a jumping-off point to explore the relevance of Hirschman's economics. Hirschman is often regarded as a maverick, not to be taken too seriously by the new generation of economists, trained as they are to jump through the hoops of econometric and mathematical techniques. While mainstream economics has dallied with some of his ideas (most notably those in his book *Exit, Voice, and Loyalty*), it has largely ignored or mangled his insights. On the other side of the coin, his ideas do not fit easily within debates about grand '-isms' (neoliberalism, imperialism) and so have never found a secure place in the work of heterodox economists.[113] We argue that many of Hirschman's ideas, as well as his methodological approach, should be central to development economics. Hirschman's methods—immersing himself in the particular and drawing general principles from close empirical observation— draw him close to Kalecki, who spent many years collecting detailed information on factories and businesses, and to Amsden. His understanding of uncertainty puts him firmly in the Keynesian tradition, while his ideas about linkages connect with the economics of Adam Smith, Allyn Young, Kaldor, and many others.

---

[112] Mondliwa and Roberts (2017).   [113] Grabel (2017).

Hirschman's observations regarding the hiding hand have more recently been taken up by others, both in work on 'adaptive efficiency' and in larger sample tests of Hirschman's claims.[114]

One of the most useful ways for policy officials to draw on Hirschman's ideas is to see in unbalanced growth a justification for a bolder selection of priorities. Bland wish lists—in government reports, consultancy advice, and international development agency strategies—are the enemies of economic development. Ideas about linkages and where they may be most concentrated, or ideas about the conditions in which large projects may or may not provoke adaptive learning, can potentially provide criteria for ranking policy support initiatives or targets for interventions. But effective interventions will require much better mechanisms to identify and respond to *failures* in economic policy.

Hirschman's 'narrow margin for failure' is not just a function of technology. The margin for failure can be a political matter and it is often reflected in urgency. China in the 1970s, for example, was keen to complete the TAZARA Railway ahead of schedule as much to make a geopolitical statement as for financial reasons. The British government, in a rush to fix its post-war foreign exchange shortage, pressed on with the Tanganyika groundnut scheme. And arguably the GERD, and the speedy push to create a floriculture industry, were given added propulsion by former Prime Minister Meles Zenawi's explicit tying of political legitimacy to delivering development gains.[115] It has been argued that the ruling Ethiopian People's Revolutionary Democratic Front (EPRDF) had, after the challenge of the 2005 election results, an even more urgent 'need to seek "performance legitimacy" through a project of economic transformation'.[116] Such is the political economy of being in a rush.

The pressure of time—contrary to the logic of gradual continuity, smooth adjustment, and balance—is another form of disequilibrium or tension that may, in a Hirschman-like way, provoke change. This can be seen in the rhetoric of development policy, from Samora Machel's exhortation to Mozambicans to achieve 'victory over underdevelopment in ten years'[117] to plans for Ethiopia to become a middle-income country by 2025. 'Rushing' has the potential to further conceal the hiding hand, increasing optimism about what can be achieved, and it may, through political urgency, create a form of narrow margin for failure. Conversely, pushing at full tilt may encourage people to overlook problems that come to undermine outcomes, or may lead to a failure to exploit gains that otherwise might have been available. Rushing may reveal, not a hiding hand, but a throttling hand. In the construction of the TAZARA Railway, there was very little training to build up Tanzanian or Zambian capabilities, which might have helped later in addressing issues related to repair work on engine and wagon

---

[114] Giezen, Bertolini, and Salet (2015); Ika (2018).   [115] De Waal (2013).
[116] Clapham (2018: 1154).   [117] Hanlon and Mosse (2010: 3).

faults. Furthermore, the hiding hand of post-war urgency in the UK was no match for problems such as erratic rainfall, inadequate soil analysis, the blight of disease, or the failure to manage labour shortages in Tanganyika.[118]

In the global floriculture air freight business, and increasingly in the textiles value chain —where styles and demand shift suddenly—profitability and competition enforce the narrow margin for failure. Even here, however, the conditions of profitability depend in turn on the political and regulatory conditions within which firms operate. A good example of the consequences of a rush (to privatization) and the collapse of regulatory institutions can be seen in the failure of South Africa to meet phyto-sanitary standards regarding citrus fruits, thereby preventing it from expanding its share of the world market.[119] Successful exporting depends on the presence and behaviour of the regulatory 'referees'. Regulatory failures can have disastrous consequences for exports in more industrialized economies too, as the collapse in exports of the Boeing 737 Max shows.[120]

---

[118] Rizzo (2006: 201).   [119] Cramer and Sender (2015).
[120] Lewis (2019); Bogaisky (2019); Travis (2019).

PART III
LABOUR, POVERTY, AND AGRICULTURAL PRODUCTIVITY

7

Wage Employment in Africa

7.1 Introduction: Sweet Dreams of Self-Employment and Nightmares of Dangerous Youth

Population and labour force data in Africa are astonishingly unreliable. But most economists and policymakers do not regard this as an obstacle to making authoritative pronouncements and dreaming up policies. They readily make use of the officially published estimates and projections to argue that there are far too few employment opportunities, especially for the surge in young rural entrants into African labour markets. This argument is made both by mainstream economists and by their most vociferous critics; these critics share with mainstream economists a pessimistic assessment of the potential for a faster rate of growth of paid—waged and salaried—employment.

The prospects for decently remunerated wage employment in productive enterprises are believed to be especially bleak. It is taken for granted that, for the foreseeable future, a proletariat is unlikely to emerge or to play a significant political or economic role. For mainstream economists there is some hope of new jobs *if* labour market flexibility can be maximized and public sector employment slashed; their critics hope to ameliorate the situation for new entrants by promoting and subsidizing cooperatives producing for the domestic mass market. Both sets of development experts place a great deal of faith in associations of the self-employed, and in supply-side skills enhancement for income-generation schemes.

Many economists now also believe that Africa is suffering from early onset deindustrialization (see Chapters 3 and 4), so most youth will have to remain *self-employed* or *unpaid family workers* in relatively low-productivity enterprises for decades. Young people will not find jobs in the higher-productivity manufacturing sector but will continue to flood into the service sector, much of which is characterized by very low productivity. Policies to increase the returns to self-employment in the service sector and/or on small-scale family farms are widely recommended, usually concentrating on supply-side policy interventions to provide new young entrants with training, extension advice, and micro-credit. But these policies involve a leap of faith, assuming that an increased supply of better-qualified micro-entrepreneurs and job-seekers will benefit from a quasi-magical automatic market mechanism ensuring that there will be sufficient demand to

African Economic Development: Evidence, Theory, Policy. Christopher Cramer, John Sender, and Arkebe Oqubay, Oxford University Press (2020). © Christopher Cramer, John Sender, and Arkebe Oqubay.
DOI: 10.1093/oso/9780198832331.001.0001

allow them to succeed. This leap of faith, involving yet another attempt to resuscitate Say's Law, has been diagnosed as 'jobs dementia'.[1]

At the end of this chapter, in Section 7.10 we develop our own arguments and policy suggestions, which are very different in both tone and content. They are less pessimistic about the possibility of increases in waged employment and they highlight the need and scope for large-scale investments in those specific economic activities most likely to generate rapid increases in demand for wage labour.

Recommendations to increase expenditure on training and micro-credit are a knee-jerk response to political leaders' fears that rural youth will flood into cities on the off-chance of finding a job, become disillusioned, and riot. Some anticipate a rural–urban flow more frightening than a flood, for example a *tsunami* or a haemorrhaging.[2] Many African elites seem to believe that potentially dangerous young people need to be trained (brainwashed) to accept individual responsibility for their own economic survival rather than depend on state handouts or, worse still, claim that the scarcity of decent jobs has been caused by the theft of state resources or misguided macroeconomic policies. The Mozambican youth who participated in the *greves* (strikes and demonstrations) of February 2008 and September 2010 were described by ministers as vandals and bandits. In response to these ministerial rebukes the youth became 'outspoken in their contempt for the current ruling elite' clustered around President Guebuza; rap musicians 'openly satirised the Frelimo elite as corrupt and out of touch', while rejecting government claims that falls in real wages were caused by adverse international prices, rather than ministerial ineptitude.[3]

The training proposed by African governments has sometimes focused directly on political views.[4] More often it aims to transform the 'aspirations' and 'values' of young people, who would otherwise be 'using substances like khat, marijuana, tobacco, and alcohol and watching football to pass the time'.[5] The laziness of youth has been disparaged in speeches by, for example, Presidents Buhari, Mogae,

---

[1] Amsden (2010: 58; 2012). Keynes believed that Say's Law, the hugely influential idea that supply creates its own demand, was 'the chief postulate he had to escape in writing the *General Theory*' (Kent, 2005: 62).

[2] Meagher (2016: 484); Meagher, Manna, and Bolt (2016: 474).

[3] Hossain et al (2014: 41). (See Azagaia lyrics in Portuguese at https://www.vagalume.com.br/azagaia/povo-no-poder.html). 'His Excellency the Ghetto President' of Uganda has been less explicit when rapping about Museveni: https://www.france24.com/en/20190725-uganda-opposition-figure-former-pop-star-bobi-wine-2021-presidential-election.

[4] Yibeltal (2017).

[5] The unrealistic aspirations of youth in developing countries are stressed in OECD (2018: 27ff.). The quote on substance abuse is from Desta, Bitga, and Boyson (2018: 41). Purdeková (2011) describes the camps established to transform the 'mindset' of youth, urban hawkers, and 'social deviants' in Rwanda. Efforts to transform the values of the unemployed are, of course, not confined to Africa: 'the personal belief systems' of individuals are the main target of training offered to groups of unemployed in Texas, who are promised 'empowerment' by 'retraining the brain', through a critique of the self rather than a critique of the economy (Thomas, 2018).

Museveni, and Zuma.[6] Similar prejudices were expressed by Africa's colonial rulers in the late 1940s: they too accused everyone without a recognized form of wage employment of not 'having a culture amenable to work';[7] these rulers justified brutal interventions because 'recalcitrance, resistance, and unwillingness to cooperate were . . . natural attitudes of lazy or uncivilized "Blacks" who had to be coerced for their own good'.[8]

African labour force and employment statistics have often been collected, classified, and analysed so as to reinforce prevailing conventional wisdoms or prejudices: these include politically convenient stories designed to pillory idle youth for having unrealistic expectations, and tales that blame a small number of 'privileged' (unionized 'core') wage workers for crowding out the possibility of faster employment growth for 'peripheral' workers—by pushing wages too high while selfishly opposing the eminently sensible recommendations of mainstream economists to reduce labour market regulation and inflexibility.[9] We aim to expose the weak underbelly of hegemonic ideas about labour market flexibility and self-employment, as well as to strengthen the neglected case for radical transformation of statistical authorities in Africa—so we devote substantial space in this chapter to discussion of the quality of officially published labour force data. We argue that the available evidence does *not* support the view that the growth of wage employment has been, or must remain, pathologically slow everywhere in Africa; and we query overconfident, generalized, and pessimistic predictions of a growing excess in the supply of labour—by discussing heterogeneous trends in total fertility rates and the real possibilities for reducing these rates.

We provide evidence that employment protection legislation (EPL) is compatible with rising levels of total (and youth) employment; and we conclude by recommending its vigorous implementation. This may have the added advantage of forcing the least efficient employers to adopt improved technology rather than continue to compete on the basis of starvation wages. At the end of this chapter, we also recommend other policies to improve employment prospects. These include policies that can sustain high levels of demand and an increasing volume of targeted public sector capital expenditure. They also include the recommendation that most investment should specifically be designed to increase *rural* wage employment, as well as the supply of basic wage goods and exports (see Chapters 4 and 5). The scope for public sector investment in irrigation and other productive

---

[6] https://www.vanguardngr.com/2018/04/nigerian-youths-not-lazy-adp-tells-president-buhari/; https://citizen.co.za/news/south-africa/350441/zuma-slams-lazy-south-africans/; Makgala (2013: 56); https://news.mak.ac.ug/2017/07/president-museveni-launches-national-mindset-education-programme.
[7] Cooper (2017: 149).   [8] Rossi (2017: 12).
[9] Organized and privileged labour has been criticized for opposing wage 'flexibility' by, for example, Nattrass and Seekings (2018: 4); the naivety and unrealistic employment expectations of African youth have been emphasized by Rankin and Roberts (2011).

rural infrastructure is immense; and these investments could accelerate the rate of growth of wage employment, including both wage employment in high-tech agribusiness activities and wage employment for millions of rural youth in Africa who have not completed primary schooling. There is a strong human welfare case for investments targeted at increasing the number of years that rural girls spend in secondary education and at dramatically improving their access to contraception, but one direct benefit is too rarely discussed: this type of investment would immediately reduce the number of new entrants into the labour market (and improve returns to their labour).

7.2 Young Africans Will Never Get Decent Jobs—Says Who?

Louise Fox, who was employed as the World Bank's Lead Economist for the Africa Region before becoming Chief Economist for United States Agency for International Development (USAID), is a leading representative of one of the variants of labour market pessimism, arguing that

> owing to the demographics and current structure of low income SSA economies, even exceptionally high economic growth rates in the non-farm sectors have not and will not generate enough new non-farm wage employment to absorb both the new entrants and those who seek to leave the agricultural sector.[10]

Two major supply-side problems will continue, in Fox's view, to afflict the region for many decades and are what lies behind these gloomy predictions. First, there will be an excess supply of labour because fertility rates in Africa will not fall rapidly, or as rapidly as they did in the more successful East Asian economies. Second, the private sector cannot be expected to expand wage employment in internationally competitive firms very fast, because it will take so long for schools in rural Africa to improve the literacy and numeracy of their students and produce sufficient new workers with a basic education.[11]

Many additional reasons for inadequate rates of growth of wage employment are given in other World Bank publications, but these reasons are rarely Africa-specific. Usually they simply repeat familiar rhetorical warnings and the diagrams from undergraduate economics textbooks cautioning against futile state intervention in all labour markets: employers will be deterred from hiring by minimum wage legislation, by legislation protecting employees from unfair dismissal, by any encouragement of collective wage bargaining, and by other regulations requiring

---

[10] Fox and Sohnesen (2012: 28). See also Filmer and Fox (2014: 5) and Fox, Thomas, and Haines (2017: ix).
[11] Filmer and Fox (2014: 21). The OECD (2018: 17) makes the same argument.

health benefits, and so on.[12] Employing the usual reactionary rhetorical devices, the World Bank argues that these types of intervention and legislation risk harming the poor—because they 'could, when too stringent, exacerbate inequity by increasing the share of workers who are either unemployed or in the informal sector'.[13] But even if governments could follow the advice of major aid donors— immediately deregulating and 'reforming' labour market institutions—the World Bank still predicts that structural shifts in African economies over the next decade will not match East Asia's achievements in expanding the role of manufacturing employment.[14]

Surprisingly similar predictions have often been published by authors who would regard themselves as bitterly opposed to the research methods and the conclusions reached by the International Monetary Fund (IMF), the World Bank, and USAID. For example, Guy Standing, who until recently played an important intellectual leadership and policy role in the International Labour Organization (ILO), believes that

> the old proletariat, the core, [is] shrinking fast all over the world. Its remnants will continue, but they no longer have the strength to develop or impose their agenda in the political domain.[15]

Franco Barchiesi is also unsympathetic to the Washington institutions and his work has been praised as 'at the cutting edge of contemporary debates on the politics of the working class'.[16] He argues that waged work in Africa has always been 'precarious' and that, 'despite few exceptions as in Nigeria during the 1970s oil boom . . . the predicament of waged workers after independence was largely unfavourable across the board'.[17] Other development sociologists agree that neoliberal policy reforms have 'forced labour out of formal labour markets into burgeoning informal economies in a process Marxist scholars refer to as "depro-letarianization"'.[18] And if some members of Africa's 'vast informal labour reserve' do become employed producing for the global economy, 'low-income unstable work' or 'adverse incorporation' is all they will be offered.[19] There is also the argument that rural women, in South Africa for instance, should now be regarded

---

[12] Storm (2019) shows the extreme weakness in the economic logic and empirical analysis behind one econometric paper that has been particularly influential in persuading governments 'in India and much of the developing world' to turn away from EPL.
[13] World Bank (2018: 28). On reactionary rhetoric, see Hirschman (1991).
[14] Fox, Thomas, and Haines (2017: 20–1). The World Bank's projections of shifts in employment in the Côte d'Ivoire reach similar conclusions about the tiny contribution that wage employment in industry will make to total employment (Christiaensen and Lawin, 2017: 60).
[15] Standing (2015: 5).   [16] Webster (2012: 88).
[17] Freund (2018); Barchiesi (2017: 22). See also Phimister and Pilossof (2017: 215); while Larmer emphasizes the weakness of Katangese trade unions and claims that the stagnation and precarity of wage labour in Copperbelt cities is typical of all urban capitalist spaces in the global south (2017: 182).
[18] Meagher, Manna, and Bolt (2016: 474–6).   [19] Meagher, Manna, and Bolt (2016: 476).

as members of a surplus population who have uncoupled their livelihoods from wage employment and are quite successfully building a '*post-wage*' existence.[20]

A particularly popular variant of this view has been disseminated through the International Development Economics Associates (IDEAs) network.[21] According to this view, Africa's rural population will *never* become wage workers. For example, in the Patnaiks' historical account: 'precapitalist producers lingered on in real history as a subordinate mass in the periphery without becoming assimilated into the capitalist workforce'.[22] This long-term failure of assimilation has recently become more acute, they argue, because of the sway of neoliberal policymaking.[23] Some of these scholars draw inspiration from Samir Amin, who (a century after Lenin) concluded that capitalism had entered into advanced senility, incapable of generating decent employment and only likely to produce a planet full of slums.[24]

Neo-Marxist explanations for the inability of capitalist development in Africa to absorb workers in productive non-agricultural wage employment often boil down to the claim that there are insuperable problems faced by capitalist industrial development in *all* economies located in the (vaguely defined) periphery of the global economy. One of these problems is described using a strand of dependency theory that used to be called technological dependency but was refreshed by Arrighi using Schumpeter's work on innovation processes. Arrighi argued that the innovation process

'tends to begin in the wealthier countries because high incomes create a favourable environment for product innovations . . . by the time the "new" products and techniques are adopted by the poorer countries they tend to be subject to intense competition and no longer bring the high returns they did in the wealthier countries'.[25]

The intensity of competition between poor countries belatedly adopting these techniques is likely to lead them into a race to the bottom (encouraged by neoliberal policies), promoting falls in real wages. Declining real wages, in turn, exacerbate another critical barrier to capitalist development in Africa and in other

---

[20] Williams (2017b).

[21] IDEAs was founded in South Africa; its funders include the Ford Foundation, United Nations Development Programme (UNDP), Christian Aid, and ActionAid International.

[22] Patnaik and Patnaik (2017: 143).

[23] Patnaik (2016: 11). Shivji agrees that throughout Africa 'the dominant tendency is for the semi-proletarianisation of labour' (2009: 76); and see Moyo (2011: 70).

[24] Amin (2015: 18). For fulsome praise of Amin's contribution see: http://roape.net/2018/08/21/a-rebel-in-the-marxist-citadel-tributes-to-samir-amin/ and Prabhat Patnaik and Jayathi Ghosh: http://www.networkideas.org/news-analysis/2018/08/obituary-samir-amin-1931-2018/.

[25] Arrighi, Silver, and Brewer (2003: 18). Rodrik follows the technological dependency line, arguing that 'new technologies disproportionately favor rich economies, well-endowed in skills and capital, rather than developing economies' (2018: 8, 11).

poor areas of the world. This barrier is the low level of domestic demand generated by the mass of impoverished people for the goods manufactured by proto-capitalist enterprises in Africa.

The political context for demand deficiency in Africa is rising inequality of income, of wealth, and of political power, as well as excessive fiscal austerity leading to deflation. Inadequate aggregate demand and an inadequate growth rate of decent jobs are not simply caused by a revival of neoliberal macroeconomic policies (including real wage cuts in the public sector) and their enthusiastic implementation by a *comprador* class, but also reflect capitalism's ineluctable trend towards stagnation. The central claim of these scholars is that a proletariat will not emerge in poor economies because, as argued by Paul Baran in 1952, (monopoly) capitalism and growth are incompatible *both* in advanced and backward areas of the world.[26] Baran's impossibilist argument was that 'while in the advanced countries capitalism leads to stagnation or militarism or both, in the underdeveloped countries it strangles all efforts at economic advance'.[27]

7.3 Contesting Ambiguous Evidence on Work for Wages

Perhaps the most reliable evidence on employment covers the small minority of African employees who are defined by the ILO as 'formally' employed. Unfortunately, the definitions of 'formality' used by the ILO have changed over time, which is one good reason for caution when making judgements about employment trends in Africa.[28] But a glance at the best available (ILO) estimates of changes in the absolute number of employees between 1991 and 2017 (in Figure 7.1) shows a consistent and unambiguous *increase* in 'formal' wage employment.

Although many economists have expressed fears about the consequences of stagnant *global* wage employment growth, the worldwide number of paid employees actually increased by almost 20 per cent between 1997 and 2017; and the share of paid employment in total global employment also increased.[29] Part of the explanation for these global trends is that China's rate of growth of 'regular' wage employment was astonishingly rapid. The rate of growth of employment in India's 'organized' manufacturing and construction sectors was also impressive over the period 1999 to 2012,[30] with particularly rapid employment growth in organized manufacturing between 2006 and 2016.[31]

---

[26] Baran's economic thought is discussed by King (1988).
[27] The quotation is from the introduction to the Penguin edition by R. B. Sutcliffe (Baran, 1973: 100). Some useful criticism of Baran can be seen in Kaldor (1958: 169).
[28] ILO (2018c: 7–8).   [29] ILOSTAT (2018).
[30] Chan, Pun, and Selden (2017: 173); Majid (2015: 27); Ghose (2015: 6).
[31] Basole and Narayan (2018: 23). Less up-to-date evidence on 'the formal organized sector' in India has been used by Jawaharlal Nehru University (JNU)-based economists to make an unconvincing argument that this sector has failed to draw in more workers: Chandrasekhar and Ghosh (2015: 12).

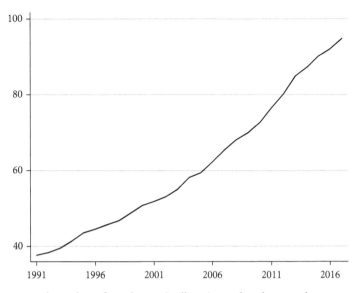

Figure 7.1 Total number of employees (millions) in sub-Saharan Africa, 1991–2017
Source: ILO Modelled Estimates (2018).

What may come as more of a surprise to many is that ILO data also suggest a rapid rise in the share of paid employees in total employment in Africa—in some African countries this share has remained low, but in others it has now reached well over 20 per cent (Ghana, Zambia, and Uganda); it is close to 40 per cent in Kenya; it is 50 per cent in Senegal; and it is rising fast in Ethiopia and, more erratically, in Tanzania and Nigeria.[32]

All calculations of the share of paid employees in Africa involve estimating the number Africans employed as '*own-account workers*' and '*contributing family workers*'; but these estimates are probably even less reliable than the data on the more visible Africans employed for a wage or a salary in the 'formal' sector. A much higher proportion of women than men are currently recorded as 'contributing family workers', but there are good grounds for believing that many of the women lumped into this category are actually doing some seasonal and/or casual *wage* work or are employed 'on commission' in a disguised wage relationship.

One of the reasons women are so often misclassified by enumerators, (both in Africa and in the USA), is that household surveys fail to probe respondents by repeatedly insisting that they provide a complete list of *all* of the different types of work that women, especially rural women, undertake over the year as a whole, rather than during the week before the survey or some other short reference

---

[32] ILO Modelled Estimates 2018.

period. Probing questions have, for example, been shown to significantly increase estimates of the proportion of paid employees among the employed in Tanzania and have identified a substantial additional amount of informal work activity in the US Current Population Survey.[33] Another important reason for the under-estimate of women's labour is the widespread use of proxy respondents in Labour Force and Household Surveys. These respondents (often male 'household heads') answer questions on behalf of other household members, but are known to provide inaccurate answers to questions about the wage employment of both women and children. For example, the prevalence of child labour increases very dramatically when children self-report.[34]

The ILO defines 'own-account workers' and 'contributing family workers' as more '*vulnerable*' than paid employees in Africa, because the latter benefit from more job security and better working conditions. It is puzzling that the declining share of 'vulnerable' employment and the rising share of paid employment (dramatically graphed in Figure 7.2) has generated so little positive comment.

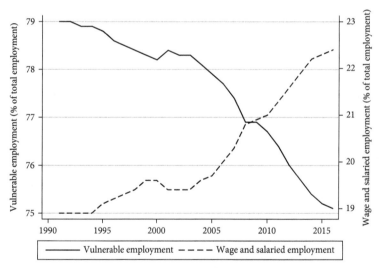

Figure 7.2 'Vulnerable', wage, and salaried employment shares in total employment, sub-Saharan Africa, 1992–2016

Note: The World Development Indicators (WDI) define 'Vulnerable Employment' as the sum of the ILO categories '*own-account workers*' and '*contributing family workers*'. The WDI defines 'Wage and Salaried Employment' as the ILO category '*employees*'.

Source: WDI (2017).

---

[33] Abraham and Amaya (2018); Serneels et al. (2010). When a longer reference period was used in the Ugandan Household Survey questionnaire, the estimate of labour force participation increased dramatically (Fox and Pimhidzai, 2011: 11).

[34] Janzen (2018).

If it is acknowledged that, for example 'in Ghana, Rwanda, Zambia and Malawi, wage employment is growing at nearly three times the rate of growth in self-employment', this important and positive trend is too often deflated by adding a downbeat warning: 'this rapid growth is starting from a very low base and thus translates into a relatively small number of jobs each year'.[35] More broadly, there is surprisingly little interest in statistical evidence in discussions of precarity.[36] Good examples of a cavalier attitude to statistical evidence (and reliance on tiny samples) can be found in the influential work of scholars such as James Ferguson and Ian Scoones.[37]

The positive trends we have identified (drawing on ILO Labour Force Surveys) are likely to be significant underestimates of wage employment. One problem is that Labour Force Surveys are out of date in most African countries: in some relatively large African countries, such as Nigeria, Ethiopia, the Democratic Republic of the Congo (DRC), Ghana, Malawi, Uganda, and Zimbabwe, although there have been important recent changes in the size of the total population and in patterns of employment and urbanization, the ILO publishes analyses based on survey data that are five (or more) years old.[38] In addition, these surveys are implemented using methods that ensure a massive undercount of precisely those forms of wage employment that have historically been particularly important for early and low-paid entrants into developing labour markets, that is, the women and children employed as domestic servants.

7.4 How to Hide Domestic Servants and Child Wage Labourers

At the beginning of the twentieth century, about 1.7 million women and girls were employed as domestic servants in England and Wales: 'Measured by employment, female and male, domestic service was bigger than agriculture in 1901, bigger than coal-mining, and bigger even than textiles.'[39] Despite their dominant position in labour markets in England and throughout Europe, these wage workers (like their colleagues now working in Africa) were often ignored: 'Servants remained in the shadows: they were employed in a sector that from the late eighteenth century had been increasingly considered unproductive; they were barely present on the political scene . . . '[40] Similarly, in Africa in the twenty-first century, the ILO confirms that National Statistical Offices undercount domestic workers, although a very substantial share of *all* wage employment for women and girls is as

---

[35] Yeboah and Jayne (2018: 820). On Rwanda see also World Bank (2016b: 55).
[36] Doogan (2015: 45). On the UK labour market evidence see also Choonara (2018).
[37] Ferguson (2019: 16); see also Ferguson and Li (2018: 2); Scoones et al. (2019: 8).
[38] ILO (2018a: table A. 7.1).   [39] Outram (2017: 893).   [40] Sarti (2014: 284).

domestic servants ('maids') employed by private households.[41] They are like the protagonist of Ralph Ellison's novel *Invisible Man*: 'I am a man of substance, of flesh and bone, of fiber and liquids—and I might even be said to possess a mind. I am invisible, understand, simply because people refuse to see me.'[42]

Research on domestic servants in Zambia, Uganda, Kenya, and several western African countries suggests not only that millions of domestic servants have been employed in both rural and urban areas in the past, but also that their number is currently growing. For example, in Lusaka households across the socio-economic spectrum employed domestic workers: 'The demand for childcare was intrinsically linked to increased female labour-force participation, as many working women sought "substitutes" to care for their children and take care of domestic tasks in their absence . . .'[43] The linkages extended further: female domestic workers themselves have sought such substitutes for their own children's care. Despite the fact that so many Africans, including mineworkers, have employed domestic servants since the 1950s or earlier, Zambian government officials, trade unionists, and civil society activists very often ignore the domestic service sector.[44] They certainly do not publicize the negative aspects of the jobs found by some of these 'maids':

> Mary expressed real distress at the way she had been treated by the children of her first employers, a Zambian couple with four children . . . the children would spit in the dregs of their tea to prevent her from drinking anything they had left.[45]

The lack of respect or recognition accorded to Mary in Lusaka is echoed in research on casual domestic servants in Nairobi.[46] Tabloid journalists in Nampula, Nairobi, and Lagos mix disdain for 'maids' and sexualized fear in a cocktail familiar to students of the early history of the Witwatersrand.[47] The number of specialized recruiting agencies and intermediaries in these cities is growing rapidly, but the total number of very young girls (and boys) currently exploited as domestic servants remains poorly recorded.[48]

---

[41] ILO (2018a: 168; 2013: 13–15, 11). Undercounts of undocumented internal migrant and child domestic workers are also important in some countries (UNCTAD, 2018a: 10).

[42] Ellison (2001: 1).

[43] Female labour force participation rates and the number of Zambian women in formal employment increased very rapidly between 2008 and 2012: 'Formal employment growth has been slightly faster for women than for men (14.6 per cent per year versus 13 per cent per year)' (Harasty, Kwong, and Ronnås, 2015: 45).

[44] Hepburn (2016: 102, 200, 85, 112, 4).   [45] Hepburn (2016: 113–14).

[46] Agaya and Asunza (2013: 8–9).

[47] On sexual fear, moral panics, and servants in rapidly urbanizing South Africa see Van Onselen (2001). In rural Southern Africa at a later date, sexual anxieties about African servants were explored by Lessing (1973). Unpaid wages, abuse, and repeated accusations in the media of the rampant sexuality of 'housegirls' in Lagos are discussed in detail by Nesbitt-Ahmed (2016).

[48] Jacquemin (2009); Nesbitt-Ahmed (2016). Underestimates of the employment of maids in Uganda are discussed in Sender and Von Uexkull (2009: 65) and in Lyon and Valdivia (2010).

Outside the major cities, there is even less quantitative information about the employment of children for wages in rural Africa, although our own research in Ethiopia and Uganda offers some data on prevalence in export crop-producing areas, as well as many disturbing examples of cruel treatment.[49] It is not easy to select the most distressing of the many accounts we recorded, but one combination of the compulsion to work as a domestic servant and as a coffee harvester in southern Ethiopia illustrates exploitation that cannot be discussed using the ILO's National Child Labour Force Survey:[50]

> At a very young age, when she was about six, Eman was driven by hunger to leave her father; she walked for more than five hours desperately trying to find an aunt she thought could help her. Her aunt did not welcome her into the family. Instead, she was put to work as a domestic servant—carrying water, preparing food for the aunt's family (which she was not allowed to eat) and was often slapped when she performed these tasks too slowly or said she was tired. It is Eman's job to cook breakfast for her aunt's children before they go to school; she is not allowed to eat this food (or go to school) and this makes her cry. Whenever coffee pickers are required she is sent to do this work in addition to domestic chores; her aunt took most of her earnings and abused her on those days when she could not find a job picking coffee. Many coffee farmers underpaid or physically abused her. She does not think she could manage to find her way home to visit her parents.[51]

7.5 How to Undercount Wage Labour in Agriculture

How is it possible to explain the failure of official surveys to capture the agricultural wage labour we have observed so easily in our fieldwork? There is no simple answer to this question. Officials and dominant classes in rural areas have always found it easy to hoodwink urban authorities and well-meaning 'useful idiot' visitors.[52] The District Agricultural Officer in Kabale denied the existence of wage labour on small vegetable farms in Uganda until we pressed him to shake

---

The World Bank analyses urban employment in Ethiopia, but ignores the labour market for domestic servants and child workers (World Bank, 2016c).

[49] Cramer et al. (2014b: Section 3.5).

[50] The National Child Labour Force Survey found hardly any children working as domestic servants in Ethiopia (ILO, 2018b: table 6.3).

[51] Cramer and Sender (forthcoming). Nelson and Brown (2017) provide very similar accounts of the experiences of child domestic servants in southern Nigeria.

[52] The *Oxford Online Dictionary* defines a useful idiot as a foreign citizen regarded by locals as naive and susceptible to manipulation for propaganda: the term was often used to describe 'sympathetic' visitors to the Soviet Union in the 1930s.

hands with a group of women in a field near his office; and an ILO-funded team has described how it was deliberately misled about child wage labour by all the local elite on the largest tea plantation in Ethiopia.[53] Efforts to impede statistical investigation—especially the collection of data on farm labour—are well documented not only in Africa, but also in Europe.[54]

Another part of the explanation for the 'missing' wage workers can be found by studying the methods used in 35 widely quoted surveys promoted and funded by the World Bank. Many of the common-sense policy proposals for rural development in Africa are based on statistical analyses of Household Budget Surveys, especially the World Bank's Living Standards Measurement Surveys (LSMS) and, more recently, the Integrated Surveys of Agriculture (LSMS-ISA). The results of these surveys are ideologically convenient; they provide the data used by the International Food Policy Research Institute (IFPRI) and mainstream agricultural economists to foster the notion that wage labour is unimportant in rural Africa and to support populist proposals to skew the allocation of resources towards 'efficient' family farms.

Both the LSMS and the LSMS-ISA are designed as nationally representative household surveys. The latter has 'a strong focus on agriculture', collecting panel data on households in eight sub-Saharan African countries.[55] Two important issues need to be raised immediately. First, as noted by the Food and Agriculture Organization (FAO) but glossed over in LSMS-ISA publications, these surveys exclude *non-household farms*. They rarely acknowledge that 'household farms are not representative of the entire agricultural sector . . . private corporate farms also play an important role and may operate a large share of the agricultural farmland in some countries'. The conclusion reached by FAO economists is that a 'substantial share of agricultural land in Malawi, Nigeria and Uganda is unaccounted for by the LSMS surveys'.[56]

A second important issue is often ignored in analyses of household surveys: not everyone living in African rural areas is a member of an 'agricultural household' or a 'farm household': migrants living in labour camps, landless or semi-landless people, who may cultivate a tiny vegetable garden rather than owning a farm or an agricultural enterprise, are unlikely to be recorded as members of agricultural households in the LSMS-ISA. For example, rural households were excluded from the sampling frame of a Tanzanian survey of farm households if they produced too little agricultural output.[57] The Agricultural Sample Surveys (ASS) in Ethiopia

---

[53] Cramer et al. (2014b) and Kifle, Getahun, and Beyene (2005: 8); see also Chapter 3.
[54] D'Onofrio (2016: ch. 5).
[55] http://surveys.worldbank.org/lsms/programs/integrated-surveys-agriculture-ISA.
[56] Lowder et al. (2016: 7–9).
[57] Of course, the same survey also excluded large-scale agricultural producers on 'estates' or 'plantations' because their output was not defined as 'household' production (Christiansen and Sarris, 2007: 163, 8).

have been the basis for many assertions about agricultural activities in Ethiopia, but the sample excludes *all* Ethiopia's large-scale farms—such as the Wush Wush and Gumaro tea plantations (and contains no information about their wage workers)—so it is rather predictable that the ASS underestimates the national number of rural wage labourers. Similarly, if urban surveys are confined to respectable residential areas and no special effort is made to sample less salubrious areas near bars and massage parlours, the number of prostitutes will probably be underestimated.[58] Waged work in agriculture is not as stigmatized as work providing sexual services. But because efforts are so often made to deny its existence, especially when child agricultural labour is involved, there is a good case for venue-based sampling of individuals in 'hotspots', rather than the conventional random selection of rural households.[59] Hotspots for child migrant labour in Africa include cotton in Burkina Faso and cocoa in Côte d'Ivoire.[60]

Most agricultural wage work is *concentrated* in specific areas and for a few enterprises, that is, in high-value (export) crop production areas for dynamic capitalist farmers. Similarly, hired workers are *not* employed evenly throughout the agricultural sector of the United States; a very small number of large farmers of fruits, vegetables, and horticultural speciality crops account for more than half of the jobs offered to hired workers, most of whom are immigrants into the USA.[61]

In Africa, hundreds of thousands of agricultural wage workers also seasonally migrate, for example, to the Western Cape deciduous fruit farms from the Eastern Cape, from Zimbabwe and elsewhere. But South Africa's first LSMS listed hardly any rural households deriving an income from agricultural wage labour in the Western Cape—they were excluded from the sample because they did not live in conventional housing or 'households'.[62] Surveys designed to obtain nationally representative information on *all* farming households will include a great many farms located far away from the most important producing and wage-employing areas—random sampling could miss the biggest concentrations of rural wage earners. Besides, pretensions to representative sampling usually depend on samples drawn from an out-of-date National Population Census and/or on the inaccurate lists of households compiled by local officials. These unreliable sources for constructing a sampling frame may well exclude the newest in-migrants, refugees, or squatters; but these excluded individuals are often important suppliers of unskilled casual wage labourer.[63]

The questionnaires used in the LSM-ISA (and in the Demographic and Health Surveys) do not probe to obtain key information about the labour market

---

[58] Ethiopia's ASS is criticized in more detail in Sender (2019).   [59] Cramer et al. (2014b).

[60] Edmonds and Shrestha (2012: 105).   [61] Martin (2012).

[62] Standing, Sender, and Weeks (1996: 240).

[63] Household surveys in Africa (and elsewhere) typically exclude the tails of the distribution of households (Carr-Hill, 2017). Attempts to exclude new arrivals from the lists of officially sanctioned rural residents are discussed in James (2013).

experience of *all* the individuals with close economic ties to rural households; the LSMS methodology requires enumerators to ask questions about the employment and labour market participation only of '*residents*' in rural households.[64] Following this protocol, a child who is a seasonal labour migrant to another rural area may well not be defined as resident at the time of the survey and will be excluded from the roster of individuals about whom the enumerators ask questions.[65] Even if these seasonal migrants are identified (by proxy respondents) as individuals remitting income to surveyed rural households, no detailed information is obtained about where they are and how they earn their income; their remittances are classified as 'transfer income' rather than wage income; and the strange assumption is made that all transfer income should be classified as 'non-agricultural'. On the basis of this misleading classification it is argued that most rural households derive a very low proportion of their income from wages.[66]

7.6 Now You See Them, Now You Don't: Estimating Factory Workers

Governments in Africa are much more willing and able to produce statistics on industrial employment. The absolute number of Africans employed in industry appears to have grown substantially since 1991.[67] In the manufacturing sector, employment has been growing in several African economies, suggesting that predictions of a generalized decline in or stifling of manufacturing employment may themselves be premature. In Ethiopia, for example, the number of people engaged in manufacturing increased from 561,000 in 1995 to 2,825,000 in 2011, while the comparable increases in Kenya and Nigeria were from 747,000 to 1,990,000 and from 1,271,000 to 2,345,000.[68] Recent increases in manufacturing wage employment should be seen in historical context: in the 1960s, a tiny number of Kenyans or Ethiopians (fewer than 50,000) found jobs in the manufacturing sector; in 1960, about 47,000 Tanzanians were engaged in the manufacturing sector, but by 2011 this sector employed about 700,000 workers.[69] Perhaps the most dramatic recent increase in recorded wage employment in Africa was in

---

[64] Cramer et al. (2014: 176–9).

[65] Survey data from Burkina Faso show how a failure to obtain data on temporarily absent migrant youth distorts analyses of inequality and poverty (Akresh and Edmonds, 2010). De Brauw, Mueller, and Woldehanna (2013), Mueller, Schmidt, and Lozano-Gracia (2015), and Yeboah and Jayne (2018) provide some quantitative evidence of the importance of rural–rural migration and of remittances to the migrants' 'home' households.

[66] It is admitted in passing that agricultural wages are an important source of the income in the case of the of the very poorest rural households (Davies, Giuseppe, and Zezza, 2017: 161; table A. 3).

[67] ILO Modelled Estimates 2018.

[68] Groningen Growth and Development Centre Database (GGDC) 10-Sector Database.

[69] The early Ethiopian and Kenyan data are from Sender and Smith (1986: 95). The Tanzanian data are from the GGDC. The growth in employment in Mozambique's manufacturing sector is very recent,

Ethiopia's construction sector: between 2005 and 2013 the number of employees tripled, increasing from 229,000 to 825,000.[70]

Government officials and foreign consultants do not count more than a fraction of the wage workers when they conduct surveys of Africa's manufacturing establishments. There are several reasons for this undercount, including: the exclusion of manufacturing establishments employing a 'small' number of workers—in some countries the threshold for inclusion is 5 workers, but in others it is as high as 10 or even 25 (in the case of Mozambique, for example);[71] the exclusion of manufacturing enterprises that are not registered by an official government agency, leading to under-sampling of thousands of smaller firms and of all enterprises unwilling to submit to state surveillance and taxation; and biased sampling frames or dated lists of manufacturing establishments that fail to take account of rapid structural change by excluding recently created firms, while listing many firms that no longer exist.[72]

7.7 How Long Will It Take for African Fertility Rates to Fall?

The evidence does not suggest that the growth of wage employment in Africa has stagnated. Nevertheless, it is often argued that wage employment growth must be regarded as too slow, because fertility rates in Africa are currently so high and, for the foreseeable future (several generations), cannot be expected to fall very rapidly: 'the decline in fertility rates has stalled—or not even started—in many African countries'.[73] The more productive sectors of the economy will be unable to absorb a labour force that is growing exceptionally rapidly in Africa—much more rapidly than in the earlier industrializers.[74]

In addition it is widely believed that, unlike the earlier industrializers, African economies cannot escape from their labour absorption problem by exporting their surplus workers to formal and informal colonies.[75] But, in some of the early industrializers, including the Netherlands, France, and Germany, emigration only reduced the local labour force by a tiny percentage between 1870 and 1910, suggesting that capitalist success in raising manufacturing employment (and wages) in these countries is unlikely to be explained by labour export opportunities. Japan's labour-intensive industrialization before the 1940s required access to

---

but extremely rapid—from about 70,000 workers in 2002 to 272,000 in 2008 (Sparreboom and Staneva, 2015: 40).

[70] Oqubay (2019: 632).   [71] Le, De Haan, and Dietzenbacher (2018: 10).
[72] Mozambique provides good examples of the problems arising from dated and inaccurate sampling frames (Schou and Cardoso, 2014).
[73] Filmer and Fox (2014: 3).   [74] Scherrer (2018: 305).
[75] Patnaik and Patnaik (2017: 56).

imports of food and raw materials; securing access to these resources was an important motive for colonial expansion—far more important than opening up new opportunities for getting rid of surplus labour through emigration.[76]

We are unconvinced by repeated reference to 'persistently high fertility' in Africa.[77] Policymakers should be suspicious whenever they are told that it is 'impossible' to achieve social change—such as a rapid improvement in women's reproductive welfare. The most reliable available source, the United Nations Population Division, has a long record of incorrect assumptions about initial demographic conditions and of underestimating the future rate of decline in fertility. This record confirms the need for more 'humility about our capacity to anticipate major social changes' and it confirms the need for African policymakers to question all data underpinning the recommendations of international agencies.[78]

The claim that fertility rates have 'stalled', like most generalizations about the subcontinent, is obviously untrue. Figure 7.3 shows the dramatic and continuing decline in the estimated total fertility rates for some large East and West African economies between 1950 and 2025–30 (see also Chapter 1).

It may be possible to achieve an even faster decline in fertility rates and extend these declining rates to a greater number of African countries. This potential exists partly because in sub-Saharan Africa there are some of the highest recorded rates

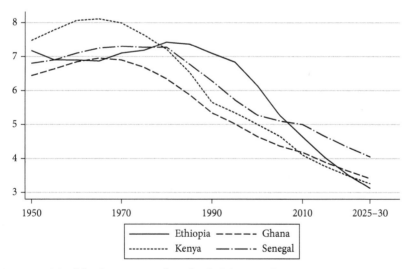

Figure 7.3 Total fertility rate in selected sub-Saharan African countries, 1950–2030
Source: UN (2017).

---

[76] Taylor and Williamson (1997: table 1); Sugihara (2004).   [77] Losch (2016: 56).
[78] Khan and Lutz (2008); Lutz and KC (2010). Bongaarts describes the extreme pessimism of researchers in the 1960s about the possibility of fertility reduction in low-income Asia, until the evidence of dramatic declines in fertility in Bangladesh undermined their pessimism (2018: 2).

of unmet need for contraception in the world and because there are some African governments that 'are still reluctant to make commitments to family planning'.[79] In Tanzania, for example, commitment to family planning was undermined in 2018, when the President described women using contraceptives as lazy and under the influence of foreigners with sinister motives.[80]

Although policy interventions have succeeded in achieving a substantial increase in the use of contraception by African women since 1980, in the majority of countries widespread use of family planning has *not* been achieved—it remains restricted to the urban, best-educated, and privileged women.[81] If investments were made to ensure the availability of modern contraceptive methods to more rural women and to raise the level of their education there could be a large impact on fertility: 'the decline in fertility could be faster than that currently foreseen by the United Nations for African countries'.[82] Reducing unplanned fertility would, of course, lead to a reduction in the growth rate of the young population.[83] Many economists continue to support fashionable (but ineffective) policies designed to support young entrepreneurs. But too little attention is paid to the economic benefits of specific interventions targeted to improve the reproductive health of rural girls and women.

7.8 Employment Policies When Ideology Trumps African Evidence

Pessimism about employment opportunities has not stemmed the flow of publications recommending supply-side policies to improve labour market outcomes for African youth. These policy proposals usually begin by stating that there is a shortage of skilled workers. A 'mismatch' between the demand for and the supply of skills is said to be a major obstacle to growth and development. In overcoming this obstacle, 'Availability of quality, relevant *training* for in-demand skills and occupations is a key factor, along with accessible and timely labour market information.'[84] In Ethiopia, for example, the World Bank's analysis is very clear: 'skills shortages in Ethiopia constitute a key constraint to growth and improved productivity in the manufacturing sector . . . In the short run, the provision of Technical and Vocational Education Training (TVET) . . . could be used to bridge the gap of skills supply to the manufacturing sector.'[85] TVET in Ethiopia,

[79] Bongaarts (2018: 5).
[80] https://www.thecitizen.co.tz/News/Magufuli-advises-against-birth-control/1840340-4751990-4h8fqpz/index.html.
[81] Towriss and Timæus (2018: 2028).   [82] Garenne (2018: 145).   [83] Bongaarts (2018: 9).
[84] International Labour Organization, Organization for Economic Cooperation and Development, and World Bank Group (2014: 17; emphasis added).
[85] World Bank (2016a: 41).

as in many other developing countries, has been promoted through state expenditures and by support for the introduction of competence-based training; employers' views about the detailed requirements for occupational competence are supposed to have an increased influence on the curriculum. The explosive growth of enrolment in TVET since about 2005—at an annual rate of about 30 per cent—reflects a major policy commitment by the Ethiopian state.[86] Ethiopia is following a global trend, described as 'a VET renaissance in both OECD and developing countries'.[87]

The model followed is to ask some employers to play the key role in developing a new and improved set of relevant qualifications. Young people, if they have access to sufficient information about labour markets, will then be able to make choices to enhance their 'employability'; they can invest to obtain these new qualifications, have their competence certified, and ensure, on the basis of their newly acquired 'human capital', a smooth transition into employment.[88] An additional reform of public policy is recommended—making this choice-theoretic model even more appealing to neoclassical economists: It is argued that training and certification should mainly be provided by private sector contractors, rather than state-run colleges or schools.

Young people in this theoretical world will use improved information about labour markets to abandon their unrealistic aspirations for white collar employment as civil servants, choose the most suitable training modules, and avoid burdening their parents/family with carrying the costs of protracted employment search. They will accept the fact that a decent full-time job as a wage worker is only a remote possibility, even if the TVET college has issued them with an embossed certificate of competence in skills selected by the managers of large firms. Most of them will end up working in small and micro-enterprises, surviving as self-employed workers and, therefore, they urgently need training in *entrepreneurial skills*. This is the vision offered by mainstream policy advisors. It is a vision shared by many of the critics of neoliberal economic policy, although their preference would be to train people to juggle a complex *bricolage* or diversified portfolio of entrepreneurial activities, or to train cooperative leaders. The consensus is that:

> Entrepreneurship training provides young people with the skills they need to create and manage a sustainable business likely to generate jobs.[89]

What have been the results of Africa's massive expenditures on TVET and the training of entrepreneurs? The expansion of training opportunities does not

---

[86] Yamada et al. (2018: 14).   [87] McGrath, Alla-Mensah, and Langthaler (2018: 12).
[88] Allais (2012: 635ff.). See King (1990: ch. 3, especially p. 69ff.) for a critique of the concept of 'human capital' (and of the theories of labour supply offered by neoclassical economists).
[89] African Development Bank (2012: 139).

appear to have reduced the risks of protests and rioting by violent youth and most evaluations agree that

> In practice, those who have followed the TVET path often take longer to find jobs and when they find employment, the jobs are perceived to be of dead-end in nature career-wise.[90]

> Technical and Vocational Skills Development systems in Africa suffer from a shortage of qualified staff, obsolete equipment, ill-adapted programmes and weak links with the job market.[91]

The unemployment rate for TVET graduates is high; few youth from rural, low-income backgrounds graduate; and even fewer of the urban and relatively privileged TVET graduates actually wish to work on a factory floor. Collaboration between TVET colleges and factories remains very limited.[92]

If education is a cumulative process, with later learning building on earlier learning, it follows that an improvement in the levels of literacy and numeracy achieved in African secondary schools could make in-employment training much more effective; and these improvements would probably have a more positive impact on labour productivity than expenditures to improve 'skills'. There is good evidence from several African countries of the disappointing performance of schools, as well as on the variability of performance within and between these countries.[93] In Organisation for Economic Co-operation and Development (OECD) economies, the decline in literacy and numeracy proficiency among young adults since the mid-1990s does appear to have reduced their ability to engage in further learning and to adapt to changes in the pattern of labour demand.[94] And it has been argued that there is a causal relationship between the maths/science scores achieved by 15-year-old school children and subsequent economic growth in developing economies.[95]

Diverting resources away from enhancing numeracy and literacy in schools to create entrepreneurial skills is a policy that has also failed to achieve employment or other economic benefits. A review of entrepreneurship training that focuses on evaluations in low- and middle-income economies—including some sub-Saharan African economies—argues that most interventions targeting micro-enterprises with up to five employees or aiming to enhance youth self-employment *cannot* be shown to have significant positive effects on employment, sales revenue, or profits. Searching for something (anything) positive to say about the results of

---

[90] Oketch (2014: 3).   [91] African Development Bank (2012: 147); Tripney et al. (2013: 77–8).
[92] Yamada (2018: 18, 40, 45, 53, 24).   [93] Jones (2017).   [94] Liu (2018).
[95] Hanushek and Woessmann (2016). Komatsu and Rappleye (2017) question the empirical link between test scores and economic growth, and the policy implications of this alleged link. Sandefur (2016) discusses problems with the comparability of the data on maths scores in Africa.

entrepreneurship training, the authors conclude by damning these interventions with very faint praise: 'Entrepreneurship training can . . . prevent non-profitable business ideas from being started.'[96]

High failure rates for self-employed businesses with no or very few employees are a global phenomenon, but the failure rates of firms managed by young people have been shown to be particularly high in a survey of about 14,000 very small firms.[97] Policymakers might wish to take account of this result and other evidence of an *oversupply* of start-up micro-enterprises in Africa by reallocating resources away from supporting the efforts of youth to establish their own survivalist start-up enterprise. Even if a few of these small enterprises do survive, evidence from Mali, Malawi, and Tanzania suggests that they will each provide relatively few wage employment opportunities for young people.[98] Worse, it is possible that:

> Encouraging more businesses into the same limited niches may further depress the incomes of existing self-employed people, or even force them out of business . . . [99]

There is good evidence from South African and other panel data that most of the net growth in national employment opportunities is provided by large rather than small firms.[100] Many young African workers looking for wage employment would be well advised, if they can cover the transport and other costs, to go to where most jobs are being created—the large and mature firms, specifically firms employing more than a hundred workers that have been in business for at least ten years. Young workers who can only find jobs in small enterprises risk losing their jobs very soon and are unlikely to get as much training or be paid wages as high as the wages received in larger firms. Page and Söderbom conclude that 'it is time to stop overselling small enterprise development as the panacea for employment creation in Africa' (see also Chapter 3).[101]

Our own research in rural Ethiopia and Uganda has confirmed the ability of larger rural enterprises to offer young people more stable employment, as well as better wages and working conditions.[102] In Chapter 8 we emphasize the similarities between the mainstream policy recommendation—vocational and entrepreneurship training—designed to increase non-agricultural employment and the policies recommended for smallholder agricultural development, especially the popular proposals to invest in agricultural extension/advice. Chapter 8 also

---

[96] Grimm and Paffhausen (2015: 74).   [97] McKenzie and Paffhausen (2017: 16).
[98] Nagler (2017: 11).   [99] Burchell et al. (2015: 38).
[100] Kerr, Wittenberg, and Arrow (2014); Aga, Francis, and Meza (2015).
[101] Page and Söderbom (2012: 20–1).
[102] Cramer et al. (2017). For West African evidence on higher wages in large than small enterprises see Mbaye and Gueye (2018: 21).

presents evidence of the costly failures of micro-credit, which is often alleged to be essential for the development of both non-agricultural enterprises and farms.

7.9 Policies to Avoid a Disabling Environment for Employment Growth

Those who blame inadequate rates of growth of employment on the deficient skills and personal attributes of Africans working in low-productivity jobs usually also advocate reforms to create a more favourable environment for private sector investors. Their argument is that 'Regulation by a low-quality bureaucracy and high taxes stifle the private formal sector . . . labor market distortions reduce productivity . . . stalling overall growth.'[103] The importance of promoting employment by reducing labour market protections for workers is stressed not only by economists working for the African Development Bank in Abidjan, but also by influential economists working in the World Bank in Washington: the Bank's flagship development report on 'The Changing Nature of Work' questions the relevance of current labour laws and institutions in all developing countries, urging that 'governments should rethink policies that deter job creation'. Governments should reform labour market rules, because 'stringent regulations make it costlier for firms to adjust the composition of their workforce'.[104] In short, it is argued that labour protection is a luxury that poor economies cannot afford.

The claim that restrictions on dismissal and requirements relating to severance payments contribute to unemployment by presenting firms with a disincentive to hire workers is not based on any empirical evidence from African economies. Instead, these proposals for labour market reform—to create a more business-friendly environment—simply echo assertions made repeatedly since the 1980s by orthodox economic policy advisers to the IMF, the OECD, and the European Union (EU) Commission. The labour market outcomes of orthodox policy in Europe were particularly disastrous in Greece, where the employment to population ratio (as recorded by ILOSTAT) plummeted from about 50 per cent in 2008 to below 39 per cent in 2013. Labour market reforms have not had better outcomes elsewhere: an analysis of panel data from 31 countries, including both the OECD economies and the 10 new EU member-states from Central and Eastern Europe, suggests that 'there is no direct link between EPL and youth unemployment . . . EPL is not a key culprit for unemployment, and thus government efforts to tackle unemployment by liberalizing employment laws alone may well be futile'.[105] Moreover, a larger panel of 117 countries and a more carefully constructed measure of comparative levels of employment protection, covering a

---

[103] Mbaye and Gueye (2018: 24).   [104] World Bank (2018b: 31, 92).
[105] Avdagic (2015: 7, 22).

longer time period (1991–2013), shows that increases in worker protection are generally associated with *rising* employment and falling unemployment, although these associations are relatively small when set against wider economic trends.[106]

The 'wider economic trends' influencing rates of growth of employment and the environment for private sector investment are conspicuously absent from and rarely mentioned in the voluminous literature fuelling the panic about youth employment in Africa. But it is a serious mistake to recommend fashionable supply-side policies while downplaying the roles of aggregate demand, Keynesian fiscal policy, and the pattern of public sector investment in influencing labour market performance. Aggregate demand has consistently been shown to be a fundamental determinant of the state of the youth labour market. Expansionary fiscal policy, especially when based on increased government investment expenditure on infrastructure, has played a major role in raising employment rates. In Europe, countercyclical discretionary fiscal policy appears to have increased youth employment rates and to have reduced long-term youth unemployment.[107]

In emerging and developing economies, the IMF has estimated that fiscal consolidations achieved through reductions in public sector investment expenditure have a massive *negative* effect on the percentage of the working age population in employment.[108] The IMF has also used a dataset covering the period 1989 to 2016 to confirm that discretionary fiscal contractions have a significant adverse effect on the unemployment rate. In this dataset, there is also *no* evidence that austerity provides an environment that encourages an expansion of the private sector; on the contrary, fiscal consolidations were linked to falls in private investment.[109]

Of course, falls in aggregate demand and employment in Africa could also be the result of increases in the price of food (or other basic wage goods) reducing the real income of wage workers. Kalecki's arguments, outlined in Chapter 3, reinforce the need for policymakers to focus on ensuring sufficient growth in the availability of wage goods as a fundamental determinant of employment growth, rather than on a narrow range of supply-side microeconomic variables. One implication of the discussion in Chapters 3 and 4 is that economic policy must be directed towards increasing output in specific sectors and activities, for example, those making a major contribution to wage good production and to labour-intensive export revenue.

But African governments are constantly lectured about the impossibility of 'picking winners'. They are told, instead, to establish a 'business-friendly' environment where market incentives are not distorted by bureaucrats, but provide the

---

[106] Adams et al. (2019: 23). An economic explanation of the links between employment protection and a rising level of employment and wages has been provided by Storm and Capaldo (2018).
[107] O'Higgins (2017: section 2.2.1).   [108] IMF (2014a: 25).
[109] Carrière-Swallow, David, and Leigh (2018: 15). For additional evidence on how public investment 'crowds in' private investment in developing countries see Furceri and Li (2017: 18).

'correct' price signals (reflecting the relative scarcity of factors of production) to all agents in all sectors of the economy as a whole. Direct, targeted state interventions to create an increase in the demand for unskilled rural wage workers, for example, would be risky and would probably fail. These warnings about the impossibility of picking winners are part of the standard 'enabling' package that includes recommendations to cut the red tape stifling entrepreneurs, deregulate the labour market, and restrict public sector investment. We have argued that the standard package cannot be expected to result in an adequate rate of growth of aggregate output in Africa. We also argue that policymakers should not be content simply to accept the increase in employment historically associated with a market determined change in *aggregate* output, that is, the aggregate employment elasticity. Instead, policies should be more interventionist, ambitious, and disaggregated, targeting sectoral and subsectoral elasticities of employment. Moreover, employment elasticities need to be calculated not only for different sectors and activities but also for different demographic groups, especially rural women.

7.10 Policies to Increase the Demand for Young and Female Rural Workers

There are some obvious patterns in employment intensity in Africa: for example, employment elasticities seem to be much lower in large-scale mining/extractive industry than in agriculture. However, empirical work shows that

> there is generally also considerable heterogeneity in the degree of employment intensity within sectors, and even within subsectors. Subsectors generally include a wide range of activities. Furthermore, even within an activity there are significant differences in production techniques, with some being more employment-intensive than others. Firm size . . . product characteristics . . . and management choices would be amongst the factors affecting employment intensity at firm level.[110]

The database on the labour content of exports currently available from the World Bank does not cover all African countries and, more importantly, provides no disaggregated information at all on the agricultural sector.[111] But this disaggregated information should be the basis for interventions to increase employment. Our own research in Southern Africa has shown that apricot production, for example, needs about seven times more labour inputs per hectare than does

---

[110] Tregenna (2015: 15).

[111] Cali, Francois, Hollweg, Manchin, Oberdabernig, Rojas-Romagosa, Rubinova and Tomberger (2016).

sugarcane; and deciduous fruit production on average requires some three hundred times more permanent labour per hectare than maize production. Similarly, crops like barley (and the production of beef or poultry) are very limited in their employment creation effects, while other crops like grapes, avocados, carrots, and blueberries are hugely more labour intensive—and most of their labour requirements are met by young women who have not had the chance to attend secondary school. In short, we have shown that there is enormous employment generation potential from expanding the area under cultivation of precisely those crops with the highest labour input requirements.

If policymakers do not have immediate or easy access to all of the relevant crop-specific data, they can nevertheless begin to make decisions on the basis of a few stylized facts about employment intensity; and they can then learn by doing, that is, adjust policy continuously, after careful monitoring and evaluation of the employment and net foreign exchange consequences of public sector expenditures and state interventions.

One important stylized fact about employment intensity in developing economies—largely ignored in conventional diagnoses of African employment crises—is that the level of public sector investment in irrigation and water control has a major influence on labour intensity. The proportion of farmland under irrigation has been shown to have a profound influence on the level of employment (labour use per hectare), as well on the intensity with which other inputs, such as agrochemicals and machinery, are used. Irrigation and water control therefore are regarded as *the leading input* in historical accounts of technical change, output, and productivity growth in the most dynamic Asian economies. In those economies, much of the required investment in irrigation schemes—plus ancillary investments in transportation, storage, and fertilizer production—was undertaken by the public sector.[112] This is in marked contrast to the African experience. Since the 1980s, technically feasible opportunities to invest in expanding the total area equipped for irrigation have been neglected in many African countries, as will be argued in Chapter 9. Moreover, there has been insufficient investment to rehabilitate existing irrigation schemes and to reduce the substantial loss of potential crop area, production, and employment arising from inefficient irrigation practices and maintenance backlogs.[113]

---

[112] Bramall (2004: 134); Pincus (2006: 208).
[113] Only a tiny fraction of the irrigated area, even in the most technologically advanced African economy, benefits from investment in drip and micro-irrigation (Cramer and Sender, 2015: 17).

8

Working Out the Solution
to Rural Poverty

8.1 Introduction

What people think they know about poverty is clouded by misleading measures, unreliable data, and ideology masquerading as common sense. Powerful common-sense ideas—that poor people are rural, that they live in large, female-headed households, and most of them live on small farms—appear to be confirmed in official surveys generating the raw data for a string of poverty measures and indexes. However, most of these indexes are confused; the surveys have serious shortcomings; and the 'rhetorical commonplaces' of poverty in Africa are wrong. It is no wonder too little poverty reduction has really been achieved in recent decades.

This chapter explains why we argue in this way. We begin by discussing issues of measurement and definition. We then try to blow off the common-sense chaff from the more useful grain of what we term stylized facts: facts that are broadly supported by carefully collected evidence and provide policy-relevant ideas about the characteristics of extreme poverty. We show that some, but not all, of these stylized facts are uncontroversial and similar to the conventional wisdoms used to identify the poor in Africa. The poorest people live in female-dominated households (not 'female-headed' households) and lack regular access to support from an adult male; the adult females and children in these households probably have not received an adequate education; they are severely threatened by the risks of teenage pregnancy; they also rely on a monotonous and undiversified diet; and the poorest people have been able to acquire barely any basic consumer wage goods. More controversially, we also show that these households are relatively *small*; and we stress the stylized fact that the poorest people in Africa depend on low-paid wage labour (not self-employment on their own farms) for their survival.

Policymakers and researchers must question the data and arguments underpinning proposals to reduce poverty in Africa. Part of the problem is that national statistical organizations (NSOs) are under-resourced and often under political pressure. There is nothing uniquely African about this: it is a common issue elsewhere and historically. We give some recent examples of difficulties experienced by African NSOs, focusing on problematic census and agricultural data.

African Economic Development: Evidence, Theory, Policy. Christopher Cramer, John Sender, and Arkebe Oqubay, Oxford University Press (2020). © Christopher Cramer, John Sender, and Arkebe Oqubay.
DOI: 10.1093/oso/9780198832331.001.0001

This chapter provides an overview of evidence about the impact of policy interventions on the poorest people in Africa (Section 8.3). We then try to explain the skewed impact of many very fashionable, but obviously failing, poverty reduction policies. We show how bad data and hegemonic ideas about how to reduce poverty in Africa are intimately connected. Our conclusion is that commonly advocated policies to reduce poverty and increase agricultural output are likely to continue to have disappointing results. The recommendations from fashionable randomized control trials (RCT) are also very unlikely to make more than very modest inroads on poverty.[1] What these RCTs actually show is often stretched into far larger claims than the method justifies.[2] At their best, RCTs can be useful in answering *limited* types of question; but they are not designed to generate understanding of distributional dynamics or the political economy of production, accumulation, and labour, let alone to generate effective policies to make structural differences to the conditions of development and poverty reduction.[3] It has also been shown that some of the flagship RCTs used to promote a much wider use of the method have not conformed to the standards of research protocol that they set out; and that their claims to statistical significance are often unfounded.[4] The policy implications that we draw from the stylized facts on rural poverty are elaborated through other chapters in this book (especially Chapters 4, 5, 7, 9, and 10). The single most important mechanism in poverty reduction (globally and in Africa) is, as it has been throughout the history of capitalism, labour market development—the growth of demand for labour in higher-productivity activities and the hard-won achievement of higher wages and some legal protections for employees. We argue that a greater difference can be made—including in the relatively short term—by prioritizing policies and investments designed to promote a rapid rate of growth of labour demand in particular types of activity (in rural and urban areas) than by pouring resources into safety nets that invariably fail the poorest or by 'nudging' the behaviour of poor people themselves through small interventions based on very sketchy empirical work.

Although a small number of countries have failed to make any progress at all in reducing monetary poverty rates since 2002—mainly small countries classified by the World Bank as 'Fragile States'[5]—boasts that poverty is falling in Africa are easily made. Some widely published data do support a less gloomy, if not a rosy, interpretation of trends in the prevalence of poverty (Figure 8.1). Although the

---

[1] Labrousse (2016a).   [2] Deaton and Cartwright (2018).
[3] Bédécarrats et al. (2019a); Pritchett and Sandefur (2013) argued that the scope of appropriate application of RCTs is 'vanishingly small'; and a group of Department for International Development (DFID) managers estimated that less than 5 per cent of development interventions are suitable for RCTs (Stern, 2012: 1, cited in Bédécarrats et al., 2019b: 10).
[4] Bédécarrats et al. (2019b): https://replicationnetwork.com/2019/04/30/bedecarrats-et-al-lessons-from-replicating-an-rct/; Young (2018).
[5] Chandy (2017: 11).

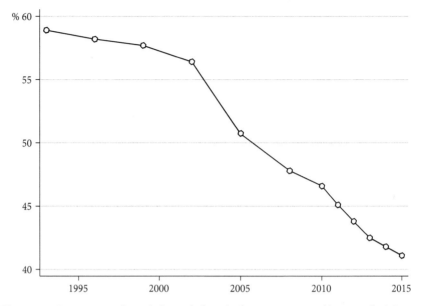

Figure 8.1 Percentage of people living below the 'extreme poverty' line in sub-Saharan Africa, 1993–2015

Note: Extreme poverty defined by the World Bank using 2011 PPP and $1.9/day poverty line.

Source: Author calculation using PovCalnet, World Bank (2019).

prevalence of extreme poverty in sub-Saharan Africa appears to have *fallen* a great deal between 1993 and 2015—from 59 per cent to 41 per cent—we will alert policymakers to serious problems that limit the usefulness of this particular measure. We emphasize, in Section 8.5, the difficulties (and the costs) of identifying poor households by estimating whether or not their consumption per capita falls below the cut-off of an international poverty line.

Boasts about poverty reduction will be contested by those who mistrust governments or are critical of their policies and wish to change them. Claims about trend reductions in poverty are also questioned by rigorous applied economists, such as Tony Atkinson, who insists that 'any estimate—of level or of change—is surrounded by a margin of error. This is often lost from sight in public pronouncements, and it is important to convey to policymakers and other users that they are operating with numbers about which there is considerable uncertainty'.[6] The broad aim of this chapter is to encourage policymakers to probe very carefully the arguments and available data underpinning fashionable proposals to reduce poverty in Africa.

---

[6] World Bank (2016d: xv–xvi, xviii).

8.2 Who Wants to Know? Struggles over Data

African political leaders such as President Kagame may be prepared to dispute statistics measuring poverty, but few are prepared, as Stalin was, to execute the nation's most senior statisticians if data in a population census fail to support implausible claims about output growth.[7] More generally, as Angus Deaton put it:

> The state decides what it needs to see and how to see it. That politics infuses every part of this is a testament to the importance of the numbers; lives depend on what they show.[8]

The NSO in Malawi was subject to intense pressure after 2005, because it had become politically imperative to exaggerate the success of the Minister of Agriculture's flagship farmer-support initiative, the Fertilizer Subsidy Programme. This political pressure was difficult to ignore because the Minister of Agriculture was also Malawi's President, who was facing an impending election. This political pressure, intensified by fiscal dependence on donors sceptical about the benefits of subsidies, perhaps explains delays in the publication of the Agricultural and Livestock Census (2006/7), which inconveniently showed that maize output in Malawi was about 60 per cent *below* previous estimates provided by agricultural extension officers. The embarrassing census also showed that the Ministry of Agriculture had been allocating expenditures on the basis of hugely inaccurate administrative estimates of the total number of farm households and their regional distribution. The result was a skewed distribution of subsidized inputs to ghost farmers and to the Northern Region, which was 'the swing voting region' critical to the electoral success of President Mutharika in 2009.[9]

A better-known African example of the political sensitivity of the census involves Nigeria, where there has not been a population census since 2006. Estimates of the size of the current population range between 140 and 200 million.[10] Political parties cultivating support in northern and southern Nigeria are continuing to obstruct and contest the production of more definitive statistics, because new and disaggregated estimates of the relative size of regional populations would have major resource (re)allocation implications. More recently, in Tanzania a political leader was arrested in November 2017 for publishing an analysis of anomalies in the statistics provided by the Bank of Tanzania and suggesting that the government had been manipulating (and exaggerating) gross

---

[7] Wilson (2019b); Merridale (1996).   [8] Deaton (2015).
[9] Jerven (2014: 10); Chinsinga and Poulton (2014: s140). See also Kilic et al. (2018: 4).
[10] Jerven (2018: 468) and additional references in Serra (2018: 662). Marivoet and de Herdt (2017) discuss census data in the Democratic Republic of Congo (DRC).

domestic product (GDP) growth rates.[11] And in 2019 (an election year) the Head of Mozambique's National Statistical Institute was forced by the President to resign after defending national census figures for the Frelimo-voting province of Gaza against what appeared to be inflated numbers in the electoral register.[12]

Africa's political leaders usually allocate limited and fluctuating resources to NSOs, leaving the funding and much of the design of statistical investigations to external donors.[13] Most NSOs in Africa are said to be 'constrained by budget instability and a lack of autonomy that leave them vulnerable to political and interest group pressures'. It is also reported that: 'ad hoc donor-funded projects generate significant revenue for statistics offices and individual NSO staff. Increasing take home pay by chasing donor-funded per diems via workshop attendance, training, and survey fieldwork is the order of the day. As a result, NSOs lack incentives to improve national statistical capacity . . . '[14] Labrousse concludes:

> Dominated by external actors (private, public, supranational), African 'statistical sovereignty' is profoundly incomplete.[15]

The World Bank has published an index of national statistical capacity for sub-Saharan African countries. Among the reasons why this index is unreliable is that it excludes important indicators, for example, data about labour force surveys.[16] Another index aims to measure the degree to which the websites of African NSOs follow best international practice in terms of coverage, accessibility, and quality of publicly accessible data.[17] Nigeria's score on this index might be regarded as surprisingly high in view of the absence of up-to-date population data; and Rwanda's relatively good scores on both these indices may raise eyebrows in the light of recent controversies over the politicization of poverty data.[18]

The meaning of all the scores on these indices, including the high score and apparent superiority of Statistics South Africa—so fiercely defended against academic critics by its recently retired leader[19]—needs to be questioned and examined alongside other evidence. In five major South African surveys, interviewer cheating and other sources of error were widespread.[20] The most politically embarrassing statistics, that is, the trends in South African inequality and real

---

[11] Human Rights Watch (2018): https://www.hrw.org/world-report/2018/country-chapters/tanzania-and-zanzibar#; Taylor (2017); *The Economist*, 14 March 2019.
[12] Hanlon (2019).   [13] Hoogeveen and Nguyen (2017).
[14] Glassman and Ezeh (2014: xii).   [15] Labrousse (2016b: 528).
[16] http://datatopics.worldbank.org/statisticalcapacity/.
[17] Hoogeveen and Nguyen (2017: appendix).
[18] http://roape.net/2018/11/21/the-cover-up-complicity-in-rwandas-lies/. For another view of the quality of Rwanda's statistics see Krätke and Byiers (2014: box 3), and Wilson and Blood (2019).
[19] Allison (2013) describes the extremely defensive response to criticism by South Africa's Statistician-General.
[20] Finn and Ranchhod (2017).

wages, are difficult to analyse because of serious data quality issues and because the officially published series has been interrupted by breaks in the measurement process.[21] The demographic impact of HIV AIDS in South Africa has also been politically sensitive; different sources of data provide very different estimates of the pattern and trends in new-born deaths, partly because 'there is uncertainty regarding the degree of completeness of reporting for young children'.[22] Earlier, President Mbeki's obsessive AIDS denialism encouraged the Department of Health to refuse medical researchers access to survey data while this department published misleading statistics on trends in the epidemic between 2006 and 2008.[23]

8.3 Ignoring Pro-Poor Policy Failures

There is accumulating evidence that allegedly pro-poor policies have an inegalitarian impact in rural Africa. Aid officials and the political elite have publicly championed a variety of anti-poverty policies and social welfare expenditures; but most of the poorest 20 per cent of the population in sub-Saharan Africa (as defined by the World Bank) failed to benefit from any of these anti-poverty programmes between 1998 and 2012.[24] An analysis for the period after 2012 examines African Development Bank and World Bank project aid to 17 African countries and also 'reveals that aid does not favor the poorest. Rather, aid disproportionately flows to regions that hold more of a country's richest people.'[25]

Data on education spending in Africa provide a particularly clear illustration of the degree to which large volumes of donor and state expenditure have been channelled to benefit the rich: the children of the rich, defined in terms of a Demographic and Health Survey (DHS) Wealth Index, are far more likely to gain access to higher levels of education; only about one in ten young people in sub-Saharan Africa are able to enter higher education, but hardly any of this small group of young people come from the poorest decile of households. Young people in poor households are particularly disadvantaged in some countries: in Ghana, for example, the poorest households only receive $16 for every $100 spent on rich households, while in Malawi poorest can expect to receive less than $10 for every $100 spent on the richest decile.[26]

Those countries having the most extreme pro-rich spending patterns usually show a consistent pattern of pro-rich public expenditure allocation at both secondary and higher education levels. By far the most extreme pro-rich bias in public expenditure on secondary schooling is found in Ethiopia (Figure 8.2).

---

[21] Wittenberg (2017).   [22] Bamford et al. (2018: 28).
[23] Dorrington and Bourne (2008); Lodge (2015).   [24] Ravallion (2015: 7, 23).
[25] Briggs (2017: 203).   [26] Ilie and Rose (2018: 637).

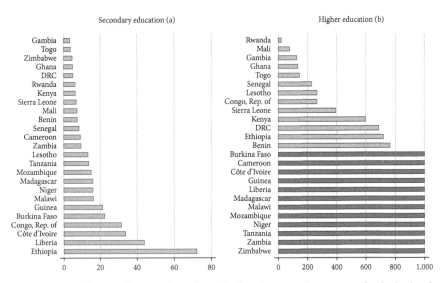

Figure 8.2 Public spending on the richest decile relative to the poorest decile, by level of education, selected sub-Saharan African countries

Note: The darker shaded bars in Table (b) indicate countries where the richest:poorest ratio exceeds 1,000.

Source: Adapted from Ilie and Rose (2017), based on UNESCO Institute of Statistics (UIS) and DHS data.

Current public spending patterns on education in Africa generally allocate large amounts to higher education at the expense of the primary and secondary sectors; these spending allocations are clearly much more regressive (pro-rich) in some African countries than in others.

By 2018, most African countries had established policies 'to protect and promote the poor and the vulnerable'; but, on average, these 'social safety net' programmes only cover a tiny percentage of the population. For example, less than 3 per cent of the population participate in public works programmes and most safety nets provide hardly any coverage of the huge internally displaced populations in Africa. And a significant proportion of Africa's social safety net expenditures benefit the *richest* quintile of households: Malawi's Social Action Fund and Ghana's Livelihood Empowerment Against Poverty programme are both good examples of benefit leakage to the richest households. A World Bank evaluation concludes that most of the poor in Africa have not benefitted from social safety net expenditure.[27]

Ethiopia's Public Safety Net Programme (PSNP) is the largest in Africa outside South Africa and its impact has been evaluated several times, leading to some

---

[27] Beegle, Coudouel & Monsalve (2018: 73–5).

rather positive conclusions.[28] Despite the size of Ethiopia's safety net programme, the bottom 10 per cent of rural households actually suffered declining consumption between 2005 and 2011—at an annual average rate of close to 2 per cent in real terms robust to the choice of deflator, while inequality as measured by a Theil Index, a measure sensitive to the share of the poorest, increased between 2000 and 2011.[29]

The beneficiaries of PSNP interventions to reduce malnutrition have been concentrated in selected districts (*woredas*), with predictably skewed nutritional results:

> Ethiopia's malnutrition rate could likely be substantially reduced by shifting some of the programs from the woredas with a high concentration of major programs into those with high malnutrition rates but no major programs.[30]

The PSNP 'excludes—by design—at least 52 per cent of vulnerable Ethiopian households'.[31] Econometric evidence suggests that this flagship anti-poverty intervention has had *no* effect on household dietary diversity or children's height-for-age in participating households.[32] Perhaps this is because the people benefitting from Ethiopia's PSNP (about one tenth of Ethiopia's population) were *not* selected by applying simple anthropometric rules or quantitative criteria.[33] People have been excluded (graduated) from the PSNP for not supporting the political elite and also because 'the criteria were subjective and no household data existed to support decision making'.[34]

This type of outcome is predictable whenever local officials beholden to politically appointed leaders are required to distribute scarce resources. The political imperatives underlying resource allocation in rural Ethiopia have been described by René Lefort and have also been illustrated by ethnographic research in seven different *kebeles*, which concludes that the 'social protection programme is being implemented in a way to eliminate opposition and . . . entrench power of the existing elite'.[35] Similarly, in Uganda, donor-funded technical reports on 'how to select' the beneficiaries of anti-poverty programmes have been brushed aside to pursue 'vote-buying clientelism', while in Tanzania the rollout of the Productive Social Safety Net and of earlier donor-funded schemes aimed at poverty reduction has been manipulated for electoral purposes and has served to strengthen the ruling party (the Chama Cha Mapinduzi; CCM).[36]

---

[28] For examples of this evaluation literature see: Favara et al. (2019) and Desalegn and Ali (2018).
[29] World Bank (2015: 12–14).   [30] Rajkumar et al. (2011: 134).
[31] World Bank (2015: 12, 49).   [32] Gebrehiwot and Castilla (2018).
[33] Sharp, Brown, and Teshome (2006: 21).
[34] Cochrane and Tamiru (2016: 657); Roelen, Devereux, and Kebede (2017: 22). See also Elias et al. (2013: 177).
[35] Lefort (2012); Cochrane and Tamiru (2016: 655).
[36] Hickey and Bukenya (2016: 18); Kjær and Joughin (2019); Jacob and Pedersen (2018: 23).

It has been argued that in rural Zimbabwe the government intentionally adopted policies to achieve 'Extreme scarcity and dependence on the state for agricultural inputs and food aid . . . [to] create an enforced loyalty that supports regime perpetuation.'[37] The extreme bias in the pattern of distribution of food aid to the rural poor by the rural cadres of Zimbabwe African National Union— Patriotic Front (ZANU–PF) has been 'discretionary, clientelistic and exclusionary'.[38] More recently, Emmerson Mnangagwa spearheaded the Command Agriculture Programme to allocate resources to securocrats and other politically important beneficiaries in rural areas.[39] Both the President and the Minister of Agriculture are said to 'have demonstrated a willingness to (ab)use food for political gain in Zimbabwe'.[40]

If policymakers and foreign advisors ignore the prevalence of violent struggles to maintain political power and to monopolize access to state resources in rural Africa, their proposals for interventions to reduce poverty are likely to be irrelevant. Resources ostensibly allocated to anti-poverty programmes, smallholder development, and food distribution are routinely diverted—to subsidize accumulation by larger farmers and/or conspicuous consumption by cronies.[41] The policy remedies proposed by the Food and Agriculture Organization (FAO), for instance, are unlikely to benefit the poor, because they so studiously avoid any discussion of African political realities: instead, FAO resorts to platitudes about the need for 'strong political commitment' as a precondition for ending extreme rural poverty.[42] Proclamations from Rome, together with the conventional surveys of rural household poverty (criticized in Section 8.5) and the increasingly complex multidimensional indicators of poverty promoted by other donor agencies, can readily be manipulated or ignored by administrative elites within Africa.

8.4 Conventional Strategies for Rural Poverty Reduction

Policymakers are repeatedly advised to focus support on smallholder farmers not only because of their allegedly superior yields per hectare but also because of a belief that, when African smallholder output increases, poverty will fall.[43] We discuss the data on the yield of small farmers in Chapter 9; here we focus on poverty reduction *mechanisms*.

John Mellor, the founder and first Director of International Food Policy Research Institute (IFPRI) and a Chief Economist for United States Agency for International Development (USAID), has argued, since 1961, that increases in

---

[37] Simpson and Hawkins (2018: 338).
[38] Chinyoka (2017: 17); Marongwe (2012: 144–5); Munyani (2005: 69–73).
[39] Simpson and Hawkins (2018: 365).   [40] Cameron (2018: 42).
[41] Jayne et al. (2018); Sender (2016).   [42] De La O Campos et al. (2018: 38).
[43] Hazell (2013: 20).

smallholder output 'generate rapid, equitable, geographically dispersed growth owing to agriculture's substantial labor intensive linkages with the non-farm economy'. The rural non-farm sector is a key source of income for the landless or semi-landless poor and opportunities in this sector are positively linked to the growth of small farmer income, because 'smallholders spend substantial portions of increased income . . . on employment-intensive, nontradable goods and services produced by the rural non-farm sector'. In contrast, according to this argument, much weaker rural consumption linkages are generated when *large* farmers' output and income grows; these farmers have 'urban-orientated consumption patterns'.[44]

Anyone who has spent time in rural Africa will agree that many poor people do depend on activities other than farming, although the poorest usually work *on* farms as casual agricultural wage workers rather than in the *non-farm* economy. But trading and village centres as well as small rural towns often provide poor rural women and men with opportunities for part-time and unskilled non-farm employment. These include many opportunities for low-paid wage employment: in construction and transport, food processing and packaging, carpentry, alcohol preparation, hairdressing, sexual services, guard work, and, of course, as domestic servants in private households. In some rural areas the main impetus for the growth of these local opportunities for wage employment may, as Mellor and many others suggest, be an increase in the agricultural revenues earned by scattered small famers. But elsewhere very different causal mechanisms have been much more important, with dramatically better outcomes for the poor.

For example, when public sector expenditure constructs a district hospital, a health clinic, a teacher training college, or a new irrigation structure, then salaried staff cadres, together with the more numerous wage workers employed as cleaners and security guards in these institutions, are likely to provide the breakthrough to a new level of local demand for wage-labour-intensive goods and services. The consequence may be increased competition for unskilled rural labour between, for example, the construction and the agricultural sector and a tightening of the labour market, leading to a rise in seasonal agricultural wages and a reduction in rural poverty. This link between public sector investment in rural areas, tightening labour markets, and rising agricultural wage rates is well documented for rural India.[45] In other rural areas, the impetus may arise when large-scale agribusinesses invest and create a new group of formal on-farm unskilled wage employees, who then stimulate a surprising array of non-farm employment. This is precisely what happened in Ziway, a town in Ethiopia that has grown very

---

[44] Mellor and Malik (2017: 2–3). In one Ethiopian simulation it is even assumed that 'all the additional income generated from increased production of these large farms is spent on urban goods, spent on imports, saved or sent abroad' (Dorosh and Mellor, 2014: 429).

[45] Sen and Ghosh (1993). For later years see: Himanshu and Kundu (2016).

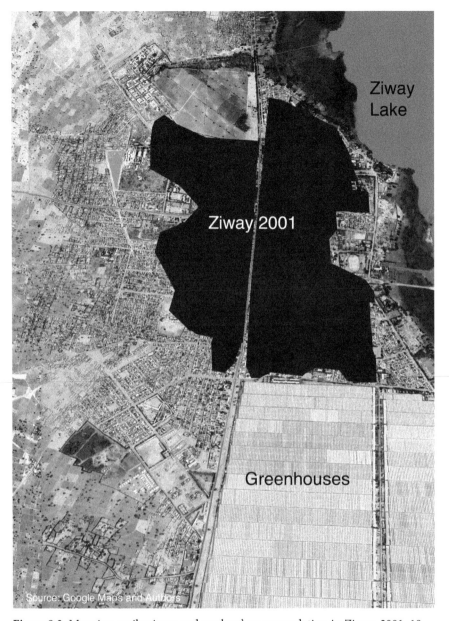

Figure 8.3 Mapping agribusiness and workers' accommodation in Ziway, 2001–18

dramatically since 2001 in the shadow of a few very large-scale floricultural and wine-producing firms.[46] Figure 8.3 illustrates some of this growth: part of the

---

[46] Cramer, Di John, and Sender (2018).

massive expansion in the area covered by greenhouses by 2018 can be seen in the bottom right-hand corner; and the degree to which the original (blacked-out) area of the town has been dwarfed by new residential areas constructed to the west and to the north is also obvious. Google's coloured satellite pictures make it clearer that the density of buildings in the original area covered by Ziway in 2001 has been transformed, with every available scrap of land converted to provide rental accommodation for migrant wage workers.

There are other examples of this type of poverty-reducing dynamic. In northern Senegal, where five large agribusiness estates have been established since 2003, there was rapid growth in the incomes of agribusiness wage employees.[47] In Tanzania, several emerging urban centres (EUCs) became 'hotspots for rural migration', often providing a range of services for large-scale agribusiness managers and their workers. When the population of salaried employees increased in the 1990s, access to schooling, health, and financial services improved—and non-crop-related wage employment opportunities for unskilled migrants from nearby and distant rural areas expanded.[48]

Strategies designed to increase the output of *all* small farm households will result, according to conventional theory, in new wage employment opportunities for people who are much poorer, because the beneficiaries will not only need to hire additional seasonal agricultural labour inputs at harvest time, but will also devote their incremental income to additional consumption of rurally produced labour-intensive goods and services. But we are not convinced about the strength of this indirect mechanism and its likely impact on poverty reduction. Even if some farmers do achieve a marginal increase in their consumption of purchased goods and services, only a few will have the capacity to use more hired labour inputs. The well-connected individuals farming on a relatively large scale will account for much of any growth in consumption stemming from state and non-governmental organization (NGO) interventions.[49] These individuals are also likely to purchase a high proportion of all hired labour days: the largest size tercile of smallholder farmers in Tanzania, for example, are much more likely to use hired labour than the smallest size tercile, and farmers who have acquired larger extents of irrigated vegetables use more hired labour than farmers with access to less irrigated land.[50] Where employers are oligopsonists in local labour markets, then the bargaining power of and the daily wage rate paid to their agricultural wage workers may be very low.[51]

If, instead, workers could find employment on much larger-scale farms, they would reduce the risk of failing to find daily employment outside peak seasons

---

[47] Van den Broeck and Maertens (2017).   [48] Lazaro et al. (2017: 24).
[49] Cramer et al. (2014a); Ragasa, Mazunda, and Kadzamira (2016: 22); Gray, Dowd-Uribe, and Kaminski (2018).
[50] Wineman and Jayne (2018: 24); Benali, Brümmer, and Afari-Sefa (2018: table 5).
[51] Bardhan and Rudra (1980a, 1980b).

and, as our own fieldwork over the past 30 years in Ethiopia, Mozambique, South Africa, and Uganda has shown, they would typically benefit from better wages and working conditions than those provided by smaller farmers.[52] Policy initiatives focused on improving the real annual wage of rural wage labourers—rather than on increasing the profits of 'small' producers—are rarely discussed or advocated in Africa by agricultural economists or donors. The need to monitor the real wages of agricultural wage workers as an indicator of poverty trends in Africa is hardly ever acknowledged.

There is no a priori reason to suppose that the non-farm linkages generated by the expenditures of rural wage workers, especially if they are paid a better wage, will be *weaker* and less poverty reducing than the linkages generated by the mini-farmers who struggle to survive by cultivating a few plants. On the contrary, we have good evidence that even the very poorest casual agricultural wage labourers in Africa aim to purchase a few locally produced consumer goods—such as a new dress, a table, bed, or cupboard.[53]

The assumption that poverty-reducing linkages can *only* stem from small farm development is also unconvincing because it has relied so heavily on strange and slippery definitions of the 'small'. Available data on the size distribution of farms in Africa is inconsistent and unreliable, but in many countries the median operated farm area per household is probably below one hectare.[54] So it is surprising that Mellor and his colleagues regard some farmers cultivating as much as 75 hectares as small. In Africa, they choose to define the top end of the distribution of all family farms (i.e. the 'commercial' and 'middle' farmers—with reliable access to water) as 'small'. In Ethiopia, for example, these authors adopt an idiosyncratic 'small' category that includes farmers who cultivate farms as large as 33 hectares.[55] Such quirky definitions can be useful when boasting that flagship policies supporting smallholders are pro-poor.[56] But it is disingenuous and extremely unhelpful for policy officials.

8.5 The Fog of Poverty Reduction: How Not to Focus on the Poorest

Angus Deaton argues that the 'gold standard'—the World Bank's central monetary measure of poverty—is 'inherently unreliable'.[57] He points out that it continues to be difficult to explain the large discrepancies between measures of consumption derived from household surveys and from national income statistics.

---

[52] Cramer et al. (20167).   [53] Sender, Cramer, and Oya (2018: 597).
[54] Lowder et al. (2016: 14).
[55] On Pakistan, see Mellor and Malik (2017: 3); on Ethiopia, see Dorosh and Mellor (2013: 423).
[56] Hazell (2019: 150).
[57] Deaton also argues against another supposed 'gold standard', that of RCTs as a means of finding out 'what works': Deaton and Cartwright (2018: 2) argue that 'any special status for RCTs is unwarranted'.

He also argues conventional methods of poverty estimation are 'clouded in a fog of technicalities'.[58] We will try to dispel this fog in our discussion of the most widely used conventional method.

The 'traditional basis', 'the core indicator' or the gold standard for identifying the poor, is the detailed information on consumption per household member collected in household surveys, especially the Living Standards Measurement Surveys (LSMS). On the basis of this costly, rather unreliable, and often dated information, everyone who lives in a household failing to achieve some minimum (cut-off) level of consumption per day is defined as 'poor'. If an individual's daily consumption expenditure is below the cut-off, defined by an international poverty line (set by the World Bank at US$1.90 in 2011 purchasing power parity (PPP) dollars), they suffer from 'extreme poverty' (see Figure 8.1).

It is not considered a good idea to use official exchange rates to compare the standard of living between countries, especially between low-income and OECD countries. At the official exchange rate, one dollar (for example) will usually be able to purchase far more goods and services in Dar es Salaam—cups of tea and haircuts—than it could in New York. A more 'correct' exchange rate would make one dollar worth the same, that is, have the same purchasing power in the low-income and the OECD country. The PPP rate is an estimate of the 'correct' exchange rate in this sense and this estimate requires the collection of millions of prices of comparable items all around the world. There is probably a 25 per cent margin of error on either side of PPP exchange rates.[59]

The mix of methods and countries used to select the US$1.90 poverty line—originally a 'dollar a day'—appears to have been strongly influenced by the Bank's own public relations requirements and a desire to achieve consistency with previous estimates, rather than by examining the lived experience of the poor. An earlier version of the current international poverty line was slightly below $1.90, but the World Bank decided to round this number up.[60] Angus Deaton labels the level of daily expenditure that has been selected as the poverty line cut-off 'a miserable pittance', while Jean Drèze points out that (even above the cut-off) the amount a 'non-poor' person could afford to spend per month on health, for example, would barely cover the cost of purchasing a single aspirin; their total monthly expenditures could not possibly 'meet the requirements of dignified living'.[61] It has been suggested that the apparently arbitrary choice of such a low cut-off line was influenced by a desire to applaud the success of governments and international agencies in achieving an impressive reduction in poverty.[62]

[58] Deaton (2016: 1223). Drèze and Deaton (2017: 66).   [59] Deaton (2013: 228).
[60] Ferreira et al. (2016: 161).
[61] Deaton (2013: 223); Drèze (2019: 55); https://www.youtube.com/watch?v=zfxH6qL9_ik.
[62] Edward and Sumner (2016: 10).

In sub-Saharan Africa the consumption level in 2015 of a huge percentage of the population (41 per cent) fell *below* this cut-off line and all these people are defined by the World Bank as living in extreme poverty. In 11 sub-Saharan African countries 'more than half of the population live in extreme poverty'.[63] No less than 86 per cent of the rural population of South Sudan is, according to the latest estimate (for 2016), living in extreme poverty.[64] A large proportion of African households are consuming at levels only very slightly above or below the level of the international poverty line.[65] One implication is that a recalculation of the PPP rate by economists in Pennsylvania, or a proposal in Washington for a very small increase/decrease in the poverty cut-off, will immediately shift millions of Africans into or out of poverty. For example, a tiny increase in the international PPP poverty line (from $1.90 to $2.00) would add 100 million people to the extreme poverty headcount.[66]

The World Bank argues that 'In 2015, more than half of the global poor resided in Sub-Saharan Africa' and forecasts that by 2030 about 87 per cent of the global poor will live in sub-Saharan Africa.[67] But the proportion of global poverty that is accounted for by sub-Saharan Africa (as opposed to South Asia) is determined by the Bank's questionable decision to set the international poverty cut-off at a relatively low level. Whether those living just above this line really are now 'non-poor' depends on whether or not we accept that someone can live decently when their level of consumption is so low. Policymakers should also be aware that trends in poverty reduction can easily be exaggerated when household survey questionnaires or methods change between surveys and when the available consumer price indices do not accurately reflect the changing consumption basket of very poor households. For example, poverty reduction has been exaggerated in Uganda for both of these reasons; and it has been exaggerated in Rwanda by manipulating the Consumer Price Index.[68]

Any optimistic assessment of trends in poverty also depends on whether or not we accept claims that household surveys reliably capture the consumption of individuals at the tail end of the distribution, for example, the meagre consumption of migrant construction workers, squatters, and agricultural wage labourers. Quite apart from the problem of these excluded individuals at the tail end, even officially included 'poor' individuals have not enjoyed the consumption gains reflected in the aggregate trend for sub-Saharan Africa as a whole: growth rates of consumption for the 'poor' were *negative* in Uganda, Zambia, Ghana, Niger, and South Africa between about 2010 and 2015 and, over roughly the same period, were barely positive in Ethiopia and Rwanda.[69] Consequently, it is not

---

[63] World Bank (2018: 27).   [64] Pape and Parisotto (2019: 3).   [65] World Bank (2018: 75).
[66] Aguilar and Sumner (2019: 2).   [67] World Bank (2018: 4).
[68] Daniels and Minot (2014); ROAPE (2018).
[69] http://iresearch.worldbank.org/PovcalNet/povOnDemand.aspx; see also Clementi, Fabiani, and Molini (2019).

surprising that the share of national income currently received by the poor is minuscule. The latest available disaggregated data on the income share of the poorest (defined as the lowest 20 per cent in Figure 8.4) show large differences between African countries, but also that the income share of the poorest

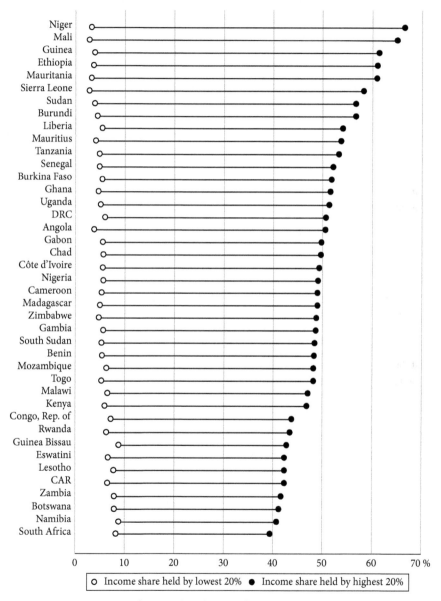

Figure 8.4 Income inequality in sub-Saharan Africa (shares of the lowest and highest 20% of population)

Source: World Bank PovCalnet (2019).

20 per cent is *always* disproportionately small; it is below—in some countries way below—10 per cent.

8.6 Alternatives to the 'Gold Standard'?

We have discussed some of the problems of using conventional consumption per capita and cut-off lines to analyse poverty. Many development economists are aware of these (and other) difficulties with LSMS data in Africa. Nonetheless, when economists advise policymakers on how to select the 'best' method of identifying the poor the only selection criterion continues to be accuracy in predicting household per capita expenditure.[70] It is not necessary for policymakers to accept this definition of the 'best' indicator: they can turn to well-established alternative indicators of poverty or socio-economic status, such as wealth or asset indices based on DHS data.

Asset indices have been used rather successfully in Africa to identify rural households containing less educated people with more health problems, higher fertility, and greater risk of child stunting than other households.[71] They can also offer other important advantages to policymakers: they are usually constructed from a few dichotomous indicators of asset ownership and housing characteristics (e.g. does the house have access to a radio, improved sanitation, or have an earth/ dung floor?). Answers to these questions do not require respondents to perform unrealistic feats of recall, and can be collected more cheaply, more quickly, and probably with less measurement error than the huge number of questions about past and current expenditures in the LSMS. (The costs of LSMS in Uganda and Tanzania amounted to about US$400 per surveyed household.[72])

The accuracy of responses to questions about ownership of inanimate items of furniture, a bed for example, can be confirmed visually by enumerators. But responses to questions about other key assets in rural Africa—the number of chickens and animals owned—are always much more unreliable.[73] And there are other important problems faced by all attempts to construct these asset indices: if the aim is to use the asset index as a proxy for wealth, researchers must either use depreciated values or make arbitrary choices about how to weight different assets; but the relevant time series of prices to estimate depreciation is unlikely to be available in poor rural areas. Besides, it will always be difficult to account for differential quality: it may be obvious to all enumerators that an Apple iPhone is not the same thing as the most common mobile phone in Africa (a Tecno T201—costing about US$15), but less obvious that the quality of one cooking utensil is very much lower than another (home-made) item, or that the

---

[70] Ngo and Christiaensen (2018).   [71] Stifel et al. (2018).   [72] Kilic et al. (2017: 21).
[73] Lesnoff (2015); Himelein, Eckman, and Murray (2014).

quality of access to sanitation varies dramatically, for example, between those with access to piped water 24/7 and those with only intermittent access.[74] Also, huge seasonal price variations have been recorded for rural assets—in Tanzania, for example, the price of a bicycle can more than double in the dry relative to the wet season.[75]

The theoretical and practical problems of how to justify the selection of the specific items to be included in an asset index—and of how to weight these items—are often side-stepped in published research on rural poverty. Most studies are content to follow conventions and procedures established by earlier social scientists. Researchers admit that there is little underlying theory to support the choice of variables to include when using statistical procedures—such as the principal components analysis (PCA) used by the DHS.[76]

Besides, unweighted indices of socio-economic status have often been found to perform just about as well in identifying low socio-economic status rural house-holds as the indices constructed using PCA to estimate weights.[77] Since many policymakers may not be inclined to unpick the meaning of the weights used or to query the arguments for including one asset rather than another, PCA (and other statistical techniques such as multiple correspondence analysis) would seem merely to lend a spurious aura of scientific, quantitative precision to conventional policy prescriptions.[78]

A bewildering smörgåsbord of implicitly or explicitly weighted indices and recondite definitions of poverty now confront policymakers in Africa. Apart from asset/wealth indices and the 'gold standard' monetary measures, a mixed assortment of new *non-monetary* indices of poverty has been added to the buffet table, including indices that make brave attempts to quantify levels of 'empowered decision-making' such as the Relative Autonomy Index (RAI), providing a direct measure of women's motivational autonomy. Another, though less fashionable, non-monetary index facetiously claims to track the quality of governance in public institutions—the Gross Toilet Index.[79] Some poverty experts mix and match, using these novel indices in combination with the increasingly fashionable Multidimensional Poverty Index (or other 'mash-up indices') to report, for example, the percentage of women 'deprived in at least three dimensions', or the proportion of children deprived in three to six dimensions.[80]

---

[74] https://humantechlab.org/2019/01/10/which-chinese-phone-giant-dominates-sales-in-africa-against-apple/; Gulyani, Rizvi, and Talukdar (2019).

[75] Kaiser, Hruschka, and Hadley (2017: 2).

[76] Tusting et al. (2016: 651); Ngo and Christiaensen (2018: 12); Rich, Desmond, and Makusha (2019: 494).

[77] Sender, Cramer, and Oya (2018): Liu, Esteve, and Treviño (2017); Kabudula et al. (2017). There is, of course, no such thing as an unweighted index; it simply means that the components of an index are given *equal weights*.

[78] Some of these statistical techniques are outlined in Vollmer and Alkire (2018).

[79] Vaz, Pratley, and Alkire (2016); Mahajan (2014).

[80] Ravallion (2012); Beegle et al. (2016: 108).

One noteworthy feature of the Multidimensional Poverty Indices is a failure to include any indicators of the fundamentally important determinants of the standard of living of rural children and adults, that is, their wages and working conditions or, in the case of children, their exposure to teenage pregnancy.[81] The World Bank has made an effort to explain its failure to include any employment indicators in its 2018 Multidimensional Poverty Index, but inconsistent and unfounded arguments citing relevance and data quality smack of ideology:

> Employment is not part of the multidimensional poverty measure presented here for two reasons. First, many of the frequently used indicators of employment in high-income countries, such as . . . wage employment, are not as relevant in low-income countries, which have very different labor market structures . . . Second, whatever relevant indicators of employment exist, these indicators are not available or not sufficiently harmonized in the different surveys considered here.[82]

Since 2009, the World Bank has promoted an index of development that is sensitive to inequality of opportunity, that is, an index that can take account of the fact while average access to education or maternal health services for women in Africa has been improving, some (rural) women have not been able to benefit very much from expanded coverage. But this Human Opportunity Index (HOI) is very highly and significantly correlated with the United Nations Development Programme's (UNDP's) Human Development Index (HDI); and the Bank's Multidimensional Poverty Indices produce a similar global poverty profile to the monetary 'gold standard' measures based on the $1.90 poverty cut-off.[83] Our conclusion is that many of the growing number of newly minted poverty indices are redundant—they may appear to satisfy NGOs' demand for non-monetary, more 'human' development measures, but they do not get us closer to identifying the realities of the economic lives of the poorest people and they do not help in sharpening the focus of policymakers on these poor people.

8.7 The Most Vulnerable People: 'Common Sense' and Uncontroversial Stylized Facts

Nicholas Kaldor used stylized facts to criticize theories and explanations published by neoclassical economists; he regarded them as guilty of producing theories based on assumptions that were not even approximately true and, therefore, could not justifiably be used for purposes of explanation or policy analysis.[84] Something

---

[81] Alkire et al. (2017: table 1).   [82] World Bank (2018: 94).
[83] Brunori, Ferreira, and Peragine (2013: 17); Aguilar and Sumner (2019: 22).
[84] Lawson (1989: 76).

similar affects much economic analysis of poverty and of contemporary African economic development. Most economists agree on several conventional wisdom propositions about African poverty. In this section we begin by listing and questioning the policy relevance of three of these popular, conventional propositions about poverty. We then introduce a selection of stylized facts about poverty—uncontroversial facts that are much *less* likely to mislead policymakers. Finally, we introduce a particular stylized fact that has too often been ignored or dismissed as irrelevant for understanding broad trends in poverty or making policy but that we argue is at the very core of the problem.

Conventional Wisdom I: Poverty is Rural

In most African countries most of the people who are poor live in rural rather than urban areas. It makes little difference how poverty is defined—with a money metric, an asset index, an anthropometric cut-off, or a mix of multidimensional indicators: rurality dominates the poverty profile. The percentage of the poor who live in rural areas in the 2010s is about three times greater than the percentage of the poor who live in urban areas.[85] About two thirds of the total population of sub-Saharan Africa live in rural areas and in some countries, for example, Burundi, Uganda, Malawi, Niger, South Sudan, and Ethiopia, more than 80 per cent do so.

But this does not help policymakers to design very precise or effective interventions.[86] A geographically defined strategy claiming to benefit 'rural' households will, for political economy reasons already discussed in Section 8.2, probably exclude the poorest households. Besides, a growing number of rural households in Africa's rapidly differentiating countryside are by no means poor; they operate medium and large-scale capitalist enterprises.[87]

The policy relevance of a simple rural–urban distinction is also questionable for another reason: the boundaries between the rural and the urban are shifting very rapidly in Africa and are often contested.[88] Many *non-poor* households are falsely classified as 'rural' when they live just outside the dated and arbitrarily drawn administrative boundaries of a city.[89] On closer examination, they are primarily engaged in urban occupations and well integrated into urban economic activities, including, in some cases, real estate speculation. If relatively prosperous urban people can make false claims to be living in 'rural' households with customary

---

[85] Beegle et al. (2016: 10); De La O Campos et al. (2018: 9).
[86] Aguilar and Sumner (2019: table 5); World Bank (2018: table 4C.1).
[87] Jayne et al. (2016); Lay, Nolte, and Sipangule (2018); Whitfield (2017); Greco (2015); Schaefer (2016).
[88] Van Noorloos and Kloosterboer (2018).   [89] Pincus and Sender (2008).

land rights, then the poorer rural households may again be at the back of any queue for allocating valuable resources.

The rural–urban gap in consumption per capita is, like the headcount rate of poverty, much larger in some countries than others. For example, Integrated Surveys of Agriculture (LSMS-ISA) suggest that the level of consumption per capita in urban Tanzania is 2.2 times higher than in rural Tanzania, while in Uganda urban consumption per capita is 3.3 times rural consumption per capita.[90] Non-monetary poverty indicators can also provide evidence of inter-country differences in the urban–rural welfare gap: for example, while the under-5 mortality rate (U5MR) is very high in rural Sierra Leone, the urban mortality rate is not much lower; but in Nigeria the urban rate is much lower than the rural rate; in Kenya, the rural–urban gap has already disappeared and the urban U5MR is now actually higher than the rural rate.[91] While these variations are important, average data for a group of 23 African countries can be used to illustrate the general disadvantages of rurality (Figure 8.5). This figure highlights the huge disadvantages faced by rural women, especially in their ability to achieve adequate education and antenatal care.

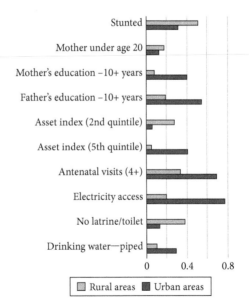

Figure 8.5 Urban and rural inequality: mean comparison for selected variables (for a group of 23 sub-Saharan African countries)
Source: Stifel et al. (2018).

---

[90] De Magalhães and Santaeulàlia-Llopis (2018: table 2).   [91] Beatriz et al. (2018: table 1).

Geographical inequality is only *one* form of inequality that can be used to investigate disparities in standards of living and to design policy, but it is conventional common sense to focus on geography and on the mapping of administrative units, rather than political economy and class analysis. The widely accepted view is that geographical mapping of poverty indicators can make a major contribution to the design of poverty reduction strategies.[92] But there is good evidence that the pattern of U5MR, as well as other indicators of risks to health, *cannot* be explained in terms of rural or urban residence. Instead, much if not all of the urban health advantage can be explained by socio-economic factors such as household wealth and maternal education.[93] For example, urbanization does *not* appear to have a direct and positive association with child nutrition outcomes and diets. When socio-economic controls are introduced into linear probability regressions, the results suggest that the rural–urban child nutrition gap does *not* remain significant; instead of geography, 'the key nutritional disadvantage of rural populations stems chiefly from social and economic poverty'.[94]

Influential populists have claimed for decades that the poor will benefit if interventions are rebalanced to favour rural rather than urban areas, but policymakers face a much more difficult task—to reduce unacceptable differences in the standard of living *within* rural and urban locations.[95] The broad claim that most of the poor in Africa are young is also not very useful for (or surprising to) policymakers; it is also true by definition because children and young people account for such a very high proportion (about 60 per cent) of Africa's total population.[96] The scatter-gun targeting of the poor as 'youth' has fuelled spurts in expenditure on tertiary education and training that, while claiming to be pro-poor, have mainly benefitted the children of richer parents and very few of the poorest young people. It is also driven by a supply-side fantasy that more education will lead neatly to more growth and employment, another nugget of conventional wisdom contradicted by the evidence.

Conventional Wisdom II: The Poorest People Live in Large Households

There is a long tradition emphasizing the negative social consequences of excessive fecundity among poor women; and these views have often fuelled regressive policy interventions and moral panics.[97] One of the founders of the London School of Economics believed that children living in large households in Britain

[92] Marivoet, Ulimwengu, and Sedano (2019); Oxford Poverty and Human Development Initiative (2018: 71); Alkire (2018: 11).
[93] Beatriz et al. (2018).   [94] Stifel et al. (2018).
[95] The high priests of the movement to reduce 'urban bias' are Bates (1980) and Lipton (2012b).
[96] United Nations (2017: 10).   [97] Shepard (2007).

at the end of the nineteenth century risked poverty because of irresponsible breeding by an inferior type of 'thriftless and irresponsible' immigrant Catholic and Jew.[98] In fact, during the nineteenth century the poorest decile of households—paupers and vagrants—lived in very small households. Unskilled labourers lived in much smaller households than richer classes.[99]

In Africa, larger households are conventionally believed to be more vulnerable to poverty. For example, an analysis of poverty in Uganda based on LSMSs concludes that 'the chronic poor have relatively large households . . . Those that have never been poor have small households.'[100] But the view that large households are more likely to be poor than other households leans towards tautology.

Households are defined as poor because household *per capita* expenditure/ consumption is below the cut-off. If the denominator (i.e. the size of the household) is large, it is not a surprising arithmetic result that the incidence of poverty is higher in larger households. It also follows arithmetically that a small reduction in the size of the denominator as a result, for example, of the death of a new-born baby, could immediately raise *per capita* household expenditure above the poverty cut-off.

Whether or not a household is classified as poor is obviously influenced by the accuracy of and the methods used to count the number of household members, that is, survey estimates of the size of the denominator. The problem is that these estimates are, in many African contexts, unreliable. They continue to rely on an a priori standardized, narrow, and inappropriate definition of 'the household' and its 'residents', despite decades of vigorous criticism showing the difficulties of using conventional (residential) definitions of the household in studying rural Africa.[101] There is no coherent account of how survey enumerators should delimit the boundaries of the household and the pattern of visits by enumerators that may be required: 'little attention has been paid to the issue of what "household" means in these surveys: how it is defined for data collection purposes and what the definition implies for the analysis and interpretation of results'.[102] Moreover, 'The probability of finding no one at home in a one person household is larger than in a multiple person household. Small households are therefore likely to be underrepresented in the survey.'[103]

---

[98]   Cited in Aldrich (2019: 19).   [99]   Schürer et al. (2018: table 9).
[100]   Van Campenhout, Sekabira and Aduayom (2016: 150). For similar views on Ethiopia see: Abebaw and Admassie (2013: 127). More generally, see Beegle, Coudouel, and Monsalve (2018: 50). See also: Beegle et al. (2016: 130) and World Bank (2018: 38).
[101]   Guyer and Peters (1987); O'Laughlin (1995); Adato, Lund, and Mhlongo (2007); Akresh and Edmonds (2010); Cramer et al. (2014b: 178–9).
[102]   Randall, Coast, and Leone (2011: 217). Estimating 'household size' in Victorian Britain is also difficult because of shifts in instructions to census enumerators (Schürer et al., 2018: tables 1 and 3).
[103]   Hoogeveen and Schipper (2006: 77–8). Poor widows are also likely to be under-represented (Randall and Coast, 2016: 150).

Although poverty has often been associated with large households on the basis of household expenditure data, very different conclusions are reached when poverty is analysed using a wealth index. For example, DHS survey data show that household size in the poorer wealth (not expenditure) quintiles in 2011 was *smaller* than in the richer quintiles in Uganda and Ethiopia. In South Africa too, the poorest decile of households are *not* significantly larger than other households, if poverty is defined in terms of an asset index rather than expenditure per capita.[104]

Historical arguments support the view that very small households face greater risks. The most distinguished historian of poverty in Africa points out that: 'In several African languages the common word for "poor" . . . implies lack of kin and friends, while the weak household, bereft of able-bodied male labour, has probably been the most common source of poverty throughout Africa's recoverable history.'[105] The intuition that successful farming may be impossible for some very small households is also supported by survey evidence from Ethiopia, Ghana, South Africa, and elsewhere: the challenges of crop production are likely to be insurmountable where small households lack sufficiently close links to adult males, or to the network of local connections necessary to acquire land, agricultural inputs, seasonal credit, and certain types of labour.[106] One implication of these difficulties was noted many years ago by Iliffe, but has since been insufficiently emphasized, that is, that in these small and very poor households the main or most reliable source of income may be casual wage labour for neighbouring, larger households.

Conventional Wisdom III: Female-Headed Households are the Poorest

In UN agencies 'there is a continued focus on comparisons between households, and especially between male-headed and female-headed units. The thorny question of how to define "female headship" is often ignored.'[107] World Bank publications also continue to argue that 'For several countries, a larger share of the multidimensional poor live . . . in female-headed households', although a number of their economists have admitted that the classification of households as either male or female headed is 'not very useful'.[108]

---

[104] Rich, Desmond, and Makusha (2018: 8). In Vietnam, LSMS results linking poverty with large households have been criticized in detail by Dinh Vu Trang Ngan, Pincus, and Sender (2012).

[105] Iliffe (1987: 7, 238). The poor in England during the Industrial Revolution lived in much smaller households than other social classes (Allen, 2019: 92).

[106] Siyoum (2012: 50ff.); Skalidou (2018: table 9); Palmer and Sender (2006).

[107] Bradshaw, Chant, and Linneker (2017: 16).

[108] World Bank (2018: 109); Boudet et al. (2018: 4). The emphasis on female-headed households is widespread among African leaders of NGOs (ACPF, 2019: 33).

There have been many attempts to link deprivation with 'female-headed households' or 'female farm managers' in sub-Saharan Africa (and elsewhere), but these typically reach ambiguous conclusions.[109] One reason is that, like 'rural' households, female-headed households are a very mixed bag. A highly educated woman on a career break can choose to spend some time bringing up children alone on her own peaceful farm; her husband may very rarely leave his highly paid urban job to visit her, but he does send her a large monthly money order. The bucolic standard of living enjoyed by this woman cannot easily be compared to the survival struggles of a landless widow or divorcee bringing up children and grandchildren in a rural area without any support from an adult male. The gulf between these two women has been papered over in key documents produced by UN Women, where 'lack of consideration of differences between women is a recurrent theme'.[110]

One problem is that 'A household is likely to report a female head if the usual male head is a migrant working out of town, in which case the household may benefit from remittances that make them less likely to be poor.'[111] More generally, we have already argued that most survey enumerators do not depart from simplistic tick-box rules and local social norms when they identify 'the head' (or list all approved 'members') of a 'household'. If enumerators were sufficiently trained and supervised to collect *all* the data necessary to understand the fluidity of residential arrangements in rural Africa and the role of labour mobility and remittances in reproduction strategies, then the gendered disadvantages faced by *individuals* (as well as households) could be highlighted. A recommendation in 2018 that poverty analysts should abandon the simple classification of households by 'headship' and gender in favour of an array of new household typologies, for example 'multiple adults, only female—with children', may be a step in the right direction.[112] But there will still be difficulties in probing respondents to enumerate *all* household members (currently resident or non-resident) and the economic relationships between them.

Domestic servants and other female (and male) migrant workers remit part of their wage earnings to other rural individuals. Unfortunately, no information is recorded in conventional surveys about the workers who remit. This information gaps make it extremely difficult to understand how the poorest rural households actually pay for children's school expenses and food; the gendered and generational dynamics of power and labour market inequalities are obscured in a rural black box 'household' especially if, as is usually the case, the education levels achieved by, and the gender of, 'non-residents' are unrecorded.

---

[109] Milazzo and van de Walle (2015); Liu, Esteve, and Treviño (2017); Djurfeldt, Dzanku, and Isinika (2018); Fransman and Yu (2019).

[110] Bradshaw, Chant, and Linneker (2017: 13).　　[111] Casteñada et al. (2018: 257).

[112] Boudet et al. (2018: 25ff.).

In our own surveys we have tried both to overcome these difficulties and to analyse gendered experiences of poverty in rural Africa—without making any attempt to identify 'household heads'. Our methodological innovations have been discussed at length elsewhere.[113] The broad aim of our research was to collect data on vulnerable wage workers, especially female workers engaged in seasonal, casual, and low-paid jobs outside major urban centres. We recognized that many of these individuals are frequently *not* 'resident' in households. They live and work for long periods in labour camps, construction sites, and illegal squatter settlements, or they have been given some space to sleep at their workplace during the harvest season, or while working as domestic servants: they are the 'nowhere people'.[114]

With more information on a larger range of individuals than are usually recorded in DHS or LSMS household rosters, we had the information to develop a clearer idea of the nature and implications of economic flows between male and female individuals, wherever they were currently located. If more than 75 per cent of the whole range of listed adults were female, then we described these households as 'female dominated'; and these households were much more likely than other households to be extremely deprived.[115] The proposed definition of female domination and how we measured 'extreme' deprivation—using a simple Deprivation Index—did not require any technically complicated weighting, smoke or mirrors. We use an index that is transparent, easy to construct, and intuitively appealing.

8.8 Selecting Stylized Facts with an Extreme Deprivation Index

Some of the rural women we met are difficult to forget, especially their embarrassed faces when they could not even offer us a seat while we talked—not even on the simplest stool or bench. They lived in utterly bare rooms. These women helped us to understand that owning a few consumer goods could result in large absolute improvements in the quality of rural life. Without reliable access to electricity, a torch makes the night safer; sleeping on earthen floors cannot be compared to sleeping on a bed; a radio and a mobile phone can expand intellectual horizons, reduce isolation, and even help in searching for casual wage employment. Respondents may also be able to benefit in less obvious ways if they own 'honorific' or 'prestige-based' consumer goods—such as a sofa. The women we have talked to in poor rural areas of Southern and Eastern Africa are, of course, well aware of these benefits and our surveys do show rather widespread ownership of this type of consumer good. For example, about half of all our respondents in

---

[113] Cramer et al. (2014b).   [114] Breman (2010: 135).
[115] Sender, Cramer, and Oya (2018: table 4).

Uganda and Ethiopia owned a radio and more than half owned a table, while 60 per cent owned a bed. It was intuitively obvious that individuals who had access to *none* or hardly any of these basic wage goods were extremely deprived.

Building on this intuition and rejecting statistically driven methods for constructing and weighting asset indices, we designed a new and very simple measure—the Extreme Deprivation Index (EDI). The practical relevance of the EDI is that it allows a quick, reliable and cost-effective way of identifying people who suffer from extreme deprivation and of assessing the distributional impact of policy interventions. The EDI takes out the 'unavoidable guesswork in establishing who is poor' that a leading proponent of RCTs seems simply to accept.[116] We made a context-specific selection of 10 *basic non-food wage goods*, each of which would probably make a difference to the quality of rural life in many areas of rural Africa. The goods we selected were: a cupboard; a metal or wooden bed; a table; a sofa; a stove or cooker; a thermos; a torch; a mobile phone; a radio; and a cassette/CD player. We did not estimate the prices of these items or attempt to justify a complex weighting system: the EDI gives a score of 1 to ownership of each of the 10 selected basic consumer goods; *the lowest scoring quintile of our respondents either scored no points or a maximum of 2.* We defined these respondents recording a score in the bottom quintile of the distribution of EDI scores as living in the 'most deprived' households.

Many other surveys have shown that a high proportion of rural African households in the lowest expenditure/wealth quintile fail to consume the amount of food necessary to prevent child stunting,[117] but these surveys also agree that relatively poor households do devote some of their expenditure to non-food consumer goods; they often do manage to acquire items very similar to the simple furniture and other basic consumer goods that we suggest should be the basis for constructing a context-specific EDI. For example, in rural Kenya, the expenditure elasticity for furniture—'beds, chairs, tables, etc.'—has been found to be very high in a random sample of poor households.[118]

We have used survey data from Uganda and Ethiopia to compare the characteristics of households in the bottom quintile of the EDI (the 'most deprived') with other households; and we found little evidence to support conventional conclusions about the vulnerability of large households or female-headed households. But we did find that a significantly higher percentage of the 'most deprived' households was *small* and *female dominated*.[119] In East African rural contexts where women and widows are often subjected to brutal forms of discrimination and gender inequalities are pervasive, it is perhaps not surprising that the 'most

---

[116] Banerjee (2015: 8).   [117] Black et al. (2013).
[118] Haushofer and Shapiro (2013: 30). For similar results in rural South Africa, see Browne, Ortmann, and Hendriks (2007: 571).
[119] Sender, Cramer, and Oya (2018).

deprived' households contain relatively few adult males and that relatively few of these households have regular access to any financial support from an adult male.[120] For example, in tea-growing areas of Uganda, about half of the 'most deprived' households had no regular male support, compared to 15 per cent of other households.

We have also used the EDI to confirm the importance of other uncontroversial stylized facts about gender relations and deprivation. For example, it is widely acknowledged that adolescent pregnancies are hazardous both for the mother and the child.[121] Teenage mothers in Africa and elsewhere are at greater risk than more mature mothers of mortality; and their lifetime labour incomes are likely to be significantly lower than the earnings of women who did not have children when they were teenagers.[122] In the 'most deprived' households identified by the EDI, young women aged between 20 and 30 years are very likely to have had a child as an adolescent. In Uganda, for example, the risks of teenage pregnancy are remarkably high in the 'most deprived' households: only a very low proportion of young women in the 'most deprived' households (17%) had their first child when they were mature (20 years old or older), while a much higher proportion of women in other households (44%) were able to delay having their first child until they were mature.

A low level of female educational attainment is widely and correctly viewed as a particularly useful marker of poverty and of the adverse longer-term consequences of deprivation in Africa, because a woman's lack of education is likely to be transmitted inter-generationally, negatively affecting the health, productivity, and lifetime earnings of her children.[123] Our analysis using the EDI confirms the relevance and policy importance of the uncontroversial stylized fact that parental education and poverty are linked: we show, for example, clear associations between the 'most deprived' households and the absence of any adult who had graduated from secondary school, the presence of children not attending school, adult failures to complete primary school, and adult functional illiteracy.[124]

Another uncontroversial and policy-relevant stylized fact is that African children are vulnerable to chronic undernutrition if their diet is monotonous—if they can only achieve a low dietary diversity score.[125] Again, our rural surveys were able to use the EDI to confirm the importance of this link. We simply asked respondents how frequently different types of food were eaten by anyone in the household.

---

[120] Marshall, Lyytikainen, and Jones (2016); Semahegn and Mengistie (2015); Bantebya, Muhanguzi, and Watson (2014); Sharp, Devereux, and Amare (2003: 56).

[121] Saloojee and Coovadia (2015: e342).   [122] Pradhan and Canning (2016: 1).

[123] Castañeda et al. (2018: 258); ICF International (http://www.statcompiler.com); Alderman and Headey (2017: 456); Bado and Sathiya Susuman (2016); Ambel and Huang (2014: 14); Keats (2018: 155). See also: Tusting et al. (2016: 653).

[124] Sender, Cramer, and Oya (2018: 7–8).

[125] Hernández (2012); Herrador et al. (2015); Hirvonen, Taffesse, and Worku Hassen (2016); Hirvonen et al. (2017); Muhoozi et al. (2016).

The EDI proved surprisingly useful in predicting dietary diversity: only about 14 per cent of the 'most deprived' claimed to eat *any* high-value food items regularly, compared to over 45 per cent of other households.

We conclude that it is possible to identify policy-relevant stylized facts about the poorest people in Africa: they live in relatively small, female-dominated households and lack regular access to support from an adult male; adult females and children in these households probably have not received or are not receiving an adequate education; these women and children are threatened by the risks of teenage pregnancy; they also risk undernutrition because they rely on a monotonous and undiversified diet; and they have been able to acquire hardly any basic consumer wage goods. The absence of these goods in their homes can rapidly (and accurately) be confirmed by enumerators, using an EDI. This index can reliably, and at low cost, predict many of the difficulties they face.

Perhaps the least controversial and easily accepted policy implication of these stylized facts would be an agreement on new funding to reduce educational deprivation, especially investment to allow rural girls to complete or even attend secondary school. Appropriate expenditures on education would probably delay pregnancy and improve the labour market prospects for rural women, but the targeting of these interventions—for example, scholarships or conditional cash transfers—towards the 'most deprived' girls would involve a major reallocation of resources (see Figures 8.2 and 8.4), and an ability to resist powerful political demands for wider inclusion and/or the retention of patriarchal and other atavistic privileges.[126]

In some African countries, advocating policies to reduce high levels of unmet demand by girls and women for contraception (Chapter 2) will also face powerful opposition. In these countries, effective policies will not be given priority as long as the relationship between teenage pregnancy and poverty is downplayed or blamed on the moral failures of girls.

8.9 Wage Labour and Poverty: The Most Controversial Stylized Fact

It is even more unlikely that the policy implications of another, often ignored, stylized fact will be accepted with any enthusiasm by aid donors, capitalist employers, and other powerful political forces in Africa. This stylized fact, emphasized both here and in Chapter 7, is that the poorest rural people depend on wage labour. We have shown that the 'most deprived' households in Uganda and Ethiopia depend on the earnings of agricultural wage workers. Similarly, a

---

[126] The strength of political demands for wide inclusion in Ghana is discussed in Abdulai (2019).

very high proportion of women in poorer Malawian households are engaged in seasonal agricultural wage labour; and an analysis of surveys covering over half of the population of sub-Saharan Africa found that 'poorer rural households tend to have a higher rate of participation in agricultural wage employment . . . the share of income from agricultural wage labor is more important for poorer households'.[127] Often, too little attention is paid to this evidence, or to research on the importance of hired labour inputs on smallholder maize and wheat farms in Eastern and Southern Africa by the Consultative Group on International Agricultural Research (CGIAR).[128] Instead, there is a romantic stress on the resilient self-sufficiency of African rural families—in the face of growing evidence that a high proportion of rural households not only purchase their food but also engage in agricultural wage labour.

We have used the EDI to analyse the recent labour market experience not only of our principal respondents but also of all other (broadly defined) members of the 'most deprived' households. We began by identifying two crude categories of job: the 'worst' and the 'more decent'. The 'worst' is a large category covering all the lowest paid and least desirable and most stigmatized types of rural wage work, especially manual labour performed in the open air. Other menial jobs in this category include working as a domestic servant for a rural private household and shining shoes. The 'more decent' jobs ranged over many different types of (mainly) non-agricultural wage employment, including: nursing, teaching, police, supervisory work inside processing plants and pack-houses, and so on. One of the largest groups of workers in this category were 'guards'. Female respondents were much less likely than male respondents to have found employment in a 'more decent' job.

Escapes from poverty are conceivable if at least *one* household member can obtain more decent employment. Unfortunately, if a respondent works as a manual agricultural wage labourer, she/he is unlikely to live in a household where anyone listed on the household roster has managed to secure a more decent job in the last 12 months. This suggests that the consequences of deprivation can be cumulative; it may never be easy to escape from poverty by building on the success in the labour market of your parents or another household member. In the USA after 1945, a surprisingly similar story can be told—of cumulative disadvantage, rooted in a labour market unable to provide adequate job opportunities for people with low education.[129]

What policy implications follow from the stylized fact that that vulnerable rural women depend on the income they earn from wage labour and, therefore, on the number of days of wage employment they are offered (and the real daily wage rate)? We are not confident that legislative interventions to improve the wages and

---

[127] Koolwal (2019: 8); Davis, Di Giuseppe, and Zezza (2017: 161 and table A2).
[128] Baudron et al. (2019).   [129] Case and Deaton (2017: 29ff.).

working conditions of these women will achieve rapid results, partly because of the well-documented failures of a battery of progressive legislation and of a relatively strong trade union movement in South Africa.[130] There is perhaps a better case for two immediate interventions: a massive increase in expenditure to monitor and publish the wage rates of poorly educated seasonal and casual workers; and a surge in investments to expand the demand (direct and indirect) for their labour in rural areas. Regular publication of these wage data may encourage long-overdue policy debates, new political demands, and even organizational successes. In Chapter 9, we focus on the untapped investment potential to increase rural wage employment and agricultural output in Africa.

---

[130] Devereux (2019).

9

Technical Change and Agricultural Productivity

9.1 Introduction: From the Missionary Position to Modern Charitable Fantasies

Rural development policy in Africa has been weighed down by a long tradition of pessimism and catastrophic prediction. Missionaries, colonial officers, and settlers all had their reasons for vociferous anxiety about disastrous land use; and their lurid visions of degradation, drought, food shortages, and starvation still colour many current official, academic, and non-governmental organization (NGO) publications.

We begin this chapter by illustrating the remarkable persistence and popularity of gloomy views about how difficult, if not impossible, it will be to sustain increases in agricultural output. We find little support in the available data for generalizations about an irreversible African environmental crisis. And we are not convinced that the barriers said to limit the adoption of Green Revolution technologies are all insuperable; on the contrary, we point to evidence, in Section 9.4, of interventions and economic policies that have been remarkably successful in increasing agricultural productivity. We argue that there is considerable agro-ecological potential to build on the success of recent interventions to increase yields.

As in Chapters 7 and 8, we insist that policymakers would be wise to question the quality of the data used in debates about agricultural technology, especially data used to justify ineffective interventions to reduce land degradation and hunger—such as brutal interventions by agronomists and others to police (and resettle) rural populations and demand changes in how they farm, or massive expenditure on the salaries of agricultural extension officers and on subsidies for micro-finance institutions (MFIs).

9.2 Panic and Paternalism

In the 1820s, the Scottish missionary Moffat 'was pre-disposed to designate the inhabitants of all the dry lands north of the Orange River as responsible for a situation of moral and environmental disorder'. Moffat depicted the Tswana as

African Economic Development: Evidence, Theory, Policy. Christopher Cramer, John Sender, and Arkebe Oqubay, Oxford University Press (2020). © Christopher Cramer, John Sender, and Arkebe Oqubay.
DOI: 10.1093/oso/9780198832331.001.0001

'environmental destroyers' in urgent need of European Christian tutelage. This Methodist missionary's disapproval was echoed by colonial forestry and conservationist officials, 'directly equating veld-burning and tree-felling carried out by Africans with moral degeneration and criminality'.[1] By the 1930s it had become increasingly fashionable to warn of the extreme dangers posed by soil erosion. The Colonial Office in London and administrators in East Africa had become convinced of the need to intervene coercively to regulate the husbandry practices of African farmers, because 'the apparently increasing incidence of drought conditions in many parts of East Africa over the period 1926 to 1935 indicated that the region was becoming progressively more arid'.[2] After the Second World War, 'the dominant colonial view was that African farmers were incompetent as they were responsible for environmental decay in the reserves'.[3] The Head of the Economic Bureau of the Colonial Office (and his French counterparts) doubted the possibility 'of any technical change at all'.[4]

In the post-colonial period, neo-Malthusian alarmism influenced agricultural policy in many African countries. The historical evidence for Africa does not provide much support for these policies, suggesting that there is no direct link between soil degradation and population growth: 'There are cases where "more people" accompanied "less erosion", as well as cases where soil degradation occurred in spite of declining population pressure.'[5] Nevertheless, officials, agricultural economists, and agronomists in Africa continue to claim that population growth leads to environmental degradation. For example, the Director of Statistics at the African Development Bank warns of the dangers of downward spirals and an immiserating rural process throughout Africa:

> Rapid population growth, inadequate food production . . . and increasing degradation of natural resources have created a vicious circle of poverty and environmental degradation, especially in rural areas.[6]

United Nations Conference on Trade and Development's (UNCTAD's) Economic Development in Africa Report highlights the same trends.[7] Some of the most influential American agricultural economists repeat these warnings, claiming that African farmers are making the wrong choices:

> [A]t present most African smallholders appear not to be choosing sustainable paths, hence the interlinked crises of rural poverty, declining per capita agricultural productivity, and environmental degradation.[8]

---

[1] Grove (1989: 166, 184).   [2] Anderson (1984: 322–3).   [3] Shanguhyia (2015: 2).
[4] Cooper (2004: 20).   [5] Koning and Smaling (2005: 5).   [6] Lufumpa (2005: 369).
[7] UNCTAD (2018: 17–18).
[8] Reardon et al. (1999: 377, 389). For similar views see: Nhamo et al. (2019: 2); and Rigaud et al. (2018: 82).

This long history of anxieties and periodic panics about impending rural catastrophe can partly be explained by elite preoccupations with political risk. There might be threats to those in power if land degradation and declining agricultural productivity cause accelerated migration by 'climate refugees' out of rural areas, swelling the slum population and the ranks of the urban dangerous classes, or the number of squatters invading more fertile capitalist farms. In Nairobi, for example, rapid migration into squatter settlements from rural areas appears to have reinforced 'the government perception that informal settlers are uneducated, unhealthy and dangerous. Indeed, the informal settlements are perceived as crime zones.'[9]

These conventional wisdom fears about migration are very weakly supported by the evidence. There are other—and well-established—facts about migration from rural Africa that subvert the conventional views: first, only a very small proportion of the projected increase in Africa's urban population will be the result of climate change impacts—about 0.1 per cent according to recent estimates; second, urban conflict and food riots in Africa have complex causes and cannot simply be attributed to an influx of 'climate refugees' or to anthropogenic climate change, variability in food production, food availability or prices;[10] third, there is evidence that climate change may—paradoxically for those unfamiliar with Hirschman's hiding hand (see Chapter 6)—create important opportunities for *rural–rural* migration and encourage investment to *increase* crop production and rural incomes, for example in new areas of coffee cultivation in the south-west highlands of Ethiopia.[11]

Internationally, moral panic about 'climate refugees' has been encouraged by some of the more xenophobic media, by NGOs, by political demagogues and the leaders of populist movements in the European Union (EU).[12] The imagined political consequences of Africa's agricultural retrogression or stagnation do not require further discussion here. Having suggested that it is important to look closely at the evidence before indulging in fervid speculation about political futures, we turn to a more detailed examination of the most prevalent (negative) assessments of rural technological change in Africa, especially the conclusion that Africa's Green Revolution has been 'delayed and weak'.

9.3 Chronicle of a Failure Foretold

The Green Revolution, when cereal yields jumped from one to two or more tonnes per hectare in a few years after the late 1960s, has been described as the most

---

[9] Kyed, Stepputat, and Albrecht (2017: 24). For the fears of the urban bourgeoisie during the British Industrial Revolution see Enzensberger (1974).
[10] Rigaud et al. (2018: 87); Selby (2014); Mach et al. (2019).   [11] Moat et al. (2017).
[12] Kelman (2019: 11); Bettini (2013).

important episode of agricultural innovation in modern history; the World Bank (and others) have spent more than a decade trying to explain why 'it didn't happen in Sub-Saharan Africa'.[13]

> [T]he impact of agricultural innovation in sub-Saharan Africa cannot be compared to its success in transforming rural economies of many Asian and Latin American countries during the 1960s–1990s.[14]

In the period after 1960, public funding was used 'to apply scientific understandings of genetics to the development of improved crop varieties that were suited to the growing conditions of developing countries'. The initial research to develop high-yielding varieties (HYVs) of wheat and rice was extraordinarily successful, resulting in an extremely rapid spread of HYVs from the research centres to many farms in similar agro-ecological areas, especially to those areas in countries with extensive irrigation and/or reliable rainfall. In other areas and for other crops, including crops that are particularly important in Africa, diffusion has taken much longer.[15] For example, in the 18 years between 1965 and 1983, HYVs of rice and wheat were adopted on more than 120 million hectares in Asia and Latin America (but only about 0.7 million hectares in sub-Saharan Africa).[16]

Africa is said to have had 'a delayed and weak Green Revolution' and this failure is explained in different ways: Africa does not have large tracts of agro-ecologically similar land, comparable to the irrigated lowlands of South East Asia or the Indo-Gangetic plane of South Asia; Africa's production environments are extremely heterogeneous and localized so that no single regional or district package of HYVs and agrochemicals can be recommended and distributed; Africa's soils are generally poor and degraded;[17] very low and stagnant levels of fertilizer use exacerbate land degradation;[18] much of the land in Africa's dry zones is currently poorly responsive to agrochemical inputs and 'generally unfavourable for agriculture'; many dryland zones are badly served by transport infrastructure so that many of the agricultural producers living in these zones (about 171 million people) face extremely long travel times to reach the nearest large town;[19] if they purchase agricultural inputs the costs will be relatively high and the farmgate prices they receive for their output are likely to be relatively low;[20] although less than 3 per cent of Africa's total cultivated area is irrigated—compared to about 39 per cent in South Asia and 29 per cent in East Asia—the rate of expansion of the irrigated area since 1961 has been very much slower than in tropical Asia, averaging only about 1 per cent per year since 1995; in several African countries

[13] World Bank (2007: 55); Goyal and Nash (2017: 7).
[14] Ogundari and Bolarinwa (2018: 19, 3).   [15] Gollin, Hansen, and Wingender (2018: 2).
[16] Fuglie and Marder (2015: 339).   [17] Tittonell and Giller (2013: 88).
[18] World Bank (2008: 55).
[19] Cervigni and Morris (2016: 115 and 49–63). See also You (2008: 1).   [20] Porteous (2020: 2).

there has been a *decline* between 2000 and 2015 in the percentage of arable land equipped for irrigation; the cost per hectare of irrigation projects in Africa has been very much higher than the cost in other regions, partly because African irrigation projects are relatively small—too small to take advantage of scale economies to reduce unit costs.[21]

The rapid development of rice and wheat HYV production appears to have depended on two earlier specific forms of investment: first, a long history of accumulating the infrastructure required for irrigation and for rural transport; and, second, decades of appropriate earlier research on wheat and rice in advanced capitalist countries prior to the 1960s. There was no similar stock of scientific knowledge about the crops—cassava, yams, millets, and sorghum—and the crop mixes that are particularly important in Africa.[22] Sorghum and pearl millet account for about one third of Africa's cropped area, but hardly any of Africa's scientists are currently working on these crops—less than 5 per cent of full-time equivalent (FTE) researchers. Since the 1960s, national agricultural research programmes in Africa have received relatively little funding, especially for their operating budgets, and their expenditure was particularly volatile and squeezed in the period from the mid-1980s to the end of the 1990s.[23]

One policy conclusion that could be drawn from this abbreviated list of the difficulties involved in cultivating areas with degraded soils and erratic rainfall patterns would be to decide to concentrate on lower hanging fruit, that is, to allocate far more resources to zones with much higher *immediate* production potential and lower risks of climate shock. The slogan that each and every administrative area should receive a similar amount of state resources to promote rural development may be politically seductive—because it addresses regional inequalities, historic neglect, or ethnic discrimination—but is likely be costly in terms of lost opportunities for accumulation and technological progress. It is a false remedy for the problem of insufficient 'inclusiveness' in resource allocation.

If Africa has failed, for all the reasons given (and others), to replicate the record-breaking speed of Asia's Green Revolution, there is no need for policy-makers to despair or accept all the pronouncements made by the prophets of ecological doom. For it is not difficult to make certain negative types of prophecy: we can confidently predict, for example, that most countries in the world will fail to produce many marathon runners *as fast as* Eliud Kipchoge or Mary Keitany. But, if we use *a less demanding criterion*, we can predict great success for many non-Kenyan aspiring athletes, that is, we can be confident that the average time they take to complete a marathon will fall substantially. Policymakers should not be browbeaten by long lists of reasons for failure; they can reject the usual story of

---

[21] Nhemachena et al. (2018: table 3); Inocencio et al. (2007).
[22] Gollin, Hansen, and Wingender (2018: 12, 8–9).
[23] Alwang (2015: 15); Beintema and Stads (2017: figures 11 and 13).

African agricultural production as shrouded in an air of dismal inevitability, of preordained productivity stagnation—failure foretold. Less stringent criteria can be used to assess African agricultural success, such as the speed of output and yield growth relative to Africa's own past performance, or relative to the agricultural growth rates achieved when Europe was industrializing.

It is important too for policymakers to recall the failures of past predictions about future trends in African agricultural output. There were many confident predictions, for example in the 1980s and 1990s, of progressive declines in agricultural production as a result of the HIV epidemic; but some of the academic prophets later published a rare *mea culpa*, admitting that 'as advocacy took over, so science flew out of the window'. When the areas that were the original source of the data used to support these catastrophic predictions were resurveyed, it was discovered that 'the AIDS epidemic seems not to have had the profound long-term impact in this part of East Africa that was predicted 20 years ago'.[24] There has not been enough reflection on the reasons for these mistakes, including the severe limitations of the researchers' aggregated conceptual model of 'a Ugandan farming system' and the unreliable (but trusted) methods of data collection.

9.4 Measuring Agricultural and Food Production

Assertions about food production in Africa have often been quite gloomy. 'Comparing the 1970s with the present', as one example has it, 'it is readily apparent that the state of African agriculture is far worse now.'[25] There is a particular anxiety that food production has suffered throughout Africa because of greater integration into global markets. Thus:

> Most developing countries have succumbed to the demand to open up and engage in free trade. This produced area diversion to export crops, led to decline in the food grains growth rate which fell below the population growth rate, resulting in falling per capita output and availability of food grains . . . we find declining per head food grains output combined with fast growing per head exportables output in every important developing region . . . and the whole of Sub-Saharan Africa.[26]

But we will argue that these assertions—often made by aid bureaucrats as well as by Marxist or neo-Marxist scholars—are questionable. This is a continuation of an

---

[24] Barnett, Dercon, and Seeley (2010: 958); Seeley, Dercon, and Barnett (2010: 333).
[25] Bryceson (2009: 56).
[26] Patnaik (2016: 145). For similar views see Sundaram and Chowdhury (2017); and Traore and Sakyi (2018: 6).

argument made more than three decades ago by one of us, who queried pessimistic pronouncements about African food production that were as popular then as they are now.[27]

Too little has changed since the mid-1980s: there are still many reasons for extreme caution when using African food and agricultural production statistics, including the fact that agricultural censuses have become less common. The Food and Agriculture Organization (FAO) itself considers that only two countries in sub-Saharan Africa have high standards in data collection, while standards in 21 other countries remain low, and the remaining African countries could not be rated.[28] Published data available on the Food and Agriculture Organization Statistical Database (FAOSTAT) and CountrySTAT sites do not always agree about the level of cereal and starchy root crop production, for example in Nigeria or Zambia.[29] The FAO has argued since the 1950s that high-standard, reliable estimates of yields can only be obtained by using their recommended 'gold standard' method, that is, a crop-cutting survey. But in a rigorous discussion of crop-cutting samples to measure yields on maize plots in Uganda several concerns were raised regarding the accuracy of even the most costly crop-cutting methods.[30]

Most commentators on hunger continue to rely on the estimates of domestic food production in the FAO's published data on food balance sheets (FBS), which are the basis for estimates of food consumption per capita in all African countries. But more reliable, individual-level national dietary surveys have established that the FAO estimates tend to either over- or underestimate consumption of most types of food.[31] These well-known problems with FAO food production and consumption data, as well as with the Gallup data on self-reported degrees of hunger, have not prevented the United Nations Development Programme (UNDP), for example, from expressing the gloomy view—based on these data—that African dietary intakes have been growing too slowly and that African food production has been growing 'at a very slow rate'.[32] Other United Nations (UN) officials including, for example, a UN Assistant Secretary-General for Economic Development, are also pessimistic about nutrition, but for very different reasons: 'In Zambia, greater use of seeds and fertilizers from agribusiness tripled maize production without reducing the country's very high rates of . . . malnutrition.'[33] No evidence is provided to support this paradoxical assertion: in fact, the prevalence of undernutrition (PoU) and of child stunting *fell* in Zambia between 2004 and 2006 and 2015 and 2017. Gloom has also been spread by Michael Lipton, who

[27] Sender and Smith (1986: 100).   [28] Carletto, Jolliffe, and Banerjee (2015: 137, 134).
[29] Luan et al. (2019: 15).   [30] Gourlay, Kilic, and Lobell (2017: 10).
[31] Del Gobbo et al. (2015). Grünberger (2014: 4). Additional criticisms of the FAO's FBS approach are summarized in de Weerdt et al. (2016).
[32] Chauvin, Mulangu, and Porto (2012: 4).   [33] Sundaram (2019).

is well aware that 'Africa's data for output of food staples are largely worthless', yet who nevertheless asserted in 2012 that 'calorie output and intake per person in most of Africa are no higher than in the early 1960s'.[34]

Despite all the dismal pronouncements quoted, it is surprisingly easy to use FAO (and United States Department of Agriculture (USDA)) data to question gloomy assessments of food and staple production in Africa and of the supply of calories available per person. We do not believe that the data used in Figures 9.1 and 9.2 are reliable. We will continue to provide policymakers with much ammunition to criticize them. But the aggregate official data on food production and food supply used in these figures can serve a similar purpose to the International Labour Organization's (ILO's) suspect data on African trends in employment presented in Chapter 7: they frame and provide a corrective perspective to the widespread pronouncements by economists about Africa's allegedly tragic performance.

We now turn attention to the rising trends in the output and yield of those basic food grains that are so critical for the consumption of Africa's poor. The trends in maize production are particularly important because maize is the most commonly

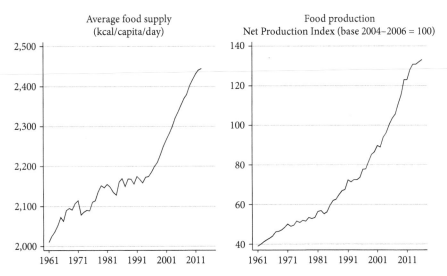

Figure 9.1 Food production and average food supply in sub-Saharan Africa, 1960–2015

Note: Countries included: Angola, Benin, Botswana, Burkina Faso, Cabo Verde, Cameroon, Central African Republic, Chad, Congo, Côte d'Ivoire, Eswatini, Ethiopia, Gabon, Gambia, Ghana, Guinea, Guinea-Bissau, Kenya, Lesotho, Liberia, Madagascar, Malawi, Mali, Mauritania, Mauritius, Mozambique, Namibia, Niger, Nigeria, Rwanda, Sao Tome and Principe, Senegal, Sierra Leone, South Africa, Togo, Uganda, United Republic of Tanzania, Zambia, Zimbabwe.

Source: FAOSTAT (2018).

[34] Lipton (2012a: 3).

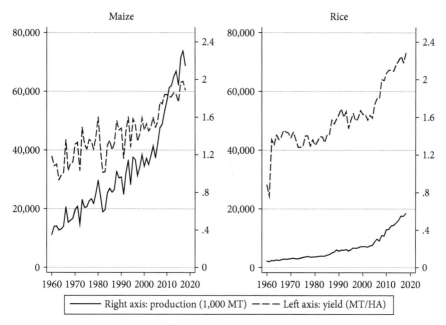

Figure 9.2 Maize and rice production and yield in sub-Saharan Africa, 1960–2018
Source: USDA (2019).

cultivated cereal in Africa.[35] Because crop failure, drought, and yield fluctuations are so common in Africa, it is always important to look at long-run data: the production data for maize and rice in Figure 9.2 cover more than fifty years.

It is also important to stress (again) the heterogeneity of African experiences: recent agricultural performance has been very much more impressive in some African countries and areas than others. For example, between 1990/2 and 2012/14, rather rapid growth rates in total and per capita agricultural production were recorded for Malawi, Ethiopia, Ghana, Mozambique, and Tanzania, while, over the same period, total and per capita agricultural output plummeted in Zimbabwe and the growth rate of per capita output was relatively slow in Senegal and the Côte d'Ivoire. Within countries, a high and probably increasing proportion of total marketed agricultural output was produced by a small number of farms, with many farmers only producing tiny or even declining amounts. The policy implications of more disaggregated agricultural production data will be discussed in Sections 9.5 and 9.7, while the mediocre growth of agricultural exports and the rapid growth of food imports—which still account for a very small percentage (about 2 per cent) of all food consumed in Africa[36]—were noted in Chapter 5.

---

[35] Wiggins (2018: 28). African evidence suggests that income elasticities are low for cereals and tubers (Choudhury and Headey, 2016: table 2.1).
[36] Vorley and Lançon (2016: 8).

The trends shown by the unreliable data in Figures 9.1 and 9.2 may be considered plausible to the extent that they are consistent with much more reliable evidence, such as such as the evidence on undernutrition (measured by child stunting and provided in the United Nations Children's Fund (UNICEF), World Health Organization (WHO), World Bank Group Joint Malnutrition Estimates). These estimates suggest that, between 1990 and 2016, there was a fall in the proportion of sub-Saharan African children under the age of 5 suffering from stunting—from 45.7 per cent to 33.6 per cent.

If food production, availability, and calorie intake were actually failing to improve in sub-Saharan Africa, then well-documented and widespread declines in child stunting become difficult to understand, because improved nutritional intake does appear to play an important role in the growth performance of African infants.[37] Apart from the decline in stunting, a more comprehensive measure also shows a very large reduction since 1990 in the health burden of chronic hunger in sub-Saharan Africa. Disability-adjusted life years (DALYs) have been used to measure the number of healthy life years lost in a population that can be directly attributed to chronic hunger. One econometric analysis suggests that Africa's rising total food supply has been associated with a lower burden of chronic hunger in Africa.[38]

The FAO (in collaboration with other international organizations monitoring food, hunger and undernutrition—International Fund for Agricultural Development (IFAD), UNICEF, WHO, and the World Food Programme (WFP)) publishes an annual report that appears to be designed to convince bilateral and other funders of the need to replenish the budgets of these organizations. In 2018, this flagship report claimed that 'Undernourishment and severe food insecurity appear to be increasing in almost all subregions of Africa.' The necessary caveats that the FAO itself makes about this self-serving headline about recent trends in the PoU are relegated to an appendix:

> Due to the probabilistic nature of the inference and the margins of uncertainty associated with estimates of each of the parameters in the model, the precision of the PoU estimates is generally low.[39]

9.5 Against the Poor Measurements behind a Defence of the Small Farm Orthodoxy

The latest donor efforts to improve the quality of data on crop production and yields, the Living Standards Measurement Study—Integrated Surveys on

---

[37] Stewart et al. (2019).   [38] Gödecke, Stein, and Qaim (2018: 25–6).
[39] FAO et al. (2018: 142). Given these margins of error, it is hard to assess the meaning of the finding that the PoU in sub-Saharan Africa 'increased' from 22.3 to 23.2 (ibid.: table 1).

Agriculture (LSMS-ISA), are funded by the Gates Foundation and managed by the World Bank rather than the FAO or African statistical agencies. Implementation began in 2010 but to date these household panel surveys cover just eight African countries. We already noted, in Chapter 7, one very important methodological limitation of the LSMS-ISA surveys: their incomplete coverage of the national agricultural sector and exclusion of the most dynamic large-scale capitalist farm enterprises. Moreover, the method used by LSMS-ISA to measure the crop yields in the sampled agricultural households is unreliable: these surveys solicit *farmer-reported* information on crop production at the plot level; but research in Uganda and Ethiopia has shown that farmer-reported data suffers from systematic measurement error and leads to biased estimates of production and yield. When compared to more reliable measures of yield—based on remote sensing and full-plot cutting, as opposed to cutting from a small sample within a plot—the farmer-reported yields are particularly likely to be overestimates on *smaller* plots; on average, these self-reported yields in Uganda were almost double the yields measured by more accurate methods.[40] Similarly, surveys of maize production in Ethiopia indicate that self-reported production is likely to be over-reported by up to 50 per cent on *small* plots, but under-reported by 25 per cent on *larger* plots.[41]

Evidence this faulty immediately calls into question an ideologically powerful piece of conventional wisdom. For the implication is that African household survey evidence supporting an inverse size–productivity relationship is deeply unreliable. Policymakers should *not* assume that smaller farms usually achieve higher yields per hectare than larger farms, or that large farms in Africa are unlikely to benefit from scale economies. Faith in the relative efficiency and productivity of smallholder farmers—a powerful nugget of common sense (see Chapter 3)—underpins almost all policy advice on rural development and poverty reduction, but this advice appears to be based on the naive view that the largest and richest farmers have actually been included in the national sampling frame used by Agricultural Household Surveys (and will usually agree to tell official surveyors the truth about output and yields on their farms) and that smallholder farmers give a precise account of their own yields.

The conventional wisdom is that 'the most productive farms will be small in most places in Sub-Saharan Africa' and that these farms, because they are 'managed and worked primarily by family members', can reduce hired-labour supervision costs and avoid shirking to achieve high yields. Furthermore, differentiation or a change in the size distribution of farms in Africa and the increasing dominance of capitalist farmers is unlikely in the foreseeable future: 'Poorly functioning land markets . . . work to help keep farms small, because they keep the risks and

---

[40] Lobell et al. (2018: 13).   [41] Desiere and Jolliffe (2018: 90–1).

costs of renting or purchasing land unnecessarily high.'[42] This conventional wisdom fuels campaigns:

> Melinda and I started to realize that the poorest people in the world shared an occupation in common: They were small farmers. The conclusion was obvious: They could lift their families up by growing more food.[43]

The Agriculture and Rural Development Team in the World Bank confirm that 'Most rural development strategies in Sub-Saharan Africa focus on improving the productivity of smallholder farms.'[44] When the evidence is ambiguous or flatly contradicts the hegemonic faith in the productive potential of these farms, some mini-farm champions—especially those trained in mainstream micro-economics—can reach for another weapon to defend their belief: they can deploy the simple neoclassical model of a unitary farm household to prove that small farmers 'could' (theoretically) be more efficient 'if' market imperfections and information asymmetries disappeared. These neoclassical economists can confidently anticipate the disappearance of such market glitches as soon as appropriate institutions, for example, cooperatives, a high-tech electronic commodity exchange, and competitive financial/insurance services, are conjured out of the air by waving a magic wand or brandishing a mobile phone.[45]

The two most important policies and expenditure priorities derived from the small farm household model and pessimism about technological progress in Africa involve efforts to provide additional credit and extension advice. Even economists critical of neoclassical methods and optimistic about African developmental prospects agree that these policies are urgently needed. Ha-Joon Chang, for example, argues that 'credit provision to small farmers has been one of the most important challenges that has faced the policy-makers in the early stages of economic development'.[46] Chang quite rightly emphasizes the significance of state provision of, subsidies to, and regulation of rural credit, but seems to put too much faith in what we have shown to be a very vague and problematic category of 'small' farmers. We question the impact of these popular policies to support extension services and private sector credit to small farmers in Section 9.6; and in Section 9.7 we discuss the potential for alternative policies and investment priorities.

---

[42] Larson, Muraoka, and Otsuka (2016: 9).
[43] https://www.gatesfoundation.org/media-center/speeches/2012/02/bill-gates-ifad.
[44] Larson, Muraoka, and Otsuka (2016: 2).
[45] The weak economic logic, patchy evidence, and dubious claims about rural poverty advanced by believers in the inverse size–productivity relationship are discussed in more detail in Sender and Johnston (2004). The myth that poor producers in rural areas use mobile phones to obtain more accurate and lower-cost information on market prices has been criticized by Burrell and Oreglia (2015).
[46] Chang (2009: 489, 494).

9.6 Do Farmers Fail without Advice and Subsidized Credit?

Farmers have good reason not to tell the truth to outsiders and rural development tourists participating in focus group discussions. But we do think that some of what they say about extension officers, or about the advice they have received from young people with technical qualifications employed by the Ministry of Agriculture, should be taken seriously. We have met successful capitalist farmers who simply laugh at the idea that inexperienced, wet-behind-the-ears advisors know what they are talking about and might have something useful to say. The poorest, especially women who cultivate very small areas and do not have the cash to purchase agrochemicals and HYVs, have told us that no advisor has ever visited their farms; they do not even know the name of the local extension officer or the precise location of his or her office.

But we do not have to rely on our own anecdotes to question the impact of agricultural extension services in Africa. Historians of the most successful episodes of technological change in rural Africa emphasize the role of African traders and capitalists—not agricultural extension officers—in explaining the introduction and extraordinarily rapid expansion of cocoa in Amansie between 1900 and 1916.[47] More recently, there have been hundreds of evaluations of the impact on agricultural production of expenditure on extension. Policymakers may find it tedious to wade through all these studies, because when polite and judicious mainstream economists are funded to evaluate the impact of extension, they usually hedge their bets on the evidence: 'Results from these studies are mixed and few generalizations can be made'; 'evidence from systematic reviews regarding the effects of extension and advisory services on poverty is extremely thin'; 'there is limited rigorous evidence on the effectiveness of . . . potentially scalable extension services provided by public agencies in developing countries'.[48] These diplomatically fudged conclusions suggest there is an elephant in the room—an awkward fact that no one wants to mention.

The uncomfortable truth is that, after many decades of devoting a high proportion of government recurrent expenditure on agriculture to paying the salaries and wages of extension staff, it cannot be shown that their work has improved agricultural productivity. Negative evaluations of extension services have sometimes led to changes in the *types* of extension projects donors are willing to fund. For example, the high recurrent cost training and visit model was all the rage at the World Bank, promoted from 1975 to 1998 in over fifty countries, but it fell out of favour in Africa to be replaced by models that purport to be more participatory, geared to farmer field schools and to the average rather than to 'progressive'

[47] Austin (1987).
[48] Alwang et al. (2019: 2); Bernstein, Johnson, and Arsalan (2019); Kondylis et al. (2017: 13); Fabregas et al. (2017: 8); Waddington et al. (2014: 37). See also Ragasa et al. (2013) and Berhane et al. (2018: 22).

farmers, sensitive to gender relations and to farmers' demands, based on farmer-to-farmer interactions, and decentralized.[49] But there is no evidence that the new fads have made much difference. In Kenya, for example, a field experiment on the impact of text messaging concluded that 'we do not find consistent evidence that advice delivered through mobile phones was effective in increasing knowledge or use of recommended inputs'.[50] In Ethiopia, research on an NGO programme in North Shewa Zone (to train farmers in soil conservation) concludes that 'there were no differences in crop productivity between attendees and non-attendees, and higher rate of participation in farmer trainings was not associated with changes in land-use intensity at the village level'.[51] An evaluation of a larger NGO programme providing training in soil fertility management to the members of farmer-based organizations in Ghana's Upper Volta Region also could not demonstrate a positive impact.[52] Government-provided advice through salaried cadres of advisors appears to have been equally ineffective in Ethiopia and Malawi, for example.[53]

Why then do so many governments, donors, and NGOs continue to devote resources to training and advising smallholders in Africa? There are several possible answers: it may be politically difficult to retrench large numbers of government workers or to disappoint college-trained young aspirants to posts in the bureaucracy; it may also be politically convenient to have eyes in the villages and a means of policing potential troublemakers, for example, by fining and imprisoning them or refusing to supply them with subsidized inputs and credit. Rwanda and Ethiopia provide good examples of rural areas where the line between state officials and party officials is blurred and an important function of the development and extension agents, the *umudugudu* leaders or 'the delegates', may be to eliminate opposition and entrench the power of the existing elite.[54]

Insistent demands to increase expenditures on agricultural extension, like proposals to increase the level of resources devoted to agricultural credit, micro-credit, and financial inclusion, have often received ideological support from mainstream economists; these demands have also been amplified by domestic and international political pressures that policymakers cannot easily ignore. According to mainstream theory, farmers and other potential capitalists in rural Africa suffer because they are cut off from the opportunities for investing, risk-taking, and risk spreading that would be available through better financial integration into larger national and global financial markets. They do not have access to critical financial services because they are 'afflicted' by fragmented, imperfect markets; in rural Africa markets do not look anything like the neoclassical ideal type—information asymmetries and the high costs of attempting to enforce

[49] Anderson, Feder, and Ganguly (2006).   [50] Fabregas et al. (2017: iii).
[51] Chesterman et al. (2019: 7).   [52] Andam, Makhija, and Spielman (2018).
[53] Bowser (2015: 22); Ragasa (2019).   [54] Cramer and Sender (2019a); Huggins (2017: 729).

contracts in rural areas are major obstacles to adopting new inputs to accelerate development.[55]

The policies prescribed by those who believe in reducing market imperfections to allow untrammelled individual entrepreneurs to spearhead African economic development are predictable: states and donors should focus on supporting institutions that ensure the legal enforcement of financial contracts, make property rights more secure, and diffuse information. Of course, states should also remove all forms of 'financial repression'—directed credit and the regulations that hinder the entry and expansion of new private (and especially foreign corporate) lenders in Africa. More recently, mainstream policy conclusions have become a little more nuanced: it is sometimes acknowledged that the private lenders and financial institutions may have to be 'crowded in'; they will need to be bribed by access to privatized assets at very low prices and by *additional* state subsidies, especially if the aim is to introduce innovative financial products (such as crop insurance now heavily subsidized by United States Agency for International Development (USAID) and the Gates Foundation).[56]

The advocates of conventional liberalization policy packages cannot avoid the unpalatable conclusion that there is a case for state and donor expenditure to subsidize rural credit, because they have been unable to find any evidence of the surge in private sector lending anticipated by the mainstream theorists of 'financial repression' (see Chapter 4), despite the space for private sector initiatives created by savage cuts in public sector agricultural credit between the 1980s and the end of the 1990s.[57] The dominant view now is that Africa's rural credit needs can effectively be provided by subsidizing MFIs that benefit from lower transaction costs and informational hurdles than larger-scale, bureaucratic, and more formal lenders such as national rural development banks. By the 1990s, the cost of the subsidies provided annually by donors to the newly fashionable micro-finance sector was about US$1 billion.[58]

Despite massive subsidies and repeated policy recommendations to increase interest rates, very few MFIs in sub-Saharan Africa show any signs of achieving operational sustainability or reaping the cost advantages of operating at scale. Those institutions that are least effective in reaching poor farmers have received more subsidies than institutions making smaller loans to the poor.[59] Most credit in rural Africa continues to be supplied by family, friends, usurious shopkeepers/traders, and employers seeking to secure labour at below the local market wage rate. Where there is access to micro-credit, it does not appear to have a discernible impact on the use of new agricultural inputs such as chemical fertilizer. This was

[55] Conning and Udry (2007: 2859–60).
[56] De Bock and Gelade (2012). The uptake and renewal rates for micro-insurance in Africa are still very low.
[57] De Bock and Gelade (2007: 2867).   [58] Hudon and Traca (2011: 966).
[59] Cull, Demirgüç-Kunt, and Morduch (2018).

the conclusion of case studies in Tanzania and Kenya, for example, where panel data also suggest that both rice yields and household income have failed to increase with credit use.[60]

There is even better evidence that most MFIs fail to provide any credit to the smallest farmers and the poorest rural people. Access to any type of formal credit by African households at the bottom of the distribution of income is very low and barely increased between 2011 and 2017.[61] The much-hyped success of the fintech innovation for digital money transfers in Kenya (M-Pesa) cannot be shown to have reduced the poverty of those Kenyans who do not have links to the relatively wealthy. In western Uganda, women's access to a micro-finance cooperative did not prove 'an unconditional blessing'. In South Africa, where the micro-credit bubble expanded at a quite extraordinary rate, the National Income Dynamics Survey panel data 2008 to 2015 suggest that access to micro- and informal loans by the poorest rural women has a *negative* effect on their quality of life.[62]

The distribution of credit in Africa usually excludes poor borrowers in rural areas and results in problems of financial sustainability. Most donors and the public relations staff of the MasterCard Foundation and Citibank now prefer to focus on MFIs' contribution to the nebulous goal of 'financial inclusion', rather than sticking to the old and widely missed target of poverty reduction.[63] Ignoring evidence on the impact of expenditures to subsidize rural credit may be convenient for other reasons: regimes often seek to attract support from influential power brokers by channelling short-term credit to wealthy and powerful rural borrowers—not merely at *de jure* rates of interest way below those charged by private sector informal lenders, but also on the implicit understanding that *de facto* there will be no repayments at all. We have argued that most expenditure to promote MFIs and on financial inclusion continues for ideological and political reasons: investment resources have *not* been allocated to those national institutions that have historically (in Japan, Brazil, South Korea, the Netherlands, Austria, and Switzerland, for example) been extraordinarily successful in providing savings and money transmission facilities to relatively poor people—post offices.[64] On the contrary, there has been donor pressure to limit the role of post offices and, in some African countries (Mali, for example), a structural adjustment programme led to the demise of the post's facilities and network.[65]

---

[60] Nakano and Magezi (2019).

[61] Awaworyi Churchill (2018); Bernards (2019: 4); Adjognon, Liverpool-Tasie, and Reardon (2017: table 5a).

[62] Bateman, Duvendack, and Loubere (2019); Bateman (2014); Meier zu Selhausen and Stam (2013); Greyling and Rossouw (2019: 10).

[63] Bateman and Chang (2012: 17).   [64] Mader (2018: 479); Rillo and Mlyamoto (2016).

[65] D'Alcantara, Dembinski, and Pilley (2014: 9).

9.7 Massive Potential to Sustain and Accelerate Increased Yields per Hectare: Policy Opportunities

There are several ways to make a more realistic assessment of Africa's potential to improve its agricultural performance. We begin by emphasizing the immense gap between the yields actually achieved on some farms and the low yields achieved by others farming in the same agro-climatic zones. An important implication of these carefully measured cropland yield divergences *within homogeneous zones* is that there is a huge potential to increase output and productivity, if currently observed best cultivating practices are diffused throughout the zone.[66] Satellite-derived images have made an important contribution to identifying hotspots of yield divergence within each African country; they could be used by policymakers to argue for concentrating investment in specific sub-districts and for closer monitoring of the impact of policy on yields.

The current level of adoption of HYVs also provides a good indicator of a potential for dramatic increases in crop production. Although the HYV adoption rate in sub-Saharan Africa probably increased by as much in the 2000s as in the four preceding decades, adoption is very far from universal, as suggested by the data on yield divergence. By 2010 the total area sown to improved varieties of food crops exceeded 37 million hectares, more than double the estimated area in 2000; but this impressive achievement represented only 35 per cent of area planted to these crops.[67] Adoption rates are, for example, only 23 per cent for improved varieties of cowpea in sub-Saharan Africa; they are as low as 20 per cent for improved varieties of a key food crop (cassava) in some countries. While improved varieties of maize are now cultivated on 57 per cent of the total maize area in West and Central Africa, some countries in this region have only managed to plant improved varieties on less than 10 per cent of the maize area; in Mozambique and Angola, improved varieties of maize are also planted on only 10 per cent of the maize area, compared to about 70 per cent in Kenya and 84 per cent in Zambia.

Increasing the proportion of African farmland cultivated with varieties developed through modern crop-breeding techniques could make a huge contribution to improving living standards and to economic growth.[68] Already, according to the estimates of one econometric model, the adoption of improved varieties in sub-Saharan Africa has boosted average net crop yields by about 0.55 tonnes per hectare, equivalent to an increase of 47 per cent above average yields achieved during the period 1976–80. Part of the explanation for the faster rate of adoption of HYVs in some African countries than others is that these countries have invested much more in agricultural research, enabling them to release larger

---

[66] Luan et al. (2019).   [67] Fuglie and Marder (2015: 338).
[68] Gollin, Hansen, and Wingender (2018: 32–3); Walker and Alwang (2015: 74–122 and 206–227).

numbers of new varieties and achieve more rapid rates of diffusion.[69] Unfortunately, in a rather large number of sub-Saharan African countries the growth rates of public agricultural research spending between 2000 and 2014 were stagnant (seven countries) or negative (five countries).[70] Even worse, in several countries a smaller share of public agricultural expenditure was devoted to research and development (R&D) than to extension services, despite the much higher estimated returns to expenditure on R&D than other types of public agricultural spending.[71] There is an urgent need for a better-informed policy debate about how to increase the level and improve the functional allocation of public agricultural spending. We argue that proposals for reallocating spending both to R&D and to export crops should now move to the top of the policy agenda. But a precondition for improving government policy is the availability of much more transparent, consistent, and accurate data on current patterns of public agricultural expenditure in Africa.[72]

The rate of adoption of HYVs, especially of new varieties of maize, rice, and vegetables, could be accelerated by prioritizing public sector investment in irrigation and water control because, as noted in Section 9.3, these investments in 'the leading input' improve the prospects for introducing not only HYVs, but also complementary inputs—such as fertilizers and agrochemicals—that farmers can use to maximize crop yields. In South Asia the irrigated area represents about 42 per cent of the cultivable area; in sub-Saharan Africa most of the area currently cropped (at least 95 per cent) is cultivated in the rainy season *without* irrigation; producers face the risk of extremely uncertain water availability both in terms of quantity and timing.[73] The potential to reduce the (often life-threatening) risks of relying on rainfed cropping systems is considerable: estimates of the precise magnitude of this potential do differ and are sensitive to underlying assumptions about cost, yields, internal rates of return, and so on, but all agree that it is *possible* to escape some of the risks of rainfed production; that the scope for economically and technically viable investment to expand the area under irrigation is considerable.

In the drylands of sub-Saharan Africa, about 5.2 million hectares are currently irrigated. There is a well-established potential to irrigate an additional 14 million hectares, equivalent to about 8 per cent of the total area that is currently being cultivated in the drylands. The impact on sub-Saharan African crop production of this realistically assessed addition to the irrigated area would be 'transformational': one estimate is that dryland cereal production could increase by 52 per cent.[74] The impact would be particularly dramatic in those countries where the area that could be developed for irrigation accounts for a large proportion of the total cultivable

---

[69] Fuglie and Marder (2015: 356–7).   [70] Beintema and Stads (2017: 7).
[71] Benin, McBride, and Mogues (2016: 115).   [72] Mogues and Caceres (2018).
[73] Walker (2016: xvi).   [74] Ward (2016: 53, 64).

area. For example, in Malawi fully 70 per cent of the cultivable area in the drylands could be brought under irrigation and in Ghana and Tanzania the comparable proportion is more than 25 per cent. Nigeria has the potential to irrigate millions of hectares of dryland, but many other countries also have the potential to irrigate large areas—200,000 hectares or more—including Angola, Burkina Faso, Chad, Ghana, Madagascar, Mali, Niger, Senegal, Somalia, South Africa, and Uganda.[75]

Successful cultivation of HYVs has usually been associated with improved water management and has depended on the extremely positive response of these seeds to fertilizer. An increase in the use of fertilizers appears to have played a key role throughout the world in raising cereal yields and promoting structural change.[76] Many farmers in sub-Saharan Africa are currently *not* benefitting sufficiently from the potential yield gains offered by plant genetic improvement because they are not applying adequate nutrients to their soils.[77] Despite recent relatively fast rates of growth of consumption in some African countries, fertilizer consumption remains way below the levels recorded in South Asia: in Bangladesh, for example, average consumption per hectare is about 280 kg, compared to the sub-Saharan African average of 15 kg per hectare. There is massive potential to increase and improve fertilizer use in Africa from a very low base, which has motivated investors such as Dangote to invest billions of US dollars in fertilizer production in a number of African countries.[78]

Policies that combine increases in Africa's irrigated area with increased (but appropriate) levels of nutrient application would increase yields in Africa. Enhanced investment in agricultural R&D should result in more disaggregated and efficient fertilizer recommendations linked to the push for public sector investment in irrigation and transport infrastructure in precisely those rural areas with the greatest potential for wage employment and export production.

---

[75] Ward (2016: 58).   [76] McArthur and McCord (2017).   [77] Tittonell and Giller (2013).
[78] Oxford Business Group (2019: 18).

PART IV

TOWARDS POSSIBILISM
IN POLICY MAKING

10

High-Yielding Variety Policies in Africa

10.1 Introduction: Proving Hamlet Wrong

Many policy seeds have been planted in African soil, but their yields have often been considered disappointing. These seeds, often older ones rather than the most recently improved cultivars and hybrids, are sown with the folkloric wisdom of the most cited and renowned economists; they represent the common varieties of policy thinking that we have drawn attention to throughout this book.

Our metaphor can be stretched to cover other similarities: following the practice of many African farmers, policy officials often to try to compensate for low and erratic yields by planting a mix of different types of seeds and plants on their fields, in the hope that some at least may thrive and even generate cash returns. Just that kind of hope and risk-averse, scatter-gun approach is reflected too in the endless wish lists and unweighted bullet-point lists of recommendations that pepper the concluding sections of government policy plans, international agency advice, and consultancy reports. What we have argued for, by contrast, is a concentration on a very small number of priorities and criteria and a commitment to ongoing research and development (R&D) to support high-yielding variety policies (HYVPs) that can be adapted to the socio-political contexts of specific African economies.

There are two kinds of R&D required if HYVPs are to flourish. First, there has to be the adaptation to specific locations and the development of the most appropriate modern policy variety, using plant stock material stored in gene banks that have been curated as a public good. There is a large stock of research to draw on for this: the analysis of 'what has worked' across a huge range of contexts historically. Throughout this book we have highlighted many policies that have been effective. They are often different to those packaged and pushed as appropriate for all African economies and we have explained why the standard packages are in fact typically inappropriate. But, second, what has worked in one context—one political, historical equivalent of a specific agro-climatic zone—does not necessarily work at all or in the same way elsewhere.

This is true for certain varieties of rice, for example: the New Rice for Africa (NERICA) varieties are the result of interspecific crosses between the *Oryza sativa* rice species from Asia and the locally adapted and multiple-stress resistant *Oryza glaberrima* African rice species: 'NERICA varieties can smother weeds, resist drought and pests and can thrive in poor soils like the African parent. Like its

African Economic Development: Evidence, Theory, Policy. Christopher Cramer, John Sender, and Arkebe Oqubay,
Oxford University Press (2020). © Christopher Cramer, John Sender, and Arkebe Oqubay.
DOI: 10.1093/oso/9780198832331.001.0001

Asian parent, NERICA has high yield.' But NERICA varieties have been far more successful for some types of farmers in some African countries and regions than others.[1] Relatively few improved rice varieties have been released that are appropriate for Africa's more difficult and complex upland and rainfed environments; the varieties used on irrigated lowlands have usually been more successful.[2] Just as the drugs developed by pharmacogenetics are effective for some patients but not others, the same is true for economic policies. Liberalizing a market—for fertilizer and seed distribution, say—may have initially positive results in one country but in another, given its specific political economy and the ability of the state to act independently under pressure from globally concentrated fertilizer producers, it may simply reconfigure concentrated market power without promoting lower prices or more efficient spread. Advocating a state-owned airline may draw on examples of success in some countries, even in one African economy (Chapter 6), but that does not mean a state-owned airline will be viable in another African economy.

That is one reason we cannot provide a policy blueprint. It would be satisfying to suggest a neat plan, and there are plenty of attempts to do so. They are the branding equivalent of Fairtrade labelling: policy officials may want to 'do the right thing' yet they have too little detailed evidence or knowledge about the complex reality they are dealing with and about the history of capitalist development, so a tidy blueprint cuts the information corner for them and guides them to what is generally believed to work. But such neat plans are largely pointless. Time and again their recommendations, even if drawn from theoretically elegant models or extrapolating from some randomized controlled trial results, fail to fruit when grafted onto different contexts. (We have also argued that they are often built on poor theory and evidence anyway.)

Setting out a branded blueprint would also be a vain exercise because of uncertainty. Fundamental uncertainty, the role of contingency within cumulative causation dynamics, and the fact that tensions, imbalance, and struggles always trump equilibrium mean that broad sweeping claims to generalizable laws of policy effectiveness cannot be trusted. Moreover, unintended consequences are not always positive ones. Green Revolution initiatives like improved varieties were part of a mix of intensification policies with social and economic, and environmental, implications. Some of these were environmentally and distributionally negative. New systems of crop production using new types of inputs have been shown to have contradictory impacts on gender and labour relations; they may well exacerbate intra-household conflict in the short run. For example, it is argued that the diffusion of a disease-resistant genetically modified banana is more likely to benefit capitalist (male) farmers in the south-west of Uganda than the large

---

[1] Arouna et al. (2017: 55).   [2] Diagne et al. (2015: 203).

number of smaller producers relying on the exploitation of female family workers in central and eastern Uganda.[3] It is also argued that the Green Revolution in Punjab and Haryana had serious environmental consequences, partly because it was associated with a level and pattern of subsidized urea applications that damaged both soil and human health.[4] High-yielding economic policy varieties will also require constant monitoring and adaptation to respond to unanticipated and damaging distributional and environmental outcomes.

So we hedge our policy discussion with doubt and issue stern warnings to officials to be alert to unintended adverse consequences. Much of the success of policies lies in allocating sufficient resources to enhancing policymakers' ability to collect the data to monitor their effects closely; and to have the flexibility to change tack if needed. High-yield crop varieties have rarely achieved their yield potential without massive investment in infrastructure, above all irrigation; high-yield policies are unlikely to be effective, or even to avoid catastrophe, without a similar commitment to investment in the infrastructure of data collection and monitoring. It is necessary to develop an institutionalized ability not only to learn, but especially to learn from failure. For this reason, we advocate a policy officials' version of the 'error cabinet' in Enzo Ferrari's head office. Ferrari often held board meetings in a room whose walls were lined with glass-fronted cabinets displaying malfunctioning motor parts. Every time a Ferrari car broke down during a race, the offending parts were studied, and advances made on the basis of learning what had gone wrong.

Nonetheless, there are some things that we can say with confidence. There are strategic decisions that the evidence suggests are important almost everywhere and that policy officials in particular countries can study, considering how they could be tweaked, modified, and adapted to local conditions. There are criteria that have to be satisfied if a dynamic of economic development is to take hold that can be sustained over time with broadly progressive effects on welfare. This chapter, pulling out some of the implications from earlier chapters, therefore highlights priority areas for policy and a small number of criteria that officials do need to consider when making resource allocation decisions.

What shapes our priorities and criteria is our commitment, shared with Hirschman and his brother-in-law Colorni (who was also an anti-fascist activist), to 'proving Hamlet wrong'. If Hamlet's endless self-questioning freezes him into inaction in Shakespeare's play, Hirschman and Colorni emphasized the productiveness of doubt: the importance of doubt *to spur action* even in the face of apparently overwhelming and barbaric obstacles—'possibilism'. Thus, with Hirschman, we would encourage in policy officials even in the poorest African economies a 'bias for hope': not a dreamy utopianism fuelled by grand theory or

---

[3] Addison and Schnurr (2016).   [4] Abrol et al. (2017).

pan-Africanist dreams but an insistence on the possible, enriched by realistic analysis and by evidence.

As with doubts about the adverse unintended ecological consequences of high-yielding Green Revolution inputs, these doubts should not lead to an impossibilist resignation to a future with low yields but to redoubled research efforts to achieve adaptation. That means that we distinguish our approach from the impossibilist gloom of many development sages and many 'dismal' economists.[5] Impossibilists continue to: make sweeping critiques of ambitious and large-scale projects; insist that global capitalism allows no space for economic development within Africa or for wage workers to develop defensive political powers; argue that straying from the purity of comparative advantage principles is ruinous; allege that state-owned enterprises are necessarily wastefully inefficient; and remain convinced that the stranglehold of rent-seeking, the politics of the belly, corruption, or what de Waal calls the 'political marketplace', means that there is no possibility of implementing progressive policy ideas.

10.2 Possibilism and Experiment

Some development economists have relatively recently come to acknowledge what before were dismissed as unsound arguments: that the development of capitalism has always owed a particular debt to the role of manufacturing; and that industrialization has always and everywhere depended on state intervention that has 'got prices wrong'. But the typical refrain of common sense is still: 'well, it may have worked before—in Taiwan, in Vietnam, or somewhere, but please please don't try this yourself!' The argument is that the risks of failure are so high (and the historical record certainly does show many failures), and capacities in Africa so low, that it would be unwise to try to emulate the 'lessons' of economic history. For example, Paul Krugman came to realize that theoretically, there was a very good case for ignoring the principle of comparative advantage, but, he argued, officials should actually stick to the principle and to producing unsophisticated goods because otherwise politics will get in the way and ruin things.[6] Rather, prudent African policy officials should bide their time, getting the elements of good governance aligned, gradually building capacities, and confining themselves to the modest work of the facilitating state. African states, this plausible version of impossibilist common sense has it, should intervene up to and not beyond their current level of capacity.

---

[5] The 'dismal science' is widely believed to refer to those classical economists (the original impossibilists), above all Malthus, who believed that capitalist growth would run aground before long (Heilbroner, 1987: 78).

[6] Krugman (1987).

Meanwhile, the other strand of impossibilist common sense rolls out a series of warnings suggesting that almost all policies or accumulation strategies simply have no chance of succeeding because the dominant material and ideological forces of global capitalism are stacked against low-income peripheral countries. Global value chains are controlled tightly by powerful systems integrators that brook no significant technological upgrading by developing country producers, who remain constrained to producing relatively simple goods on a lowly rung of the ladder. The world market prices for all the goods produced in poor countries are so volatile that the imports required for dynamic growth and political stability cannot reliably be acquired. The World Trade Organization (WTO) imposes rules so binding on developing countries that they are now unable to avail themselves of the kinds of policies in the trade and financial sectors used successfully by earlier 'catching-up' countries.

We acknowledge that it is easier to fail than to succeed with development policy—often more for domestic political reasons than reasons of measurable technocratic 'capacity'. For example, in Ghana and Kenya political pressures were able—at some times more than others—to overwhelm sophisticated economic technocrats.[7] We also acknowledge that the external financial and economic environment confronting developing country economies and governments is prone to wild fluctuations, often hostile, and poses risks to improving welfare. But there is still significant, proven scope for governments to intervene in support of an accelerated dynamic of accumulation, structural change, and not insignificant welfare improvement. And there is scope for governments to intervene beyond their current capacity levels, to experiment.

10.3 The Political Origins of Economic Institutions and Shifts in Policy

Keynes emphasized the fundamental uncertainty that might stall investment by rational actors. Something, for example the sentiments of a mimetic rush of animal spirits sparked by government spending, was needed to provoke private investors into action. By analogy, rational officials working for a state faced with a list of constricting rules of global governance and weighed down by the evidence of many failures in other African and Latin American economies might, like Hamlet, do nothing decisive. Something is required to push them to act in effective ways.

That something has eluded textbook economists: it cannot be modelled. It probably takes different forms and these may include a flush of nationalism or an

---

[7] Fahnbulleh (2006).

impending external military threat. Our greater understanding in recent years of the economic role and impact of institutions 'has not been matched by our understanding of their political origins'.[8] There are accounts of African economic development that consider being in a 'bad neighbourhood' one of the key 'traps' that prevents growth;[9] being surrounded by countries mired in instability and violence can of course have negative spill-over effects, but it would not be wise to take this so literally, for the regional effect (just like being landlocked, for example—another 'trap') may provoke creative policy responses that lead to *faster* growth. Wars, and the presence of both internal and external threats, have historically played a significant role in prompting shifts in growth, in state organization and capability, in fiscal revenues and in the coherence of policymaking. Generally, jolts of political crisis have tended to be more important spurs to substantial reshaping of economic policy and production than the steady assembly of preconditions (of governance, of capability, of comparative advantage). It is the same with reductions in inequality: 'Across the full sweep of history, every single one of the major compressions of material inequality we can observe in the record was driven by one or more of these levelers': calamitous war that drew in societies as a whole, similarly violent revolutions, state collapse, or appalling pandemics that raised the wages of poorer (and suddenly scarcer) people.[10]

Similarly, historically, states have made war and war has made states. The main mechanism through which this has worked is resource mobilization. Needing to find ways to mobilize people to fight and to mobilize the resources to keep fighting forces fed, transported, clothed, and armed, states have resorted to all manner of extortion, borrowing, and, over time, above all, taxation. Those states that have most effectively raised revenue have not only won wars and secured the state but also created lasting institutions of statehood.[11] War has also often—very far from always—led to shifts in the extent and types of state intervention in economies and societies that is politically acceptable (even imaginable). It has had major effects on the organization of large capitalist firms and their links to state institutions that have often survived long after the end of wars.[12]

In the North East Asian economies of South Korea and Taiwan, for example, 'systemic vulnerability' played a very important role in the political origins of institutions and policies associated with 'developmental states' and rapid economic growth. One argument is that such institutions only emerge 'when political leaders confront extraordinarily constrained political environments', specifically where they stare down the barrels of

[8] Doner, Ritchie, and Slater (2005: 327).   [9] Collier (2008).   [10] Scheidel (2017: 36).
[11] Tilly (1992).   [12] Cramer (2020).

three different guns: (1) the credible threat that any deterioration in the living standards of popular sectors could trigger unmanageable mass unrest; (2) the heightened need for foreign exchange and war matériel induced by national insecurity; and (3) the hard budget constraints imposed by a scarcity of easy revenue sources.[13]

Similar constraints lay behind the shift in Ethiopia—associated with the then Prime Minister Meles Zenawi—towards efforts to create a 'democratic developmental state'. Without copious natural resource rents and in one of the very poorest nations in the world, the Ethiopian People's Revolutionary Democratic Front (EPRDF) took power in a context characterized precisely by 'a scarcity of easy revenue sources'. Violent insecurity in neighbouring countries and tense relations with some of these countries, including military intervention by Ethiopia in Somalia and a war with Eritrea, resulted in a 'heightened need for foreign exchange and war matériel induced by national insecurity'. And national insecurity was also fragile in a context of the fundamental strains on Ethiopian political economy. There was tension between the long historical source of political power in the highlands while the sources of economic reproduction were greater in the lowland peripheries.[14] This tension at the heart of an unfinished project of creating a coherent 'imagined community'[15] of the Ethiopian nation state was exacerbated by rapid population growth, accelerating urbanization, continued poverty, and rising political challenges in the 2000s to the EPRDF.[16] The EPRDF then committed, under Meles and his successor as Prime Minister, Hailemariam Desalegn, to delivering economic development in the pursuit of legitimacy. The latest dramatic turn of policy direction—in 2019—may perhaps be explained by the fact that sustained and remarkably rapid economic growth had failed to resolve this systemic vulnerability, and that the foreign exchange shortage was becoming even more pressing.

Dramatic political upheaval has been at the heart of major leaps in the national organization of production and productivity in the history of the USA, too. In the wake of the War of Independence from Great Britain, Alexander Hamilton famously pioneered American industrial policy. Hamilton's practical policy involvement led him, in his *Report on the Subject of Manufactures*, to argue that Adam Smith's academic approach led to propositions that were 'geometrically true' but 'practically false'.[17] The American Civil War in the 1860s led to a range of technological, organizational, and policy innovations with lasting consequences.[18] And much later, when the USA entered the Second World War, President Roosevelt launched his campaign to build an 'Arsenal of Democracy'. The strategy to produce victory involved creating 'a production system that linked

---

[13] Doner, Ritchie, and Slater (2005: 328).   [14] Clapham (2017).   [15] Anderson (1987).
[16] Markakis (2011).   [17] McNamara (1998).   [18] Cramer (2006).

technological innovations in weapons with the production capability to absorb and integrate technological change', in other words to graft the mass production system pioneered in the USA onto a technologically advanced war production system.[19] The 'industrial empire' that ensued was financed through 'public-sector entrepreneurship', in the form of a non-market leasing system through which the state financed two thirds of war-oriented private sector production.[20]

10.4 Priorities for Strategies of Economic Development

One of the main uses of our book is to offer practical suggestions about how to argue against fashionable policies that are not rooted in evidence or are theoretically incoherent. We also offer a guide to implementing some other and less-discussed economic policies, although we are aware that this guide may only prove useful in particular political conditions.

The evidence and arguments presented here, especially in Chapters 4–9, lead us to propose the following broad, strategic priorities.

Objective 1: A High Investment Ratio

Governments should promote a high investment ratio as an urgent priority. Stimulating a sustained high investment to gross domestic product (GDP) ratio is fundamental to prospects for rapid and lasting growth and structural change. The historical evidence shows this clearly. The state has to lead this investment push by making a commitment to economically productive public spending. This does *not* have to be financed by deregulation of the financial sector. Indeed, liberalizing the financial sector too much and too rapidly, the evidence shows, undermines such a strategic objective.

Objective 2: National Champion Firms

Rather than supply-side small-is-beautiful entrepreneurship programmes, policy officials should prioritize the creation and subsidize the success of large national champions and ensure the complementarity of public and private initiatives. These large firms are the ones that can capture the productivity gains from increasing returns to scale, they are more likely to survive than small and medium-sized enterprises (SMEs) (among which there are typically high rates of

---

[19] Best (2018: 27).   [20] Best (2018: 24–54).

collapse), they make a disproportionate contribution to exports, and they are more likely to create large numbers of decent and unionized jobs.[21]

Officials should acknowledge the historical evidence that major private sector investing firms have typically developed thanks to state support. This support has taken a wide variety of forms, including: protectionist and 'infant industry' policies, the creation of state-owned enterprises, procurement policies, supporting legal cartels, laying the base for private sector firms through public research and development, and other mechanisms of the 'entrepreneurial state', as well as effective management of social conflicts and security provision to secure the conditions of capitalist investment and production. These are not just policies of historical interest. They are what governments around the world do (in advanced Organisation for Economic Co-operation and Development (OECD) economies and in middle and lower-income economies)—with varying degrees of success—to support successful large firms. It is what the Brazilian state has done in supporting second-generation bio-tech firms, through innovative financing mechanisms. Sometimes, major firms emerge from mutual interests in a tangle of calculation among politicians and business—winners picking states just as much as states picking winners. A case in point is Aliko Dangote, founder of the immense Nigerian and now continent-wide cement firm. Dangote had made strenuous efforts to develop very close political ties, including to General Obasanjo, over many years of accumulating rents from a number of 'crony capitalist' trading enterprises. 'Dangote used his close connection to Obasanjo to influence the Nigerian government to adopt and sustain a Backward Integration Policy (BIP) for the cement industry in Nigeria.'[22] There is clearly an element of the contingent in these histories, but it certainly helps for officials to be aware of the scope of the possible, rather than to continue wasting resources chasing fantasies of development and structural change through tiny start-ups.

Objective 3: A Rapid Rate of Increase in Imports and in Exports

A publicly led investment boost will necessarily imply a faster rate of growth of imports. This is only sustainable if there is a rapid rate of increase in exports. Investment booms tend to lead to debt problems. This is natural. What matters is preventing a debt *problem* becoming a debt *crisis*. There are all sorts of ways of negotiating and managing external debt, all of them an important part of a shrewd strategy, including: ensuring a sensible spread of debt maturities, limiting non-concessional borrowing, renegotiating repayment structures, preventing

---

[21] On 'national champions' in China and China's industrial policy learning from other East Asian economies, see Li and Chen (2020).
[22] Akinyoade and Uche (2018: 835).

unregulated private sector borrowing abroad, and others. Investment–import booms in Africa can also be financed in part by resort to concessional foreign funds or aid. But just as exposure to commercial debt is risky, so is too great a reliance on too few sources of foreign aid, because individual donors may be unreliable, and because the strings attached to some aid are difficult to reconcile with the strategic objectives of sustained economic growth. The real key to managing a rapid rate of growth of imports is to promote very rapid export expansion. Despite naysayers, this remains possible. While improving the scope for (and reducing costs of) intra-African trade may be a boon to economic activity, it is most unlikely to be an effective substitute for maximizing exports to demanding (in terms of quality and phyto-sanitary or labour or other standards) large higher income markets. Intra-African trade should be a complement to, not a refuge from, a strategy of wider global economic integration.

Objective 4: Promoting Investment in Specific Types of Economic Activity

Investment, especially public investment in infrastructure and state-owned enterprises, and government policies designed to encourage private sector productive investment, needs to be targeted—directed towards particular types of activity. There are three particularly important criteria to bear in mind here. First, investment will have a greater economic and social impact if it is concentrated in those activities most likely to create growth of demand for the labour of women with little education. (This should be combined with measures to keep girls in school longer: both to improve their own knowledge and skills and to tighten the labour market.) Such investment may be in high-value agriculture (not just 'agro-processing'), which should be recognized as industrial, complex, and sophisticated production, as well as in urban/peri-urban manufacturing factories. Complementary policies might support both types of investment by reducing the financial and social costs of labour mobility as labour shifts from low to higher-productivity forms of employment (low-cost accommodation, travel, the cost of phone network usage for communicating with family and transferring savings home, or to rural post offices).

Second, investment is needed to underpin rapid export growth. If possible, the selected activities absorbing unskilled female labour migrants from rural areas should therefore also make a rapid net contribution to foreign exchange earnings. That involves a range of policies including the competitive undervaluation of the exchange rate.

Third, and complementary to investment in export capacity, we have shown that it is extremely important to allocate investment resources to increase the supply of food and other basic wage goods, which in turn underpins dynamics of investment. Investments are required to monitor real wages and to intervene rapidly in food markets to smooth price spikes. In the longer term, investments to accelerate agricultural production of wage goods and exports requires R&D expenditures and targeted infrastructure provision focused on particular crops (e.g. coffee and avocados for exports and cassava or yams—rather than dairy and poultry—for the poorest consumers); and it requires betting on the strong, that is, on farms with a proven track record either in expanding exports or in producing large marketed surpluses of basic foods for domestic consumers. Clearly, it would be desirable to combine several strategic objectives, selecting national and 'export' champions that also employ large numbers of, especially, women from poor rural backgrounds, or selecting the most dynamic and efficient producers of wage goods for a low-income domestic mass market that also employ large numbers of unskilled wage workers (see Chapter 3).

Objective 5: Develop Capability for Monitoring and Disciplining

Designing incentives for well-targeted investment promotion is not difficult. But it is bordering on pointless to introduce incentives to firms if there is no parallel development of capacity to monitor performance and to discipline firms (including by withdrawing access to exemptions or subsidies, etc.). This quid pro quo— the reciprocal control mechanism to ensure that firms meet targets for exports, investment, employment, and productivity– is a *sine qua non* of effective policy.

If labour productivity is to improve and if absolute poverty is to be reduced, there is one aspect of the performance of capitalist firms that it is particularly important to monitor. In return for state support, firms need to be set targets not only to increase exports, but also to encourage the organization and effective voice of the workers they employ. We are well aware that firms can and do evade modest levels of employment protection legislation in Africa (and elsewhere). But minimum wage, health and safety rules, child protection, gender rights, and other legislation to enforce decent working conditions may nevertheless be expected to have *positive* effects, encouraging the growth of trade unions and strengthening their negotiating capacity. Even when states appear unable to impose strict discipline on capitalists—ensuring that all subsidized enterprises comply with agreed rules—employment protection legislation can provide a rallying cry and a reference point for struggles to organize workers. Workers' organizations and professional associations, together with relatively efficient compliant firms, may also put pressure on state institutions to monitor and discipline those firms continuing to compete on the basis of illegal working conditions and low labour productivity.

There are many good reasons for policymakers to make a serious effort to create the institutions and mechanisms to monitor (preferably on a monthly basis) the real wages of all wage workers, especially the lowest-paid female workers. Publishing trends in these wages would improve the quality of public debate about poverty reduction and support Objective 6. It would also help to rapidly identify failing investment projects and to legitimate strict disciplinary action by governments against errant subsidized capitalists. Most importantly, it would provide emerging workers' organizations with the information necessary to target their limited resources towards particular sectors and employers.

Objective 6: Protecting Welfare, Profitability, and Political Stability through Grain Market Management

A key feature of the analysis in this book (chiefly in Chapters 4 and 7) has been to highlight the importance of a non-inflationary supply of basic wage (especially food) goods. This protects the ability of firms employing workers to ensure that profitability is not eroded by wage hikes necessary to allow workers to meet rising costs of basic living; and it protects politicians from the political consequences of wages not rising sufficiently in such circumstances. Part of the strategy, (Objective 4) involves promoting investment in the supply of basic food goods (especially those cereals purchased by the poorest wage workers). But the evidence from elsewhere (especially in Asia) is that part of the strategy also has to involve direct intervention in food grain markets to prevent price spikes. If export revenues are increasing and the long-run real international market prices of certain foods are declining, a successful accumulation strategy in Africa (as elsewhere) will involve *increases* in the volume of food imports (and the manipulation of tariffs on food imports to smooth domestic price fluctuations).

10.5 Conclusion: Impossible is Nothing

In conclusion, we emphasize two features of the analysis and argument in this book. First, we have argued that variation matters. Descriptively, identifying variation in policies and in performance is crucial to analysis and is often smothered in averages. Closer attention to variation reveals, for example, that there is usually more variation *within* sub-Saharan African countries—in undernutrition, in wealth, in access to education, and so on—than there is between African countries, while, nonetheless, the variation between countries is itself more significant than often acknowledged. But we have also argued that it matters to ask: variation in what? Much poverty analysis, for example, focuses on categories—simple geographical distinctions like rural/urban or categories such as 'female-headed households'—that can be misleading. These analyses, we have argued, obscure 'intra-category' variation, for example, inequality within areas classified as rural or huge diversity of living standards among 'smallholders' or 'female-headed households'. And we have suggested some examples of what we argue are more useful categorical distinctions. The same is the case for distinctions between broad economic 'sectors', which we have argued have become even less useful analytically than they may have been in the past. The blurring of boundaries captured in the idea of 'servicification' and of 'the industrialization of freshness' is a prompt to recalibrate the assessment of which kinds of activity are most relevant for the objectives of economic policy, which then leads to the identification of new kinds of variation.

Variation can then become a source of policy possibilism. That it has been possible to achieve very steep declines in fertility rates in Rwanda compared to Burundi, despite many similarities of 'structure', history, and endowments, or in Kenya compared to Uganda, or Ghana compared to Nigeria (Chapter 2) suggests a clear role for policy. And the policy history of these countries confirms a clear commitment to meeting women's contraceptive needs—sustained over a lengthy period—in those countries with sharp fertility declines. Again, the variation in the incidence of insecticide-treated bed nets or in the equity of their distribution cannot simply be 'read off' from indices of endowments but reflects purposive policy design and implementation. Similarly, the fact that some farms have managed to generate far higher agricultural yields than others within the same agro-ecological zones suggests a clear role for officials to identify why and to pursue policies that can clearly secure higher yields on a much larger area. And differences between African countries in the rate of adoption of high-yield variety (HYV) seeds reflect variation in an important policy choice: public spending on agricultural research (Chapter 9). It is also extremely important to emphasize, as in Chapter 4, that some African countries have adopted policies to achieve much higher and more sustained levels of public sector investment than others.

Second, we have not only shown that mainstream economic analysis and policy advice is empirically unfounded, has deep theoretical weaknesses, and has not produced the results insistently claimed, but we have also provided a coherent (and possibilist) alternative. But criticizing the mainstream is relatively easy and also commonplace. Subjecting alternatives to a non-mainstream critique is more uncommon and, we argue, necessary. Because these alternatives have so readily and uncritically been accepted by non-economists in Africa and by heterodox economists, it has been all too easy for orthodox economists and advisers to deploy dodgy quantitative evidence to brush these alternative policy proposals aside. We have therefore, at the risk of alienating those we have worked with and often agreed with, also tried to offer an alternative to the most widespread forms of critique of the mainstream: these oscillate between stifling impossibilism and fanciful expectations of capitalism with a human face, of South–South solidarity, of homogeneous and mutually supportive rural societies, of the triumph of small-scale capitalism (based on millions of very small farmers and entrepreneurs).

Above all, we have sought to contribute analysis and evidence that make it easier for policy officials to pursue some variant of what Meles Zenawi called the 'Sinatra model' of policymaking—assessing what has been effective in a range of contexts and adapting to specific African contexts, and then doing it 'my way'.

References

Abdulai, A.-G. (2019). *Rethinking Elite Commitment to Social Protection in Ghana: Insights from an Adapted Political Settlements Approach* (ESID Working Paper No. 112). Manchester: Global Development Institute, School of Environment, Education and Development, University of Manchester.

Abebaw, D., & Admassie, A. (2013). 'Correlates of extreme poverty in Ethiopia'. In J. Von Braun & F. W. Gatzweiler (eds), *Marginality Addressing the Nexus of Poverty, Exclusion and Ecology*. New York: Springer.

Abraham, K. G., & Amaya, A. (2018). *Probing for Informal Work Activity* (Working Paper No. 24880). Cambridge, MA: National Bureau of Economic Research.

Abrol, Y. P., Adhya, T. K., Aneja, V. P., Raghuram, N., Pathak, H., Kulshrestha, U., Sharma, C., & Singh, B. (eds). (2017). *The Indian Nitrogen Assessment: Sources of Reactive Nitrogen, Environmental and Climate Effects, Management Options, and Policies*. Duxford: Elsevier.

Acemoglu, D., Johnson, S., & Robinson, J. A. (2001). 'The colonial origins of comparative development: an empirical investigation', *American Economic Review*, 91/5: 1369–401.

Acemoglu, D., Johnson, S., & Robinson, J. A. (2002). 'Reversal of fortune: geography and institutions in the making of the modern world income distribution', *Quarterly Journal of Economics*, 117/4: 1231–94.

Achebe, C. (1987). *Anthills of the Savannah*. African Writers Series. Oxford: Heinemann.

ACLED (Armed Conflict Location & Event Data Project). (2017). 'Armed Conflict Location & Event Data Project'.

ACPF (African Child Policy Forum). (2019). *For Lack of Will: Child Hunger in Africa*. Addis Ababa: African Child Policy Forum (ACPF). Retrieved from: http://www.africanchildforum.org/ipc/documents-media/.

Adam, I. O., Musah, A., & Ibrahim, M. (2017). 'Putting the cart before the horse? Re-examining the relationship between domestic savings and economic growth in selected sub-Saharan African countries', *Journal of African Business*, 18/1: 102–23.

Adams, Z., Bishop, L., Deakin, S., Fenwick, C., Garzelli, S. M., & Rusconi, G. (2019). 'The economic significance of laws relating to employment protection and different forms of employment: analysis of a panel of 117 countries, 1990–2013', *International Labour Review*, 158/1: 1–35.

Adato, M., Lund, F., & Mhlongo, P. (2007). 'Methodological innovations in research on the dynamics of poverty: a longitudinal study in KwaZulu-Natal, South Africa', *World Development*, 35/2: 247–63.

Addison, L., & Schnurr, M. (2016). 'Growing burdens? Disease-resistant genetically modified bananas and the potential gendered implications for labor in Uganda', *Agriculture and Human Values*, 33/4: 967–78.

Adelman, J. (2013). *Worldly Philosopher: The Odyssey of Albert O. Hirschman*. Princeton, NJ: Princeton University Press.

Adelzadeh, A. (2019). *Economic Policy Scenarios for Growth and Development of South Africa: 2019–2030*. Folsom, CA: Applied Development Research Solutions (ADRS).

African Development Bank. (ed.). (2012). *African Economic Outlook: Promoting Youth Employment*. Paris: OECD.

Aga, G., Francis, D. C., & Meza, J. R. (2015). *SMEs, Age, and Jobs: A Review of the Literature, Metrics, and Evidence*. Washington, DC: World Bank.

Agarwal, B. (2019). 'Does group farming empower rural women? Lessons from India's experiments', *Journal of Peasant Studies*, 1–32.

Agaya, B. M., & Asunza, M. (2013). *Report of a Baseline Survey of Women Domestic Workers in Mukuru Informal Settlement, Nairobi, Kenya*. Nairobi: OXFAM.

Aggarwal, V. K., & Evenett, S. J. (2014). 'Do WTO rules preclude industrial policy? Evidence from the global economic crisis', *Business and Politics*, 16/4: 481–509.

Aguilar, G. R., & Sumner, A. (2019). *Who Are the World's Poor? A New Profile of Global Multidimensional Poverty* (CGD Working Paper No. 499). Washington, DC: Center for Global Development. Retrieved from: https://www.cgdev.org/publication/who-are-worlds-poor-new-profile-global-multidimensional-poverty.

Ahmed, S., Appendino, M., & Ruta, M. (2015). *Depreciations without Exports? Global Value Chains and the Exchange Rate Elasticity of Exports*. Washington, DC: World Bank.

Akinyoade, A., & Uche, C. (2018). 'Development built on crony capitalism? The case of Dangote Cement', *Business History*, 60/6: 833–58.

Akresh, R., & Edmonds, E. (2010). *The Analytical Returns to Measuring a Detailed Household Roster* (IZA Discussion Papers No. 4759). Bonn: Institute for the Study of Labor (IZA).

Aksoy, M. A., & Yagci, F. (2012). *Mozambique Cashew Reforms Revisited* (Policy Research Working Paper No. 5939). Washington, DC: World Bank. Retrieved from: http://hdl.handle.net/10986/3224.

Alacevich, M. (2012). *Visualizing Uncertainties, or How Albert Hirschman and the World Bank Disagreed on Project Appraisal and Development Approaches*. Washington, DC: World Bank.

Alderman, H., & Headey, D. D. (2017). 'How important is parental education for child nutrition?', *World Development*, 94: 448–64.

Aldrich, J. (2019). *Eugenics in British Economics from Marshall to Meade*. Economics Department, University of Southampton. Retrieved from: http://www.economics.soton.ac.uk/staff/aldrich/0%20aldrich%20eugenics.pdf.

Alexander, J., & McGregor, J. (2013). 'Introduction: politics, patronage and violence in Zimbabwe', *Journal of Southern African Studies*, 39/4: 749–63.

Alkire, S. (2018). *Multidimensional Poverty Measures as Relevant Policy Tools* (OPHI Working Papers No. 118). Oxford: Oxford Poverty and Human Development Initiative, University of Oxford.

Alkire, S., Jindra, C., Vaz, A., & Robles-Aguilar, G. (2017). *Multidimensional Poverty Reduction among Countries in Sub-Saharan Africa* (OPHI Working Papers No. 112). Oxford: Oxford Poverty and Human Development Initiative, University of Oxford.

Allais, S. (2012). 'Will skills save us? Rethinking the relationships between vocational education, skills development policies, and social policy in South Africa', *International Journal of Educational Development*, 32/5: 632–42.

Allen, R. C. (2019). 'Class structure and inequality during the Industrial Revolution: lessons from England's social tables, 1688–1867', *Economic History Review*, 72/1: 88–125.

Allison, S. (2013). 'Don't touch me on my statistics: Pali Lehohla pulls the plug on UNECA speaker'. *Daily Maverick*. 26 September. Kenilworth.

Alwang, J. (2015). 'Investments in and impacts of crop improvement research in Africa'. In K. Fuglie, J. Marder, T. Walker, & J. Alwang (eds), *Crop Improvement, Adoption and*

Impact of Improved Varieties in Food Crops in Sub-Saharan Africa. Boston, MA: CGIAR and CAB International.

Ambel, A. A., & Huang, W. (2014). 'Maternal education, linkages and child nutrition in the long and short-run: evidence from the Ethiopia demographic and health surveys', *International Journal of African Development*, 1/2: 5–28.

Amin, S. (2015). 'Food sovereignty and the agrarian question: constructing convergence of struggles within diversity'. In R. Herrera & K. C. Lau (eds), *The Struggle for Food Sovereignty: Alternative Development and the Renewal of Peasant Societies Today.* London: Pluto Press.

Amsden, A. H. (1992). *Asia's Next Giant: South Korea and Late Industrialization.* New York: Oxford University Press.

Amsden, A. H. (2001). *The Rise of 'the Rest': Challenges to the West from Late-Industrializing Economies.* Oxford: Oxford University Press.

Amsden, A. H. (2009). *Escape from Empire: The Developing World's Journey through Heaven and Hell.* Cambridge, MA, & London: MIT Press.

Amsden, A. H. (2010). 'Say's Law, poverty persistence, and employment neglect', *Journal of Human Development and Capabilities*, 11/1: 57–66.

Amsden, A. H. (2013). *Securing the Home Market: A New Approach to Korean Development* (Research Papers No. 2013-1). Geneva: UNRISD.

Amsden, A. H., & Hikino, T. (2000). 'The bark is worse than the bite: new WTO law and late industrialization', *Annals of the American Academy of Political and Social Science*, 570/1: 104–14.

An, Z., Jalles, J. T., & Loungani, P. (2018). *How Well Do Economists Forecast Recessions?* (IMF Working Paper No. WP/18/39). Washington, DC: Research Department, IMF.

Andam, K., Makhija, S., & Spielman, D. (2018). *Evaluation of the Impacts of a Soil Fertility Training Project on Farm Productivity in the Volta Region of Ghana.* New Delhi: International Initiative for Impact Evaluation (3ie).

Anderson, B. (1987). *Imagined Communities: Reflections on the Origin and Spread of Nationalism.* London: Verso.

Anderson, D. L. (1984). 'Depression, dust bowl, demography and drought: the colonial state and soil conservation in East Africa during the 1930s', *African Affairs*, 83/332: 321–43.

Anderson, J. R., Feder, G., & Ganguly, S. (2006). *The Rise and Fall of Training and Visit Extension: An Asian Mini-drama with an African Epilogue* (World Bank Policy Research Working Paper No. 3928). World Bank: Washington, DC.

Anderson, P. (2000). 'Editorial: renewals', *New Left Review*, 1/1: 1–20.

Ang, Y. Y. (2016). *How China Escaped the Poverty Trap.* Cornell Studies in Political Economy. Ithaca, NY, & London: Cornell University Press.

Ansar, A., Flyvbjerg, B., Budzier, A., & Lunn, D. (2014). 'Should we build more large dams? The actual costs of hydropower megaproject development', *Energy Policy*, 69: 43–56.

Arestis, P. (2005). *Financial Liberalization and the Relationship between Finance and Growth* (Centre for Economic and Public Policy (CEPP) Working Paper No. 05/05). Cambridge: Department of Land Economy.

Arewa, O. (2012). *The Rise of Nollywood: Creators, Entrepreneurs, and Pirates* (UC Irvine School of Law Research Paper). Irvine: University of California Irvine School of Law.

Arizala, F., Gonzalez-Garcia, M. J. R., Tsangarides, M. C. G., & Yenice, M. (2017). *Growth Breaks and Growth Spells in Sub-Saharan Africa* (African Department Working Paper). Washington, DC: IMF.

Arouna, A., Lokossou, J. C., Wopereis, M. C. S., Bruce-Oliver, S., & Roy-Macauley, H. (2017). 'Contribution of improved rice varieties to poverty reduction and food security in sub-Saharan Africa', *Global Food Security*, 14: 54–60.

Arrighi, G., Silver, B. J., & Brewer, B. D. (2003). 'Industrial convergence, globalization, and the persistence of the North–South divide', *Studies in Comparative International Development*, 38/1: 3.

Austin, G. (1987). 'The emergence of capitalist relations in South Asante cocoa-farming, c. 1916–33', *Journal of African History*, 28/2: 259–79.

Austin, G. (2008). 'The "reversal of fortune" thesis and the compression of history: perspectives from African and comparative economic history', *Journal of International Development*, 20/8: 996–1027.

Avdagic, S. (2015). 'Does deregulation work? Reassessing the unemployment effects of employment protection', *British Journal of Industrial Relations*, 53/1: 6–26.

Awaworyi Churchill, S. (2018). 'Sustainability and depth of outreach: evidence from microfinance institutions in sub-Saharan Africa', *Development Policy Review*, 36: O676–O695.

Bado, A. R., & Sathiya Susuman, A. (2016). 'Women's education and health inequalities in under-five mortality in selected sub-Saharan African countries, 1990–2015', *PLoS ONE*, 11/7: e0159186.

Baffes, J., Kabundi, A., Nagle, P., & Ohnsorge, F. (2018). *The Role of Major Emerging Markets in Global Commodity Demand* (Policy Research Working Paper No. 8495). Washington, DC: World Bank.

Bahri, A. (2016). 'Handling WTO disputes with the private sector: the triumphant Brazilian experience', *Journal of World Trade*, 50/4: 641–74.

Bakken, I. V., & Rustad, S. A. (2018). *Conflict Trends in Africa, 1989–2017* (Conflict Trends Paper No. 06–2018). Oslo: PRIO. Retrieved from: https://www.prio.org/Publications/Publication/?x=11048.

Balchin, N., Booth, D., & te Velde, D. W. (2019). *How Economic Transformation Happens at the Sector Level: Evidence from Africa and Asia*. London: ODI.

Bamford, L. J., McKerrow, N. H., Barron, P., & Aung, Y. (2018). 'Child mortality in South Africa: fewer deaths, but better data are needed', *South African Medical Journal*, 108/3: 25–32.

Bantebya, G. K., Muhanguzi, F. K., & Watson, C. (2014). *Adolescent Girls in the Balance: Changes and Continuity in Social Norms and Practices around Marriage and Education in Uganda* (Country Report). London: ODI. Retrieved from: http://resourcecentre.savethechildren.se/sites/default/files/documents/9180.pdf.

Banerjee, A. (2015). *Policies for a Better-fed World* (Working Paper No. 21623). National Bureau of Economic Research.

Baran, P. (1973). 'On the political economy of backwardness'. In P. Baran (ed.), *The Political Economy of Development and Underdevelopment*. New York: Random House.

Barchiesi, F. (2017). 'The precariousness of work in postcolonial Africa'. In E. Armano, A. Bove, & A. Murgia (eds), *Mapping Precariousness, Labour Insecurity and Uncertain Livelihoods*. London: Routledge.

Bardhan, P., & Rudra, A. (1980a). 'Labour employment and wages in agriculture: results of a survey in West Bengal, 1979', *Economic and Political Weekly*, 15/45–6: 1943–9.

Bardhan, P., & Rudra, A. (1980b). 'Types of labour attachment in agriculture: results of a survey in West Bengal, 1979', *Economic and Political Weekly*, 15/35: 1477–84.

Barnett, T., Dercon, S., & Seeley, J. (2010). 'Response by the authors', *Tropical Medicine & International Health*, 15/8: 958–9.

Barro, R. J., & Sala-i-Martin, X. (1992). 'Convergence', *Journal of Political Economy*, 100/2: 223–51.

Basole, A., & Narayan, A. (2018). *Long-Run Performance of the Organised Manufacturing Sector in India: Aggregate Trends and Industry-Level Variation* (CSE Working Paper). Centre for Sustainable Employment: Azim Premji University.

Bateman, M. (2014). *South Africa's Post-Apartheid Microcredit-Driven Calamity: Comparing 'Developmental' to 'Anti-Developmental' Local Financial Models* (Working Paper No. 47). Vienna: Austrian Foundation for Development Research (ÖFSE).

Bateman, M., & Chang, H.-J. (2012). 'Microfinance and the illusion of development: from hubris to nemesis in thirty years', *World Economic Review*, 1: 13–36.

Bateman, M., Duvendack, M., & Loubere, N. (2019). 'Is fin-tech the new panacea for poverty alleviation and local development? Contesting Suri and Jack's M-Pesa findings published in *Science*', *Review of African Political Economy*, 46/161: 1–16.

Bates, R. H. (1980). *States and Political Intervention in Markets: A Case Study from Africa* (Social Science Working Paper No. 345). Pasadena, CA: California Institute of Technology. Retrieved from: https://authors.library.caltech.edu/82223/.

Bates, R. H. (2017). 'Politics, Academics, and Africa', *Annual Review of Political Science*, 20: 1–14.

Baudron, F., Misiko, M., Getnet, B., Nazare, R., Sariah, J., & Kaumbutho, P. (2019). 'A farm-level assessment of labor and mechanization in Eastern and Southern Africa', *Agronomy for Sustainable Development*, 39/2.

Bayart, J.-F. (1993). *The State in Africa: The Politics of the Belly*. London: Longmans.

Bayly, C. A. (2008). *Indigenous and Colonial Origins of Comparative Economic Development: The Case of Colonial India and Africa* (Policy Research Working Papers). Washington, DC: World Bank.

Beatriz, E. D., Molnar, B. E., Griffith, J. L., & Salhi, C. (2018). 'Urban–rural disparity and urban population growth: a multilevel analysis of under-5 mortality in 30 sub-Saharan African countries', *Health & Place*, 52: 196–204.

Bédécarrats, F., Guérin, I., & Roubaud, F. (2019a). 'All that glitters is not gold: the political economy of randomized evaluations in development', *Development and Change*, 50/3: 735–62.

Bédécarrats, F., Guérin, I., Morvant-Roux, S., & Roubaud, F. (2019b). 'Estimating micro-credit impact with low take-up, contamination and inconsistent data.', *International Journal for Re-Views in Empirical Economics*, 3/2019-3: 1–53.

Beegle, K., Christiaensen, L., Dabalen, A., & Gaddis, I. (2016). *Poverty in a Rising Africa*. Washington, DC: World Bank.

Beegle, K., Coudouel, A., & Monsalve, E. (eds). (2018). *Realizing the Full Potential of Social Safety Nets in Africa*. Africa Development Forum Series. Washington, DC: World Bank.

Beintema, N., & Stads, G.-J. (2017). *A Comprehensive Overview of Investments and Human Resource Capacity in African Agricultural Research* (ASTI Synthesis Report). Washington, DC: International Food Policy Research Institute.

Benali, M., Brümmer, B., & Afari-Sefa, V. (2018). 'Smallholder participation in vegetable exports and age-disaggregated labor allocation in Northern Tanzania', *Agricultural Economics*, 49/5: 549–62.

Bench Marks Foundation. (2012). *Communities in the Platinum Minefields: A Review of Platinum Mining in the Bojanala District of the North West Province—A Participatory Action Research Approach* (Policy Gap 6). Johannesburg: Bench Marks Foundation.

Bengtsson, E. (2019). 'The Swedish Sonderweg in question: democratization and inequality in comparative perspective, c. 1750–1920', *Past & Present*, 244/1: 123–61.

Benin, S., McBride, L., & Mogues, T. (2016). 'Why do African countries underinvest in agricultural R&D?' In J. Lyman, N. Beintema, J. Roseboom, & O. Badiane (eds), *Agricultural Research in Africa: Investing in Future Harvests*. Washington, DC: International Food Policy Research Institute.

Benjamin, W. (1992). *Illuminations*. Fontana: London.

Bennhold, K. (2010). 'In Greek debt crisis, a window to the German psyche'. *New York Times*. 4 May.

Benshaul-Tolonen, A. (2018). 'Local industrial shocks and infant mortality', *The Economic Journal*, 129/620: 1561–92.

Bernards, N. (2019). 'The poverty of fintech? Psychometrics, credit infrastructures, and the limits of financialization', *Review of International Political Economy*, 26/5: 815–38.

Bernstein, J., Johnson, N., & Arsalan, A. (2019). *Meta-Evidence Review on the Impacts of Investments in Agricultural and Rural Development on Sustainable Development Goals 1 and 2* (IFAD Research Series No. 38). Rome: IFAD.

Best, M. H. (2018). *How Growth Really Happens: The Making of Economic Miracles through Production, Governance, and Skills*. Princeton, NJ, & Oxford: Princeton University Press.

Bettini, G. (2013). 'Climate barbarians at the gate? A critique of apocalyptic narratives on "climate refugees"', *Geoforum*, 45: 63–72.

Bharadwaj, K. (1974). *Production Conditions in Indian Agriculture: A Study Based on Farm Management Surveys* (University of Cambridge Department of Applied Economics Occasional Paper No. 33). London & New York: Cambridge University Press.

Bianchi, A.M. (2011). *Albert Hirschman and his controversial research report*. Working paper no.2011-03. Department of Economics, FEA/USP: São Paulo.

Birdsall, N.M, Campos, J., Kim, C.S, Corden, W.M., MacDonald, L., Pack, H., Page, J., Sabor, R., Stiglitz, J. (1993). *The East Asian miracle: economic growth and public policy*. A World Bank Policy Research Report. New York: OUP.

Black, R. E., Victora, C. G., Walker, S. P., Bhutta, Z. A., Christian, P., De Onis, M., Ezzati, M., Grantham-Macgregor, S., Katz, J., & Martorell, R. (2013). 'Maternal and child undernutrition and overweight in low-income and middle-income countries', *The Lancet*, 382/9890: 427–51.

Blanchard, O. (2012). 'Monetary policy in the wake of the crisis'. In O. Blanchard, D. Romer, M. Spence, & J. Stiglitz (eds), *In the Wake of the Crisis: Leading Economists Reassess Economic Policy*. Cambridge, MA: MIT Press.

Bloom, N., Fischer, G., Rasul, I., Rodriguez-Clare, A., Suri, T., Udry, C., Verhoogen, E., et al. (2014). *Firm Capabilities and Economic Growth* (International Growth Centre Evidence Paper). London: LSE.

Boardman, A. E., Siemiatycki, M., & Vining, A. (2016). 'The theory and evidence concerning public–private partnerships in Canada and elsewhere', *School of Public Policy*, 9/12, University of Calgary. Retrieved from: https://www.policyschool.ca/wp-content/uploads/2016/05/p3-boardman-siemiatycki-vining.pdf.

Bodenstein, F. (2018). 'Rawson and the Moor: the capture of Benin City (1897)'. *Translocations. Anthologie*. Retrieved from: https://translanth.hypotheses.org/ueber/rawson-moor.

Bogaisky, J. (2019). 'Boeing 737 MAX raises concerns over how FAA will ensure the safety of autonomous aircraft'. *Forbes*. 24 April.

Bompani, B., & Brown, S. T. (2015). 'A "religious revolution"? Print media, sexuality, and religious discourse in Uganda', *Journal of Eastern African Studies*, 9/1: 110–26.

Bongaarts, J. (2018). 'The evolution of family planning programs', *Studies in Family Planning*. May, 1–11.

Booth, L., & Starodubtseva, V. (2015). *PFI: Costs and Benefits* (Briefing Paper No. 6007). London: House of Commons Library.

Boudet, A. M. M., Buitrago, P., de la Briere, B. L., Newhouse, D., Matulevich, E. R., Scott, K., & Suarez-Becerra, P. (2018). *Gender Differences in Poverty and Household Composition through the Life-Cycle: A Global Perspective* (Policy Research Working Papers). Washington, DC: The World Bank.

Bourbonniere, M. (2013). 'Ripple effects: the groundnut scheme failure and railway planning for colonial development in Tanganyika, 1947–1952', *Canadian Journal of African Studies/Revue canadienne des études africaines*, 47/3: 365–83.

Bowser, W. H. (2015). 'The long and short of returns to public investments in fifteen Ethiopian villages', *3ie Replication Series Paper*, 4. https://www.3ieimpact.org/evidence-hub/publications/replication-papers/long-and-short-returns-public-investments-fifteen

Bradshaw, S., Chant, S., & Linneker, B. (2017). 'Gender and poverty: what we know, don't know, and need to know for Agenda 2030', *Gender, Place & Culture*, 24/12: 1667–88.

Bramall, C. (2004). 'Chinese land reform in long-run perspective and in the wider East Asian context', *Journal of Agrarian Change*, 4/1–2: 107–41.

Branson, N., & Byker, T. (2018). 'Causes and consequences of teen childbearing: evidence from a reproductive health intervention in South Africa', *Journal of Health Economics*, 57: 221–35.

Brautigam, D., & Hwang, J. (2016). *Eastern Promises: New Data on Chinese Loans in Africa, 2000 to 2014* (SAIS China Africa Research Initiative Working Paper No. 2016/4). Washington, DC: School of Advanced International Studies, Johns Hopkins University.

Breman, J. (2010). 'A poor deal', *Indian Journal of Human Development*, 4/1: 133–42.

Briggs, J. (1992). 'The Tanzania–Zambia railway: review and prospects', *Geography*, 77/3: 264–8.

Briggs, R. C. (2017). 'Does Foreign Aid Target the Poorest?', International Organization, 71/01: 187–206.

Broadberry, S. & Wallis, J. (2017). 'Growing, shrinking, and long run economic performance: historical perspectives on economic development.' Working paper 23343. NBER: Cambridge, MA.

Broich, T. (2017). *U.S. and Soviet Foreign Aid during the Cold War: A Case Study of Ethiopia* (Working Paper Series No. 2017-010). Maastricht: Maastricht Economic and social Research Institute on Innovation and Technology (UNU–MERIT).

Browne, M., Ortmann, G. F., & Hendriks, S. (2007). 'Expenditure elasticities for rural households in the Embo ward, Umbumbulu, KwaZulu-Natal', *Agrekon*, 46/4: 566–83.

Bruce, D. (2014). *Political Killings in South Africa* (Policy Brief No. 64). Pretoria: Institute for Security Studies (ISS).

Brunori, P., Ferreira, F. H., & Peragine, V. (2013). *Inequality of Opportunity, Income Inequality and Economic Mobility: Some International Comparisons* (Policy Research Working Paper No. 6304). Washington, DC: World Bank.

Bryceson, D. F. (2009). 'Sub-Saharan Africa's vanishing peasantries and the specter of a global food crisis', *Monthly Review*, 61/3: 48–62.

Burchell, B., Coutts, A., Hall, E., & Pye, N. (2015). *Self-Employment Programmes for Young People: A Review of the Context, Policies and Evidence* (Employment Working Paper No. 198). Geneva: International Labour Organization.

Burke, M., Heft-Neal, S., & Bendavid, E. (2016). 'Sources of variation in under-5 mortality across sub-Saharan Africa: a spatial analysis', *Lancet Global Health*, 4/12: e936–e945.

Burrell, J., & Oreglia, E. (2015). 'The myth of market price information: mobile phones and the application of economic knowledge in ICTD', *Economy and Society*, 44/2: 271–92.

Cali, M., Francois, J., Hollweg, C.H., Manchin, M., Oberdabernig, D.A., Rojas-Romagosa, H., Ruvinova, S., & Tomberger, P. (2016). *The labor content of exports database*. Policy Research Working Paper No. 7615, World Bank: Washington, DC.

Cameron, H. (2018). 'State-organized starvation: a weapon of extreme mass violence in Matabeleland South, 1984', *Genocide Studies International*, 12/1: 26–47.

Campbell, I. (2017). *The Addis Ababa Massacre: Italy's National Shame*. London: Hurst & Co.

Carletto, C., Jolliffe, D., & Banerjee, R. (2015). 'From tragedy to renaissance: improving agricultural data for better policies', *Journal of Development Studies*, 51/2: 133–48.

Carr-Hill, R. (2017). 'Improving population and poverty estimates with citizen surveys: evidence from East Africa', *World Development*, 93: 249–59.

Carrière-Swallow, Y., David, A., & Leigh, D. (2018). *The Macroeconomic Effects of Fiscal Consolidation in Emerging Economies: Evidence from Latin America* (IMF Working Paper). Washington, DC: IMF.

Cascão, A. E. (2008). 'Ethiopia: challenges to Egyptian hegemony in the Nile basin', *Water Policy*, 10/S2: 13–28.

Case, A., & Deaton, A. (2017). 'Mortality and morbidity in the 21st century'. Presented at the Brookings Panel on Economic Activity, 17 March (draft version).

Cashin, P., & Pattillo, C. (2006). 'African terms of trade and the commodity terms of trade: close cousins or distant relatives?', *Applied Economics*, 38/8: 845–59.

Castañeda, A., Doan, D., Newhouse, D., Nguyen, M. C., Uematsu, H., & Azevedo, J. P. (2018). 'A new profile of the global poor', *World Development*, 101: 250–67.

Cervigni, R., & Morris, M. (eds). (2016). *Confronting Drought in Africa's Drylands: Opportunities for Enhancing Resilience*. Africa Development Forum Series. Washington, DC: World Bank.

Chakraborty, S. (2012). 'Is export expansion of manufactured goods an escape route from terms of trade deterioration of developing countries?' *Journal of South Asian Development*, 7/2: 81–108.

Chan, J. (2019). 'State and labor in China, 1978–2018', *Journal of Labor and Society*, 22/2: 461–75.

Chan, J., Pun, N., & Selden, M. (2017). 'Apple, Foxconn, and China's new working class'. In H. F. Hung & M. Selden (eds), *The Cambridge History of Communism*, vol. 3: *Endgames? Late Communism in Global Perspective, 1968 to the Present*. Cambridge: Cambridge University Press.

Chandra, V., Lin, J. Y., & Wang, Y. (2013). 'Leading dragon phenomenon: new opportunities for catch-up in low-income countries', *Asian Development Review*, 30/1: 52–84.

Chandrasekhar, C. P., & Ghosh, J. (2015). *Growth, Employment Patterns and Inequality in Asia: A Case Study of India* (Working Paper). Geneva: International Labour Organization.

Chandy, L. (2017). *No Country Left Behind: The Case for Focusing Greater Attention on the World's Poorest Countries*. Washington, DC: Global Economy and Development at the Brookings Institution.

Chang, H.-J. (2006). *The East Asian Development Experience: The Miracle, the Crisis and the Future*. London: Zed.

Chang, H.-J. (2009). 'Rethinking public policy in agriculture: lessons from history, distant and recent', *Journal of Peasant Studies*, 36/3: 477–515.

Chauvin, N. D., Mulangu, F., & Porto, G. (2012). *Food Production and Consumption Trends in Sub-Saharan Africa: Prospects for the Transformation of the Agricultural Sector* (Working Paper No. WP 2012–011). New York: UNDP Regional Bureau for Africa.

Cheng, K. C., Hong, G. H., Seneviratne, D., & van Elkan, R. (2016). 'Rethinking the exchange rate impact on trade in a world with global value chains', *International Economic Journal*, 30/2: 204–16.

Cherif, R., & Hasanov, F. (2019). *The Return of the Policy that Shall Not Be Named: Principles of Industrial Policy*. Washington, DC: IMF. Retrieved from: https://www.imf.org/en/Publications/WP/Issues/2019/03/26/The-Return-of-the-Policy-That-Shall-Not-Be-Named-Principles-of-Industrial-Policy-46710.

Chesterman, N. S., Entwistle, J., Chambers, M. C., Liu, H.-C., Agrawal, A., & Brown, D. G. (2019). 'The effects of trainings in soil and water conservation on farming practices, livelihoods, and land-use intensity in the Ethiopian highlands', *Land Use Policy*, 87: https://www.sciencedirect.com/science/article/pii/S026483771831411X.

Chinsinga, B., & Poulton, C. (2014). 'Beyond technocratic debates: the significance and transience of political incentives in the Malawi farm input subsidy programme (FISP)', *Development Policy Review*, 32/s2: s123–s150.

Chinyoka, I. (2017). *Poverty, changing political regimes, and social cash transfers in Zimbabwe, 1980–2016* (WIDER Working Paper No. 2017/88). Helsinki: The United Nations University World Institute for Development Economics Research.

Chong, K., & Tuckett, D. (2015). 'Constructing conviction through action and narrative: how money managers manage uncertainty and the consequence for financial market functioning', *Socio-Economic Review*, 13/2: 309–30.

Choonara, J. (2018). 'An examination of employment precarity and insecurity in the UK'. PhD Thesis, Middlesex University.

Choudhury, S., & Headey, D. D. (2016). *What Drives Diversification of National Food Supplies? A Cross-Country Analysis*, vol. 1581. Washington, DC: International Food Policy Research Institute.

Christiaensen, L., & Lawin, G. (2017). 'Jobs within the structural transformation: insights for Côte d'Ivoire'. In L. Christiaensen & P. Premand (eds), *Côte d'Ivoire Jobs Diagnostic: Employment, Productivity, and Inclusion for Poverty Reduction*. Washington, DC: World Bank.

Christiansen, L. J., & Sarris, A. (eds) (2007). *Rural Household Vulnerability and Insurance against Commodity Risks: Evidence from the United Republic of Tanzania* (FAO Commodities and Trade Technical Paper). Rome: Food and Agriculture Organization of the United Nations, Trade and Markets Division.

Chuhan-Pole, P., Angwafo, M., Dennis, A., Korman, V., Sanoh, A., Buitano, M., Devaranjan, S., & Fengler, W. (2017a). 'An analysis of issues shaping Africa's economic future', *Africa's Pulse*, Office of the Chief Economist for the Africa Region, 9. Washington, DC: World Bank.

Chuhan-Pole, P., Dabalen, A., Land, B. C., Lewin, M., Sanoh, A., Smith, G., & Tolonen, A. (2017b). *Mining in Africa: Are Local Communities Better Off?* Africa Development Forum. Washington, DC: World Bank.

Cimoli, M., Dosi, G., & Stiglitz, J. E. (eds) (2009). *Industrial Policy and Development: The Political Economy of Capabilities Accumulation*. Initiative for Policy Dialogue Series. Oxford & Toronto: Oxford University Press.

Clapham, C. (1994). 'Review: the "longue durée" of the African state'. *African Affairs*, 93/372: 433–9.

Clapham, C. S. (2017). *The Horn of Africa: State Formation and Decay*. Oxford: Oxford University Press.

Clapham, C. S. (2018). 'The Ethiopian developmental state', *Third World Quarterly*, 39/6: 1151–65.

Clark, N. L. (1994). *Manufacturing Apartheid: State Corporations in South Africa*. New Haven, CT: Yale University Press.

Clementi, F., Fabiani, M., & Molini, V. (2019). 'The devil is in the detail: growth, inequality and poverty reduction in Africa in the last two decades', *Journal of African Economies*, 28/4: 408–34.

Co, C. Y. (2014). *Supply-Side Constraints, Capital Goods Imports, and the Quality of Sub-Saharan African Countries' Exports* (WIDER Working Paper). Helsinki: WIDER.

Cochrane, L., & Tamiru, Y. (2016). 'Ethiopia's productive safety net program: power, politics and practice', *Journal of International Development*, 28/5: 649–65.

Cohen, G. A. (2001). *Karl Marx's Theory of History: A Defence*, expanded edn. Princeton, NJ: Princeton University Press.

Cole, J., & Booth, S. S. (2007). *Dirty Work: Immigrants in Domestic Service, Agriculture, and Prostitution in Sicily*. Lanham, MD: Lexington Books.

Collier, P. (2008). *The Bottom Billion: Why the Poorest Countries are Failing and What Can Be Done about It*. New York: Oxford University Press.

Collier, P., & Gunning, J. W. (1999). 'Why has Africa grown slowly?', *Journal of Economic Perspectives*, 13/3: 3–22.

Collier, P., Kirchberger, M., & Söderbom, M. (2015). 'The cost of road infrastructure in low- and middle-income countries', *World Bank Economic Review*, 30/3: 522–48.

Collier, P., & O'Connell, S. (2008). 'Opportunities and choices'. In B. J. Ndulu, S. O'Connell, R. H. Bates, P. Collier, & C. Soludo (eds), *The Political Economy of Economic Growth in Africa, 1960–2000*. Cambridge: Cambridge University Press.

Commission on Growth and Development. (2008). *The Growth Report: Strategies for Sustained Growth and Inclusive Development*. Washington, DC: World Bank. Retrieved from: http://hdl.handle.net/10986/6507.

Conning, J., & Udry, C. (2007). 'Rural financial markets in developing countries'. In R. Evenson, P. Pingali, & T. Schultz (eds), *Handbook of Agricultural Economics*, vol. 3. Oxford & Amsterdam: North-Holland.

Cooper, D., Harries, J., Moodley, J., Constant, D., Hodes, R., Mathews, C., Morroni, C., & Hoffman, M. (2016). 'Coming of age? Women's sexual and reproductive health after twenty-one years of democracy in South Africa', *Reproductive Health Matters*, 24/48: 79–89.

Cooper, F. (1992). 'Colonizing time: work rhythms and labor conflict in colonial Mombasa'. In N. Dirks (ed.), *Colonialism and Culture*. Ann Arbor, MI: University of Michigan Press.

Cooper, F. (2004). 'Development, modernization, and the social sciences in the era of decolonization: the examples of British and French Africa', *Revue d'histoire des sciences humaines*, 1: 9–38.

Cooper, F. (2017). 'From enslavement to precarity? The labour question in African history'. In W. Adebanwi (ed.), *The Political Economy of Everyday Life in Africa: Beyond the Margins*. Woodbridge: James Currey.

Corcoran, J. (1998). 'Consequences of adolescent pregnancy/parenting: a review of the literature', *Social Work in Health Care*, 27/2: 49–67.

Cotterill, J. (2017). 'State loans at heart of Mozambican debt scandal', *Financial Times*, 25 June.

Cotterill, J. (2018). 'National airline tests Ramaphosa's ability to reform state companies', *Financial Times*, 27 November.

Cotula, L., Oya, C., Codjoe, E. A., Eid, A., Kakraba-Ampeh, M., Keeley, J., Kidewa, A. L., Makwarimba, M., Seide, W., & Nasha, W.O. (2014). 'Testing claims about large land deals in Africa: findings from a multi-country study', *Journal of Development Studies*, 50/7: 903–25.

Coutts, K., & Laskaridis, C. (2019). 'Financial balances and the development and the Ethiopian economy'. In F. Cheru, C. Cramer, & A. Oqubay (eds), *The Oxford Handbook of the Ethiopian Economy*. Oxford: Oxford University Press.

Coyle, D. (2015). *GDP: A Brief but Affectionate History*. Princeton, NJ: Princeton University Press.

Cramer, C. (2006). *Civil War Is Not a Stupid Thing: Accounting for Violence in Developing Countries*. London: Hurst & Co.

Cramer, C. (2010). 'Racionalidad económica y terrorismo: una fórmula explosiva', *Análisis Político*, 23/70: 3–24.

Cramer, C. (2020). 'War economies and war economics.' mimeo, Department of Development Studies, SOAS, University of London.

Cramer, C., Di John, J., & Sender, J. (2018). *Poinsettia Assembly and Selling Emotion: High Value Agricultural Exports in Ethiopia* (AFD Research Papers Series No. 2018-79, September). Paris: Agence Français de Développement.

Cramer, C., Johnston, D., Mueller, B., Oya, C., & Sender, J. (2014). 'How to do (and how not to do) fieldwork on Fair Trade and rural poverty', *Canadian Journal of Development Studies/Revue canadienne d'études du développement*, 35/1: 170–85.

Cramer, C., Johnston, D., Oya, C., & Sender, J. (2014a). 'Fairtrade cooperatives in Ethiopia and Uganda: uncensored', *Review of African Political Economy*, 41 (Supplement 1): S115–S127.

Cramer, C., Johnston, D., Oya, C., & Sender, J. (2014b). *Fairtrade, Employment and Poverty Reduction in Ethiopia and Uganda: Final Report to DFID*. London: SOAS, University of London.

Cramer, C., Johnston, D., Mueller, B., Oya, C., & Sender, J. (2017). 'Fairtrade and labour markets in Ethiopia and Uganda', *The Journal of Development Studies*, 53/6: 841–856'

Cramer, C., & Sender, J. (2015). *Agro-Processing, Wage Employment and Export Revenue: Opportunities for Strategic Intervention* (TIPS Working Paper for the Department of Trade and Industry). Pretoria: Trade and Industrial Policy Strategies.

Cramer, C., & Sender, J. (2017). *Putting Coffee at the Centre of Ethiopia's Structural Change* (Report for the Prime Minister's Office). Addis Ababa: Prime Minister's Office.

Cramer, C., & Sender, J. (2019a). 'Oranges are not only fruit: the industrialization of freshness and the quality of growth'. In S. M. R. Kanbur, A. Noman, & J. E. Stiglitz (eds), *The Quality of Growth in Africa*. Initiative for Policy Dialogue at Columbia: Challenges in Development and Globalization. New York: Columbia University Press.

Cramer, C., & Sender, J. (2019b). 'Policy, political economy, and performance in Ethiopia's coffee sector'. In F. Cheru, C. Cramer, & A. Oqubay (eds), *Oxford Handbook of the Ethiopian Economy*. Oxford: Oxford University Press.

Cramer, C., & Sender, J. (forthcoming). '"Only the desperate work": the economics of family, labour markets, and disappointment in rural Ethiopia and Uganda'.

Cramer, C., & Tregenna, F. (2020). 'Heterodox approaches to industrial policy, the shifting boundaries of the industrial, and the implications for industrial hubs'. In A. Oqubay & J. F. Lin (eds), *The Oxford Handbook of Industrial Hubs*. Oxford: Oxford University Press.

Crehan, K. (2011). 'Gramsci's concept of common sense: a useful concept for anthropologists?', *Journal of Modern Italian Studies*, 16/2: 273–87.

Croke, K. (2012). 'The political economy of child mortality decline in Tanzania and Uganda, 1995–2007', *Studies in Comparative International Development*, 47/4: 441–63.

Cuddington, J. T., & Urzúa, C. M. (1989). 'Trends and cycles in the net barter terms of trade: a new approach', *The Economic Journal*, 99/396: 426–42.

Cull, R., Demirgüç-Kunt, A., & Morduch, J. (2018). 'The microfinance business model: enduring subsidy and modest profit', *World Bank Economic Review*, 32/2: 221–44.

D'Alcantara, G., Dembinski, P. H., & Pilley, O. (2014). *Postal Financial Services, Development and Inclusion: Building on the Past and Looking to the Future*. Fribourg: Université de Fribourg.

D'Onofrio, F. (2016). *Observing Agriculture in Early Twentieth-Century Italy: Agricultural Economists and Statistics*. London & New York: Routledge.

Dafe, F. (2017). 'The politics of finance: how capital sways African central banks', *Journal of Development Studies*, 55/2: 1–17.

Daniels, L., & Minot, N. (2014). 'Is poverty reduction over-stated in Uganda? Evidence from alternative poverty measures', *Social Indicators Research*, 121/1: 1–19.

Dasgupta, P., Sen, A., & Marglin, S. (1972). *Guidelines for Project Evaluation*. New York: UNIDO.

Dashwood, H. S. (1996). 'The relevance of class to the evolution of Zimbabwe's development strategy, 1980–1991', *Journal of Southern African Studies*, 22/1: 27–48.

Davies, R. (2004). 'Memories of underdevelopment: a personal interpretation of Zimbabwe's economic decline'. In B. Raftopoulos & T. Savage (eds), *Zimbabwe: Injustice and Political Reconciliation*. Cape Town: Institute for Justice and Reconciliation.

Davis, B., Di Giuseppe, S., & Zezza, A. (2017). 'Are African households (not) leaving agriculture? Patterns of households' income sources in rural Sub-Saharan Africa', *Food Policy*, 67: 153–74.

Day, C., & Gray, A. (2017). 'Health and related indicators'. In A. Padarath & P. Barron (eds), *South African Health Review 2017*. Durban: Health Systems Trust.

De Aghion, B. A. (1999). 'Development banking', *Journal of Development Economics*, 58/1: 83–100.

De Bock, O., & Gelade, W. (2012). *The Demand for Microinsurance: A Literature Review* (ILO Microinsurance Innovation Facility Research Paper No. 26). ILO: Geneva.

De Brauw, A., Mueller, V., & Woldehanna, T. (2013). 'Motives to remit: evidence from tracked internal migrants in Ethiopia', *World Development*, 50: 13–23.

De La O Campos, A. P., Villani, C., Davis, B., & Takagi, M. (2018). *Ending Extreme Poverty in Rural Areas: Sustaining Livelihoods to Leave no one Behind*. Rome: FAO.

De Magalhães, L., & Santaeulàlia-Llopis, R. (2018). 'The consumption, income, and wealth of the poorest: an empirical analysis of economic inequality in rural and urban sub-Saharan Africa for macroeconomists', *Journal of Development Economics*, 134: 350–71.

De Waal, A. (2013). 'The theory and practice of Meles Zenawi', *African Affairs*, 112/446: 148–55.

De Waal, A. (2018). *The Future of Ethiopia: developmental state or political marketplace*. World Peace Foundation, Fletcher School, Tufts University: Somerville, MA.

De Weerdt, J., Beegle, K., Friedman, J., & Gibson, J. (2016). 'The challenge of measuring hunger through survey', *Economic Development and Cultural Change*, 64/4: 727–58.

Deane, P. (2011). *Colonial Social Accounting*, vol. 11. Cambridge: Cambridge University Press.

Deaton, A. (2009). *Instruments of Development: Randomization in the Tropics, and the Search for the Elusive Keys to Economic Development* (NBER Working Paper No. w14690). Cambridge, MA: National Bureau of Economic Research. Retrieved from: http://www.nber.org/papers/w14690.pdf.

Deaton, A. (2013). *The Great Escape: Health, Wealth, and the Origins of Inequality*. Princeton, NJ: Princeton University Press.

Deaton, A. (2015). 'Statistical objectivity is a cloak spun from political yarn'. *Financial Times*. November 2nd.

Deaton, A. (2016). 'Measuring and understanding behavior, welfare, and poverty', *American Economic Review*, 106/6: 1221–43.

Deaton, A., & Cartwright, N. (2018). 'Understanding and misunderstanding randomized controlled trials', *Social Science & Medicine*, 210: 2–21.

Del Gobbo, L. C., Khatibzadeh, S., Imamura, F., Micha, R., Shi, P., Smith, M., Myers, S. S., & Mozaffarian, D. (2015). 'Assessing global dietary habits: a comparison of national estimates from the FAO and the Global Dietary Database', *American Journal of Clinical Nutrition*, 101/5: 1038–46.

Desalegn, G., & Ali, S. N. (2018). *Review of the Impact of Productive Safety Net Program (PSNP) on Rural Welfare in Ethiopia* (ZEF Working Paper Series No. 173). Bonn: Center for Development Research, University of Bonn.

Desiere, S., & Jolliffe, D. (2018). 'Land productivity and plot size: is measurement error driving the inverse relationship?', *Journal of Development Economics*, 130: 84–98.

Desta, Z. F., Bitga, A., & Boyson, J. (2018). *USAID/Ethiopia Cross-Sectoral Youth Assessment Situational Analysis*. USAID and Youth Power. Retrieved from: https://www.youthpower.org/sites/default/files/YouthPower/resources/Ethiopia%20CSYA%20Situational%20Analysis_1.5.2018v2.pdf.

Devereux, S. (2019). 'Violations of farm workers' labour rights in post-apartheid South Africa', *Development Southern Africa*, 1–23.

Di John, J. (2009). *From Windfall to Curse? Oil and Industrialization in Venezuela, 1920 to the Present*. University Park, PA: Penn State University Press.

Di John, J. (2016). *What Is the Role of National Development Banks in Late Industrialisation?* (Issues Papers on Structural Transformation and Industrial Policy No. 010-2016). Addis Ababa: Ethiopian Development Research Institute (EDRI) and Agence Française de Développement.

Diagne, A., Kinkingninhoun-Medagbe, F. M., Amovin-Assagba, E., Nakelse, T., Sanni, K., & Toure, A. (2015). 'Evaluating the key aspects of the performance of genetic improvement in priority food crops and countries in sub-Saharan Africa: the case of rice'. In T. S. Walker & J. Alwang (eds), *Investments in and Impacts of Crop Improvement Research in Africa*. Boston, MA: CGIAR and CAB International.

Dickens, C. (2003). *A Tale of Two Cities*. Collectors Library. London: CRW.

Djurfeldt, A. A., Dzanku, F. M., & Isinika, A. C. (eds) (2018). *Agriculture, Diversification, and Gender in Rural Africa: Longitudinal Perspectives from Six Countries*. Oxford: Oxford University Press.

Doner, R. F., Ritchie, B. K., & Slater, D. (2005). 'Systemic vulnerability and the origins of developmental states: Northeast and Southeast Asia in comparative perspective', *International Organization*, 59/2: 327–61.

Donham, D. L., & Mofokeng, S. (2011). *Violence in a Time of Liberation: Murder and Ethnicity at a South African Gold Mine, 1994*. Durham, NC: Duke University Press.

Doogan, K. (2015.) 'Precarity: minority condition or majority experience?' In D. Della Porta, T. Silvasti, S. Hänninen, & M. Siisiäinen (eds), *The New Social Division: Making and Unmaking Precariousness*. New York: Springer.

Doro, E., & Kufakurinani, U. (2018). 'Resource curse or governance deficit? The role of parliament in Uganda's oil and Zimbabwe's diamonds', *Journal of Southern African Studies*, 44/1: 43–57.

Dorosh, P. A., & Mellor, J. W. (2013). 'Why Agriculture Remains a Viable Means of Poverty Reduction in Sub-Saharan Africa: The Case of Ethiopia', *Development Policy Review*, 31/4: 419–441.

Dorrington, R., & Bourne, D. (2008). 'Has HIV prevalence peaked in South Africa? Can the report on the latest antenatal survey be trusted to answer this question?', *SAMJ: South African Medical Journal*, 98/10: 754–5.

Dow, S. C. (2012). 'Uncertainty about uncertainty'. In S. C. Dow (ed.), *Foundations for New Economic Thinking*. London: Palgrave Macmillan.

Drèze, J. (2019). *Sense and Solidarity: Jholawala Economics for Everyone*. Oxford: Oxford University Press.

Drèze, J., & Deaton, A. (2017). 'Squaring the poverty circle'. In J. Drèze (ed.), *Sense and Solidarity: Jholawala Economics for Everyone*. Oxford: Oxford University Press.

Du Toit, A., & Neves, D. (2007). 'In search of South Africa's second economy: chronic poverty, economic marginalisation and adverse incorporation in Mt. Frere and Khayelitsha', Chronic Poverty Research Centre Working Paper no. 102. University of Manchester: Manchester.

Easterly, W. (2009). 'The ideology of development', Foreign Policy, 13 October. Retrieved from: https://foreignpolicy.com/2009/10/13/the-ideology-of-development/.

Easterly, W., & Levine, R. (1997). 'Africa's growth tragedy: policies and ethnic divisions', Quarterly Journal of Economics, 112/4: 1203–50.

Economist. (2012). 'Exit Albert Hirschman', The Economist, 22nd December. https://www.economist.com/business/2012/12/22/exit-albert-hirschman

Edmonds, E. V., & Shrestha, M. (2012). 'Independent child labor migrants'. In A. F. Constant & K. F. Zimmerman (eds), International Handbook of the Economics of Migration. London: Edward Elgar.

Edward, P., & Sumner, A. (2016). Global Inequality and Global Poverty since the Cold War: How Robust is the Optimistic Narrative? (Global Challenges Working Paper Series No. 1). Bergen: University of Bergen. Retrieved from: http://bora.uib.no/handle/1956/13048.

Egne, R. M. (2014). 'Gender equality in public higher education institutions of Ethiopia: the case of science, technology, engineering, and mathematics', Discourse and Communication for Sustainable Education, 5/1: 3–21.

El-Gizouli, M. (2019). 'The fall of al-Bashir: mapping contestation forces in Sudan', Arab Reform Initiative, 12 April.

Elias, A., Nohmi, M., Yasunobu, K., & Ishida, A. (2013). 'Effect of agricultural extension program on smallholders' farm productivity: evidence from three peasant associations in the highlands of Ethiopia', Journal of Agricultural Science, 5/8: 163–81.

Ellison, R. (2001). Invisible Man. Penguin Classics. London: Penguin Books.

Elmquist, D. (2005). 'A bird cloaked in guns: post conflict sculpture from Maputo', Politique Africaine, 100: 198–213.

Enzensberger, H. M. (1974). 'A critique of political ecology', New Left Review, 1/84. https://newleftreview-org.ezproxy.soas.ac.uk/issues/I84/articles/hans-magnus-enzensberger-a-critique-of-political-ecology

Epstein, G. (2013). 'Developmental central banking: winning the future by updating a page from the past', Review of Keynesian Economics, 1/3: 273–87.

Eriksson, Å. (2017). 'Farm worker identities contested and reimagined: gender, race/ethnicity and nationality in the post-strike moment', Anthropology Southern Africa, 40/4: 248–60.

Erk, J. (2015). 'Iron houses in the tropical heat: decentralization reforms in Africa and their consequences', Regional & Federal Studies, 25/5: 409–20.

Esping-Andersen, G., & Przeworski, A. (2001). 'Quantitative cross-national research methods'. In N. Smelser & P. Baltes (eds), International Encyclopedia of the Social and Behavioral Sciences, vol. 18. Amsterdam: Elsevier.

Ezra, K. (1992). Royal Art of Benin: The Perls Collection in the Metropolitan Museum of Art. New York: Metropolitan Museum of Art.

Fabregas, R., Kremer, M., Robinson, J., & Schilbach, F. (2017). Evaluating Agricultural Information Dissemination in Western Kenya (3iE Impact Evaluation Report No. 67). New Delhi: International Initiative for Impact Evaluation.

Fahnbulleh, M. N. (2006). 'The elusive quest for industrialisation in Africa: a comparative study of Ghana and Kenya, c1950–2000'. PhD Thesis, London School of Economics and Political Science (University of London).

FAO, IFAD, UNICEF, WFP, & WHO (Food and Agriculture Organization, International Fund for Agricultural Development, United Nations Children's, World Food Programme, & Fund World Health Organization). (2018). *The state of food security and nutrition in the world: Building Climate Resilience for Food Security and Nutrition.* Rome: FAO.

FAOSTAT. (2019). Food and Agriculture Organization (FAO); International Labour Organization (ILO); International Union of Food, Agricultural, Hotel, Restaurant, Catering, Tobacco and Allied Workers' Associations (IUF).

Fauvelle-Aymar, C., & Segatti, A. (2012). 'People, space and politics: an exploration of factors explaining the 2008 anti-foreigner violence in South Africa'. In L. B. Landau (ed.), *Exorcising the Demons Within: Xenophobia, Violence and Statecraft in Contemporary South Africa.* Tokyo, Paris, & New York: United Nations University Press.

Fauvet, P., & Mosse, M. (2003). *Carlos Cardoso: Telling the Truth in Mozambique.* Cape Town: Juta & Co. Ltd.

Favara, M., Porter, C., & Woldehanna, T. (2019). 'Smarter through social protection? Evaluating the impact of Ethiopia's safety-net on child cognitive abilities', *Oxford Development Studies,* 47/1: 79–96.

Felipe, J., & McCombie, J. (2017). *The Debate about the Sources of Growth in East Asia after a Quarter of a Century: Much Ado about Nothing* (Asian Development Bank Economics Working Paper Series No. 512). SSRN. Retrieved from: https://papers.ssrn.com/sol3/papers.cfm?abstract_id=2982882.

Ferguson, J. (2019). 'Proletarian politics today: on the perils and possibilities of historical analogy', *Comparative Studies in Society and History,* 61/1: 4–22.

Ferguson, J., & Li, T. M. (2018). *Beyond the 'Proper Job': Political-Economic Analysis after the Century of Labouring Man* (Working Paper No. 51). Cape Town: PLAAS, University of the Western Cape.

Ferreira, F. H. G., Chen, S., Dabalen, A., Dikhanov, Y., Hamadeh, N., Jolliffe, D., Narayan, A., Prydz, E.B, Revenga, A., Sangraula, P., Serajuddin, U., & Yoshida, N. (2016). 'A global count of the extreme poor in 2012: data issues, methodology and initial results', *Journal of Economic Inequality,* 14/2: 141–72.

Ferreira, M. E., & Soares de Oliveira, R. (2018). 'The political economy of banking in Angola', *African Affairs,* 118/470: 49–74.

Filmer, D., & Fox, L. (2014). *Youth Employment in Sub-Saharan Africa.* Washington, DC: World Bank.

Findlay, R. (1987). 'Comparative advantage'. In J. Eatwell, M. Milgate, & P. Newman (eds), *New Palgrave Dictionary of Economics.* London: Macmillan.

Fine, B. (1992). 'Total factor productivity vs. realism: the South African coal mining industry', *South African Journal of Economics,* 60/3: 277–92.

Fine, B. (2002). 'Economics imperialism and the new development economics as Kuhnian paradigm shift?', *World Development,* 30/12: 2057–70.

Fine, B. (2006). 'Financial programming and the IMF: the developmental state and the political economy of development'. In B. Fine & K. S. Jomo (eds), *The New Development Economics: After the Washington Consensus.* New Delhi: Tulika.

Fine, B., & Milonakis, D. (2009). *From Economics Imperialism to Freakonomics: The Shifting Boundaries between Economics and other Social Sciences.* London: Routledge.

Fine, B., & Rustomjee, Z. (1996). *The Political Economy of South Africa: From Minerals Energy Complex to Industrialisation.* Boulder, CO: Westview Press.

Fine, B., & Van Waeyenberge, E. (2013). *A Paradigm Shift that Will Never Be? Justin Lin's New Structural Economics* (Department of Economics Working Paper No. 179). London: SOAS, University of London.

Finn, A., & Leibbrandt, M. (2018). *The Evolution and Determination of Earnings Inequality in Post-Apartheid South Africa* (WIDER Working Paper No. 2018/83). Helsinki: United Nations University World Institute for Development Economics Research.

Finn, A., & Ranchhod, V. (2017). 'Genuine fakes: the prevalence and implications of data fabrication in a large South African survey', *World Bank Economic Review*, 31/1: 129–57.

Fitzgerald, E. V. (1980). 'A note on capital accumulation in Mexico: the budget deficit and investment finance', *Development and Change*, 11/3: 391–417.

Flyvbjerg, B. (2011). 'Over budget, over time, over and over again: managing major projects'. In Morris, P.W.G., Pinto, J., and Söderlund, J. (eds). *The Oxford Handbook of Project Management*. Oxford: OUP.

Flyvbjerg, B. (2014). 'What you should know about megaprojects and why: an overview', *Project Management Journal*, 45/2: 6–19.

Flyvbjerg, B. (2016). 'The fallacy of beneficial ignorance: a test of Hirschman's hiding hand', *World Development*, 84: 176–89.

Fosu, A. K. (2012). 'The African economic growth record, and the roles of policy syndromes and governance'. In A. Noman, K. Botchwey, H. Stein, & J. E. Stiglitz (eds), *Good Growth and Governance in Africa: Rethinking Development Strategies*. Oxford: Oxford University Press.

Fox, L., & Pimhidzai, O. (2011). *Is Informality Welfare-Enhancing Structural Transformation? Evidence from Uganda* (Policy Research Working Papers). Washington, DC: World Bank.

Fox, L., & Sohnesen, T. P. (2012). *Household Enterprises in Sub-Saharan Africa: Why They Matter for Growth, Jobs, and Livelihoods*. Washington, DC: World Bank.

Fox, L., Thomas, A. H., & Haines, C. (2017). *Structural Transformation in Employment and Productivity: What Can Africa Hope For?* Washington, DC: International Monetary Fund.

Frankema, E., & van Waijenburg, M. (2018). 'Africa rising? A historical perspective', *African Affairs*, 117/469: 543–68.

Frankema, E., Woltjer, P., Dalrymple-Smith, A., & Bulambo, L. (2018). 'An introduction to the African commodity trade database, 1730–2010', *Research Data Journal*, 3: 1–14.

Fransman, T., & Yu, D. (2019). 'Multidimensional poverty in South Africa in 2001–16', *Development Southern Africa*, 36/1: 50–79.

Freeman, J. B. (2018). *Behemoth: A History of the Factory and the Making of the Modern World*. New York: W. W. Norton & Co.

Frenkel, R., & Rapetti, M. (2014). *The Real Exchange Rate as a Target of Macroeconomic Policy* (MPRA Paper). Retrieved from: https://mpra.ub.uni-muenchen.de/59335/.

Freund, B. (2018). 'Sub-Saharan Africa'. In M. van der Linden & K. Hofmeester (eds), *Handbook Global History of Work*. Berlin & Boston, MA: De Gruyter Oldenberg.

Freund, B. (2019). *Twentieth-Century South Africa: A Developmental History*. Cambridge & New York: Cambridge University Press.

Freund, C., & Pierola, M. D. (2012). 'Export surges', *Journal of Development Economics*, 97/2: 387–95.

Fuglie, K., & Marder, J. (2015). 'The diffusion and impact of improved food crop varieties in sub-Saharan Africa'. In T. S. Walker & J. R. Alwang (eds), *Crop Improvement, Adoption and Impact of Improved Varieties in Food Crops in Sub-Saharan Africa*. Boston, MA: CGIAR and CAB International.

Fujii, E. (2017). *What Does Trade Openness Measure?* (CESifo Working Paper No. 6656). Munich: Munich Society for the Promotion of Economic Research—CESifo GmbH.

Furceri, D., & Li, B. G. (2017). *The Macroeconomic (and Distributional) Effects of Public Investment in Developing Economies* (IMF Working Paper No. WP/17/217). Washington, DC: IMF Research Department.

Gallagher, K. P. (2007). 'Understanding developing country resistance to the Doha Round', *Review of International Political Economy*, 15/1: 62–85.

García-Cardona, J. (2016). *Value-added initiatives: distributional impacts on the global value chain for Colombia's coffee*. PhD thesis. University of Sussex: Brighton.

Garenne, M. (2018). 'Family planning and fertility decline in Africa: from 1950 to 2010'. In Z. Amarin (ed.), *Family Planning*. InTech. Retrieved from: https://www.intechopen.com/books/family-planning/family-planning-and-fertility-decline-in-africa-from-1950-to-2010.

Gebreeyesus, M. (2014). *A Natural Experiment of Industrial Policy: Floriculture and the Metal and Engineering Industries in Ethiopia* (WIDER Working Paper No. 2014/163). World Institute for Development Economics Research.

Gebrehiwot, T., & Castilla, C. (2018). 'Do safety net transfers improve diets and reduce undernutrition? Evidence from rural Ethiopia', *Journal of Development Studies*, 55/9: 1947–66.

Gerschenkron, A. (1962). *Economic Backwardness in Historical Perspective: A Book of Essays*. Cambridge, MA: Belknap Press.

Ggombe, K. M., & Newfarmer, R. S. (2018). 'From devastation to services: first transformation'. In R. S. Newfarmer, J. Page, & F. Tarp (eds), *Industries without Smokestacks*. UNU-WIDER Studies in Development Economics. Oxford: Oxford University Press.

Ghazanchyan, M., & Stotsky, J. G. (2013). *Drivers of Growth: Evidence from Sub-Saharan African Countries*. Washington, DC: International Monetary Fund.

Ghose, A. K. (2015). *India Needs Rapid Manufacturing-LED Growth* (IHD Working Paper WP 01/2015). New Delhi: Institute for Human Development.

Ghosh, J. (2018). 'Global instability and the development project: is the twenty-first century different?', *European Journal of Economics and Economic Policies: Intervention*, 15/2: 193–207.

Ghosh, J. (2019). 'A brave new world, or the same old story with new characters?', *Development and Change*, 50/2: 379–93.

Gibbon, P. (2011). *Experiences of Plantation and Large-Scale Farming in 20th-Century Africa* (DIIS Working Paper No. 2011:20). Copenhagen: Danish Institute for International Studies.

Giezen, M., Bertolini, L., & Salet, W. (2015). 'Adaptive capacity within a mega project: a case study on planning and decision-making in the face of complexity', *European Planning Studies*, 23/5: 999–1018.

Glassman, A., & Ezeh, A. (2014). *Delivering on the Data Revolution in Sub-Saharan Africa*. Washington, DC: Center for Global Development.

Glyn, A. (2007). *Capitalism Unleashed: Finance, Globalization, and Welfare*. Oxford: Oxford University Press.

Gödecke, T., Stein, A. J., & Qaim, M. (2018). 'The global burden of chronic and hidden hunger: trends and determinants', *Global Food Security*, 17: 21–9.

Godley, W. (1999). *Seven Unsustainable Processes* (Special Report). Annandale-on-Hudson, NY: Levy Institute. Retrieved from: http://www.levyinstitute.org/pubs/sr/sevenproc.pdf.

Gollin, D., Hansen, C. W., & Wingender, A. (2018). *Two Blades of Grass: The Impact of the Green Revolution* (Working Paper No. 24744). National Bureau of Economic Research. Retrieved from: http://www.nber.org/papers/w24744.

Gourlay, S., Kilic, T., & Lobell, D. (2017). *Could the Debate Be Over?* (Policy Research Working Paper No. 8192). Washington, DC: World Bank.

Grabel, I. (2011). 'Not your grandfather's IMF: global crisis, "productive incoherence" and developmental policy space', *Cambridge Journal of Economics*, 35/5: 805–30.

Grabel, I. (2017). *When Things Don't Fall Apart: Global Financial Governance and Developmental Finance in an Age of Productive Incoherence*. Cambridge, MA: MIT Press.

Graetz, N., Friedman, J., Osgood-Zimmerman, A., Burstein, R., Biehl, M. H., Shields, C., Mosser, J. F., Casey, D., Deshpande, A., Earl, L, Reiner, R., Ray, S., Fullman, N., Levine, A., Stubbs, R., Mayala, B., Longbottom, J., Browne, A., Bhatt, S., Weiss, D., Gething, P., Mokdad, A., Lim, S., Murray, C., Gakidou, E., & Hay, S. (2018). 'Mapping local variation in educational attainment across Africa', *Nature*, 555/7694: 48–53.

Gramsci, A. (1971). *Selections from the Prison Notebooks*, ed. and tr. Q. Hoare & G. Nowell Smith. New York: International Publishers.

Gray, L. C., Dowd-Uribe, B., & Kaminski, J. (2018). 'Weaving cotton-led development? Liberalization, cotton producer organizations, and uneven development in Burkina Faso', *Journal of Agrarian Change*, 18/4: 831–47.

Greco, E. (2015). 'Landlords in the making: class dynamics of the land grab in Mbarali, Tanzania', *Review of African Political Economy*, 42/144: 225–44.

Green, E. (2008). *District Creation and Decentralisation in Uganda*. London: Crisis States Research Centre.

Green, F. (2013). 'Youth entrepreneurship.' Background paper for OECD Centre for Entrepreneurship, SMEs, and Local Development. OECD: Paris.

Greyling, T., & Rossouw, S. (2019). 'Access to micro-and informal loans: evaluating the impact on the quality of life of poor females in South Africa', *South African Journal of Economic and Management Sciences*, 22/1: 14.

Grimm, M., & Paffhausen, A. L. (2015). 'Do interventions targeted at micro-entrepreneurs and small and medium-sized firms create jobs? A systematic review of the evidence for low- and middle-income countries', *Labour Economics*, 32: 67–85.

Grove, R. (1989). 'Scottish missionaries, evangelical discourses and the origins of conservation thinking in Southern Africa 1820–1900', *Journal of Southern African Studies*, 15/2: 163–87.

Grünberger, K. (2014). *Estimating Food Consumption Patterns by Reconciling Food Balance Sheets and Household Budget Surveys* (Statistics Division Working Paper No. ESS/14-08). Rome: FAO.

Gulyani, S., Rizvi, A., & Talukdar, D. (2019). *Are They Really Being Served?* (Policy Research Working Paper No. 8750). Washington, DC: World Bank.

Gurara, D., Klyuev, M. V., Mwase, M., Presbitero, A., Xu, X. C., & Bannister, M. G. J. (2017). *Trends and Challenges in Infrastructure Investment in Low-Income Developing Countries*. Washington, DC: International Monetary Fund.

Guyer, J. I., & Peters, P. E. (1987). 'Introduction', *Development and Change*, 18/2: 197–214.

Guzman, M., Ocampo, J. A., & Stiglitz, J. E. (2017). *Real Exchange Rate Policies for Economic Development* (Working Paper No. 23868). National Bureau of Economic Research. Retrieved from: http://www.nber.org/papers/w23868.

Haddad, M., & Pancaro, C. (2010). *Can Real Exchange Rate Undervaluation Boost Exports and Growth in Developing Countries? Yes, But Not for Long* (Economic Premise No. 20). Washington, DC: World Bank. Retrieved from: https://openknowledge.worldbank.org/handle/10986/10178.

Hahn, F. (1984). *Money and Inflation*. Mitsui Lectures in Economics. Oxford: Blackwell.

Hallward-Driemeier, M., & Nayyar, G. (2017). *Trouble in the Making? The Future of Manufacturing-Led Development*. Washington, DC: World Bank Publications.

Handal, A. J., & Harlow, S. D. (2009). 'Employment in the Ecuadorian cut-flower industry and the risk of spontaneous abortion', *BMC International Health and Human Rights*, 9/25.

Hanlon, J. (2019). 'Respected statistics head forced out over Gaza by vitriolic Nyusi', *Club of Mozambique*, 30 August. Retrieved from: https://clubofmozambique.com/news/mozambique-respected-statistics-head-forced-out-over-gaza-by-vitriolic-nyusi-by-joseph-hanlon-140628/.

Hanlon, J., & Mosse, M. (2010). *Mozambique's Elite: Finding Its Way in a Globalized World and Returning to Old Development Models*. Helsinki: WIDER.

Hanushek, E. A., & Woessmann, L. (2016). 'Knowledge capital, growth, and the East Asian miracle', *Science*, 351/6271: 344–5.

Haraguchi, N., Cheng, C. F. C., & Smeets, E. (2017). 'The importance of manufacturing in economic development: has this changed?', *World Development*, 93: 293–315.

Harasty, C., Kwong, M., & Ronnås, P. (2015). *Inclusive Growth and Productive Employment in Zambia* (Employment Working Paper No. 179). Geneva: International Labour Organization.

Hardy, V., & Hauge, J. (2019). 'Labour challenges in Ethiopia's textile and leather industries: no voice, no loyalty, no exit?', *African Affairs*, 118/473: 712–36.

Harris, T., Collinson, M., & Wittenberg, M. (2016). *Aiming for a Moving Target: The Dynamics of Household Electricity Access in a Developing Context* (Working Paper No. 195). Cape Town: South Africa Labour and Development Research Unit.

Harrison, A. E., Lin, J. Y., & Xu, L. C. (2014). 'Explaining Africa's (dis) advantage', *World Development*, 63: 59–77.

Hartzenburg, T. (2011). *Regional Integration in Africa* (Staff Working Paper No. ERSD-2011-14). Geneva: WTO.

Haushofer, J., & Shapiro, J. (2013). *Household Response to Income Changes: Evidence from an Unconditional Cash Transfer Program in Kenya* (Poverty Action Lab Working Paper). Abdul Latif Jameel Poverty Action Lab. Cambridge, MA: MIT.

Hazell, P. (2019). Urbanization, agriculture, and smallholder farming'. In R. Serraj & P. L. Pingali (eds), *Agriculture and Food Systems to 2050: Global Trends, Challenges and Opportunities*. Hackensack, NJ: World Scientific.

Hazell, P. B. R. (2013). 'Options for African agriculture in an era of high food and energy prices', *Agricultural Economics*, 44/s1: 19–27.

Headey, D. D., & Martin, W. J. (2016). 'The impact of food prices on poverty and food security', *Annual Review of Resource Economics*, 8/1: 329–51.

Heilbroner, R. L. (1987). *The Worldly Philosophers: The Lives, Times, and Ideas of the Great Economic Thinkers*. Harmondsworth: Penguin.

Hein, E., & Vogel, L. (2007). 'Distribution and growth reconsidered: empirical results for six OECD countries', *Cambridge Journal of Economics*, 32/3: 479–511.

Hepburn, S. (2016). 'A social history of domestic service in post-colonial Zambia, c. 1964–2014'. PhD Thesis, University of Oxford.

Hermes, C. L. M., & Lensink, B. W. (2014). *Financial Liberalization and Capital Flight: Evidence from the African Continent*. In Ajayi, S.I. & Ndikumana, L. (eds). Capital Flight from Africa: causes, effects, and policy issues. OUP: Oxford.

Hernández, V. M. (2012). 'Are wealth indices good predictors of diet quality? Using alternative socio-economic measures to determine welfare in Ethiopia'. MSc Development Economics Dissertation, SOAS, University of London.

Herrador, Z., Perez-Formigo, J., Sordo, L., Gadisa, E., Moreno, J., Benito, A., Aseffa, A., Custodio, E., & van Wouwe, J. (2015). 'Low dietary diversity and intake of animal source foods among school aged children in Libo Kemkem and Fogera districts, Ethiopia', *PLOS ONE*, 10/7: e0133435.

Herrerias, M. J., & Orts, V. (2013). 'Capital goods imports and long-run growth: is the Chinese experience relevant to developing countries?', *Journal of Policy Modeling*, 35/5: 781–97.

Hickey, S., & Bukenya, B. (2016). *The Politics of Promoting Social Cash Transfers in Uganda* (ESID Working Paper No. 69). Manchester: Effective States and Inclusive Development Research Centre, University of Manchester. Retrieved from: https://papers.ssrn.com/sol3/papers.cfm?abstract_id=2893028.

Hilmarsson, H. T. (1995). *Cashew Pricing and Marketing in Mozambique* (World Bank Working Paper) prepared for a seminar in June.

Hilton, B. (2006). *A Mad, Bad, and Dangerous People? England, 1783–1846*. Oxford & New York: Oxford University Press.

Himanshu, & Kundu, S. (2016). 'Rural wages in India: recent trends and determinants', *Indian Journal of Labour Economics*, 59/2: 217–44.

Himelein, K., Eckman, S., & Murray, S. (2014). 'Sampling nomads: a new technique for remote, hard-to-reach, and mobile populations', *Journal of Official Statistics*, 30/2: 191–213.

Hirschman, A. O. (1958). *The Strategy of Economic Development*. New Haven, CT: Yale University Press.

Hirschman, A. O. (1967). *Development Projects Observed*. Washington, DC: Brookings Institution Press.

Hirschman, A. O. (1971). *A Bias for Hope: Essays on Development and Latin America*. New Haven, CT: Yale University Press.

Hirschman, A. O. (1981a). *Essays in Trespassing: Economics to Politics and Beyond*. Cambridge & New York: Cambridge University Press.

Hirschman, A. O. (1981b). 'The rise and decline of development economics'. *Annales. Economies, Sociétés, Civilisations*, 36: 725–44.

Hirschman, A. O. (1991). *The Rhetoric of Reaction*. Cambridge, MA: Harvard University Press.

Hirschman, A. O. (1994). 'The on-and-off connection between political and economic progress', *American Economic Review*, 84/2: 343–8.

Hirschman, A. O. (2013). *The Passions and the Interests: Political Arguments for Capitalism before Its Triumph*. Princeton, NJ: Princeton University Press.

Hirvonen, K., Hoddinott, J., Minten, B., & Stifel, D. (2017). 'Children's diets, nutrition knowledge, and access to markets', *World Development*, 95: 303–15.

Hirvonen, K., Taffesse, A. S., & Worku Hassen, I. (2016). 'Seasonality and household diets in Ethiopia', *Public Health Nutrition*, 19/10: 1723–30.

Hochschild, A. (1999). *King Leopold's Ghost: A Story of Greed, Terror and Heroism in Colonial Africa*. London: Macmillan.

Hoff, K., & Stiglitz, J. E. (1993). 'Imperfect information and rural credit markets: puzzles and policy perspectives'. In K. Hoff, A. Braverman, & J. E. Stiglitz (eds), *The Economics of Rural Organization: Theory, Practice and Policy*. Washington, DC: World Bank.

Holmes, S. M. (2013). *Fresh Fruit, Broken Bodies: Migrant Farmworkers in the United States*. Berkeley, CA: University of California Press.

Honeyman, K. (2016). *Child Workers in England, 1780–1820: Parish Apprentices and the Making of the Early Industrial Labour Force*. London: Routledge.

Hoogeveen, J., & Nguyen, N. T. V. (2017). 'Statistics reform in Africa: aligning incentives with results', *Journal of Development Studies*, 55/4: 1–18.

Hoogeveen, J. G., & Schipper, Y. (2006). 'Correcting survey non-response with census data', *Journal of African Statistics*, 3 (November): 77–88.

Horrell, S., & Humphries, J. (2018). *Children's Work and Wages, 1270–1860* (Oxford Economic and Social History Working Paper No. 163). University of Oxford, Department of Economics. Retrieved from: https://econpapers.repec.org/paper/oxfesohwp/_5f163.htm.

Hossain, N., Brito, L., Jahan, F., Joshi, A., Nyamu-Musembi, C., Patnaik, B., Sambo, M., Shankland, A., Scott-Villiers, A., Sinha, D., Kalita, D., & Benequista, N. (2014). *Them Belly Full (But We Hungry): Food Rights Struggles in Bangladesh, India, Kenya, and Mozambique*. Brighton: Institute of Development Studies, University of Sussex.

Howard, M. C., & King, J. E. (1992). *A History of Marxian Economics*, vol. 2: *1929–1990: Radical Economics*. Basingstoke: Macmillan.

Hudon, M., & Traca, D. (2011). 'On the efficiency effects of subsidies in microfinance: an empirical inquiry', *World Development*, 39/6: 966–73.

Hudson, J., & Mosley, P. (2008). 'The macroeconomic impact of aid volatility', *Economics Letters*, 99/3: 486–9.

Huggins, C. (2017). 'Discipline, governmentality and "developmental patrimonialism": insights from Rwanda's pyrethrum sector', *Journal of Agrarian Change*, 17/4: 715–32.

Human Security Report. (2013). *Human Security Report 2013: The Decline in Global Violence: Evidence, Explanation and Contestation—World*, 13 March. Retrieved from: https://reliefweb.int/report/world/human-security-report-2013-decline-global-violence-evidence-explanation-and.

Hundsbæk Pedersen, R., & Bofin, P. (2019). 'Muted market signals: politics, petroleum investments and regulatory developments in Tanzania', *Journal of Eastern African Studies*, 13/3: 1–19.

Ifeanyi, D. (2016). 'The rise and demise of Nigeria Airways', *AviationTribune*, 25 October.

Igwe, E. (2018). 'Formalizing Nollywood: gentrification in the contemporary Nigerian film industry'. PhD Thesis, Birmingham City University.

Ika, L. A. (2018). 'Beneficial or detrimental ignorance: the straw man fallacy of Flyvbjerg's test of Hirschman's hiding hand', *World Development*, 103: 369–82.

Ilie, S., & Rose, P. (2018). 'Who benefits from public spending on higher education in South Asia and sub-Saharan Africa?', *Compare: A Journal of Comparative and International Education*, 48/4: 630–47.

Iliffe, J. (1987). *The African Poor: A History*. Cambridge: Cambridge University Press.

ILO (International Labour Organization). (2013). *Domestic Workers across the World: Global and Regional Statistics and the Extent of Legal Protection*. Geneva: ILO.

ILO (International Labour Organization). (2018a). *Care Work and Care Jobs for the Future of Decent Work*. Geneva: ILO.

ILO (International Labour Organization). (2018b). *Ethiopia National Child Labour Survey 2015*. Addis Ababa: International Labour Office, Fundamental Principles and Rights at Work Branch; Central Statistical Agency (CSA).

ILO (International Labour Organization). (2018c). *Women and Men in the Informal Economy: A Statistical Picture*. Geneva: ILO.

ILOSTAT. (2018). *Paid Employment vs Vulnerable Employment: A Brief Study of Employment Patterns by Status in Employment* (Spotlight on Work Statistics No. 3). Geneva: ILO.

Imam, P., & Salinas, G. (2008). *Explaining Episodes of Growth Accelerations, Decelerations, and Collapses in Western Africa* (Working Paper No. 08/287). Washington, DC: IMF.

IMF (International Monetary Fund). (2014a). *Fiscal Monitor—Back to Work: How Fiscal Policy Can Help*. Washington, DC: IMF.

IMF (International Monetary Fund). (2014b). *Long-Run Growth and Macroeconomic Stability in Low-Income Countries: The Role of Structural Transformation and Diversification* (IMF Policy Paper). Washington, DC: IMF.

IMF (International Monetary Fund). (2016). *The Federal Democratic Republic of Ethiopia: 2016 Article IV Consultation; Press Release; Staff Report; and Statement by the Executive Director for the Federal Democratic Republic of Ethiopia*. Washington, DC: IMF.

IMF (International Monetary Fund). (2018). 'Commodity prices'. Retrieved from: https://www.imf.org/en/Research/commodity-prices.

Inocencio, A., Kikuchi, M., Tonosaki, M., Maruyama, A., Merrey, D. J., Sally, H., & de Jong, I. (2007). *Costs and Performance of Irrigation Projects: A Comparison of Sub-Saharan Africa and other Developing Regions* (IWMI Research Report No. 109). Colombo: International Water Management Institute.

International Labour Organization, Organisation for Economic Co-operation and Development, & World Bank Group. (2014). *G20 labour markets: outlook, key challenges and policy responses* (Report prepared for the G20 Labour and Employment Ministerial Meeting). Melbourne.

Irwin, T., Mazraani, S., & Saxena, S. (2018). *How to Control the Fiscal Costs of Public–Private Partnerships*. Washington: IMF.

Isaacman, A. F., & Isaacman, B. (2013). *Dams, Displacement, and the Delusion of Development: Cahora Bassa and Its Legacies in Mozambique, 1965–2007*. New African Histories. Athens: Ohio University Press.

Isaacs, G., & Kaltenbrunner, A. (2018). 'Financialization and liberalization: South Africa's new forms of external vulnerability', *Competition & Change*, 22/4: 437–63.

Ivanic, M., Martin, W., & Zaman, H. (2012). 'Estimating the short-run poverty impacts of the 2010–11 surge in food prices', *World Development*, 40/11: 2302–17.

Jackson, P. (2006). *Civilizing the Enemy: German Reconstruction and the Invention of the West*. Ann Arbor, MI: University of Michigan Press.

Jacob, T., & Pedersen, R. H. (2018). *Social Protection in an Electorally Competitive Environment (1): The Politics of Productive Social Safety Nets (PSSN) in Tanzania* (ESID Working Paper No. 109). Manchester: Effective States and Inclusive Development Research Centre (ESID) Global Development Institute, School of Environment, Education and Development, University of Manchester.

Jacquemin, M. (2009). '(In)visible young female migrant workers: "little domestics" in West Africa: comparative perspectives on girls and young women's work'. Presented at the Child and Youth Migration in West Africa: Research Progress and Implications for Policy, June. Accra: Development Research Centre on Migration, Globalisation and Poverty University of Sussex and Centre for Migration Studies, University of Ghana.

James, D. (2013). 'Citizenship and land in South Africa: from rights to responsibilities', *Critique of Anthropology*, 33/1: 26–46.

Jamieson, L., Berry, L., Lake, L., University of Cape Town, & Children's Institute. (2017). *South African Child Gauge 2017*. Cape Town: Children's Institute, University of Cape Town.

Janzen, S. A. (2018). 'Child labour measurement: whom should we ask?', *International Labour Review*, 157/2: 169–91.

Jayne, T. S., Chamberlin, J., Traub, L., Sitko, N., Muyanga, M., Yeboah, F. K., Anseeuw, W., Chapoto, A., Wineman, A., Nkonde, C., & Kachule, R. (2016). 'Africa's changing farm size distribution patterns: the rise of medium-scale farms', *Agricultural Economics*, 47/S1: 197–214.

Jayne, T. S., Mason, N. M., Burke, W. J., & Ariga, J. (2018). 'Review: taking stock of Africa's second-generation agricultural input subsidy programs', *Food Policy*, 75: 1–14.

Jeha, D., Usta, I., Ghulmiyyah, L., & Nassar, A. (2015). 'A review of the risks and consequences of adolescent pregnancy', *Journal of Neonatal-Perinatal Medicine*, 8/1: 1–8.

Jerven, M. (2011). 'The quest for the African dummy: explaining African post-colonial economic performance revisited', *Journal of International Development*, 23/2: 288–307.

Jerven, M. (2013). *Poor Numbers: How We Are Misled by African Development Statistics and What to Do about It*. Ithaca, NY: Cornell University Press.

Jerven, M. (2014). 'The political economy of agricultural statistics and input subsidies: evidence from India, Nigeria and Malawi', *Journal of Agrarian Change*, 14/1: 129–45.

Jerven, M. (2018). 'Beyond precision: embracing the politics of global health numbers', *The Lancet*, 392/10146: 468–9.

Jessop, B. (2013). 'Putting neoliberalism in its time and place: a response to the debate', *Social Anthropology*, 21/1: 65–74.

Jewkes, R., & Abrahams, N. (2002). 'The epidemiology of rape and sexual coercion in South Africa: an overview', *Social Science & Medicine*, 55/7: 1231–44.

Jewkes, R. K., Dunkle, K., Nduna, M., & Shai, N. (2010). 'Intimate partner violence, relationship power inequity, and incidence of HIV infection in young women in South Africa: a cohort study', *The Lancet*, 376/9734: 41–8.

Johnston, A. (1996). 'Politics and violence in KwaZulu-Natal', *Terrorism and Political Violence*, 8/4: 78–107.

Jones, N., Tefera, B., Emirie, G., & Presler-Marshall, E. (2018). '"Sticky" gendered norms: change and stasis in the patterning of child marriage in Amhara, Ethiopia'. In C. Harper, N. Jones, A. Ghimire, R. Marcus, & G. Kyomuhendo Bantebya (eds), *Empowering Adolescent Girls in Developing Countries: Gender Justice and Norm Change*. London & New York: Routledge.

Jones, S. (2017). 'Do schools in low income countries really produce so little learning?'. University of Copenhagen, Denmark. https://economics.handels.gu.se/digitalAssets/1643/1643680_17.-sam-jones-2017-02-20.schoolprod.v2.pdf

Jourdan, P., Chigumira, G., Kwesu, I., & Chipumho, E. (2012). *Mining Sector Policy Study*. Zimbabwe Economic Policy Analysis and Research Unit (Zeparu). Harare: Zeparu.

Kabudula, C. W., Houle, B., Collinson, M. A., Kahn, K., Tollman, S., & Clark, S. (2017). 'Assessing changes in household socioeconomic status in rural South Africa, 2001–2013: a distributional analysis using household asset indicators', *Social Indicators Research*, 133/3: 1047–73.

Kagame, P. (2009). 'The backbone of a new Rwanda'. In M. Fairbanks, M. Fal, M. Escobar-Rose, & E. Hooper (eds), *In the River They Swim: Essays from around the World on Enterprise Solutions to Poverty*. West Conshohocken, PA: Templeton Press.

Kahneman, D. (2012). *Thinking, Fast and Slow*. London: Penguin .

Kaiser, B. N., Hruschka, D., & Hadley, C. (2017). 'Measuring material wealth in low-income settings: a conceptual and how-to guide', *American Journal of Human Biology*, 29/4: e22987.

Kaldor, N. (1958). 'Review of *The Political Economy of Growth*', *American Economic Review*, 48/1: 164–70.

Kaldor, N. (1972). 'The irrelevance of equilibrium economics', *The Economic Journal*, 82/328: 1237–55.

Kalecki, M. (1955). 'The problem of financing economic development.' *Indian Economic Review*, 2/3: 1–22.

Kalecki, M. (1976). *Essays on Developing Economies*. Hassocks: Harvester Press & Atlantic Highlands, NJ: Humanities Press.

Kalecki, M., & Sachs, I. (1966). 'Forms of foreign aid: an economic analysis', *Social Science Information*, 5/1: 21–44.

Kannan, K.P. & Raveendran, G. (2009). 'Growth sans employment: a quarter century of jobless manufacturing growth in India's organized manufacturing', *Economic and Political Weekly*, 44/10: 80-91.

Kaplinsky, R., & Morris, M. (2008). 'Do the Asian drivers undermine export-oriented industrialization in SSA?', *World Development*, 36/2: 254–73.

Karwowski, E., Shabani, M., & Stockhammer, E. (2017). *Financialization: Dimensions and Determinants: A Cross-Country Study* (Kingston University London Discussion Paper No. 1). Kingston upon Thames: Kingston University..

Keats, A. (2018). 'Women's schooling, fertility, and child health outcomes: evidence from Uganda's free primary education program', *Journal of Development Economics*, 135: 142–59.

Kehoe, T., & Meza, F. (2011). 'Catch-up growth followed by stagnation: Mexico 1950–2008', *Latin American Journal of Economics*, 48/2: 227–68.

Kelman, I. (2019). 'Imaginary numbers of climate change migrants?', *Social Sciences*, 8/5: 131.

Kent, R. J. (2005). 'Keynes and Say's Law', *History of Economics Review*, 41/1: 61–76.

Kentikelenis, A. E., Stubbs, T. H., & King, L. P. (2016). 'IMF conditionality and development policy space, 1985–2014', *Review of International Political Economy*, 23/4: 543–82.

Kerr, A., Wittenberg, M., & Arrow, J. (2014). 'Job creation and destruction in South Africa', *South African Journal of Economics*, 82/1: 1–18.

Kerr, P., & Durrheim, K. (2013). 'The dilemma of anti-xenophobia discourse in the aftermath of violence in De Doorns', *Journal of Southern African Studies*, 39/3: 577–96.

Keynes, J. M. (1936). *The General Theory of Employment, Interest and Money*. Miami, FL: BN Publishing.

Keynes, J. M. (1937). 'The general theory of employment', *Quarterly Journal of Economics*, 51/2: 209–23.

Khan, H. T., & Lutz, W. (2008). 'How well did past UN population projections anticipate demographic trends in six South-East Asian countries?', *Asian Population Studies*, 4/1: 77–95.

Khan, M. (2012). 'Governance and growth: history, ideology and methods of proof'. In A. Noman, K. Botchwey, H. Stein, & J. Stiglitz (eds), *Good Growth and Governance in Africa: Rethinking Development Strategies*. Oxford: Oxford University Press.

Kifle, A., Getahun, B., & Beyene, A. (2005). *The Rapid Assessment Study on Child Labor in Selected Coffee and Tea Plantations in Ethiopia*. Geneva: International Labour Organization.

Kilic, T., Moylan, H., Ilukor, J., Mtengula, C., & Pangapanga-Phiri, I. (2018). *Root for the Tubers* (Policy Research Working Paper No. 8618). Washington, DC: World Bank.

Kilic, T., Serajuddin, U., Uematsu, H., & Yoshida, N. (2017). *Costing Household Surveys for Monitoring Progress toward Ending Extreme Poverty and Boosting Shared Prosperity* (Policy Research Working Paper No. 7951). Washington, DC: World Bank,

Development Data Group & Poverty and Equity Global Practice Group. Retrieved from: https://papers.ssrn.com/sol3/papers.cfm?abstract_id=2905440.

Killick, T. (1993). *Issues in the Design of IMF Programmes* (Working Paper No. 71). London: ODI.

Kim, M. (2011). 'Gender, work and resistance: South Korean textile industry in the 1970s', *Journal of Contemporary Asia*, 41/3: 411–30.

King, J. E. (1988). *Economic Exiles*. London: Palgrave Macmillan.

King, J. E. (1990). *Labour Economics*. London: Macmillan International Higher Education.

King, J. E. (2009a). 'Economists and the global financial crisis', *Global Change, Peace & Security*, 21/3: 389–96.

King, J. E. (2009b). *Nicholas Kaldor*. Great Thinkers in Economics Series. London: Palgrave Macmillan.

King, J. E. (2012). *The Microfoundations Delusion: Metaphor and Dogma in the History of Macroeconomics*. Cheltenham & Northampton, MA: Edward Elgar.

King, J.E. (2013a). *David Ricardo*. Basingstoke: Palgrave Macmillan.

King, J. E. (2013b). 'A brief introduction to post-Keynesian macroeconomics', *Wirtschaft und Gesellschaft—WuG*, 39/4: 485–508.

King, J. E. (2013c). 'A case for pluralism in economics', *Economic and Labour Relations Review*, 24/1: 17–31.

King, J. E. (2015). *Advanced Introduction to Post-Keynesian Economics*. Elgar Advanced Introductions Series. Cheltenham & Northampton, MA: Edward Elgar.

Kingkaew, S. (2012). 'What are the factors that determine the position of firms from developing countries within the global value chain? The case of Thai firms in the chicken and canned tuna industries.' PhD Thesis, Cambridge University.

Kitching, G. N. (1989). *Development and Underdevelopment in Historical Perspective: Populism, Nationalism, and Industrialization*. Development and Underdevelopment Series. London & New York: Routledge.

Kjær, A. M., & Joughin, J. (2019). 'Send for the cavalry: political incentives in the provision of agricultural advisory services', *Development Policy Review*, 37/3: 367–83.

Knight, F. H. (1921). *Risk, Uncertainty and Profit*. New York: Riverside Press.

Komatsu, H., & Rappleye, J. (2017). 'A new global policy regime founded on invalid statistics? Hanushek, Woessmann, PISA, and economic growth', *Comparative Education*, 53/2: 166–91.

Kondylis, F., Mueller, V., & Zhu, J. (2017). 'Seeing is believing? Evidence from an extension network experiment', *Journal of Development Economics*, 125: 1–20.

Koning, N., & Smaling, E. (2005). 'Environmental crisis or "lie of the land"? The debate on soil degradation in Africa', *Land Use Policy*, 22/1: 3–11.

Koolwal, G. B. (2019). *Improving the Measurement of Rural Women's Employment: Global Momentum and Survey Research Priorities* (World Bank Policy Research Working Paper No. 8840). Washington, DC: World Bank.

Kose, M. A., Prasad, E. S., & Taylor, A. D. (2009). *Thresholds in the Process of International Financial Integration* (Working Paper No. 14916). National Bureau of Economic Research. Retrieved from: http://www.nber.org/papers/w14916.

Krätke, F., & Byiers, B. (2014). *The Political Economy of Official Statistics Implications for the Data Revolution in Sub-Saharan Africa* (Paris 21 Discussion Paper No. 5). Maastricht: ECDPM.

Krebs, R. R., & Jackson, P. T. (2007). 'Twisting tongues and twisting arms: the power of political rhetoric', *European Journal of International Relations*, 13/1: 35–66.

Kroll. (2017). 'Independent audit related to loans contracted by Proindicus S.A., Ematum S. A., and Mozambique Asset Management S.A.'. Report prepared for the Office of the Public Prosecutor of the Republic of Mozambique, 23 June. Retrieved from: https://www.open.ac. uk/technology/mozambique/sites/www.open.ac.uk.technology.mozambique/files/files/ 2017-06-23_Project%20Montague%20-%20Independent%20Audit%20Executive% 20Summary%20English%20(REDACTED%20FOR%20PUBLISHING).pdf.

Krugman, P. (1987). 'Is free trade passé?', *Journal of Economic Perspectives*, 1/2: 131–44.

Krugman, P. (1993). 'The narrow and broad arguments for free trade', *American Economic Review*, 83/2: 362–6.

Krugman, P. (1994a). 'The myth of Asia's miracle', Foreign Affairs, (November/December): 62–78.

Krugman, P. (1994b). 'The fall and rise of development economics'. Retrieved from: https:// web.mit.edu/krugman/www/dishpan.html.

Krugman, P. (2000). 'Reckonings: a real nut case'. *New York Times*. April 19th.

Kyed, H. M., Stepputat, F., & Albrecht, P. (2017). *Urban Insecurity, Migrants and Political Authority Nairobi, Beiru, Hargeisa and Yangon*. Copenhagen: Danish Institute for International Studies (DIIS). Retrieved from: https://www.diis.dk/en/research/urban-insecurity-migrants-and-political-authority

Labrousse, A. (2016a). 'Not by technique alone: a methodological comparison of development analysis with Esther Duflo and Elinor Ostrom', *Journal of Institutional Economics*, 12/2: 277–303.

Labrousse, A. (2016b). 'Poor numbers: statistical chains and the political economy of numbers', Annales. Histoire, Sciences Sociales: English Edition, 71/4: 507–38.

Lamb, G. (2018). 'Police militarisation and the "war on crime" in South Africa', *Journal of Southern African Studies*, 44/5: 1–17.

Landry, D. G. (2018). *The Risks and Rewards of Resource-for-Infrastructure Deals: Lessons from the Congo's Sicamines Agreement* (Working Paper No. 2018/16). China-Africa Research Initiative, School of Advanced International Studies. Washington, DC: Johns Hopkins University. Retrieved from: https://foreignpolicy.com/wp-content/uploads/ 2018/06/01911-sicomines-workingpaper-landry-v6.pdf

Lang, V. F., & Presbitero, A. F. (2018). 'Room for discretion? Biased decision-making in international financial institutions', *Journal of Development Economics*, 130: 1–16.

Larmer, M. (2017). 'Permanent precarity: capital and labour in the Central African copper-belt', *Labor History*, 58/2: 170–84.

Larson, D. F., Muraoka, R., & Otsuka, K. (2016). *On the Central Role of Small Farms in African Rural Development Strategies* (Policy Research Working Paper No. 7710). Development Research Group Agriculture and Rural Development Team. Washington, DC: World Bank. Retrieved from: https://elibrary.worldbank.org/doi/pdf/ 10.1596/1813-9450-7710.

Lavopa, A., & Szirmai, A. (2012). *Industrialization, Employment and Poverty* (UNU-MERIT Working Papers No. 2012-081). Maastricht: Economic and Social Research Institute on Innovation and Technology and Graduate School of Governance.

Law, R. (1985). 'Human sacrifice in pre-colonial West Africa', *African Affairs*, 84/334: 53–87.

Lawson, T. (1989). 'Abstraction, tendencies and stylised facts: a realist approach to economic analysis', *Cambridge Journal of Economics*, 13/1: 59–78.

Lawson, T. (2007). 'What has realism got to do with it?'. In D. Hausman (ed.), *The Philosophy of Economics: An Anthology*. Cambridge: Cambridge University Press.

Lay, J., Nolte, K., & Sipangule, K. (2018). *Large-Scale Farms and Smallholders: Evidence from Zambia* (Working Paper No. 310). Hamburg: German Institute of Global and Area Studies (GIGA).

Lazaro, E., Agergaard, J., Larsen, M. N., Makindara, J., & Birch-Thomsen, T. (2017). *Rural Transformation and the Emergence of Urban Centres in Tanzania* (IGN Report, October). Copenhagen: Department of Geosciences and Natural Resource Management, Faculty of Science, University of Copenhagen.

Lazzarini, S. G., Musacchio, A., Bandeira-de-Mello, R., & Marcon, R. (2015). 'What do state-owned development banks do? Evidence from BNDES, 2002-09', *World Development*, 66: 237–53.

Le, V. H., De Haan, J., & Dietzenbacher, E. (2018). 'Industry wages across countries and over time: a new database of micro survey data', *Review of Income and Wealth*, 64/1: 1–25.

Lectard, P., & Rougier, E. (2018). 'Can developing countries gain from defying comparative advantage? Distance to comparative advantage, export diversification and sophistication, and the dynamics of specialization', *World Development*, 102: 90–110.

Lee, K., Brewer, E., Christiano, C., Meyo, F., Miguel, E., Podolsky, M., Rosa, J., & Wolfram, C. (2014). *Barriers to Electrification for 'Under Grid' Households in Rural Kenya* (Working Paper No. 20327). Cambridge, MA: National Bureau of Economic Research.

Lefort, R. (2012). 'Free market economy, 'developmental state' and party–state hegemony in Ethiopia: the case of the "model farmers"', *Journal of Modern African Studies*, 50/4: 681–706.

Leibbrandt, M., Finn, A., & Woolard, I. (2012). 'Describing and decomposing post-apartheid income inequality in South Africa', *Development Southern Africa*, 29/1: 19–34.

Lensink, R., & Morrissey, O. (2000). 'Aid instability as a measure of uncertainty and the positive impact of aid on growth', *Journal of Development Studies*, 36/3: 31–49.

Lerche, J. (2007). 'A global alliance against forced labour? Unfree labour, neo-liberal globalization and the International Labour Organization', *Journal of Agrarian Change*, 7/4: 425–52.

Lesnoff, M. (2015). 'Uncertainty analysis of the productivity of cattle populations in tropical drylands', *Animal*, 9/11: 1888–96.

Lessing, D. (1973). *The Grass is Singing*. Oxford: Heinemann.

Levine, R., & Renelt, D. (1992). 'A sensitivity analysis of cross-country growth regressions', *American Economic Review*, 82/4: 942–63.

Lewis, M. (2017). *The Undoing Project: A Friendship that Changed the World*. London: Allen Lane.

Lewis, M. (2019). 'Against the rules'. Podcast. Retrieved from: https://atrpodcast.com/about.

Lewis, W. A. (1954). 'Economic development with unlimited supplies of labour', *The Manchester School*, 22/2: 139–91.

Li, C., & Chen, M. (2020). 'National champions, reforms, and industrial policy in China'. In H.-J. Chang, C. Cramer, R. Kozul-Wright, & A. Oqubay (eds), *Oxford Handbook of Industrial Policy*. Oxford: Oxford University Press.

Li, T. M. (2017). 'After development: surplus population and the politics of entitlement: development and change distinguished lecture 2016', *Development and Change*, 48/6: 1247–61.

Lichtenstein, A. C. (1996). *Twice the Work of Free Labor: The Political Economy of Convict Labor in the New South*. The Haymarket Series. London & New York: Verso.

Lin, J., & Chang, H.-J. (2009). 'Should industrial policy in developing countries conform to comparative advantage or defy it? A debate between Justin Lin and Ha-Joon Chang', *Development Policy Review*, 27/5: 483–502.

Lipton, M. (1977). *Why Poor People Stay Poor: A Study of Urban Bias in World Development*. Cambridge, MA: Harvard University Press.

Lipton, M. (2012a). 'Income from work: The food–population–resource crisis in the 'short Africa'. Leontief Prize lecture, Tufts University, Medford, MA.

Lipton, M. (2012b). 'Why the poor stay poor'. In R. Jolly (ed.), *Milestones and Turning Points in Development Thinking*. New York: Springer.

Little, I. M., & Mirrlees, J. A. (1974). *Project Appraisal and Planning for Developing Countries*. New York: Basic Books.

Liu, C., Esteve, A., & Treviño, R. (2017). 'Female-headed households and living conditions in Latin America', *World Development*, 90: 311–28.

Liu, H. (2018). *Education Systems, Education Reforms, and Adult Skills in the Survey of Adult Skills (PIAAC)* (OECD Education Working Papers No. 182). Retrieved from: https://www.oecd-ilibrary.org/education/education-systems-education-reforms-and-adult-skills-in-the-survey-of-adult-skills-piaac_bef85c7d-en.

Lobell, D. B., Azzari, G., Burke, M., Gourlay, S., Jin, Z., Kilic, T., & Murray, S. (2018). *Eyes in the Sky, Boots on the Ground: Assessing Satellite-and Ground-Based Approaches to Crop Yield Measurement and Analysis in Uganda* (Policy Research Working Papers). Washington, DC: World Bank.

Lodefalk, M. (2017). 'Servicification of firms and trade policy implications', *World Trade Review*, 16/1: 59–83.

Lodge, T. (2015). 'The politics of HIV/AIDS in South Africa: government action and public response', *Third World Quarterly*, 36/8: 1570–91.

Loizos, K. (2018). 'The financial repression–liberalization debate: taking stock, looking for a synthesis', *Journal of Economic Surveys*, 32/2: 440–68.

Losch, B. (2016). *Structural Transformation to Boost Youth Labour Demand in Sub-Saharan Africa: The Role of Agriculture, Rural Areas and Territorial Development* (Employment Policy Department Working Paper No. 204). Geneva: ILO.

Lowder, S. K., Bertini, R., Karfakis, P., & Croppenstedt, A. (2016). 'Transformation in the size and distribution of farmland operated by household and other farms in select countries of sub-Saharan Africa'. 2016 African Association of Agricultural Economists (AAAE) Fifth International Conference, Addis Ababa, Ethiopia, 23–26 September.

Loxley, J. (2013). 'Are public–private partnerships (PPPs) the answer to Africa's infrastructure needs?', *Review of African Political Economy*, 40/137: 485–95.

Luan, Y., Zhu, W., Cui, X., Fischer, G., Dawson, T. P., Shi, P., & Zhang, Z. (2019). 'Cropland yield divergence over Africa and its implication for mitigating food insecurity', *Mitigation and Adaptation Strategies for Global Change*, 24/5: 707–34.

Lufumpa, C. L. (2005). 'The poverty–environment nexus in Africa', *African Development Review*, 17/3: 366–81.

Lutz, W., & KC, S. (2010). 'Dimensions of global population projections: what do we know about future population trends and structures?', *Philosophical Transactions of the Royal Society B: Biological Sciences*, 365/1554: 2779–91.

Lyon, S., & Valdivia, C. (2010). *Towards the Effective Measurement of Child Domestic Workers: Building Estimates Using Standard Household Survey Instruments* (Working Paper). Rome: Understanding Children's Work (UCW) Programme.

Mach, K. J., Kraan, C. M., Adger, W. N., Buhaug, H., Burke, M., Fearon, J. D., Field, C. B., Hendrix, C., Maystadt, J-F., O'Laughlin, J., Roessler, P., Scheffran, J., Schultz, K., & Von Uexkull, N. (2019). 'Climate as a risk factor for armed conflict', *Nature*, 571/7764: 193–7.

Macmillan, M., Rodrik, D., & Welch, K. H. (2002). *When Economic Reform Goes Wrong: Cashews in Mozambique*. National Bureau of Economic Research.

Maddison, A. (1991). *Dynamic Forces in Capitalist Development: A Long-Run Comparative View*. Oxford & New York?: Oxford University Press.

Maddison Project. (2018). 'Maddison historical development statistics'. Groningen Growth and Development Centre. Retrieved from: https://www.rug.nl/ggdc/historicaldevelopment/maddison/.

Mader, P. (2018). 'Contesting financial inclusion: debate: contesting financial inclusion', *Development and Change*, 49/2: 461–83.

Magalhães Prates, D., & Farhi, M. (2015). 'From IMF to the troika: new analytical framework, same conditionalities', *Économie et Institutions*, 23: 41–71.

Mahajan, S. (2014). 'The gross toilet index', *Economic and Political Weekly*, 49/12: 74–5.

Majid, N. (2015). *The Great Employment Transformation in China* (Employment Working Paper No. 195). Geneva: Employment Policy Department, Employment and Labour Market Policies Branch, International Labour Organization.

Makgala, C. J. (2013). 'Discourses of poor work ethic in Botswana: a historical perspective, 1930–2010', *Journal of Southern African Studies*, 39/1: 45–57.

Mancini, L., & Paz, M. J. (2018). 'Oil sector and technological development: effects of the mandatory research and development (R&D) investment clause on oil companies in Brazil', *Resources Policy*, 58: 131–43.

Marais, H. (2013). *South Africa Pushed to the Limit: The Political Economy of Change*. London: Zed Books.

Marconi, N., Reis, C. F. de B., & Araújo, E. C. de. (2016). 'Manufacturing and economic development: the actuality of Kaldor's first and second laws', *Structural Change and Economic Dynamics*, 37 (Supplement C): 75–89.

Marivoet, W., Ulimwengu, J., & Sedano, F. (2019). 'Spatial typology for targeted food and nutrition security interventions', *World Development*, 120: 62–75.

Marivoet, W., & De Herdt, T. (2017). *From figures to facts: making sense of socioeconomic surveys in the Democratic Republic of the Congo (DRC)* (Analysis and Policy Brief No. 23). Antwerp: University of Atwerp, Institute of Development Policy and Management.

Markakis, J. (2011). *Ethiopia: The Last Two Frontiers*. Woodbridge: Boydell & Brewer.

Marois, T. (2016). 'State-owned banks and development: dispelling mainstream myths'. In M. Mustafa Erdogdu & B. Christiansen (eds), *Handbook of Research on Comparative Economic Development Perspectives on Europe and the MENA Region*. Hershey, PA: IGI Global.

Marongwe, N. (2012). *Rural women as the invisible victims of militarised political violence: the case of Shurugwi district, Zimbabwe, 2000-2008* (PhD Thesis). University of the Western Cape.

Marques de Morais, R., & Falcão de Campos, R. (2005). 'Lundas: the stones of death'. *Maka Angola*. Retrieved from: https://www.makaangola.org/wp-content/uploads/2013/07/Lundas_AsPedrasDaMorte_EN.pdf .

Marshall, A. (1920/1997). *Principles of Economics*. Great Minds Series. Amherst, NY: Prometheus Books.

Marshall, W.C. (2018). 'The Trump administration and the neoliberal project', *Theory in Action*, 11/3.

Marshall, E. P., Lyytikainen, M., & Jones, N. (2016). *Child Marriage in Ethiopia*. https://www.unicef.org/ethiopia/reports/child-marriage-ethiopia

Martin, P. (2012). 'Hired farm workers', *Choices*, 27/2. Retrieved from: http://choicesmagazine.org/choices-magazine/theme-articles/immigration-and-agriculture/hired-farm-workers.

Martínez, E., Odhiambo, A., & Human Rights Watch (Organization) (2018). *Leave No Girl Behind in Africa: Discrimination in Education against Pregnant Girls and Adolescent Mothers*. Human Rights Watch. https://www.hrw.org/sites/default/files/report_pdf/au0618_web.pdf

Marx, K. (1993). *Grundrisse: Foundations of the Critique of Political Economy*, trans. M. Nicolaus. London: Penguin Classics.

Marx, K. (2010). *Capital: A Critique of Political Economy*. Madison Park, WA: Pacific Publishing.

Mayosi, B. M., & Benatar, S. R. (2014). 'Health and health care in South Africa: 20 years after Mandela', *New England Journal of Medicine*, 371/14: 1344–53.

Mayer, J. (2013). *Towards more balanced growth strategies in developing countries: issues related to market size, trade balances, and purchasing power* (Discussion Paper No.214).

Mazzucato, M., & Penna, C. C. (2016). 'Beyond market failures: the market creating and shaping roles of state investment banks', *Journal of Economic Policy Reform*, 19/4: 305–26.

Mbaye, A. A., & Gueye, F. (2018). *Labor Markets and Jobs in West Africa* (Working Paper Series No. 297). Abidjan: African Development Bank.

McArthur, J. W., & McCord, G. C. (2017). 'Fertilizing growth: agricultural inputs and their effects in economic development', *Journal of Development Economics*, 127: 133–52.

McCombie, J. S. (1989). '"Thirlwall's Law" and balance of payments constrained growth: a comment on the debate', *Applied Economics*, 21/5: 611–29.

McGrath, S., Alla-Mensah, J., & Langthaler, M. (2018). *Skills for Decent Work, Life and Sustainable Development: Vocational Education and the Sustainable Development Goals* (Austrian Foundation for Development Research (ÖFSE) Briefing Paper No. 18). Retrieved from: https://www.econstor.eu/handle/10419/182458.

Mckenzie, D. J., & Paffhausen, A. L. (2017). *Small Firm Death in Developing Countries* (Policy Research Working Papers). Washington, DC: World Bank.

McKinsey Global Institute. (2010). *Lions on the Move: The Progress and Potential of African Economies*. Washington, DC: McKinsey Global Institute.

McKinsey Global Institute. (2018). *Outperformers: High-Growth Emerging Economies and the Companies that Propel Them*. Washington, DC: McKinsey Global Institute.

McMillan, M. S., & Rodrik, D. (2011). *Globalization, Structural Change and Productivity Growth*. Washington, DC: National Bureau of Economic Research.

McNamara, P. (1998). *Political Economy and Statesmanship: Smith, Hamilton, and the Foundation of the Commercial Republic*. DeKalb, IL: Northern Illinois University Press.

Meade, J. (1975). 'The Keynesian revolution'. In M. Keynes (ed.), *Essays on John Maynard Keynes*. Cambridge: Cambridge University.

Meagher, K. (2016). 'The scramble for Africans: demography, globalisation and Africa's informal labour markets', *Journal of Development Studies*, 52/4: 483–97.

Meagher, K., Manna, L., & Bolt, M. (2016). 'Introduction: globalization, African workers and the terms of inclusion', *Journal of Development Studies*, 52/4: 471–82.

Meek, J. (2014). *Private Island: Why Britain Now Belongs to Someone Else*. London: Verso.

Meier, G. M., & Seers, D. (1984). *Pioneers in Development*. Oxford: Oxford University Press for the World Bank.

Meier zu Selhausen, F., & Stam, E. (2013). *Husbands and Wives: The Powers and Perils of Participation in a Microfinance Cooperative for Female Entrepreneurs* (Discussion Paper Series/Tjalling C. Koopmans Research Institute No. 13/10). Retrieved from: https://dspace.library.uu.nl/bitstream/handle/1874/290875/13-10.pdf

Melese, A. (2015). *Living wage report: non-metropolitan Ethiopia – Ziway region, context provided in the horticulture sector.* Global Living Wage Coalition, Series 1, Report 6.

Mellor, J. W., & Malik, S. J. (2017). 'The impact of growth in small commercial farm productivity on rural poverty reduction', *World Development*, 91: 1–10.

Merridale, C. (1996). 'The 1937 census and the limits of Stalinist rule', *The Historical Journal*, 39/1: 225.

Milazzo, A., & van de Walle, D. P. (2015). *Women Left Behind? Poverty and Headship in Africa* (World Bank Policy Research Working Paper No. 7331). Retrieved from: https://papers.ssrn.com/sol3/papers.cfm?abstract_id=2622317.

Milberg, W. (2004). *The Changing Structure of International Trade Linked to Global Production Systems: What Are the Policy Implications?* (Working Paper No. 33). Geneva: ILO.

Mills, G., Herbst, J., Obasanjo, O., & Davis, D. (2017). *Making Africa Work: A Handbook.* London: Hurst & Co.

Millward, R., & Baten, J. (2010). 'Population and living standards, 1914–1945'. In S. Broadberry & K. O'Rourke (eds), *The Cambridge Economic History of Modern Europe*, vol. 2. Cambridge: Cambridge University Press.

Minten, B., Schäfer, F., & Worako, T. K. (2019). 'Performance and institutions of the Ethiopian coffee sector'. In C. Fantu, A. Oqubay, & C. Cramer (eds), *Oxford Handbook of the Ethiopian Economy*. Oxford: Oxford University Press.

Mitullah, W., Kamau, P., & Kivuva, J. M. (2017). *Employment Creation in Agriculture and Agro-Processing Sector in Kenya in the Context of Inclusive Growth: Political Economy & Settlement Analysis* (Research Working Paper No. 020). Nairobi: Partnership for African Social and Governance Research.

Mkandawire, T. (2014). 'The spread of economic doctrines and policy making in post-colonial Africa', *African Studies Review*, 57/1: 171–98.

Mlilo, S., & Misago, J. P. (2019). *Xenophobic Violence in South Africa: 1994–2018: An Overview.* Johannesburg: Xenowatch, African Centre for Migration and Society, University of the Witwatersrand.

Moat, J., Williams, J., Baena, S., Wilkinson, T., Gole, T. W., Challa, Z. K., Demissew, S., & Davis, A. P. (2017). 'Resilience potential of the Ethiopian coffee sector under climate change', *Nature Plants*, 3/7: 1–14.

Moene, K. O., & Wallerstein, M. (2008). 'Social democracy as a development strategy'. In D. Austen-Smith, J. A. Frieden, M. A. Golden, K. O. Moene, & A. Przeworski (eds), *Selected Works of Michael Wallerstein*. Cambridge: Cambridge University.

Mogues, T., & Caceres, L. (2018). 'Unpacking the "black box" of public expenditure data in Africa: quantification of agricultural spending using Mozambique's budget reports', *Data Science Journal*, 17: 9.

Mold, A., & Mukwaya, R. (2016). 'Modelling the economic impact of the tripartite free trade area: its implications for the economic geography of Southern, Eastern and Northern Africa', *Journal of African Trade*, 3/1–2: 57–84.

Mold, A., & Prizzon, A. (2010). *Fragile States, Commodity Booms and Export Performance: An Analysis of the Sub-Saharan African Case* (EUI Working Paper RSCAS No. 21). Florence: Robert Schuman Centre for Advanced Studies.

Moller, L. C., & Wacker, K. M. (2017). 'Explaining Ethiopia's growth acceleration: the role of infrastructure and macroeconomic policy', *World Development*, 96 (Supplement C): 198–215.

Mondliwa, P., & Roberts, S. (2017). *Economic Benefits of Mozambican Gas for Sasol and South African Government* (Working Paper No. 23/2017). Johannesburg: Centre for Competition, Regulation and Economic Development (CCRED).

Monson, J. (2005). 'Freedom railway: The unexpected successes of a Cold War development project', *Boston Review*: 1–6. Retrieved from: https://digitalcommons.carleton.edu/hist_faculty/2.

Moore, M., Prichard, W., & Fjeldstad, O.-H. (2018). *Taxing Africa: Coercion, Reform and Development*. African Arguments Series. London: Zed Books.

Mousseau, F. (2019). *The Bukanga Lonzo Debacle: The Failure of Agro-Industrial Parks in DRC*. Oakland, CA: Oakland Institute. Retrieved from: https://www.oaklandinstitute. org/sites/oaklandinstitute.org/files/bukanga-lonzo-debacle.pdf.

Moyo, D. (2009). 'Why foreign aid is hurting Africa'. *Wall Street Journal*, March 21. Retrieved from: https://www.wsj.com/articles/SB123758895999200083.

Moyo, S. (2011). 'Primitive accumulation and the destruction of African peasantries'. In U. Patnaik & S. Moyo (eds), *The Agrarian Question in the Neoliberal Era: Primitive Accumulation and the Peasantry*. Oxford: Pambazuka Press.

Mrema, E. J., Ngowi, A. V., Kishinhi, S. S., & Mamuya, S. H. (2017). 'Pesticide exposure and health problems among female horticulture workers in Tanzania', *Environmental Health Insights*, 11: 117863021771523. 'Retrieved from: https://pdfs.semanticscholar.org/18b2/ ddaf16232dce1dea36cc62bc4e468c32fab4.pdf'

Mueller, V., Schmidt, E., & Lozano-Gracia, N. (2015). 'Household and spatial drivers of migration patterns in Africa: evidence from five countries'. Presented at the Urbanization and Spatial Development of Countries Research Workshop, World Bank, Washington, DC.

Muhoozi, G. K. M., Atukunda, P., Mwadime, R., Iversen, P. O., & Westerberg, A. C. (2016). 'Nutritional and developmental status among 6- to 8-month-old children in south-western Uganda: a cross-sectional study', *Food & Nutrition Research*, 60/1: 30270.

Munyani, R.M. (2005). *The Political economy of food aid: a case of Zimbabwe*. MA Thesis. Univesity of the Western Cape: Cape Town.

Muriithi, S. (2017). 'African small and medium enterprises (SMEs) contributions, challenges and solutions', *European Journal of Research and Reflection in Management Sciences*, 5/1: 36–48.

Museru, M., Toerien, F., & Gossel, S. (2014). 'The impact of aid and public investment volatility on economic growth in sub-Saharan Africa', *World Development*, 57: 138–47.

Mussa, M., & Savastano, M. (2000). 'The IMF approach to economic stabilization', *NBER Macroeconomics Annual 1999*, 14: 79–128.

Mwanawina, I., & Mulungushi, J. (2008). 'Zambia'. In B. J. Ndulu, S. A. O'Connell, S. J. P., Azam, R. H. Bates, A. K. Fosu, J. W. Gunning, & D. Njinkeu (eds), *The Political Economic of Growth in Africa 1960-2000: Case Studies*. Cambridge, UK: Cambridge University Press.'

Myrdal, G. (1957). *Rich Lands and Poor*. New York: Harper.

Nagler, P., & Naudé, W. (2014). *Labor Productivity in Rural African Enterprises: EMPIRICAL Evidence from the LSMS-ISA* (IZA Discussion Papers No. 8524). Bonn: Institute for the Study of Labor (IZA).

Nagler, P. (2017). *A profile of non-farm household enterprises in Sub-Saharan Africa* (UNU-MERIT Working Papers No. 2017-048). Maastricht: United Nations University-Maastricht Economic and Social Research Institute on Innovation and Technology.

Nakano, Y., & Magezi, E. F. (2019). *The Impact of Microcredit on Agricultural Technology Adoption and Productivity: Evidence from Randomized Control Trial in Tanzania* (JICA-RI Working Paper No. 193). Tokyo: JICA Research Institute.

Nannyonjo, J. (2013). 'Enabling agricultural cooperatives through public policy and the state'. Presented at the Conference on Potential and Limits of Social and Solidarity Economy, UNRISD, Geneva.

NAO (National Audit Office). (2018). *PF1 and PF2: Report by the Comptroller and Auditor General*. London: National Audit Office.

Nattrass, N., & Seekings, J. (2018). *Labour Market Reform is Needed for Inclusive Growth* (Viewpoints No. 4). Johannesburg: Centre for Development and Enterprise.

Naudé, W., & Krugell, W. (2002). 'African economic growth: wrong to rely on small businesses?', *Journal of Small Business & Entrepreneurship*, 16/2: 21–44.

Ndikumana, L., & Boyce, J. (2018). *Capital Flight from Africa: Updated Methodology and New Estimates* (PERI Research Report). Amherst, MA: Political Economy Research Institute, University of Massachusetts.

Ndulu, B. J., & O'Connell, S. A. (2008). 'Policy plus: African growth performance 1960–2000'. In B. J. Ndulu, R. H. Bates, P. Collier, S. A. O'Connell, & C. Soludo (eds), *The Political Economy of Economic Growth in Africa, 1960–2000*, vol. 1. Cambridge: Cambridge University Press.

Nelson, E-U., & Brown, A. (2017). 'Rural Poverty and Urban Domestic Child Work: Qualitative Study of Female House Maids in Uyo, Nigeria', *International Journal of Social Sciences*, 11/1: 58–67.

NEPAD (New Partnership for Africa's Development). (2013). *Agriculture in Africa: Transformation and Outlook*. Midrand: NEPAD.

Nesbitt-Ahmed, Z. D. (2016). 'The same, but different: the everyday lives of female and male domestic workers in Lagos, Nigeria'. PhD Thesis, London School of Economics and Political Science (LSE).

Ngan, D., Pincus, J., & Sender, J. (2012). *Migration, Employment and Child Welfare in Ho Chi Minh City and the Surrounding Provinces* (Working Paper No. 2). Ho Chi Minh City: Fulbright Economics Teaching Program. Retrieved from: http://www.fetp.edu.vn/en/working-paper-series/migration-employment-and-child-welfare-in-ho-chi-minh-city-and-the-surrounding-provinces/

Ngo, D., & Christiaensen, L. (2018). *The Performance of a Consumption Augmented Asset Index in Ranking Households and Identifying the Poor* (Policy Research Working Paper No. 8362). Washington, DC: World Bank, Social Protection and Labor Global Practice.

Nhamo, L., Matchaya, G., Mabhaudhi, T., Nhlengethwa, S., Nhemachena, C., & Mpandeli, S. (2019). 'Cereal production trends under climate change: impacts and adaptation strategies in Southern Africa', *Agriculture*, 9/2: 474–81.

Nhemachena, C., Matchaya, G., Nhlengethwa, S., & Nhemachena, C. R. (2018). 'Exploring ways to increase public investments in agricultural water management and irrigation for improved agricultural productivity in Southern Africa', *Water SA*, 44/3: 474–81.

Nightingale, P., & Coad, A. (2013). 'Muppets and gazelles: political and methodological biases in entrepreneurship research', *Industrial and Corporate Change*, 23/1: 113–43.

Nolan, P., Zhang, J., & Liu, C. (2008). 'The global business revolution, the cascade effect, and the challenge for firms from developing countries', *Cambridge Journal of Economics*, 32/1: 29–47.

Nurkse, R. (1966). *Problems of Capital Formation in Underdeveloped Countries*. Oxford: Blackwell.

Nyambura, H., & Genga, B. (2016). 'Kenya central bank staff cited in alleged $439 million fraud'. 13 December. Retrieved from: https://www.bloomberg.com/news/articles/2016-12-13/kenyan-central-bank-officials-involved-in-bank-fraud-court-told.

O'Higgins, N. (2017). *Rising to the Youth Employment Challenge: New Evidence on Key Policy Issues.* Geneva: ILO.

O'Laughlin, B. (1995). 'Myth of the African family in the world of development'. In D. F. Bryceson (ed.), *Women Wielding the Hoe: Lessons from Rural Africa for Feminist Theory and Development Practice.* Oxford & Washington, DC: Berg.

OECD (Organisation for Economic Co-operation and Development). (2018). *The Future of Rural Youth in Developing Countries: Tapping the Potential of Local Value Chains.* Paris: OECD.

Ogundari, K., & Bolarinwa, O. D. (2018). *Agricultural Innovations, Production, and Household Welfare in Africa* (Working Paper Series No. 294). Abidjan: African Development Bank.

Oh, S.-Y. (2015). 'How China outsmarts WTO rulings in the wind industry', *Asian Survey*, 55/6: 1116–45.

Oketch, M. (2014). *Education policy, vocational training, and the youth in Sub-Saharan Africa.* (WIDER Working Paper No. 2014/069). United Nations University World Institute for Development Economics Research: Helsinki.

Olawale, F., & Garwe, D. (2010). 'Obstacles to the growth of new SMEs in South Africa: a principal component analysis approach', *African Journal of Business Management*, 4/5: 729–38.

Olorunfemi, F., & Onwuemele, A. (2017). 'Process and project failures in dam-building in Nigeria: the case of Zamfara Hydropower Dam'. In G. Siciliano & F. Urban (eds), *Chinese Hydropower Development in Africa and Asia.* London: Routledge.

Onselen, C. V. (2001). *New Babylon, New Nineveh: Everyday Life on the Witwatersrand, 1886–1914.* Johannesburg: Jonathan Ball. Vol.2.

Oqubay, A. (2016). *Made in Africa: Industrial Policy in Ethiopia.* Oxford: Oxford University Press.

Oqubay, A. (2019). 'The structure and performance of the Ethiopian manufacturing sector'. In F. Cheru, C. Cramer, & A. Oqubay (eds), *The Oxford Handbook of the Ethiopian Economy.* Oxford: Oxford University Press.

Oqubay, A., & Tesfachew, T. (2019). 'The journey of Ethiopian Airlines', *How They Did It*, 2/1: 1–16.

Osakwe, P. N., Santos-Paulino, A. U., & Dogan, B. (2018). 'Trade dependence, liberalization, and exports diversification in developing countries', *Journal of African Trade*, 5/1–2: 19–34.

Ossowski, R., & Halland, H. (2016). *Fiscal Management in Resource-Rich Countries: Essentials for Economists, Public Finance Professionals, and Policy Makers.* Washington, DC: World Bank.

Outram, Q. (2017). 'The demand for residential domestic service in the London of 1901', *Economic History Review*, 70/3: 893–918.

Owens, T., & Wood, A. (1997). 'Export-oriented industrialization through primary processing?', *World Development*, 25/9: 1453–70.

Oxfam International. (2016). *Position Paper on Gender Justice and the Extractive Industries.* London: Oxfam International. Retrieved from: https://www.oxfamamerica.org/static/media/files/EI_and_GJ_position_paper_v.15_FINAL_03202017_green_Kenny.pdf.

Oxford Business Group. (2019). *THE REPORT: Agriculture in Africa 2019*. Retrieved from: https://oxfordbusinessgroup.com/sites/default/files/blog/specialreports/949525/africa_2019_special_report.pdf.

Oxford Poverty and Human Development Initiative. (2018). *Global Multidimensional Poverty Index 2018: The Most Detailed Picture to Date of the World's Poorest People*. Oxford: University of Oxford.

Oya, C. (2019). 'Building an industrial workforce in Ethiopia'. In F. Cheru, C. Cramer, & A. Oqubay (eds), *The Oxford Handbook of the Ethiopian Economy*. Oxford: Oxford University Press.

Page, J. M., & Söderbom, M. (2012). *Is Small Beautiful? Small Enterprise, Aid and Employment in Africa*. Helsinki: UNU World Institute for Development Economics Research.

Palma, J. G. (2012). *How the Full Opening of the Capital Account to Highly Liquid Financial Markets Led Latin America to Two and a Half Cycles of 'Mania, Panic and Crash'*. (Cambridge Working Papers in Economics No. 1201). Cambridge: University of Cambridge, Faculty of Economics.

Palmer, K., & Sender, J. (2006). 'Prospects for on-farm self-employment and poverty reduction: an analysis of the South African income and expenditure survey 2000', *Journal of Contemporary African Studies*, 24/3: 347–76.

Pankhurst, R. (1996). 'Post-World War II Ethiopia: British military policy and action for the dismantling and acquisition of Italian factories and other assets, 1941–2', *Journal of Ethiopian Studies*, 29/1: 35–77.

Pape, U. J., & Parisotto, L. (2019). *Estimating Poverty in a Fragile Context: The High Frequency Survey in South Sudan* (Policy Research Working Papers). Washington, DC: World Bank.

Papier, J. (2017). 'Improving college-to-work transitions through enhanced training for employment', *Research in Post-Compulsory Education*, 22/1: 38–48.

Partridge, N., & Pienaar, L. (2015). 'Developing a multi-variate product index to prioritise agri processing investments in South Africa'. Presented at the 54th Conference of the Agricultural Economics Association of South Africa, Western Cape Department of Agriculture, Cape Town.

Pasinetti, L. L. (2000). 'Critique of the neoclassical theory of growth and distribution', *BNL Quarterly Review*, 53/215: 383–431.

Patnaik, U. (2016). 'Capitalist trajectories of global interdependence and welfare outcomes: the lessons of history for the present'. In B.B. Mohanty (ed.), *Critical Perspectives on Agrarian Transition*. New Delhi: Routledge India.

Patnaik, U., Moyo, S., & Shivji, I. G. (2011). *The Agrarian Question in the Neoliberal Era: Primitive Accumulation and the Peasantry*. Oxford: Pambazuka.

Patnaik, U., & Patnaik, P. (2017). *A Theory of Imperialism*. New York: Columbia University Press.

Patnaik, P. (2016). 'Globalization and the impasse of capitalism', *Social Scientist* 44/11/12: 3-14.

Penvenne, J. (2015). *Women, Migration and the Cashew Economy in Southern Mozambique 1945–1975*. Oxford: James Currey.

Pettersson, T., & Eck, K. (2018). 'Organized violence, 1989–2017', *Journal of Peace Research*, 55/4: 535–47.

Pfaffenzeller, S. (2018). 'Which terms of trade–recent developments in relative commodity prices'. *Global Commodity Markets and Development Economics*, Routledge Studies in Development Economics. London and New York: Routledge.

Phimister, I., & Pilossof, R. (2017). 'Wage labor in historical perspective: a study of the de-proletarianization of the African working class in Zimbabwe, 1960–2010', *Labor History*, 58/2: 215–27.

Pilling, D. (2018). 'Nigerian economy: why Lagos works'. *Financial Times*, 25 March. Retrieved from: https://www.ft.com/content/ff0595e4-26de-11e8-b27e-cc62a39d57a0.

Pilling, D. (2019). *The Growth Delusion: The Wealth and Well-Being of Nations*. London: Bloomsbury.

Pincus, J. (2006). 'Green Revolution and biotechnology'. In D. Clark (ed.), *The Elgar Companion to Development Studies*. Cheltenham: Edward Elgar.

Pincus, J., & Sender, J. (2008). 'Quantifying poverty in Viet Nam: who counts?', *Journal of Vietnamese Studies*, 3/1: 108–50.

Piza, C., Cravo, T., Taylor, L., Gonzalez, L., Musse, I., Furtado, I., Sierra, A. C., & Abdelnour, S. (2016). *Business Support for Small and Medium Enterprises in Low- and Middle-Income Countries: A Systematic Review* (3ie Systematic Review No. 25). London: International Initiative for Impact Evaluation.

Plümper, T., & Neumayer, E. (2006). 'The unequal burden of war: the effect of armed conflict on the gender gap in life expectancy', *International Organization*, 60/3: 723–54.

Pollen, G. (2018). 'From total factor productivity to structural change: interrogating economic growth and structural transformation from a developing country perspective, with reference to Zambia'. PhD Thesis, SOAS University of London. Retrieved from: http://eprints.soas.ac.uk/30263/.

Ponte, S., Kelling, I., Jespersen, K. S., & Kruijssen, F. (2014). 'The Blue Revolution in Asia: upgrading and governance in aquaculture value chains', *World Development*, 64: 52–64.

Poole, D. L. (2016). *Entrepreneurship and SME Sector Development in Post-Genocide Rwanda: A Search for the 'Missing Middle'*. London: SOAS, University of London.

Porteous, O. (2020). 'Trade and agricultural technology adoption: evidence from Africa', *Journal of Development Economics*, 44/May: 102440.

Posel, D., Casale, D., & Vermaak, C. (2014). 'Job search and the measurement of unemployment in South Africa', *South African Journal of Economics*, 82/1: 66–80.

Power, M., & Kirshner, J. (2019). 'Powering the state: the political geographies of electrification in Mozambique', *Environment and Planning C: Politics and Space*, 37/3: 498–518.

Pradhan, E., & Canning, D. (2016). *The Effect of Schooling on Teenage Fertility: Evidence from the 1994 Education Reform in Ethiopia* (Working Paper No. 128). Department of Global Health and Population, Harvard School of Public Health. Retrieved from: http://econpapers.repec.org/RePEc:gdm:wpaper:12816.

Presbitero, A. F. (2016). 'Too much and too fast? Public investment scaling-up and absorptive capacity', *Journal of Development Economics*, 120: 17–31.

Preston, P. (2012). *The Spanish Holocaust: Inquisition and Extermination in Twentieth-Century Spain*. London: HarperPress.

Pritchett, L., & Sandefur, J. (2013). *Context Matters for Size: Why External Validity Claims and Development Practice Don't Mix* (Center for Global Development Working Paper No. 336). Retrieved from: http://dx.doi.org/10.2139/ssrn.2364580.

Purdeková, A. (2011). *Rwanda's Ingando Camps: Liminality and the Reproduction of Power* (Working Paper Series No. 80). Oxford University: Refugee Studies Centre, Oxford Department of International Development.

Purdy, D. (2014). 'Crisis and regime change in Britain', *Soundings*, 57 (summer): 95–105.

Raftopoulos, B., & Mlambo, A. (eds). (2009). *Becoming Zimbabwe: A History from the Pre-Colonial Period to 2008*. Harare: Weaver Press.

Ragasa, C., Berhane, G., Tadesse, F., & Taffesse, A. S. (2013). 'Gender differences in access to extension services and agricultural productivity', *Journal of Agricultural Education and Extension*, 19/5: 437–68.

Ragasa, C., Mazunda, J., & Kadzamira, M. (2016). *The Impact of Agricultural Extension Services in the Context of a Heavily Subsidized Input System: The Case of Malawi* (IFPRI Discussion Paper). Washington, DC: IFPRI.

Rajkumar, A. S., Gaukler, C., & Tilahun, J. (2011). *Combating Malnutrition in Ethiopia: An Evidence-Based Approach for Sustained Results*. The World Bank.

Raleigh, C., Choi, H. J., & Kniveton, D. (2015). 'The devil is in the details: an investigation of the relationships between conflict, food price and climate across Africa', *Global Environmental Change*, 32: 187–99.

Randall, S., & Coast, E. (2016). 'The quality of demographic data on older Africans', *Demographic Research*, 34: 143–74.

Randall, S., Coast, E., & Leone, T. (2011). 'Cultural constructions of the concept of household in sample surveys', *Population Studies*, 65/2: 217–29.

Rankin, N. A., & Roberts, G. (2011). 'Youth unemployment, firm size and reservation wages in South Africa', *South African Journal of Economics*, 79/2: 128–45.

Rapetti, M., Skott, P., & Razmi, A. (2012). 'The real exchange rate and economic growth: are developing countries different?', *International Review of Applied Economics*, 26/6: 735-753.

Ravallion, M. (2012). 'Mashup indices of development', *World Bank Research Observer*, 27/1: 1–32.

Ravallion, M. (2015). *Are the World's Poorest Being Left Behind?* (Working Paper Series). Verona: Society for the Study of Economic Inequality. Retrieved from: http://www.ecineq.org/milano/WP/ECINEQ2015-369.pdf.

Rawson, G. (2017). 'Economies and strategies of the northern rural poor: the mitigation of poverty in a West Riding township in the nineteenth century', *Rural History*, 28/1: 69–92.

Razmi, A. (2018). *The Real Exchange Rate Policy Trilemma in Developing Economies* (UMASS Amherst Economics Working Papers No. 249). Retrieved from: https://scholarworks.umass.edu/econ_workingpaper/249?utm_source=scholarworks.umass.edu%2Fecon_workingpaper%2F249&utm_medium=PDF&utm_campaign=PDFCoverPages.

Reardon, T., Barrett, C., Kelly, V., & Savadogo, K. (1999). 'Policy reforms and sustainable agricultural intensification in Africa', *Development Policy Review*, 17/4: 375–95.

Reati, A. (2001). 'Total factor productivity: a misleading concept', *BNL Quarterly Review*, 54/218: 313–32.

Rhoda, N., Velaphi, S., Gebhardt, G. S., Kauchali, S., & Barron, P. (2018). 'Reducing neonatal deaths in South Africa: progress and challenges', *South African Medical Journal*, 108/3 (Supplement 1): S9–S16.

Rich, K., Desmond, C., & Makusha, T. (2019). 'Welfare measures and the composition of the bottom decile: the example of gender and extreme poverty in South Africa', *Development Southern Africa*, 36/4: 491–503.

Rigaud, K. K., de Sherbinin, A., Jones, B., Bergmann, J., Clement, V., Ober, K., Schewe, J., Adamo, S., McCusker, B. & Heuser, S. (2018). *Groundswell: Preparing for Internal Climate Migration*. Washington, DC: World Bank.

Rillo, A. D., & Miyamoto, J. (2016). *Innovating Financial Inclusion: Postal Savings System Revisited* (Policy Brief No. 3). Tokyo: Asian Development Bank Institute.

Rizzo, M. (2006). 'What was left of the groundnut scheme? Development disaster and labour market in Southern Tanganyika 1946-1952', *Journal of Agrarian Change*, 6/2: 205–38.

ROAPE (Review of African Political Economy). (2018). 'The cover up: complicity in Rwanda's lies'. Retrieved from: https://www.google.com/url?sa=t&rct=j&q=&esrc=s& source=web&cd=1&cad=rja&uact=8&ved=2ahUKEwj0huLnkN7gAhWPDewKHdDZD aoQFjAAegQIAxAB&url=http%3A%2F%2Froape.net%2F2018%2F11%2F21%2Fthe-cover-up-complicity-in-rwandas-lies%2F&usg=AOvVaw2O86vx5HGZ5x1JKCO9wFCA.

Robin, C. (2017). *The Reactionary Mind: Conservatism from Edmund Burke to Donald Trump*. Oxford: Oxford University Press.

Robinson, J. (1964). 'Kalecki and Keynes'. *Collected Economic Papers*, vol III, Oxford: Blackwell Oxford: Pergamon.

Robinson, J. (1977). 'The guidelines of orthodox economics', *Journal of Contemporary Asia*, 7/1: 22–6.

Rodríguez, F. (2008). 'What can we really learn from growth regressions?', *Challenge*, 51/4: 55–69.

Rodríguez, F., & Rodrik, D. (2001). 'Trade policy and economic growth: a skeptic's guide to the cross-national evidence'. In B. Bernanke and K. Rogoff (eds), *NBER Macroeconomics Annual 2000*, vol. 15. Cambridge, MA: MIT Press.

Rodrik, D. (1996). 'Coordination failures and government policy: a model with applications to East Asia and Eastern Europe', *Journal of International Economics*, 40/1–2: 1–22.

Rodrik, D. (2008). 'The real exchange rate and economic growth', *Brookings*. Retrieved from: https://www.brookings.edu/bpea-articles/the-real-exchange-rate-and-economic-growth/.

Rodrik, D. (2011). *The Future of Economic Convergence* (NBER Working Papers No. 17400). Cambridge, MA: NBER.

Rodrik, D. (2016). 'Premature deindustrialization', *Journal of Economic Growth*, 21/1: 1–33.

Rodrik, D. (2018). *New Technologies, Global Value Chains, and the Developing Economies* (No. 1). Pathways for Prosperity Commission Background Paper Series. Oxford: Blavatnik School of Government.

Roelen, K., Devereux, S., & Kebede, D. (2017). 'Evaluation of the UNICEF Social Cash Transfer Pilot Programme in SNNPR, Ethiopia. Midline Report (Final)'. Centre for Social Protection, Institute of Development Studies, United Kingdom; REBRET Business and Consultancy, Ethiopia. Retrieved from: https://opendocs.ids.ac.uk/opendocs/bitstream/handle/20.500.12413/13444/Evaluation_UNICEF_Social_Cash_Transfer_Pilot_SNNPR_Ethiopia.pdf?sequence=175'

Romer, P. M. (1992). 'Two strategies for economic development: using ideas and producing ideas', *The World Bank Economic Review*, 6/suppl_1: 63–91.

Romer, P. M. (1994). 'The origins of endogenous growth', *Journal of Economic Perspectives*, 8/1: 3–22.

Romer, P. M. (1996). *Why, Indeed, in America? Theory, History, and the Origins of Modern Economic Growth*. Washington, DC: National Bureau of Economic Research.

Romero, J. P., & McCombie, J. S. L. (2018). 'Thirlwall's Law and the specification of export and import functions', *Metroeconomica*, 69/2: 366–95.

Room, G. (2018). 'The hiding hand: a rejoinder to Flyvbjerg on Hirschman', *World Development*, 103: 366–8.

Ros, J. (2012). *Institutional and Policy Convergence with Growth Divergence in Latin America* (Estudios y Perspectivas No. 139). Mexico City: CEPAL.

Rosenstein-Rodan, P. N. (1943). 'Problems of industrialisation of Eastern and South-Eastern Europe', *The Economic Journal*, 53: 202–11.

Rosenstein-Rodan, P. N. (1961). 'Notes on the theory of the "big push"'. In H. S. Ellis (ed.), *Economic Development for Latin America: Proceedings of a Conference Held by the*

International Economic Association. International Economic Association Series. London: Palgrave Macmillan.

Rossi, B. (2017). 'What "development" does to work', *International Labor and Working-Class History*, 92: 7–23.

Rothschild, E. (2002). *Economic Sentiments: Adam Smith, Condorcet, and the Enlightenment*. Cambridge, MA, & London: Harvard University Press.

Rowthorn, R., & Coutts, K. (2013). *De-industrialisation and the Balance of Payments in Advanced Economies* (Future of Manufacturing Project: Evidence Paper No. 31). London: Foresight, Government Office for Science.

Rusca, M., dos Santos, T., Menga, F., Mirumachi, N., Schwartz, K., & Hordijk, M. (2018). 'Space, state-building and the hydraulic mission: crafting the Mozambican state', *Environment and Planning C: Politics and Space*, 37/5: 868–88.

Rutherford, B. (2018). 'Mugabe's shadow: limning the penumbrae of post-coup Zimbabwe', *Canadian Journal of African Studies/Revue canadienne des études africaines*, 52/1: 53–68.

Ruttan, V. W. (1998). 'The new growth theory and development economics: a survey', *Journal of Development Studies*, 35/2: 1–26.

Saad Filho, A., & Johnston, D. (2005). *Neoliberalism: A Critical Reader*. Chicago: University of Chicago Press.

SALGA (South African Local Government Association). (2017). *Violence in Democracy: The Political Killing and Intimidation of Local Representatives and Administrators*. Pretoria: South African Local Government Association (SALGA).

Saloojee, H., & Coovadia, H. (2015). 'Maternal age matters: for a lifetime, or longer', *The Lancet Global Health*, 3/7: e342–e343.

Sandbu, M. (2017). 'How I learnt to love current account deficits'. *Financial Times*, 10 November.

Sandefur, J. (2016). 'The case for global standardized testing', Center for Global Development, 27 April. Retrieved from: https://www.cgdev.org/blog/case-global-standardized-testing.

Sanoh, A., & Coulibaly, M. (2015). *Socio-Economic and Fiscal Impact of Large-Scale Gold Mining in Mali* (Policy Research Working Paper No. 7467). Washington, DC: World Bank.

Santos, A. (2011). 'Carving out policy autonomy for developing countries in the world trade organization: the experience of Brazil and Mexico', *Virginia Journal of International Law*, 52: 551.

Sarti, R. (2014). 'Historians, social scientists, servants, and domestic workers: fifty years of research on domestic and care work', *International Review of Social History*, 59/2: 279–314.

Sato, H. (2005). '"Total factor productivity vs. realism" revisited: the case of the South Korean steel industry', *Cambridge Journal of Economics*, 29/4: 635–55.

Sawyer, M. (2017). 'The processes of financialisation and economic performance', *Economic and Political Studies*, 5/1: 5–20.

Schaefer, F. (2016). 'Revisiting the agrarian question: coffee, flowers and Ethiopia's new capitalists'. PhD Thesis, SOAS, University of London.

Schaefer, F., & Abebe, G. (2015). *The Case for Industrial Policy and Its Application in the Ethiopian Cut Flower Sector* (EDRI Working Paper No. 12). Addis Ababa: Ethiopian Development Research Institute.

Schaffner, J.A. (2001). 'Job stability in developing and developed countries: evidence from Colombia and the United States', *Economic Development and Cultural Change*, 49/3: 511–535.

Scheidel, W. (2017). *The Great Leveler: Violence and the History of Inequality from the Stone Age to the Twenty-First Century*. Princeton Economic History of the Western World Series. Princeton, NJ, & Oxford: Princeton University Press.

Scherrer, C. (2018). 'Labour surplus is here to stay: why "decent work for all" will remain elusive', *Journal of Social and Economic Development*, 20/2: 293–307.

Schneider, F. (2005). 'Shadow economies around the world: what do we really know?', *European Journal of Political Economy*, 21/3: 598–642.

Schou, S., & Cardoso, J. (2014). *How Many Manufacturing Firms Are There in Mozambique?* (Working Paper No. 2014/084). Helsinki: WIDER. Retrieved from: http://www.wider.unu.edu/publications/working-papers/2014/en_GB/wp2014-084/.

Schumpeter, J. A. (1942). *Capitalism, Socialism, and Democracy*. New York: Harper & Row.

Schürer, K., Garrett, E. M., Jaadla, H., & Reid, A. (2018). 'Household and family structure in England and Wales (1851–1911): continuities and change', *Continuity and Change*, 33/3: 365–411.

Scoones, I., Mavedzenge, B., Murimbarimba, F., & Sukume, C. (2019). 'Labour after land reform: the precarious livelihoods of former farmworkers in Zimbabwe', *Development and Change*, 50/3: 805–35.

Seedat, M., Van Niekerk, A., Jewkes, R., Suffla, S., & Ratele, K. (2009). 'Violence and injuries in South Africa: prioritising an agenda for prevention', *The Lancet*, 374/9694: 1011–22.

Seekings, J. (2013). *Economy, Society, and Municipal Services in Khayelitsha* (Report for the Commission of Inquiry into Allegations of Police Inefficiency in Khayelitsha and a Breakdown in Relations between the Community and the Police in Khayelitsha). Cape Town: Centre for Social Science Research, University of Cape Town.

Seeley, J., Dercon, S., & Barnett, T. (2010). 'The effects of HIV/AIDS on rural communities in East Africa: a 20-year perspective', *Tropical Medicine & International Health*, 15/3: 329–35.

Selby, J. (2014). 'Positivist climate conflict research: a critique', *Geopolitics*, 19/4: 829–56.

Semahegn, A., & Mengistie, B. (2015). 'Domestic violence against women and associated factors in Ethiopia; systematic review', *Reproductive Health*, 12: 78.

Sen, A., & Ghosh, J. (1993). 'Trends in rural employment and the poverty–employment linkage'. International Labour Organization, New Delhi, India, Asian Regional Team for Employment Promotion Working Papers.

Sender, J. (1999). 'Africa's economic performance: limitations of the current consensus', *Journal of Economic Perspectives*, 13/3: 89–114.

Sender, J. (2016). 'Backward capitalism in rural South Africa: prospects for accelerating accumulation in the Eastern Cape', *Journal of Agrarian Change*, 16/1: 3–31.

Sender, J. (2019). 'Assessing poverty trends in Ethiopia, 1990–2015'. In F. Cheru, C. Cramer, & A. Oqubay (eds), *The Oxford Handbook of the Ethiopian Economy*. Oxford: Oxford University Press.

Sender, J., Cramer, C., & Oya, C. (2005). *Unequal Prospects: Disparities in the Quantity and Quality of Labour Supply in Sub-Saharan Africa*. Washington, DC: World Bank. Social Protection Unit, Human Development Network.

Sender, J., Cramer, C., & Oya, C. (2018). 'Identifying the most deprived in rural Ethiopia and Uganda: a simple measure of socio-economic deprivation', *Journal of Eastern African Studies*, 12/3: 594–612.

Sender, J., & Johnston, D. (2004). 'Searching for a weapon of mass production in rural Africa: unconvincing arguments for land reform', *Journal of Agrarian Change*, 4/1–2: 142–64.

Sender, J., & Smith, S. (1986). *The Development of Capitalism in Africa*. London & New York: Methuen.

Sender, J., & Von Uexkull, E. (2009). *A Rapid Impact Assessment of the Global Economic Crisis on Uganda*. Geneva: ILO.

Serneels, P., Bardasi, E., Beegle, K., & Dillon, A. (2010). *Do Labor Statistics Depend on How and to Whom the Questions Are Asked? Results from a Survey Experiment in Tanzania* (Policy Research Working Paper No. 5192). Washington, DC: World Bank.

Serra, G. (2018). '"Hail the census night": trust and political imagination in the 1960 population census of Ghana', *Comparative Studies in Society and History*, 60/3: 659–87.

Shanguhyia, M. S. (2015). 'British war-effort programme and the making of the land degradation narrative in colonial western Kenya', *Journal of Colonialism and Colonial History*, 16/2.

Sharan, M., Ahmed, S., May, J., & Soucat, A. (2011). 'Family planning trends in sub-Saharan Africa: progress, prospects, and lessons learned'. In P. Chuhan-Pole & M. Angwafo (eds), *Yes Africa Can: Success Stories from a Dynamic Continent*. Washington, DC: International Bank for Reconstruction and Development/World Bank.

Sharp, K., Brown, T., & Teshome, A. (2006). *Targeting Ethiopia's Productive Safety Nets Programme*. London: ODI.

Sharp, K., Devereux, S., & Amare, Y. (2003). *Destitution in Ethiopia's Northeastern Highlands (Amhara National Regional State), Final Report*. Brighton: Institute of Development Studies and SC-UK Ethiopia.

Shepard, B. (2007). 'Sex panic and the welfare state', *Journal of Sociology and Social Welfare*, 34/1: 155–72.

Shin, J.-S. (2013). *The Economics of the Latecomers: Catching-Up, Technology Transfer and Institutions in Germany, Japan and South Korea*. New York: Routledge.

Shivji, I. G. (2009). *Accumulation in an African Periphery: A Theoretical Framework*. Dar es Salaam: Mkuki na Nyota Publishers.

Silal, S. P., Penn-Kekana, L., Harris, B., Birch, S., & McIntyre, D. (2012). 'Exploring inequalities in access to and use of maternal health services in South Africa', *BMC Health Services Research*, 12: 120.

Simpson, M., & Hawkins, T. (2018). *The Primacy of Regime Survival*. Cham: Springer International Publishing.

Simson, R. (2017). '(Under) privileged bureaucrats? The changing fortunes of public servants in Kenya, Tanzania and Uganda, 1960–2010'. PhD Thesis, London School of Economics and Political Science (LSE).

Singh, A. (1986). 'Tanzania and the IMF: the analytics of alternative adjustment programmes', *Development and Change*, 17/3: 425–54.

Siyoum, A. D. (2012). 'Broken promises: food security interventions and rural livelihoods in Ethiopia'. PhD Thesis, Wageningen University. Retrieved from: http://library.wur.nl/WebQuery/wurpubs/fulltext/231226.

Skalidou, D. (2018). 'In or out? Exploring selection processes of farmers in cocoa sustainability standards and certification programmes in Ghana'. PhD Thesis, University of East Anglia, School of International Development.

Skidelsky, R. J. A. (2010). *Keynes: The Return of the Master*. London: Penguin Books.

Slade, R., & Renkow, M. (2013). 'Independence or influence: tradeoffs in development policy research'. Presented at the New Directions in the Fight against Hunger and Malnutrition: A Festschrift in Honor of Per Pinstrup-Andersen, Cornell University, Ithaca, NY.

Smith, D. R. (1985). *The Influence of the Fabian Colonial Bureau on the Independence Movement in Tanganyika*. Monographs in International Studies Series. Athens, OH: Ohio University, Center for International Studies.

Smith, M. W. (2010). 'Boston's "big dig": a socio-historical and political analysis of malfeasance and official deviance', *National Social Science Journal*, 34/2: 148–63.

Smith, S., & Sender, J. (1983). 'A reply to Samir Amin', *Third World Quarterly*, 5/3: 650–6.

Smits, J. (2006). 'Economic growth and structural change in sub-Saharan Africa during the twentieth century: new empirical evidence'. Presented at Session 41 'International Differences in Economic Welfare: A Long-Run Perspective', at the International Economic History Association Conference, Helsinki.

Solow, R. M. (1994). 'Perspectives on growth theory', *Journal of Economic Perspectives*, 8/1: 45–54.

Sparks, S. (2016). 'Between "artificial economics" and the "discipline of the market": Sasol from parastatal to privatisation', *Journal of Southern African Studies*, 42/4: 711–24.

Sparks, S. J. (2012). 'Apartheid modern: South Africa's oil from coal project and the history of a company town'. PhD Thesis, University of Michigan, Ann Arbor.

Sparreboom, T., & Staneva, A. (2015). *Structural Change, Employment and Education in Mozambique* (Employment and Labour Market Policies Branch. Employment Working Paper No. 174). Geneva: International Labour Organization.

Spraos, J. (1980). 'The statistical debate on the net barter terms of trade between primary commodities and manufactures', *The Economic Journal*, 90/357: 107–28.

Squire, L., & Van der Tak, H. G. (1975). *Economic Analysis of Projects*. Washington, DC: World Bank Publications.

Standing, G. (2015). 'The precariat and class struggle', *RCCS Annual Review*, 7/7: 3–16.

Standing, G., Sender, J., & Weeks, J. (1996). *Restructuring the Labour Market: The South African Challenge*. Geneva: International Labour Organization.

Stapledon, N. (2013). 'Australia's major terms of trade and commodity shocks, 1800–2013: sources and impacts', *Centre for Economic History Discussion Paper Series*, 2013–10. Retrieved from: https://www.cbe.anu.edu.au/researchpapers/CEH/WP201310.pdf.

Stern, E., Stame, N., Mayne, J., Forss, K., Davies, R., & Befani, B. (2012). *Broadening the range of designs and methods for impact evaluations* (Working Paper No. 36). London: Department for International Development.

Stewart, C. P., Dewey, K. G., Lin, A., Pickering, A. J., Byrd, K. A., Jannat, K., Ali, S., Rao, G., Dentz, H. N., & Kiprotich, M. (2019). 'Effects of lipid-based nutrient supplements and infant and young child feeding counseling with or without improved water, sanitation, and hygiene (WASH) on anemia and micronutrient status: results from 2 cluster-randomized trials in Kenya and Bangladesh', *American Journal of Clinical Nutrition*, 109/1: 148–64.

Stewart, F. (1991). 'The many faces of adjustment', *World Development*, 19/12: 1847–64.

Stifel, D., Headey, D., You, L., & Guo, Z. (2018). 'Remoteness, urbanization and child nutrition in Sub-Saharan Africa'. Presented at the 30th International Conference of Agricultural Economists, Vancouver.

Stiglitz, J. E. (1992). 'Comment on "Toward a Counter-Counterrevolution in Development Theory," by Krugman', *World Bank Economic Review*, 6 (Supplement 1): 39–49.

Stiglitz, J. E. (2002). *Globalization and its Discontents*. New York: Norton.

Storm, S. (2015). 'Structural change', *Development and Change*, 46/4: 666–99.

Storm, S. (2019). *The Bogus Paper that Gutted Workers' Rights*. Institute for New Economic Thinking. Retrieved from: https://www.ineteconomics.org/perspectives/blog/the-bogus-paper-that-gutted-workers-rights.

Storm, S., & Capaldo, J. (2018). *Labor Institutions and Development under Globalization* (Working Paper No. 76). Institute for New Economic Thinking. Retrieved from: Retrieved from: https://www.google.com/url?sa=t&rct=j&q=&esrc=s&source=web&cd=

1&ved=2ahUKEwi96K6bhZfnAhVmzMQBHdzBDC0QFjAAegQIAhAB&url=https%
3A%2F%2Fwww.ineteconomics.org%2Fuploads%2Fpapers%2FWP_76-revised-Storm_
Capaldo.pdf&usg=AOvVaw04OOe_N5YE5hfnpL3pa0v_.

Storm, S., & Naastepad, C. W. M. (2005). 'Strategic factors in economic development: East
Asian industrialization 1950–2003', *Development and Change*, 36/6: 1059–94.

Streeck, W. (2016). *How will capitalism end? Essays on a failing system*. London: Verso.

Stringer, L. C. (2009). 'Testing the orthodoxies of land degradation policy in Swaziland',
Land Use Policy, 26/2: 157–68.

Sugihara, K. (2004). *Japanese Imperialism in Global Resource History* (Department of
Economics No. Working Paper No. 07/04). Osaka: University of Osaka.

Sundaram, J. K. (2019). 'Agribusiness is the problem, not the solution'. *News and Views
from the Global South: Opinion*. IPS Inter Press Service. Retrieved from: http://www.
ipsnews.net/2019/02/agribusiness-problem-not-solution/.

Sundaram, J. K., & Chowdhury, A. (2017). 'Hunger in Africa, land of plenty'. *IDEAs Blogs*.
Retrieved from: https://www.networkideas.org/news-analysis/2017/10/hunger-in-africa-
land-of-plenty/.

Sutcliffe, R. B. (1964). 'Balanced and unbalanced growth', *Quarterly Journal of Economics*,
78/4: 621–40.

Szirmai, A. (2013). 'Manufacturing and economic development'. In A. Szirmai, W. Naudé,
& L. Alcorta (eds), *Pathways to Industrialization in the Twenty-First Century: New
Challenges and Emerging Paradigms*. Oxford: Oxford University Press.

Tang, K., & Shen, Y. (2020). 'Do China-Financed Dams in Sub-Saharan Africa Improve the
Region's Social Welfare? A Case Study of the Impacts of Ghana's Bui Dam', *Energy Policy*
136: 111062. DOI: 10.1016/j.enpol.2019.111062.

Tavares de Araujo Jr, J. (2013). 'The BNDES as an instrument of long run economic policy
in Brazil.' Centro de Estudos de Integração e Desenvolvimento (CINDES): Rio de
Janeiro.

Taylor, A. M., & Williamson, J. G. (1997). 'Convergence in the age of mass migration',
European Review of Economic History, 1/1: 27–63.

Taylor, B. (2017). 'Has Zitto revealed fake news on Tz economic growth?' *Mtega*. Retrieved
from: https://mtega.com/2017/11/has-zitto-revealed-fake-news-on-tz-economic-growth/.

Taylor, C., Florey, L., & Ye, Y. (2017). 'Equity trends in ownership of insecticide-treated
nets in 19 sub-Saharan African countries', *Bulletin of the World Health Organization*,
95/5: 322–32.

Taylor, L. (1997). *The Revival of the Liberal Creed: The IMF and the World Bank in a
Globalized Economy*. Amsterdam: Elsevier.

Taylor, R. (2002). 'Justice denied: political violence in KwaZulu-Natal after 1994', *African
Affairs*, 101: 473–508.

Therborn, G. (2016). 'An age of progress?', *New Left Review*, 2/99: 27–37.

Thirlwall, A. P. (2003). *The Nature of Economic Growth: An Alternative Framework for
Understanding the Performance of Nations*. Cheltenham: Edward Elgar.

Thirlwall, A. P. (2005). *Growth and Development*, vol. 2. Basingstoke: Palgrave Macmillan.

Thirlwall, A. P. (2011). *Balance of Payments Constrained Growth Models: History and
Overview* (Studies in Economics Working Paper No. 1111). School of Economics,
University of Kent. Retrieved from: https://ideas.repec.org/p/ukc/ukcedp/1111.html.

Thirlwall, A. P., & Pacheco-López, P. (2017). *Economics of Development: Theory and
Evidence*. Basingstoke: Palgrave.

Thomas, I. (2018). 'Ideological training for the new economy', *Jacobin*. Retrieved from:
'https://jacobinmag.com/2018/01/job-search-clubs-unemployment-economy.

Thomson, C. (1938). 'Norway's industrialization', *Economic Geography*, 14/4: 372–80.

Tilly, C. (1992). *Coercion, Capital, and European States, AD 990–1992*. Studies in Social Discontinuity Series. Cambridge, MA: Blackwell.

Tilly, C. (1999). *Durable Inequality*. Berkeley, CA: University of California Press.

Tily, G. (2009). 'John Maynard Keynes and the development of national accounts in Britain, 1895–1941', *Review of Income and Wealth*, 55/2: 331–59.

Timmer, C. P. (2010). 'Reflections on food crises past', *Food Policy*, 35/1: 1–11.

Timmer, C. P., & Dawe, D. (2007). 'Managing food price instability in Asia: a macro food security perspective', *Asian Economic Journal*, 21/1: 1–18.

Tiquet, R. (2018). 'Challenging colonial forced labor? Resistance, resilience, and power in Senegal (1920s–1940s)', *International Labor and Working-Class History*, 93: 135–50.

Tittonell, P., & Giller, K. E. (2013). 'When yield gaps are poverty traps: the paradigm of ecological intensification in African smallholder agriculture', *Field Crops Research*, 143: 76–90.

Tlou, B. (2018). 'Underlying determinants of maternal mortality in a rural South African population with high HIV prevalence (2000–2014): a population-based cohort analysis' (ed. S. Gebhardt), *PLOS ONE*, 13/9: e0203830.

Todrys, K. W., & Kwon, S.-R. (2011). *'Even Dead Bodies Must Work': Health, Hard Labor, and Abuse in Ugandan Prisons*. New York: Human Rights Watch.

Tondo, L., & Kelly, A. (2017). 'Raped, beaten, exploited: the 21st-century slavery propping up Sicilian farming'. *The Guardian*, 12 March.

Tooze, A. (2014). *A Small Village in the Age of Extremes: The Häusern Experiment*. Mimeo, Yale University Agrarian Studies. Retrieved from: https://www.google.com/url?sa=t& rct=j&q=&esrc=s&source=web&cd=1&ved=2ahUKEwikjPuAjZfnAhUJbcAKHZYNCH YQFjAAegQIBxAB&url=https%3A%2F%2Fagrarianstudies.macmillan.yale.edu%2Fsites% 2Fdefault%2Ffiles%2Ffiles%2Fpapers%2FAdamToozeAgrarianStudies.pdf&usg=AOvVaw 1HE1VHmzIwcWaUTVzUjPPi.

Towriss, C., & Timaeus, I. (2018). 'Contraceptive use and lengthening birth intervals in rural and urban Eastern Africa', *Demographic Research*, 38: 2027–52.

Towriss, D. (2013). 'Buying loyalty: Zimbabwe's Marange diamonds', *Journal of Southern African Studies*, 39/1: 99–117.

Traore, F., & Sakyi, D. (2018). 'Africa's global trade patterns'. In O. Badiane, S. Odjo, & J. Collins (eds), *Africa Agriculture Trade Monitor 2018*. Washington, DC: International Food Policy Research Institute (IFPRI).

Travis, G. (2019). 'How the Boeing 737 Max disaster looks to a software developer', *IEEE Spectrum*, 18 April. Retrieved from: https://spectrum.ieee.org/aerospace/aviation/how-the-boeing-737-max-disaster-looks-to-a-software-developer.

Tregenna, F. (2011). 'A new growth path for South Africa?', *Review of African Political Economy*, 38/130: 627–35.

Tregenna, F. (2012). 'Sources of subsectoral growth in South Africa', *Oxford Development Studies*, 40/2: 162–89.

Tregenna, F. (2015). *Sectoral Dimensions of Employment Targeting* (Employment Working Paper No. 166). Geneva: International Labour Organization.

Tripney, J., Hombrados, J., Newman, M., Hovish, K., Brown, C., Steinka-Fry, K., & Wilkey, E. (2013). *Post-Basic Technical and Vocational Education and Training (TVET) Interventions to Improve Employability and Employment of TVET Graduates in Low- and Middle-Income Countries*. Oslo: Campbell Collaboration. Retrieved from: Retrieved from: https://scholar.google.co.uk/scholar?output=instlink&q=info:nCCBT56zcZIJ:scholar.goo gle.com/&hl=en&as_sdt=0,5&scillfp=5376749398305671254&oi=lle.

Tuckett, D. (2011). *Minding the Markets: An Emotional Finance View of Financial Instability*. Basingstoke & New York: Palgrave Macmillan.

Tusting, L. S., Rek, J. C., Arinaitwe, E., Staedke, S. G., Kamya, M. R., Bottomley, C., Johnston, D., Lines, D., Dorsey, G., & Lindsay, S. W. (2016). 'Measuring socioeconomic inequalities in relation to malaria risk: a comparison of metrics in rural Uganda', *American Journal of Tropical Medicine and Hygiene*, 94/3: 650–8.

UN (United Nations). (2017). *World Population Prospects: The 2017 Revision, Key Findings and Advance Tables* (Working Paper No. ESA/P/WP/248). New York: Department of Economic and Social Affairs, Population Division.

UNAIDS (Joint United Nations Programme on HIV/AIDS). (2016). *Global AIDS Update 2016*. Geneva: UNAIDS.

UNCTAD (United Nations Conference on Trade and Development) (ed.). (2013). *Adjusting to the Changing Dynamics of the World Economy* (Trade and Development Report). New York & Geneva: United Nations.

UNCTAD (United Nations Conference on Trade and Development) (ed.). (2014). *Global Governance and Policy Space for Development* (Trade and Development Report). New York: United Nations.

UNCTAD (United Nations Conference on Trade and Development). (2016). *The Role of Development Banks in Promoting Economic Growth and Sustainable Development in the South*. Geneva: UNCTAD.

UNCTAD (United Nations Conference on Trade and Development). (2018a). *Migration for Structural Transformation* (Economic Development in Africa Report). New York & Geneva: United Nations.

UNCTAD (United Nations Conference on Trade and Development). (2018b). *Handbook of Statistics 2018*. Retrieved from: https://unctadstat.unctad.org/EN/.

UNECA (United Nations Economic Commission for Africa). (2016). *Transformative Industrial Policy for Africa*. Addis Ababa: UNECA.

UNECA, African Union, and African Development Bank. (2017). *Bringing the Continental Free Trade Area about*. Assessing Regional Integration in Africa VII. Addis Ababa.

UNSD (United Nations Statistics Division). (n.d.). *Violence against Women Data Portal*. United Nations Statistics Division. Retrieved from : https://unstats.un.org/unsd/gender/vaw/.

Van Bergeijk, P. A. G. (2018). 'Heterogeneity and geography of the world trade collapses of the 1930s and 2000s', *Tijdschrift voor economische en sociale geografie*, 109/1: 36–56.

Van Campenhout, B., Sekabira, H., & Aduayom, D. H. (2016). 'Poverty and its dynamics in Uganda'. In A. Channing, A. McKay, & F. Tarp (eds), *Growth and Poverty in Sub-Saharan Africa*. Oxford: Oxford University Press.

Van den Broeck, G., & Maertens, M. (2017). 'Moving up or moving out? Insights into rural development and poverty reduction in Senegal', *World Development*, 99: 95–109.

Van Noorloos, F., & Kloosterboer, M. (2018). 'Africa's new cities: the contested future of urbanisation', *Urban Studies*, 55/6: 1223–41.

Van Waeyenberge, E., Fine, B., & Bayliss, K. (2011). *The World Bank, Neo-Liberalism and Development Research*. London: Pluto Press.

Vansina, J. (2010). *Being Colonized: The Kuba Experience in Rural Congo, 1880–1960*. Madison, WI, & London: University of Wisconsin Press.

Vaz, A., Pratley, P., & Alkire, S. (2016). 'Measuring women's autonomy in Chad using the relative autonomy index', *Feminist Economics*, 22/1: 264–94.

Verhagen, M. (2017). *Flows and Counterflows: Globalisation in Contemporary Art*. Berlin: Sternberg Press.

Verheul, S. (2013). '"Rebels" and "good boys": patronage, intimidation and resistance in Zimbabwe's attorney general's office after 2000', *Journal of Southern African Studies*, 39/4: 765–82.

Viviers, W., Kuhn, M.-L., Steenkamp, E., & Berkman, B. (2014). 'Tru-Cape fruit marketing, South Africa: managing the export market diversification challenge', *International Food and Agribusiness Management Review*, 17: 193–7.

Vollmer, F., & Alkire, S. (2018). *Towards a Global Asset Indicator: Re-assessing the Asset Indicator in the Global Multidimensional Poverty Index* (OPHI Research in Progress No. 53a). Oxford: Oxford Poverty and Human Development Initiative, University of Oxford.

Von Holdt, K. (2014). 'On violent democracy', *The Sociological Review*, 62/2 (Supplement): 129–51.

Vorley, B., & Lançon, F. (2016). *Food Consumption, Urbanisation and Rural Transformation: The Trade Dimensions*. London: IIED.

Vos, R. (1982). 'External dependence, capital accumulation, and the role of the state: South Korea, 1960–77', *Development and Change*, 13/1: 91–121.

Wade, R. (2013). 'How high inequality plus neoliberal governance weakens democracy', *Challenge*, 56/6: 5–37.

Wade, R. (2003). 'What strategies are viable for developing countries today? The world trade organization and the shrinking of "development space"', *Review of International Political Economy*, 10/4: 621–44.

Wainaina, B. (2005). 'How to write about Africa', *Granta*, 92: 92–5.

Walker, T. (2016). *Improved Crop Productivity for Africa's Drylands*. Washington, DC: World Bank.

Walker, T. S., & Alwang, J. R. (eds) (2015). *Crop Improvement, Adoption and Impact of Improved Varieties in Food Crops in Sub-Saharan Africa*. Boston, MA: CGIAR and CAB International.

Ward, C. (2016). *Improved Agricultural Water Management for Africa's Drylands*. Washington, DC: World Bank.

Waugh, E. (2010). *Remote People*. London: Penguin.

Webster, E. (2012). 'Work in post-apartheid South Africa: the promise and the reality', *South African Review of Sociology*, 43/1: 87–91.

Webster, E. & Englert, T. (2020). 'New dawn or end of labour: from South Africa's East Rand to Ekurhuleni', *Globalizations*, 17/2: 279-93.

Wedig, K., & Wiegratz, J. (2018). 'Neoliberalism and the revival of agricultural cooperatives: the case of the coffee sector in Uganda', *Journal of Agrarian Change*, 18/2: 348–69.

Weeks, J. (1999). 'Commentary: stuck in low GEAR? Macroeconomic policy in South Africa, 1996–98', *Cambridge Journal of Economics*, 23/6: 795–811.

Weiss, J. (2005). *Export growth and industrial policy: lessons from the East Asian miracle experience*. ADB Institute Discussion Papers No.26. Asian Development Bank Institute: Tokyo.

Weiss, J. (2010). 'Changing trade structure and its implications for growth', *The World Economy*, 33/10: 1269–79.

Weiss, J. (2015). 'The role of development banks in developing countries'. Retrieved from: http://www.john-weiss.net/uploads/6/9/2/7/6927327/development_banks-2.pdf.

Wells, H., & Thirlwall, A.P. (2003). 'Testing Kaldor's Growth Laws across the countries of Africa', *African Development Review*, 15/2–3: 89–105.

White, S., Steel, W., & Larquemin, A. (2017). *Financial Services and Small and Medium-Sized Enterprise Growth and Development*. Research for Development Outputs series, Rapid Evidence Review. London: Department for International Development (DfID).

Whitfield, L. (ed.). (2009). *The Politics of Aid: African Strategies for Dealing with Donors.* Oxford & New York: Oxford University Press.

Whitfield, L. (2017). 'New paths to capitalist agricultural production in Africa: experiences of Ghanaian pineapple producer-exporters', *Journal of Agrarian Change*, 17/3: 535–56.

WHO & UNICEF (World Health Organization & United Nations Children's Fund). (2015). *Progress on Sanitation and Drinking-Water: 2015 Update.* Geneva & New York: World Health Organization/UNICEF.

Wiggins, S. (2018). *Agricultural Growth Trends in Africa* (Agricultural Policy Research in Africa Working Paper No. WP 13). Brighton: Institute of Development Studies, University of Sussex.

Wilde, O. (2006). *The Picture of Dorian Gray.* New York: Oxford University Press.

Wiles, P. (1995). 'Capitalist triumphalism in the Eastern European transition'. In H.-J. Chang & P. Nolan (eds), *The Transformation of the Communist Economies.* London: Palgrave Macmillan.

Williams, M. (2017a). '"Practicing" women's agency and the struggle for transformation in South Africa', *Journal of Contemporary African Studies*, 35/4: 525–43.

Williams, M. (2017b). 'Women in rural South Africa: a post-wage existence and the role of the state', *Equality, Diversity and Inclusion: An International Journal*, 37/4: 392–410. Retrieved from: https://doi.org/10.1108/EDI-05-2017-0110.

Williams, T. (2009). 'An African success story: Ghana's cocoa marketing system', *IDS Working Papers*, 2009/318: 1–47.

Williamson, J. (1990). 'What Washington means by policy reform'. In J. Williamson (ed.), *Latin American Adjustment: How Much Has Happened?* Washington, DC: Petersen Institute for International Economics.

Wilson, T. (2019a). 'Ethiopia takes first step towards liberalising finance sector'. *Financial Times*, 8 August.

Wilson, T. (2019b). 'Rwanda's Kagame dismisses FT story as Western propaganda'. *Financial Times,* 15 August.

Wilson, T., & Blood, D. (2019). 'Rwanda: where even poverty data must toe Kagame's line'. *Financial Times*, 13 August.

Wineman, A., & Jayne, T. (2018). 'Factor market activity and the inverse farm size–productivity relationship in Tanzania'. Presented at the 30th International Conference of Agricultural Economists, Vancouver.

Wise, S. (2009). *The Life and Death of a Victorian Slum.* London: Vintage.

Wittenberg, M. (2017). 'Wages and wage inequality in South Africa 1994–2011: Part 1—wage measurement and trends', *South African Journal of Economics*, 85/2: 279–97.

Wolf, C. (2017). 'Industrialization in times of China: domestic-market formation in Angola', *African Affairs*, 116/464: 435–61.

Wolf, C. (2018). 'Industrialisation in times of China: a demand-side perspective on China's influence on industrialisation processes in Sub-Saharan African countries through the example of Angola between 2000 and 2014'. PhD Thesis, SOAS, University of London.

Wood, A. (2017). *Variation in Structural Change around the World, 1985–2015: Patterns, Causes and Implications* (WIDER Working Paper 2017/34). Helsinki: United Nations University—World Institute for Development Economics Research.

World Bank. (1993). *The East Asian Miracle: Economic Growth and Public Policy.* Washington, DC: World Bank.

World Bank. (1997). *World Development Report 1997: The State in a Changing World.* Washington, DC: World Bank.

World Bank. (2007). *World Development Report 2008: Agriculture for Development.* Washington, DC & London: World Bank.

World Bank. (2013). 'Africa's pulse: an analysis of issues shaping Africa's future.' Vol.7/April. Washington, DC: World Bank.

World Bank. (2015). *Ethiopia Poverty Assessment* (Poverty Global Practice Africa Region Report No. ACS12005). Washington, DC: World Bank.

World Bank. (2016a). *Monitoring Global Poverty: Report of the Commission on Global Poverty.* Washington, DC: World Bank.

World Bank.(2016b). *Rwanda at Work* (Rwanda Economic Update No. Issue No. 9). Washington, DC: World Bank. Retrieved from: https://www.google.com/url?sa=t&rct= j&q=&esrc=s&source=web&cd=3&cad=rja&uact=8&ved=2ahUKEwjF8oLhu4PfAhVME ywKHUG5DKsQFjACegQIBxAC&url=http%3A%2F%2Fdocuments.worldbank.org% 2Fcurated%2Fen%2F126991468197359041%2Fpdf%2F103618-WP-P156677-PUBLIC-Rwanda-Economic-Update-Feb-25-2016.pdf&usg=AOvVaw3P73n5A50Vu13VRx_wVlDn.

World Bank. (2016c). *Why so Idle? Wages and Employment in a Crowded Labor Market* (5th Ethiopia Economic Update). Washington, DC: World Bank.

World Bank. (2016d). *World Development Report 2016: Digital Dividends.* Washington, DC: World Bank.

World Bank. (2018a). *Piecing Together the Poverty Puzzle.* Washington, DC: World Bank.

World Bank.(2018b). *World Development Report 2019: The Changing Nature of Work.* Washington, DC: World Bank.

Wrong, M. (2005). *I Didn't Do it for You: How the World Betrayed a Small African Nation.* London: Fourth Estate.

Wuyts, M. (2011). 'The working poor: a macro perspective'. Presented at the Institute for Social Studies, The Hague, Netherlands.

Yamada, S., Otchia, C. S., Shimazu, Y., Taniguchi, K., & Nigussie, F. (2018). *Bridging the Supply–Demand Gaps of the Industrial Workforce: Findings from a Skills Assessment of Garment Workers in Ethiopia* (Skills and Knowledge for Youth Project Interim Report). Nagoya University. Retrieved from: https://www.researchgate.net/profile/Shoko_Yamada2/ publication/327987724_Bridging_the_Supply-Demand_Gaps_of_the_Industrial_Workforce_ Findings_from_a_Skills_Assessment_of_Garment_Workers_in_Ethiopia_Skills_and_ Knowledge_for_Youth_Research_Project/links/5bb223e845851574f7f40dd9/Bridging-the-Supply-Demand-Gaps-of-the-Industrial-Workforce-Findings-from-a-Skills-Assessment-of-Garment-Workers-in-Ethiopia-Skills-and-Knowledge-for-Youth-Research-Project.pdf.

Yeboah, F. K., & Jayne, T. S. (2018). 'Africa's evolving employment trends', *Journal of Development Studies,* 54/5: 803–32.

Yibeltal, K. (2017). 'Never again? Inside Ethiopia's "retraining" programme for thousands of detained protesters', *African Insiders Newsletter,* African Arguments, 28 January.

Yongzhi, H., & Kun, J. (2020). 'Review and prospects of China's medium and long-term development: the perspective of the economic drivers of structural changes'. In Jin Zhang and Zhang Laiman (eds), *China 1978–2018: Economy, Society and Environment.* London: Routledge.

You, D., Hug, L., Ejdemyr, S., Idele, P., Hogan, D., Mathers, C., Gerland, P., New, J. R., & Alkema, L. (2015). 'Global, regional, and national levels and trends in under-5 mortality between 1990 and 2015, with scenario-based projections to 2030: a systematic analysis by the UN inter-agency group for child mortality estimation', *The Lancet,* 386/10010: 2275–86.

You, L. Z. (2008). *Africa: Irrigation Investment Needs in Sub-Saharan Africa* (Background Paper No. 9). Washington, DC: Environment and Production Technology Division of the International Food Policy Research for the World Bank Institute. Retrieved from: https://openknowledge.worldbank.org/handle/10986/7870.

Young, A. (1928). 'Economic progress', *Economic Journal*, 38: 527–42.

Young, A. (1992). 'A tale of two cities: factor accumulation and technical change in Hong Kong and Singapore', *NBER Macroeconomics Annual*, 7: 13–54.

Young, A. (2018). 'Channeling Fisher: randomization tests and the statistical insignificance of seemingly significant experimental results', *Quarterly Journal of Economics*, 134/2: 557–98.

Zalk, N. (2017). *The Things We Lost in the Fire: The Political Economy of Post-Apartheid Restructuring of the South African Steel and Engineering Sectors*. London: SOAS, University of London.

Index